PENGUIN BOOKS

CHURCHILL

Geoffrey Best is one of Britain's most distinguished historians. His many books include *War and Law since 1945*, *Humanity in Warfare* and *Mid-Victorian Britain*. He has been Professor of History at the Universities of Edinburgh and Sussex, and a Visiting Fellow at Harvard and Chicago. He is currently a Senior Member of St Antony's College, Oxford.

D0048874

GEOFFREY BEST

Churchill

A STUDY IN GREATNESS

PENGUIN BOOKS
In association with Hambledon and London

PENGUIN BOOKS

Published by the Penguin Group
Penguin Books Ltd, 80 Strand, London, WC2R ORL, England
Penguin Putnam Inc., 375 Hudson Street, New York, New York 10014, USA
Penguin Books Australia Ltd, 250 Camberwell Road, Camberwell, Victoria 3124, Australia
Penguin Books Canada Ltd, 10 Alcorn Avenue, Toronto, Ontario, Canada M4V 3B2
Penguin Books India (P) Ltd, 11 Community Centre, Panchsheel Park, New Delhi – 110 017, India
Penguin Books (NZ) Ltd, Cnr Rosedale and Airborne Roads, Albany, Auckland, New Zealand
Penguin Books (South Africa) (Pty) Ltd, 24 Sturdee Avenue, Rosebank 2196, South Africa

Penguin Books Ltd, Registered Offices: 80 Strand, London, WC2R ORL, England

www.penguin.com

First published by Hambledon and London 2001
Published in Penguin Books 2002
7

Printed in England by Clays Ltd, St Ives plc

ISBN-13: 978–0–141–01122–6
ISBN-10: 0–141–01122–X

Contents

Illustrations

Illustration Acknowledgements

The author and the publishers are grateful to the following for permission to reproduce illustrations: the Master and Fellows of Churchill College, Cambridge, 5; the Conservative Party Archive and the Bodleian Library, 8, 16, 17; the Imperial War Museum, 1, 4, 9–15; the National Portrait Gallery, 2, 3, 6, 7.

Prologue

It was in the spring of 1940 that Winston Churchill suddenly became the most important person in my mind's eye, dominant in my boyhood conception of the war my country was engaged in. Until then the war, well characterised as the 'Phoney War', had hardly felt real. Just as it did become real, Churchill became real too; super-real, even, in as much as no other human being was so familiar to us through the combination of image and voice, principle and sentiment. His broadcasts to the nation were quasi-religious events for us. When in 1942 I won a prize at school, and was asked what book I wanted, I asked for the first volume of Churchill's *War Speeches*. My copy of his excellent book about the First World War, *The World Crisis*, carries the date 1943. He was for me Pitt the Elder, Horatio Nelson and Benjamin Disraeli rolled into one; the cartoonists' John Bull too, no doubt, but a John Bull with culture, intelligence, style and what came over as the common touch.

At some time towards the end of the war, his dominance in my conception of it (as also, I now know, that of many others) began to diminish; to such effect that his replacement as Prime Minister, even by so different-looking and different-sounding a person as Clement Attlee, felt less dramatic than political historians, writing about the event at a growing distance from it, have made it appear. We were to finish the war and enter the unknown beyond it without Winston at our helm. The odd thing was that, despite what he was well known to regard as a humiliation and a defeat, and notwithstanding my adolescent sympathy with the principles of his political opponents, my conviction that he was a great man and an extraordinary character never wavered. Through the years that followed, I noted with interest and pleasure his repeated reappearances on the national and international stages; and when, dying at last, he was accorded the singular honour of a state funeral, I was glued to the television screen deeply moved as by no televised event before or since.

So much for the first phase of my interest in the man: early years of personal experience, even a sort of emotional attachment, and continuing though distant respect thereafter. The second phase, which has come to its natural culmination in this book, began in the early 1970s when my interests as an historian turned from the social history of eighteenth- and nineteenth-century Britain to international history and the modern history of warfare. I learned something about the history of the European empires, how they had been acquired and how maintained; the Churchill I found in Africa and, even more, India was not easy to assimilate to my wartime hero. I also learned a good deal about the wars of 1914–18 and 1939–45; and, although my main, and always my most enjoyable, sources for long were his own famous books about them, I was made aware that some of the many books being written by other participants and by historians were making his parts in both wars look stranger and more interesting than I had imagined. I began to learn too about the very full and unusual life he led when war was not engaging his attention. And all through those years I could not help becoming aware that the steady stream of publications was making the man seem a more complicated and, in some respects, a more contradictory character than, way back in the first place, I would have thought possible.

In this book I have noted and accepted his complications and contradictions without making any elaborate attempt to explain them. His childhood was in some respects miserable and it seems impossible to believe that the extraordinary personality of his adult years was not largely forged by it, or in reaction to it. His private life no doubt interacted significantly with his public life. It mattered hugely, for example, that from the age of thirty-three he had a clever, supporting and loving wife. Home was a comfortable place for him and, at times of trial, a refuge. It must be significant also, and was another mark of difference from many of his social and political associates, that he showed no inclination for affairs outside marriage. But I have not felt it necessary to linger on psychological speculation. I have been content to fix upon the main points of the public life of a man who was in the public eye from the age of twenty-one, who liked being there and who indeed, through his early years, positively strove to be there. It is partly because he figured in this way over so many years, in so many different roles and ultimately in such internationally prominent roles, that he is so remarkable and interesting. But, after all, what is most remarkable about him is his heroic role as leader of the people of Britain and the Empire through the years of total war, 1940–1945. His performance in this role, the particular target of criticism and questioning in recent years, was what I was most eager to find out about. Having done so, I find no cause to overturn the earlier consensus judgement: that he was, as A. J. P. Taylor famously affirmed in the potted biography of Churchill in his *English History, 1914–1945*, 'the saviour of his country'.

It is right and proper, and only to be expected, that such a man should have been, as the Duke of Wellington plaintively remarked of himself, much exposed to authors. Prominent on the shelves of Churchilliana is the monumental biographical work begun by Winston's son Randolph and finished by Sir Martin Gilbert. The roll of biographers and commentators includes some of the best historians of our time. Every significant phase and episode of his life has by now been subjected to expert scrutiny, and recollections have been published by almost everybody who had anything to do with him. I have dredged this open-cast mine of material for most of my information, I have been pleased to adopt other writers' judgements where they have said things better than I could have done or have at any rate said them first. I am grateful to have found so many sturdy shoulders to stand upon. I trust they will consider their assistance adequately acknowledged. Regarding the many aspects of Churchill's life which have become matters of persisting controversy, however, I have enjoyed making my own mind up. They are so numerous that to list these matters is to sketch the outline of Churchill's public life: his two performances as First Lord of the Admiralty; his ardent promotion of the Dardanelles expedition; his emphatic interventions in the Russian Revolution; his involvement in the Irish struggle for independence and the Indian movement for self-government; his opposition to the British government's policy of appeasement in the later 1930s; his leadership during the Second World War; his leadership of the European Movement for a few years after it; his invention of the 'Special Relationship' between Britain and the USA; his insights regarding international relations in the shadow of the Bomb. Interest in what he said and what he did in these connections will never cease. Not many modern men have left so many marks on history.

I have used Churchill's own words as much as possible, finding no good reason to let my prose or anyone else's take precedence over that of one of the great masters of the English language. I have kept the notes to a decent minimum. Scholarly readers like to have books lavishly sprinkled with footnotes, but such a presentation can be distracting for the non-specialists and general readers for whom this book is primarily designed. I have indicated the sources of all direct quotations, not least the numerous ones from Churchill himself, his wife and his daughter Mary. The sources of everything else, in so far as it has not come out of my fifty years' experience as an historian or is not specified in the notes, will be found in the books listed at the back, in among those recommended for further reading.

At the head of my list of acknowledgements must come all those historians and other writers upon whose books I have relied greatly. Next, the unfailingly courteous and helpful staffs of the libraries where I have found those books; which means above all the Bodleian, Codrington and St Antony's

College libraries in Oxford, the Churchill Archives Centre in Cambridge, and the Royal Academy in London. In photographic collections I have met with equal helpfulness; I think particularly of the Imperial War Museum and the National Portrait Gallery in London, the New Bodleian (where the Conservative Central Office's collection is held), the Churchill Archives Centre again, and the National Portrait Gallery in Washington, DC (although in the end we decided not to use anything from it). Various forms of help, inspiration and correction have been gratefully received from Paul Addison, Matthew Anderson, Piers Brendon, Robert Brown, Jane Carmichael, Robert Dann, Ann Deighton, Paddy Griffith, Sir Michael Howard, Peter Mangold, Henry Probert, Lady Soames, Hew Strachan and Neil Young. But the greatest measures of encouragement and guidance have been those received from Tony Morris and Martin Sheppard, my publishers, and Marigold Best, my wife.

In conclusion: I hope that my book will convey a fair all-round impression of this extraordinary human being. Writing it has satisfied my curiosity about him, and I trust it will satisfy the curiosity of readers of the generation younger than my own; too young to have been aware of the living Churchill, but old enough to be interested to find out why he has been called with justification the greatest Englishman of the twentieth century, and why he is certainly one of the most interesting.

'I should have made nothing
if I had not made mistakes'

CHURCHILL

1

Unwillingly to School

'I was what grown-up people in their off-hand
way call "a troublesome boy".'

My Early Life, chapter 16

The nation and society into which Winston Leonard Spencer Churchill was
born, the place in which he was born, and the parents to whom he was
born, were all remarkable.

The world into which he was born, on 30 November 1874, was one in
which the United Kingdom of Great Britain and Ireland was, to put it
bluntly, 'top nation'. Its industries and commerce had caused it to be known
as the 'workshop of the world'. Its merchant shipping fleet outstripped all
others and its shipyards made many of the others' ships. London was
Europe's biggest city and the world's financial capital. Britain's foreign
investments and all the informal authority that went with them far exceeded
those of France and the Netherlands, its nearest rivals. The overseas Empire
subject to British sovereignty was unmatched in scale and resources; a global
fact to which the attention of other powers was drawn by two events closely
following Winston's birth: Prime Minister Disraeli's bold acquisition of a
controlling share in the Suez Canal in 1875; and the spectacular proclamation
of Queen Victoria as Empress of India in 1877. The British navy, by far the
world's largest and most prestigious, was proudly believed to maintain over
the world's waterways a beneficent Pax Britannica. Only very, very few
Britons of peculiar insight or specialised information were as yet aware that
this global grandeur and naval supremacy was not bound to last – was
indeed already, however imperceptibly, on the decline. To youngsters in all
classes, provided they had the ability and the will to travel beyond the
homeland, this world with their nation's political and economic empires
stretching all over it was their oyster. Not surprisingly it was so for the
young Winston Churchill. Less predictably, grand and even grandiose concepts of this great Empire, and of the proper weight in the world of its
metropolis, went on colouring Churchill's mind throughout the rest of his
long life. Britons and their allies in the Second World War had no cause

to regret this persistent passion of his; but it certainly made difficulties for him from time to time, and contributed to the singular mixture of favourable and unfavourable judgements which people would make about him.

He was born into this great empire's governing elite. His father was a younger son of the seventh Duke of Marlborough, and little Winston, either two months premature or conceived before wedlock (as Manchester believes), was actually delivered into the world in Blenheim Palace, the grandest of England's stately homes. Although such lineage and status did not infallibly guarantee success in life, it was a good start. The political and social elites overlapped in membership and intermingled in the places and on the occasions which were as fixed in their calendars as sacred events: races at Goodwood and Ascot, cricket at Lords, regattas at Henley, the solemn rituals of the hunt, the shoot and point-to-point, the unending rounds of countryhouse parties, London clubs and, above all, the London Season. English society (with a small s, and infinitely diverse) was to all appearances capped and crowned by Society (with a capital, and tightly exclusive). The young Churchill would have understood Lady Bracknell's admonition of her nephew: 'Never speak disrespectfully of Society, Algernon. Only people who can't get into it do that.'[1] Churchill himself recalled this unique phenomenon in his 1930 classic, *My Early Life*.

> In those days English Society still existed in its old form. It was a brilliant and powerful body ... In a very large degree every one knew every one else and who they were. The few hundred great families who had governed England [sic] for so many generations and had seen her rise to the pinnacle of her glory, were inter-related to an enormous extent by marriage. Everywhere one met friends and kinsfolk. The leading figures of Society were in many cases the leading statesmen in Parliament, and also the leading sportsmen on the Turf. Lord Salisbury was accustomed scrupulously to avoid calling a Cabinet when there was racing at Newmarket, and the House of Commons made a practice of adjourning for the Derby. [The] glittering parties at Lansdowne House, Devonshire House or Stafford House comprised all the elements which made a gay and splendid social circle in close relation to the business of Parliament, the hierarchies of the Army and Navy, and the policy of the State ... I am glad to have seen, if only for a few months, this vanished world.[2]

The elegiac and valedictory tones sprang not only from his historian's sense of the changes wrought by time (remarkably little time, in this case) and of his romantic regret that the age of chivalry was past. There may also have been some degree of consciousness that, although a sociological classifier could hardly have avoided placing him in the aristocracy, he became as his adult years wore on less obviously of the aristocracy. His political association with the Liberal firebrand David Lloyd George, and the radical attitudes they shared in the years before 1914, indeed caused him to be viewed by many of the aristocracy as a traitor to his class. Of course he mixed with its members, when he met them (some of the Tory ones cut him), on equal terms. He continued throughout life to socialise with chosen members of the nobility and, when he had time, to participate in a few classic social rituals. But he never felt easy about wasting time and, more and more as the years went by, his friends and his pastimes diverged from the norms of his birth-class to form his own peculiar mix. His circle came to include the literary and (not always the same thing) the press, the raffish, the eccentric and the merely rich. He hunted and shot in his earlier years, but his most passionate sporting activity, until he grew too old or busy to play it, was the relatively exotic polo. As a golfer he was scarcely competent. Where others drove fast cars, he flew aeroplanes; until, having nearly been killed several times, his wife and friends persuaded him to give it up. Established from 1924 in his country house at Chartwell in Kent, he eschewed most conventional county enjoyments in favour of such relative eccentricities as bricklaying and oil-painting, if outdoors; if indoors, reading, talking and writing – which often amounted to much the same thing as talking, since most of what he authored began in dictation. His hours were thoroughly idiosyncratic; working in bed till lunchtime, and usually from after dinner until two or three a.m. His consuming interest, once he had woken up to the workings of 'the deep tides of destiny', was whither they were driving him and what they were doing to his country and its empire. He could have ended up in the House of Lords, but chose not to. He preferred to remain the Great Commoner.

His father, Lord Randolph Churchill, was famous or infamous, according to your political point of view. Born in 1849 and Member for the family seat of Woodstock from 1874 until its abolition by the third Reform Bill in 1885 (after which he sat for Paddington South), he was the most conspicuous young Conservative in the House of Commons and, with his prominent eyes, ferocious moustache and jaunty bearing, one of the political cartoonists' darlings. By the early 1880s he was recklessly pursuing celebrity and power. He was the leading light in a parliamentary ginger group which, calling itself 'the Fourth Party', delighted in making things hot not only for the Prime Minister, Gladstone, and his Liberal administration but also for his own party's staid leader in the Commons, Sir Stafford Northcote, whose ingrained respect for the Prime Minister was such that he had difficulty in remembering that his constitutional task was to lead the Opposition. This Opposition Lord Randolph was only too willing to provide, and his talents as parliamentarian, orator and (to a growing extent) demagogue were such that he became, for those few years, the most widely known Tory politician of the day, the most entertaining, and the most democratic-seeming one. (There continues to be disagreement about how democratic he actually was.) It was natural that observers of the parliamentary scene should speak of him as perhaps a future Prime Minister. His appointment as Chancellor of the Exchequer in the Marquess of Salisbury's administration in July 1886 looked like a step in that direction. But he pushed his luck too far. Too bold and abrasive to be a comfortable Cabinet colleague, he found no support when he ventured on a trial of strength with the formidable Prime Minister, and lost. His retirement was simply accepted. His political career thereafter ran downhill. He became increasingly resentful, unbalanced and isolated; a decline undoubtedly due principally to the disease which brought him through tragic phases of physical incapacity and mental disturbance to the grave in 1894. (For long this trouble was supposed, not without malice on some people's part, to have been syphilis, but it has recently been persuasively argued that it was more probably a brain tumour, on top of an already depressive disposition.) [3]

From this strange father, whom by Winston's own account he scarcely knew, the son evidently derived a great deal, in one way or another. What must have been the effects on him of his father's general neglect and even dislike, which were obvious despite the boy's attempts to believe otherwise, one can only guess. Writers of psychoanalytic skill or inclination have attributed much of his adult personality to his childhood and boyhood experience of parental chill and what the boy felt to be rejection. So far as the world could see, he had for his father nothing but admiration and loyalty, which issued before many years were out in an elaborate biography of the lost hero and a presentation of him as the son's model to follow. And there were obviously many inherited or shared characteristics: egotism, boldness, a need to be noticed, political ambition, bouts of depression, the ability to master complicated subjects, quickness of conception, energy, loquacity, cheek, humour, oratorical talent, impetuousness, irreverence, and sometimes disastrous tactlessness and failure of judgement. People who had known the father recognised the son as a chip off the old block. But how much of that was in the genes, and how much in the hero-worship of a wishfully adoring but neglected son, it is impossible to say.

Vigorous genes may also have come to him from his mother, Jennie. She was American; eldest of the three daughters of a New York businessman, Leonard Jerome, and living in Paris when Randolph wooed and won her. The Jerome sisters were not the sort of American girls who longed to get back to their homeland. Contentedly Europeanised, all three girls married into the aristocracy of the United Kingdom; the other two less well than Jennie. The father, prosperous enough to be able to settle £2000 a year on her, was taken aback to discover that an English aristocratic bridegroom expected the marriage settlement to come, for the most part anyway, to him. Jennie's father stood his ground firmly enough through the prolonged haggling with the family lawyers for Randolph and Jennie to end up with £1000 a year each; which was in fact not very much by current heiress-hunting standards. Beautiful, clever, lively and extravagant, she bore him two sons – Winston's brother John, a much less uncommon but well-loved character always known as Jack, was born six years after Winston in 1880 – before the ardours of marriage cooled and her life began to become the flighty one it conspicuously remained through the many years between the termination of Randolph's illness and her death in 1921. Before he became incapable of managing his own affairs, Randolph made a lot of money by investments on the Rand, but most of it had to go on settling debts when he died. Jennie was left with about £2700 a year and the two boys to launch. The years of her widowhood witnessed persistent financial troubles, some 'affairs' of the kind Society readily accommodated, two remarriages (both to men younger than herself), and a divorce.

Of Jennie's affection for Winston, and her anxiety concerning his welfare once she was widowed and he was out in the world in the 1890s, there can be no doubt; nor any doubt of his lasting affection for her. But none of that had much chance to show during the years of his boyhood, when he shared the experience common to most children of such families of being kept out of the parents' way, intermittently looked after by female relatives, including his grandmother at Blenheim ('He is a clever boy and really not naughty but he wants a firm hand')[4] and his aunt Lady Wimborne at Bournemouth, before being sent away or, what seems as often to have been the case, got rid of to school at the earliest opportunity. His letters to his parents from school pathetically show him persistently seeking more interest and affection than they could or would give. Most of the womanly affection he got came from another quarter. Young Winston's good fortune it was to be cosseted by his nurse and nanny, Mrs Everest. His cousin Clare, Jennie's sister's child, who saw quite a lot of him when they were children (and who was amazed by the way he 'organised wars' between 'thousands of lead soldiers ... with an interest that was no ordinary child game'), was struck by how much 'Winston loved "Everest"'.[5] They exchanged letters while he was away from home (a typical one, newsy and solicitous, dated 21 January 1891, begins 'My darling Winny' and ends 'Lots of love and kisses from your loving WOOM'),[6] and he missed her sorely when the time came for her to leave the household, and unhuggable figures of governesses and tutors appeared in her stead. But she remained in the family service as housekeeper of the Grosvenor Square establishment his parents for a while

shared with the seventh Duke's widow, and Winston protested nobly (and
not unsuccessfully) when his parents, short of money as usual, proposed
to cast her off, Winston never lost touch with her. When news came of
her mortal illness, he not only secured for her good medical attention but
rushed back from Aldershot to north London next day to be with her in
what proved to be her last moments. She is immortalised in one of the
most moving, and revealing, passages in *My Early Life.*

> Death came very easily to her. She had lived such an innocent and loving life of
> service to others and held such a simple faith that she had no fears at all, and
> did not seem to mind very much. She had been my dearest and most intimate
> friend during the whole of the twenty years I had lived ...[7]

His school years were not distinguished, and had much unhappiness in
them. Three boarding schools successively had some part in his education.
He was packed off to St George's at Ascot at the age of eight. This was a
new school opened by a well-connected lawyer-turned-clergyman in 1877.
The original building is still visible amidst the many extensions which have
come to surround it since it became St George's School for Girls in 1904.
The Reverend Herbert William Sneyd-Kynnersley's system of preparing little
boys for Eton and other so-called public schools included, besides the usual
classics-by-rote, birching their bare bottoms until they bled. This was too
much, even in an age when spirited boys were expected to get into trouble
and when punishment was normally corporal. Winston suffered a lot there,
and not just from the headmaster. He was not big or strong for his age,
and would have liked to have ended up a bit taller than he did. He was
prone to illnesses, and would remain so. He had a stammer and slight lisp
(the former, he worked hard to conquer when he set out on public life),
and he was a natural target for bullies, to whom schools like this one gave
ample opportunity. It is an easy mistake to suppose that the man who
talked tough, and liked to look tough, was actually (at any rate physically)
particularly tough. In some ways he was not. He liked luxuries and cosseting.
Churchill the man could be tough when he had to be (as, for instance,
during his escape from Pretoria in 1899, his weeks in the trenches in 1916,
and his journeys in unheated aeroplanes in 1942–44), but that came from
colossal will-power, not colossal physique. And while he was a small schoolboy, the will-power was more likely to get him into trouble than out of it.
He was so unhappy and maltreated at St George's, Ascot, that even his
parents took notice. Concern for his wellbeing as much as for his unhappiness led to his removal in 1884 to a less prestigious and altogether more
liberal establishment recommended by his father's physician. It was run by
a pair of maiden ladies, the Misses Thomson, in Brunswick Road on the

Hove side of Brighton. From there he duly moved on to Harrow, where he stayed from April 1888 to December 1892.

The pages about school in *My Early Life* read as if he could not make up his mind whether school had been for him a waste of time or not. Winston Churchill the schoolboy remains a bit of a puzzle. 'Somehow or other, Winston could not make up his mind to fit into the pattern imposed by school discipline, by the curriculum and by the examination system.'[8] Churchill himself later affirmed that these years formed 'not only the least agreeable, but the only barren and unhappy period of my life'.[9] He would obviously have liked to have shone more, and recorded with pride his one signal distinction of having won the public schools fencing championship. In most other respects his teachers and, consequently, his parents felt he was not trying as hard as he could, and he spent much time in hot water or the doghouse. He very sensibly felt that the study of Latin and Greek had more of a cachet than it deserved, and wrote with excellent humour about his grapplings with the former. Mathematics – all-important for entry into the Royal Military College at Sandhurst – never ceased to be a minefield to him. Yet he evidently learned a good deal while he was at Brighton and Harrow, and in his later years he enjoyed going back to Harrow for its festivals. He lapped up the patriotic and imperial history that was usual in those years, mostly kings and queens, wars and battles and heroes. He learned the usual sort of general-knowledge geography: physical features, national borders, ports and products. He learned how to write good English and he began to appreciate, and memorise, English literature. He became able to get along in French – an Anglicised 'pidgin' sort of French in which he remained robustly fluent, although he didn't always understand what was said back to him. He even, at the third shot (and with much special tutoring and 'cramming'), mugged up enough maths to pass the Sandhurst exam in 1893. And, after all, it is no uncommon thing for a great man of action to have been an indifferent schoolboy. What makes Churchill's case more surprising is that he turned out also to be not merely a great man of action but a man of letters and a wit, a capable painter, a tireless politician, a famous speech-maker and an internationally respected statesman. Since Harrow was his last experience of formal education, and since by his own account he only began to study seriously after he had left school, we have to classify him as, in significant measure, self-educated.

2

Willingly to War

'War is an intense form of life.'

Cosmopolitan, April 1926

Sandhurst suited him better than Harrow. He had no trouble with the work there, got into no serious scrapes (the one nearest to seriousness, involving some slight damage to property and his first public oration to a rowdy crowd at the Empire Theatre, is amusingly described in *My Early Life*), excelled on the equestrian side, and passed out with honours, eighth out of 150.[1] The original family plan had been for him to go into the infantry, but, to his hard-up mother's distress, he insisted on accepting the embrace of a very smart, exclusive and expensive cavalry regiment, the 4th Hussars. The life of an officer in so prestigious and gorgeously-apparelled an outfit, once he was through the painful rigours of the riding school, was easy and delightful, but the glamour of manoeuvres, the luxuries of the mess, the excitements of the polo field, and the social round of parties and balls (where in any case he was not at his best), did not for long satisfy him. From when he was commissioned in February 1895 until he became a Member of Parliament five years later, Winston was a soldier, but a soldier of a most uncommon kind; and not only because he quickly tired of routine soldiering and spent as much time as he could away from his regiment. He also improved his mind by serious solitary study while seeking to prepare himself for public life by making himself 'a celebrity'; he shamelessly pulled strings to involve himself in such active service adventures as garrison duty could not provide, and he discovered that he could earn a handsome income by journalism (war correspondence), book-writing (campaign histories and a novel) and public-speaking.

There can have been few if any other young cavalry or infantry officers in the 1890s, and probably not many Oxbridge undergraduates either, who got through as many good books – 'history, philosophy, economics, and things like that' – as Winston's mother faithfully mailed out to him in Bangalore, his base from October 1896. He began with Gibbon and Macaulay, and moved on through Plato, Aristotle, Schopenhauer, Malthus and Darwin, Fawcett, Hallam, Lecky, Adam Smith, Winwood Reade and (a very sensible suggestion of his mother's in view of his growing political ambitions) the *Annual Register of World Events*; and others unspecified.

> It was a curious education. First because I approached it with an empty, hungry mind, and with fairly strong jaws; and what I got I bit; secondly because I had no one to tell me: 'This is discredited', 'You should read the answer to that by so and so; ... and so forth.'[2]

In this lavish though somewhat haphazard course of historical and political literature we can see the sources of many of Churchill's later achievements: his own good prose, always lucid and muscular, handy with irony and wit, sometimes too heavy or florid, too much of Gibbon and Macaulay for delicate tastes; his moral foundations in western culture, his historical foundations in the centuries of European expansion and British military glory. We may see also, especially in Winwood Reade and Gibbon, the sources of the personal philosophy which, as he himself rather laboriously explained, came to replace the conventional Anglicanism he had so far unquestioningly followed. Paul Addison's sketch of it cannot be bettered:

> For orthodox religion, Churchill substituted a secular belief in historical progress, with a strong emphasis on the civilising mission of Britain and the British Empire. This was accompanied by a mystical faith, alternating with cynicism and depression, in the workings of Providence. He was inclined to believe that Providence had intervened on a number of occasions to save his life, and that he was being protected in order to fulfil his destiny – whatever that was.[3]

At the same time, on top of being by nature conceited, impetuous and self-willed, he shared one of the characteristics of the autodidact: though his mind was capacious, powerful and retentive, it had no training in critical method (as in this passsage he freely admitted), and he was not always as well-informed as he felt himself to be. Furthermore, he learned nothing of any consequence about the India that spread itself, vast and wonderful, beyond the confines of his cantonment. The only Indian people he knew anything about were, on the one hand, the princely and cavalry officer types encountered in maharajahs' palaces, on the polo field and infrequently on special mess occasions; and, on the other, the servants, who made his life luxurious, and the hostile tribes, who made it dangerous when he was adventuring.

His motives for that adventuring, which took him successively to Cuba, the North-West Frontier of India, the Sudan and South Africa, were mixed to an extent that is difficult to understand. The highly readable accounts of them given in *My Early Life*'s retrospect from thirty years later convey little of the extraordinary mixed state of mind in which he undertook them, as revealed in his letters to his mother: risk-taking on his own account but critical of the pointless risks taken by inept generals; self-admiring yet self-critical; now living for the desperate moment, now coolly calculating his chances; more and more sure that he wanted to quit the army and enter politics, maintaining nevertheless his military connections because they provided the best-lit stage on which to perform; and explicitly desirous of making a mark in the world. The image he presents of himself is more that of a hyperactive, hotheaded and rather alarming teenager than of the Sandhurst-educated officer and gentleman he technically was.

He had been in the cavalry for little more than half a year when, the normal five month winter season of leave coming round, his restless eye lit on Cuba, where the Spanish government's campaign to suppress the Cuban national liberation movement was reaching its climax. His colonel and colleagues 'generally looked with favour upon a plan to seek professional experience at a seat of war. It was considered as good or almost as good as a season's serious hunting'.[4] The Spanish military authorities were so far taken with, or taken in by, his letters of introduction, and no doubt also by his own presentation of himself, that he was treated as a guest of honour, allowed to accompany a mobile column for a couple of weeks, and in the course of it given a first taste of (desultory) military action; also a life-long liking for Havana cigars and the Hispanic institution of the siesta, to both of which he would remain addicted for the rest of his life.

He was home in time for the next seven months of professional soldiering, which in his memoir appear to have been passed largely on the polo field and in Society. His regiment sailed for India in 1896 and his home for the remainder of his service as a cavalry officer was at Bangalore, except when he was on leave, either back in England or, his first imperial adventure, on India's North-West Frontier with General Sir Bindon Blood's 'Malakand Field Force', the latter becoming the subject not only of several exciting (and sometimes amusingly Gibbonian) chapters in his memoir, but also of his first book. The military operations in which he participated this time, in the autumn of 1897, were not much more successful than those in Cuba, but the fighting he experienced was very much rougher and more unpleasant. The Pathan tribes whom it was the object of the expedition to 'pacify' were ulti-mately unpacifiable, and in battle neither gave nor were given quarter. Winston witnessed at first hand the behaviour that prompted Kip-ling's grim lines:

> When you're wounded an' out on Afghanistan's plains
> An' the women come out to cut up what remains,
> Jest roll to your rifle an' blow out your brains,
> An' go to your Gawd like a soldier.[5]

(Except that, on these occasions, the men didn't wait for the women.) Undaunted by these distressing experiences of 'uncivilised warfare' and, as he privately considered, ill-conceived operations, he and his ever-loyal mother ('she left no wire unpulled, no stone unturned, no cutlet uncooked') pleaded and wangled to find him a lodging in another such expedition in the same region, this time to deal with the ferocious Afridis in Tirah, 'a region of tremendous mountains lying to the north of Peshawar and east of the Khyber Pass'.⁶ Again they succeeded. To the increasing irritation of his regimental colleagues, in early 1898 he was off again. But he got no further than Peshawar, to which, after some days of inactivity, came the unwelcome news of an outbreak of peace.

His next object was the Sudan. The government's long-nourished plans to avenge the death of General Gordon and to oust the Mahdi from control over the Sudan were coming close to fruition. The head, or 'Sirdar', of the Egyptian army, Sir Herbert Kitchener, was ready to begin the great advance up the valley of the Nile, and Winston, back in Britain again in the summer of 1898, was desperate to get in on the act. He found it difficult. To the character of a pushy individualist was by now added the reputation of a wire-puller, an adventurer, a scribbler (though his merits as a war correspondent and military historian were undeniable), and – what did him no good at all in higher military circles – a soldier so unfaithful to his vocation that he wanted to enter that trade loathsome to every proper officer, politics. Kitchener declined to take him on but he circumvented the Sirdar by means of a family friend's friendship with the Adjutant-General. With temporary commissions from both the 21st Lancers and the *Morning Post*, he sped to join the avenging host on its way to Khartoum. He took an active and dashing part in the fighting, on 1 September 1898, sharing in the last great cavalry charge in British history at the battle of Omdurman, 'the last link in the long chain of those spectacular conflicts whose vivid and majestic splendour has done so much to invest war with glamour'.⁷ Again he was several times within an inch of death. Yet he survived, justifying to himself what he described to his mother as his 'faith – in what, I do not know – that I shall not be hurt'. Another letter about the same time ingenuously displays his unique mix of conceit, courage and calculation. He had been invited to join the Egyptian cavalry, he told her, but his own colonel wouldn't let him go, because he was too useful. 'He [the colonel] is quite right but it is a pity, as I should have stood a much better chance of getting something out of the business with the Egyptians.'⁸

Adventure in South Africa and entry into politics by now peremptorily beckoning, it was urgently necessary to return to Bangalore and to resign from the regular army. This he did, early in 1899; not however before taking part in his regiment's glorious triumph in the inter-regimental polo tournament. Then it was back to England, to write his second book, to fight a by-election at Oldham, to secure an even better contract with the *Morning Post*, and then to leave for Cape Town in early October on the *Dunnottar Castle*, which happened also to be carrying the Commander-in-Chief Sir Redvers Buller and his staff. It was fortunate for him that he had not yet enlisted in the Yeomanry by the middle of November, when, pirouetting as usual on the sharp edge of whatever operations were locally going on, he was captured by the Boers. His status was so questionable that he could easily have been shot. He had taken a prominent part in facilitating the escape, under fire, of the locomotive of an armoured train, which the Boers had sought to capture. He had been behaving in an officer-like manner. He had a revolver holster on his belt; the revolver itself, by a stroke of extremely good luck, was on the escaped locomotive. His pockets contained standard-issue dum-dum bullets, which he prudently threw away when no one was looking. His argument that he was just a simple newspaper correspondent cut no ice with his captors. Nor did it help that the local English-language newspapers described him as the heroic 'Lieutenant Churchill'. He was taken to Pretoria, for the time being at any rate, as a prisoner-of-war.

Before a month was out, he had escaped. He, together with the officer who had let him onto the armoured train in the first place and an Afrikaans-speaking colonial sergeant major, planned to scale the wall together. The officer, Haldane, subsequently alleged that Churchill's imprudence and prima donna-like behaviour spoiled his companions' chances; the evidence, printed in full by his son Randolph, is of an atmosphere so rich in misgivings, bungling and bad temper that mishaps and misunderstandings were all too likely.[9] Churchill was first to go, and successfully evaded the vigilance of the sentries. He waited for the others, but they failed to appear. Ill-equipped as he was (plenty of English money but no map, no food other than chocolate, and of course no Afrikaans), and not, as it happened, in the best of health, he set out on his own, walked nonchalantly out of town, and had the good fortune to strike a railway line and a goods train heading towards the neutral territory of Mozambique. Alighting from it before the sun was up, hiding through the next day, and becoming desperate for help, he had the further good fortune to run into a mine manager of English origin who was willing to take the risk of sheltering him. By now the hunt was on, and notices were posted all over the place offering £25 for the capture, dead or alive, of 'the escaped prisoner of war Churchill ... 25 years old, about 5ft 8in tall, average build, walks with a slight stoop, pale appearance, red brown hair, almost invisible small moustache [a temporary feature, never to reappear], speaks through the nose [presumably the way his upper-class English sounded to Afrikaners], cannot pronounce the letter "s", cannot speak Dutch, has last been seen in a brown suit of clothes'.[10]

The mine manager and the workers he could trust hid Churchill for nearly a week – the first few days down the mine in company with rats which ate his candles – and then arranged with an Anglophile merchant to send him off towards Lourenço Marques in a cunningly-made tunnel within a tarpaulin-covered truck of bales of wool. That journey took three days, longer than expected, but he remained undiscovered, turning up ten days after his escape at the office of the British consul in Lourenço Marques. He took the first ship back to British Durban, and became at once fêted and celebrated. Now he did enlist properly, in the South African Light Horse. In deference to his character as a hero and a generally exceptional person, he was allowed also to continue to function as a war correspondent. After six months of continuous writing and fighting, including another close-to-death experience at Dewetsdorp, he sailed for home in July 1900. So ended five years of lively doings, about which the British public had been kept well informed.

His activities as war correspondent and campaign historian merit particular notice because, besides giving him the financial independence indispensible for embarking on a political career, they marked the beginning of a lifetime as a fine writer and a famous orator. He early discovered that he could write both quickly and well, and that he enjoyed writing, when he could make time for it. 'It was great fun writing a book. One lived with it. It became a companion ...'[11] His income from writing would often be of the first importance for a public man who from time to time – and all the time from 1929 to 1939 – held no public office; but he also went on writing also through his later years of relative affluence. He was, on top of everything else, a born writer, and he discovered early the time-saving knack of dictating what he wanted to write.

His father in his last years had made good money as a special correspondent and this may well have encouraged young Winston in his first effort: five 'Letters from the [Cuban] Front' for the *Daily Graphic* in the winter of 1895/6, their source sufficiently evident in the initials 'WSC'. He was furious when his next batch of letters, from the North-West Frontier to the *Calcutta Pioneer* and, much more important from a career point of view, the *Daily Telegraph*, were attributed in the latter simply to 'A Young Officer'; he had written them, he told his mother, 'with design, a design which took form as the correspondence advanced, of bringing my personality before the electorate'.[12] No such blanket was ever again allowed to conceal his identity. Those letters, and the book which soon followed them, *The*

Story of the Malakand Field Force, established his reputation as a competent war correspondent and a readable military historian, with more irreverence in him than in the conventional practitioner in that genre. Later that year, 1898, he completed his only-ever venture into fiction: a *Prisoner of Zenda* type novel, *Savrola*, with a lot of fighting in it and a hero remarkably like himself. Although it is creditable evidence of his versatility, he never claimed that it was anything more than a potboiler, and he shared the general amusement when there appeared in the United States a professional novelist of exactly the same name barring the 'Spencer', with whom he exchanged humorous courtesies and whose works may still be confused with his in second-hand bookshops. From his Sudan adventure came a series of signed letters to the famously Conservative *Morning Post* and, about a year later, a 950-page, two-volume study of the whole campaign and its historical background, *The River War*. From the South Africa adventure came another, even better paid, series of letters to the same newspaper, and two more books: *London to Ladysmith* and *Ian Hamilton's March* (six weeks from Bloemfontein to Pretoria), both published in 1900.

His career as orator, tactfully setting aside the impromptu speech to the mob at the Empire in 1894, he dated from the day late in 1898 when, anxious to set foot on the political ladder, he went as celebrity guest speaker to a Primrose League fête in a rich Conservative's park overlooking the city of Bath. With the example of his famously speech-making father to encourage him, he took enormous pains over the preparation, writing it all out and learning it by heart as he was to go on doing, with all his major utterances, for many years to come. He found the task easy and enjoyable: 'I very soon had enough to make several speeches. However, I had asked how long I ought to speak, and being told that about a quarter of an hour would do, I confined myself rigorously to twenty-five minutes.' His speech, rousingly larded with imperialist and party clap-trap, went down very well. The *Morning Post* did him the honour of a full column and, moreover, 'wrote an appreciative leaderette upon the arrival of a new figure on the political scene'.[13] After that, he had no more fear of speaking in public than he had ever had of speaking in private. He performed efficiently at the Oldham by-election in early 1899, and during the winter of 1900–1 further capitalised on his South African experiences by going on an exhausting but lucrative couple of lecture tours on both sides of the Atlantic.

All this activity had its designed effect. It made him widely well-known, which was politically desirable, and made him richer to the tune of about £10,000, serious money in those days. Invested on his behalf by Sir Ernest Cassel, one of the series of financiers and businessmen often to be found in his circle of acquaintances, this kept him going for several years. Writing at the end of the 1920s and (because he had by then, after all, held several remunerated public offices) with a degree of exaggeration betraying grand ideas of what was necessary for a good life, he proudly recorded that until 1919, when he received an unexpected legacy, 'I was entirely dependent upon my own exertions. During all these twenty years I maintained myself, and later on my family, without ever lacking anything necessary to health or enjoyment'.[14]

Most of his writing and speaking having been about war in one form or another, this is an appropriate place for dealing with the controversial topic of Churchill's attitude towards it. It is controversial because his reputation in some liberal and leftish circles has been the unpleasant one of a 'militarist' (a term which demands more definition than it usually receives) and a 'warmonger'. That he was interested in, indeed fascinated by, war from his earliest years is obvious. The boy's fascination developed through the young soldier's experience into the thinking adult's recognition of the truth – recognised indeed by every international historian, though few of them would affirm it to such flesh-creeping effect as he did in beginning a striking piece of journalism in 1924 – that 'The story of the human race is War'.[15] War to him was an exciting, problematical, natural phenomenon, to which he devoted much study. But he was more self-aware about this side of himself than can have been realised by those who didn't like it. Consider for example these two passages, the first in one of his letters from South Africa to the *Morning Post* and the second from Würzburg (where he had been to observe the German army's annual manoeuvres) to his wife ten years later:

> Ah, horrible war, amazing medley of the glorious and the squalid, the pitiful and the sublime, if modern men of light and leading saw your face closer, simple folk would see it hardly ever ...

> Much as war attracts me and fascinates my mind with its tremendous situations – I feel more deeply every year – and can measure the feeling here in the midst of arms – what vile and wicked folly and barbarism it is.[16]

Notwithstanding this confusion of feelings, he was entirely a man of his day in sharing with all the military men of his age, and without doubt the majority of educated civilians, an unquestioning acceptance of war as the ultimate arbiter of disputes between states and a normal accompaniment of imperial expansion and defence. In these early years, he would slip now and then into a tough Social Darwinist style of talk about war and its value as a test of a nation's quality. But that was only the logical conclusion of what was on all conservative and imperial minds. The national debate about 'national efficiency' which followed the Boer War was at bottom about little else.

Did his military enthusiasms unbalance his judgement in great questions of war and peace, and was he prone to encourage military actions that might otherwise have been avoided? In one connection, the answers have to be yes. His obsession with Bolshevism in 1918–19 and persistence in feeding the fires of the Russian Civil War attracted criticism from political allies as well as from political opponents. The Labour Party's idea of him as a warmonger became fixed at that time, producing in the 1930s some unfortunate misunderstandings of his attitude to Nazism. But he did not have war-making on his mind all the time. When there was no war in view, he could give his whole mind and energies to the works of peace – including, when it seemed the right thing to do, the cutting of armed services down to size. From his first weeks in the Commons, he had a sharp eye for War Office bungling; indeed, he may be said to have been at times unreasonably critical of the higher army command. He was never in favour of armed services without a clear defensive and diplomatic purpose. In 1909 he said to a big meeting in Manchester, 'I hope that you will not expect me to advocate a braggart and sensational policy of expenditure on armaments'.[17] As Chancellor of the Exchequer, in the later 1920s, he was a consistent pruner of military budgets and thus, when skies had darkened, incurred some of the blame for the country's military unpreparedness.

On the other hand, when war was in view, and especially when the safety of Britain and its Empire were at risk, the intensity of his interest was liable to boil over into excessive excitement. His vast appetite for investigating military matters and his considerable understanding of the conditions governing military operations did not save him from exasperating military chiefs by advice and queries which they often considered neither timely nor sensible. (Not that the opinions of military chiefs need be considered as infallible as military historians sometimes assume them to be.) None of this however qualifies, on the strict Ludendorffian definition, as militarism. The looser term 'war-lover' may be applicable, but if readiness to engage heart and soul in a war believed to be justifiable makes a man a war-lover, many millions of twentieth-century fighters must qualify. As for 'warmonger', that charge had no justification when it was revived in the later 1930s by all those on the left, and indeed across the whole span of British politics, who couldn't make up their minds whether they were willing to resist Hitler with force of arms or not. The one eminent politician whose views on the matter never wavered was bound to be unpopular. He actually felt flattered that the loudest cry of 'Warmonger!' came from Adolf Hitler.

3

Clementine and the Commons

'We are all worms. But I do believe that I am a glow-worm.'

Violet Bonham Carter, *Winston Churchill*
as I Knew Him, chapter 1 (1906)

Churchill entered the House of Commons as MP for Oldham and, to nobody's surprise, as a Conservative Unionist. Nothing else was to be expected of so conspicuous a son of so conspicuous a Conservative father. What was surprising, and to the great majority of Conservatives offensive, was that within four years the son had crossed the floor to join the Liberals.

This was the first of the string of pools of political hot water through which he would have to swim; and it was potentially the most embarrassing, for it concerned the qualities most revered in family and political life: loyalty of son to father, and loyalty of member to party. The question concerning the father is the easier to deal with, for his father's Conservatism was undeniably idiosyncratic. Lord Randolph had been anything but the party manager's ideal of being one of the MPs who, as the Palace of Westminster sentry sings of them in Gilbert and Sullivan's *Iolanthe*, 'do just what their leaders tell 'em to'. Lord Randolph's associates then, and historians since, have found it difficult to make out where opportunism ended and principle began. They have been unable to determine how radical and democratic his vaunted Tory Democracy actually was. There was, however, no doubt that he had enjoyed flirting with Liberalism in his last years, even to the point of remarking that Home Rule – the Gladstonian Liberals' proposed solution to the Irish question, a measure abhorrent to good imperialists – was the only obstacle between them and him. Winston made the most of these Liberal and democratic inclinations in the heavyweight biography of his father on which he soon began working. Its two volumes came out in January 1906 and – another example of his uncommon literary and scholarly abilities – the work was at once admitted to that distinguished club, the Great Victorian Biography, where it has remained ever since. The painstaking biographer disclosed rather more than the admiring son intended. Lord Randolph was presented in a manner sufficiently true to life that no thoughtful reader could fail to realise why the man had become distrusted and, in some quarters, disliked. It became one of the many puzzles, for those trying to understand the son, that he seems not to have understood this. He was often strangely lacking in self-awareness.

Winston, on his entry upon the political stage, behaved at first very much as his father had done. He became one of the leading lights of a ginger group of young Conservatives who rejoiced in being known as the 'Hughligans' or 'Hooligans' (the other leading light being Lord Hugh Cecil), and who enjoyed socialising with interesting seniors of whatever party; one of them, to whom Winston became for a while particularly close, was the Liberal Unionist *éminence grise* Lord Rosebery. This little gang's *raison d'être* was presumed to be having fun, showing off, and seeking advancement by making minor nuisances of themselves. Winston to begin with spoke, of course, with a certain authority on South Africa, but otherwise he specialised in the matters of army reform and economy, consistently making a good case, as his father had done before him, against Britain's paying for any more elaborate an army than was required for imperial security and home defence. This sort of anti-militarism (as it might loosely be described) showed Liberal leanings. So did the interest in social reform which Rosebery did something to encourage. As Winston had done in India some years before, and as he was to do many times again, on becoming interested in a subject new to him he buckled down to reading recommended books so that he would understand the issues and know what he was going to be talking about. In this instance, the principal book was Seebohm Rowntree's *Poverty: A Study in Town Life*, which evidently confirmed in him the sentiment of sympathy (to put the minimal interpretation on it) with the have-nots which remained part of his character through the rest of his life. His political opponents on the left would never concede that it was anything more than sentiment. Whether it was so or not, it weighed heavily enough in 1902–3 to have a part in the switch from Conservative to Liberal which he was about to make, and to begin his preparation for appearance as Lloyd George's lieutenant when the Liberals seriously set about the work of social reform later in the decade.

The ostensible primary cause of that switch, however, was Winston's adherence to the doctrine of Free Trade. The two main parties had sung the same tune about Free Trade for half a century but it now joined Home Rule as one of the great divisive political questions of the age. The Conservative Party had already had one split over the same issue when pressed by Sir Robert Peel to divorce Protectionism in 1846. Some members had never forgotten their first love; and now Joseph Chamberlain's call to remarry her, dressed *à la mode* as Imperial Preference, was certain to agitate the party again. Conservative politicians were at first a good deal divided among themselves and it seemed not impossible that those who wanted to stick with Free Trade might win the day. Churchill was active as a member of the group within the party, the Unionist Free Trade League, which put the case against tariff reform at its principled strongest.

But now came into play two counter-principles which were, for most Conservatives, even stronger: reluctance to split the party and loyalty to the party leadership. The Prime Minister, Arthur Balfour, sailed through the storm with his customary aplomb and took on the Liberal Joseph Chamberlain's programme with enough modifications to make almost all Conservatives accept the new course they were going to steer. Churchill, however, could not stomach even so cautious and Empire-sustaining a dalliance with tariffs. Somehow or other, he was not a sound party man. No such a man would have had the dealings with the enemy implied in his exploration of the possibility of a tactical alliance between his minority group and the Liberals. No such a man would have made the speeches he did, in the House and around the country, denouncing the direction which the leaders of his party were taking. A fair sample of his style and of his state of mind at this time is the article he contributed to the November 1903 issue of the *Monthly Review*.

> The position which many moderate people occupy today is one of great difficulty. They lie between the party organizations. They take a sincere pride and pleasure in the development and consolidation of the Empire, but they are not prepared to see Imperialism exploited as a mere electioneering dodge ... The great question is – are political organizations made for men or men for political organizations? ... Fifty years ago there were a score of private members in the House of Commons whose word weighed in the councils of the nation not less than the word of distinguished Ministers. Now the private member is an antic. If he is silent he is a fool. If he lifts his voice he is a knave – disappointed because his pretensions are ignored ... The first set of tariffs may indeed be framed to serve the trade of the country. The second will be arranged to suit the fortunes of a party. This to catch the iron vote, that to collar the cotton; this other, again, to rope in the woollens. Every dirty little monopolist in the island will have his own 'society' to push his special trade; and for each and all the watchword will be 'Scratch my back', and the countersign, 'I'll scratch yours'.[1]

The outcome was never in doubt. The Conservative whip was withdrawn from him in January 1904. He began to hob-nob with Lloyd George and other young Liberal lions. He finally crossed the floor of the House in May 1904, characteristically taking the seat where his father used to sit while in Opposition. Denounced as a turncoat, he ran into a lasting squall of political and social hostility. He was blackballed by the Hurlingham Club, which stood to polo as Lords did to cricket. When four years later he married a wife, she found that certain Tory houses where she was accustomed to go closed their doors to her.[2] His constituency association lost confidence in him. He offered to resign but, fearing a by-election embarrassment, the association asked him to stay on until the next general election, which in any case might not be far away. It did not in fact occur until January 1906. The next Parliament saw him take his seat, after a lively and much-publicised struggle, as Liberal and Free Trade Member for Manchester North West and, what would have been surprising had he not been the most obviously rising young man in the Commons at the time, as Parliamentary Under-Secretary for the Colonies.

Was Churchill a politician of principle? If he wasn't, he must be labelled an 'opportunist'. (Citizens not bound by those conventions might note that the terms 'man of principle' and 'opportunist' seem as interchangeable, according to the point of view, as 'freedom-fighter' and 'terrorist'.) It was as an opportunist that the party rank and file, the conventional foot-soldiers of politics, tended to think of him. The bright stars of politics, however, were not so bothered; Lord Hugh Cecil, for example, remained a close enough friend to act as best man at Churchill's marriage; by which time one of Churchill's best friends was the rising young Conservative star F. E. Smith. This question might not have become so bothersome had he not changed parties again, in the early 1920s, when he went back to being a Conservative. One way of looking at each occasion is that he quit a party (more correctly, in the later case, part of a party) which was losing its way, to associate instead with a party which seemed to have more future. Another way of looking at the same events is that, on each occasion, he quit a party the majority of whose members refused to accept that he was right and they were wrong.

For British politicians generally, loyalty to party (which in practice has to mean the party leadership) was the supreme morality. Their reasoning contained more sense and virtue than might be suggested by the obvious parallel with the primitive patriot's cry: 'my country right or wrong; and, right or wrong, my country'. The British philosophy of party politics maintains that policy disagreements, which are of course only to be expected among members of large parties in free countries, are best discussed and contained within the party, so that it goes before the electorate looking united and with a programme of action from which, over the coming session, it may not budge. This is admired not only as standing by principle but also as making for strong government; which in fact it does, within the two-party and the first-past-the-post representative system. It does not seem so admirable to advocates of systems of proportional representation, for whom coalitions of parties and malleable programmes hold no such horrors. No one was talking of proportional representation in Churchill's time, but they might, in an atmosphere of crisis and cautiously, talk of that other bugbear of party loyalists, coalition. Churchill, never cautious, was one of those most inclined to do so. The idea of a cross-party 'national' government, which by definition was what the nation could be expected to need in time of crisis, did not present itself to his mind as unnatural. He therefore failed to qualify as a sound party man on not just one but two grounds. Nevertheless he had to operate with parties and within parties if he was to hold office, exercise power and fulfil that somewhat mystical 'destiny' to which he recurrently referred. His political life was so much the more exciting and unpredictable.

With the Conservatives' resignation in December 1905, and the popular confirmation of the Liberals as their replacement at the general election of January 1906, began for Churchill ten years of ministerial hard labour which took him through, successively, the Colonial Office, the Board of Trade and the Home Office to the military heights of the Admiralty. His ministerial apprenticeship was served as Under-Secretary of State for the Colonies. At that office his senior was the ninth Earl of Elgin. They made an odd couple. Queen Victoria found the solemn and bearded Whig peer 'very shy and most painfully silent', and so did everyone else in London.[3] He never spoke in the House of Lords or the Cabinet on any matters other than those for which he felt responsible; a characteristic reductive of political usefulness. But he was stolidly impressive, a pillar of the Liberal Party in Scotland, and he had been a competent Viceroy of India. He had the administrative experience that Churchill lacked. Shrewd observers of the political scene supposed that Churchill asked for this Under-Secretaryship, in preference to the smarter post he was first offered, not just because he would be the department's sole representative in the Commons but also because he could shine like the sun beside such a ministerial moon. But if Churchill had further supposed that he would be able to run the show, he was to be disappointed. Elgin was content to let Churchill have his head on lesser issues and glad to have him in the firing-line in the Commons, where certain Liberals specialised in sniping at anything they could call a colonial scandal or bungle, and he showed patience in argument about larger issues. He was, however, immovable as granite when convinced that his excitable younger colleague was wrong. At the end of their twenty-eight months together, they parted on good terms, Churchill even admitting to having learned something from his superior about the conduct of official business.

The Colonial Office at this time was one of the 'Public Offices' in the huge Italianate block erected thirty years earlier between Downing Street and Charles Street, at the Parliament end of Whitehall. It was responsible for every part of the British Empire other than India, for which there was the separate and splendid India Office, and Egypt and the Sudan, semi-independent under the Foreign Office. All three departments (plus the Home Office) shared the same building. 'Colonies' at that date still included the big self-governing ones which would very soon be distinguished as 'Dominions' and have a department of their own: as in the cases of Canada, which had been self-governing since 1867, New Zealand and Australia, which had become so more recently, and what would in 1910 become the Union of South Africa.

South Africa demanded the most immediate attention. British hegemony had been reasserted, peace restored and white supremacy implicitly assured in 1902, but on what terms the Boers were to be incorporated within the Empire remained uncertain. Churchill held fast to the belief which he had boldly avowed while the passions of war were still high; that, once British imperial right had been vindicated, peace should be made on generous terms. Even before he had navigated the rapids of the general election in January 1906, he had written a heavyweight memorandum on the subject which impressed Lord Elgin and others in the Cabinet to whom he showed it, and which had its part in determining the new government to depart radically from the Conservatives' existing plan.[4] Churchill's effective speeches in the Commons elaborated the same argument. The Boer-subduing style of the Conservatives' admired 'Proconsul' Alfred Milner was short-sighted and doomed to failure. The Boers of Transvaal and Orange Free State must be brought into the nascent Union of South Africa on terms of equality with the British settler population of the Cape and Natal. The Boers, shown the respect due from honourable victor to gallant opponent and from one white man to another, would, so Churchill believed, become subjects of the British crown just as loyal as, he did not doubt, the French in Canada; all of them after all shared the advantage of being of European stock, and all were engaged in the same work of taking over territories from un- or sub-civilised 'natives'. The wisdom of hindsight may tell us that such optimism about white solidarity was misplaced and that such condescension to non-whites was ignorant and insulting, but such convictions were common in the heyday of British imperial pride. More confidence was placed in the colour white than turned out to be politically justified; too little in the colours black and brown. The interests of the indigenous African, the immigrant Indian and the racially-mixed populations in South Africa were casually passed over. Churchill accepted unquestioningly, though without gloating or unkindness, the then prevalent notion of white superiority. He seems never subsequently to have thought differently.

Not black or brown but, in the colour-code of imperialism, yellow was the South African problem which demanded instant attention and which raised tempers highest: 'Chinese Labour'. The mineowners on the Rand had run into a difficulty common throughout the Empire: a shortage of reliable manual workers. Indigenous peoples rarely proved to be such, unless they could be formally enslaved – which was out of the question by 1900. So workers had to be imported. Milner had allowed the Randlords to import gangs of labourers from China. Inevitably they were put into guarded compounds and kept hard at work. What turned this predictable situation into a sensational one was, first, the fact that Milner had permitted the mineowners illegally to include flogging among their disciplinary measures; and, secondly, the story that these wretched Chinese were indulging in 'unnatural vice'. The British public went into one of its periodic fits of prurient morality; and, Milner being one of the anti-imperialists' prime bogeymen although by now retired, some Liberal MPs sought formally to censure him. The main part of the problem was gradually got over; but not before Churchill had scored one of his many entries in the books of quotations by saying that the situation of the Chinese could be called 'slavery' only at 'some risk of terminological inexactitude'.[5] The Transvaal government set up under the new constitution reversed the Milner policy and most of the Chinese were sent home when their contracts expired. Churchill's speech to head off the censure of Milner, although successful in that aim, might have been thought needlessly offensive to so eminent a gentleman; a just-retired 'proconsul' whom many, not on the Opposition side of the House alone, regarded as a great public servant; and, what prudence might have whispered in Winston's ear, a man capable of reappearing in high office at home.

That speech, on 22 February 1906, displayed one of the characteristics that remained with Churchill throughout his life: a tendency to overdo the rhetoric, to sound too extreme and even violent, in presenting an argument; and, once he had got going on a prepared speech, to stick and be stuck with it whether it was going down well or not. His performance at the Colonial Office displayed other characteristics. For one thing, he could not keep quiet or still. He had always to be doing. When there were no important matters on which he could use his energies, he used them on small ones. Important items of business he could deal with very well. He mastered materials quickly. His official memoranda and state papers were as finely constructed and powerfully-argued as his set-piece speeches and might be very sensible; colleagues rarely had cause to grudge expenditure of time on them. But he lacked skill at distinguishing what was worth spending time on from what was not. He would bore or annoy colleagues (and others) by writing and talking too much about matters that did not interest or grip them. They concluded that he lacked a sense of proportion.

Then there was the love of adventure and of dicing with death. There was no real need for a minister personally to inspect Britain's recently-acquired territories in East Africa, but Churchill thought it would be a good idea; also that he and his party (secretary, manservant and sporting uncle) could incidentally shoot some big game, make a safari to the headwaters of the Nile, and begin the journey home in style by steamer via Khartoum; the whole to be paid for by articles in the *Strand Magazine* (five articles at £150 apiece), which subsequently came out as a book, *My African Journey* (another £500).[6] Characteristically, he never forgot business in the midst of these risky pleasures, which lasted from mid 1907 until January 1908. If Elgin and the civil servants had hoped to escape for a while from the normal bombardment of bright ideas, they were to be disappointed.

A third characteristic that would remain with Churchill the minister, when dealing with officials nominally under him, with others who had to report to him, and with anyone who simply wanted to meet him, was disregard of the rules of hierarchy, readiness to rebuke and correct whatever he perceived as slovenliness and ineptitude, impatience and brusquerie. It showed good nature to espouse the causes of underlings whom he perceived to be mistreated, but to do it too often or too openly could look like snubbing their superiors and unprofessional interference. His tactless rebukes and corrections caused much offence, especially when he was younger than the men he was dealing with. This characteristic was only found forgiveable during the years of his premierships, 1940–45 and 1951–55, by those who could view it as the foible of an eccentric grand old man. The senior civil servants at the Colonial Office in 1906–7 did not like him; their chief, who sounds like a very stuffy and hidebound type, complained to Lord Elgin that Churchill was 'most tiresome to deal with'.[7] One may indeed suppose that Churchill often had right and reason on his side. It must also be noted that some officials, for example Eddie Marsh, his secretary and then his friend over nearly fifty years, were quite content with him. His host in Kampala, after much difficulty in getting him to be civil to three bishops whom etiquette required him to visit, recorded 'he is a difficult fellow to handle', but went on at once to add 'but I can't help liking him'.[8] Not everybody who had to deal with him came to that conclusion. His infringements of the rules of hierarchy, the pride of office-holders and even common civility were often, at the least, tactless.

In the later months of 1907 Churchill began to show a heightened interest in the great matters of social policy with which other members of the government, his new friend David Lloyd George at their head, had from its beginning been concerned. Contemporaries and subsequent commentators of cynical and suspicious disposition attributed this new interest to restless ambition and opportunism; social reform being a more popular cause than colonial administration, and probably offering a quicker way into the Cabinet. Churchill certainly wanted to get into the Cabinet, a necesary move en route to achieving his aim of becoming – as he confided to the flabbergasted Colonial Office man in Uganda – Prime Minister by his early forties. But there is no cause to doubt the sincerity of commitment which turned his mind from imperial affairs to domestic ones and very soon presented him in the role of a radical reformer. He was only giving the whole of his attention to a field of action which had now and then engaged his sympathies ever since the last days of Mrs Everest and which, moreover, he perceived as one of his father's legacies. Before this phase of his career had fully begun, however, there occurred the most important event in his life: his marriage.

Clementine Ogilvy Hozier became his wife on 12 September 1908 as the culmination of a whirlwind courtship. We know a great deal about it, and about the marriage itself, first because they wrote so many letters to one another and the letters have survived, secondly because his youngest daughter Mary, Lady Soames, published in 1979 an exceptionally good biography of her mother, broadly enough conceived to be in effect a history of their fifty-seven years together. This long partnership began when he was thirty-three, she twenty-three. Clementine was not the first young woman whom he, a normally susceptible young man, had attempted to marry. Mary Soames lists Pamela Plowden, whom he first met in India; Muriel Wilson, a shipping heiress; and the actress Ethel Barrymore. They seem all to have found him interesting and to some extent likeable, but to have been put off by his erratic behaviour, the evident intensity of his commitment to politics and, until his parliamentary success was assured, the uncertainty of his future.

  Clementine was the product of an ill-suited marriage between the clever and strong-willed daughter of a Scottish peer, the Earl of Airlie, and an older, bad-tempered ex-officer who on retirement from the army achieved distinction in the City as Secretary of Lloyd's. She was only six when her parents separated, and her upbringing thereafter had been in somewhat reduced circumstances, saved from descent into bourgeois depths by the benevolent interest of her many titled relations. (It was one of these, who happened also to be a relation by marriage of Winston, who invited her to the party where Winston fell for her.) She was beautiful, serious-minded, sensitive and – a most uncommon achievement for a girl of her background

– had achieved a Higher School Certificate in French, German and Biology, the conclusion of four happy years at Berkhamsted High School. Her excellent headmistress wanted her to go to university but her mother by now had had enough of such eccentricities. Clementine was eighteen and it was time for her to be launched into as much of Society as they could afford and their relations could provide.

For a young woman such as Clementine, the next few years were not very satisfactory. She was twice tempted towards marriage, each time with a man a good deal older (and duller) than herself, and on the second occasion got so close to it that wedding presents had started to arrive before she decided it would be a terrible mistake. This embarrassing experience determined her not to make a mistake again. Since she had briefly come across Winston four years before, and had not thought much of him, she cannot have expected anything dramatic to happen when she found that the empty place next to her at Lady St Helier's dinner-table at 52 Portland Place, in March 1908, was where Mr Winston Churchill MP would sit when, unpunctual as usual, he at last arrived. But this was to be their enchanted evening. Winston gave Clementine the whole of his attention (characteristically being thereby rather rude to Lady Lugard on the other side) and began correspondence with her directly afterwards. He saw as much as he could of her in the succeeding weeks, persuaded his cousin the ninth Duke to invite her to Blenheim in August, and, having nearly spoiled everything by leaving her embarrassedly on her own at breakfast, proposed to her that same afternoon, 11 August 1908, while they were out in the park, taking shelter from a rainstorm. The marriage ceremony followed a month later, at St Margaret's Westminster on 12 September. Mary Soames discerningly notes that Madame Tussaud's put Winston into its permanent exhibition on the same day.

Thus began one of the most remarkable marriages of any great man in twentieth-century political public life. Others which for a while seemed glossier – one thinks of the Kennedys, the Trudeaus, the Peróns – have looked less happy under the critical microscope. Others again which maintained unbroken public fronts – Lloyd George's, F. D. Roosevelt's – are known not to have been good marriages at all. Some wives who are known to have been faithfully loved by great men and important to them, like Mme de Gaulle, nevertheless remained in the domestic background. The Churchills, however, were very often in the public eye, whether doing things together or, as was increasingly the case as their children grew up, separately. Despite his many idiosyncrasies and demanding public commitments, they managed to have a recognisably ordinary family life and to raise four children. (A fifth child, Marigold, died tragically when very young.) Everyone who knew them at all well knew that it was Clementine who kept the complicated, controversial Winston Churchill show on the road.

How was so extraordinary a marriage possible? The explanation appears to be that Winston loved Clementine with all the heart and mind which could be detached from the public affairs that commanded his enduring attention. That his love was deep and disinterested from the start was demonstrated to the material-minded, commonplace members of Edwardian Society by his marrying a relatively indigent young woman. It is as if he had taken the advice of his mother's second husband, George Cornwallis-West. A couple of years previously, Cornwallis-West had gone on from commenting on the break-up of Winston's cousin the ninth Duke's marriage to Consuelo Vanderbilt to write: 'Take my advice and if ever you do marry, do it from motives of affection and none other. No riches in the world can compensate for anything else ...'[9] Having married for love, Churchill won the commendation of the austere Beatrice Webb, who famously recorded going to lunch 'with Winston C. and his bride – a charming lady, well bred and pretty, and earnest withal – but not rich, by no means a good match, which is to Winston's credit'.[10] As for Clementine, she was a big enough personality to be able to give Winston her entire devotion, while maintaining the integrity of her own strong character and a capacity for objective and somewhat fastidious judgement which enabled her to see Winston as others saw him. She admired his ambitions, shared them, and sought to support his heroic endeavours to achieve them; doing so as often by tactful advice, even occasional reproof, as by encouragement and good counsel. The neat summary of their relationship in the 1961–70 *Dictionary of National Biography* – 'Her invariably sound advice was always cheerfully received but rarely taken. Since "Clemmie" was primarily interested in Winston and so was Winston, their relationship to each other was always closer than that with their five children'[11] – invites the footnote that by the time it was penned, three of them had in one way or another gone off the rails. But their childhoods offered no warning of unhappinesses to come. Churchill was very fond of his children and, by the standards of his class and age, unusually loving. If he had a fault in this area, it was that he was too loving. Everyone who saw the father and son together got the impression that the boy Randolph was overindulged.

4

Board of Trade and Home Office

'Democracy properly understood means the association
of all through the leadership of the best.'

Speech in Burnley, 7 November 1909

British society and politics were entering an exceptionally turbulent and
bad-tempered phase just when Clementine joined Winston. The primary
sources of disturbance and disorder lay in the flexing by the working-class
movement of its muscles, an unprecedented conflict between the Lords
and Commons, and trouble as usual in Ireland. There were also the Suffragettes, of whose increasing violence Clementine, a dedicated non-violent
Suffragist, disapproved. (Her prompt rescue action seems to have saved
Winston from being pushed under a train at Bristol by one of the aggressive
sort.) The Liberal government, which had achieved little on the home front
in the first two years of office, revitalised itself with a change of Prime
Ministers in 1908, Asquith replacing Campbell-Bannerman, and an explicit
engagement with social reforms calculated (according to one's point of
view) to appease labour or to do justice to its demands. On top of all this
was the party's awkward but ultimately inescapable commitment to deliver
on its long-standing promise of Home Rule for Ireland.

With this 'New Liberalism', Churchill found himself in eager sympathy;
discovering, as usual, that where circumstances and ambition led him it
was his destiny to go. His shift away from the Conservatives between 1900
and 1904 had been speeded by a perception that imperialist intoxication
and suburban smugness were making them insensitive to the mood of the
country, and myopic regarding the conditions in which its labouring masses
worked and died. By now Churchill was one of the leading lights of the
Liberal movement for social and democratic reform, and from April 1908
(and after the re-election, as a Member for Dundee, made necessary by
his promotion) was in the forefront of the battle with a seat in the Cabinet
as President of the Board of Trade, a department whose spreading responsibilities included conciliation in trade disputes and conditions of labour.
He determined to spread its responsibilities wider.

The demands of Labour were made known in two ways. The potentially less alarming to the propertied classes was parliamentary. The Liberal Party for many years had been accustomed to work with or even absorb respectable trade union dignitaries; one such, John Burns, had come so far along this road that he was now in the Cabinet as President of the Local Government Board. The recently formed Labour Party had twenty-nine Members in the House of Commons, all of them dependent on trade unions for their exiguous incomes. (MPs had no incomes as such until 1911.) These men were not socialists, and New Liberalism had little difficulty in working with them to remove or at least to reduce the causes of working-class discontent. But socialism and its impetuous stepsister syndicalism were alive and well in Britain, with much more capacity for alarming action than appeared in the tiny Independent Labour Party and among well-bred *soi-disant* socialist intellectuals like Sidney and Beatrice Webb, who were content to feed collectivist ideas and plans to ministers and officials. Most of British heavy labour by now was unionised, and the years 1908–13 produced more strikes, and more violent strikes, than any government had ever previously had to cope with. The very social disorders which the 'newer' Liberals had been fearing were actually happening. Free Traders in principle but pragmatically interventionist, they hustled to introduce legislation to remedy the injustices which prompted strikes and riots, and to cut the ground from under the socialists and worse who egged them on.

Churchill prepared himself for this new line of work in his accustomed way by reading recommended books and by consulting relevant experts. He even mugged up on socialism in the course of his African trip. Neither then nor at any later date could he abide socialism; but no socialist's language could have been more extreme than his, at this time, in conducting 'the war against poverty' on behalf of (a striking phrase, curiously antici-patory of the Blair government's programme ninety years later) 'the left-out millions'. While he was still in Africa, and evidently under the influence of his socialist studies, he sketched his ideas of social reform – 'minimum standards of wages and comfort, insurance in some effective form or other against sickness, unemployment, old age' – in a letter to the editor of the *Westminster Gazette*, upon the language of which no socialist could have improved: 'They [the masses] will not tolerate the existing system by which wealth is acquired, shared and employed ... they will set their faces like flint against the money power – heir of all other powers and tyrannies overthrown – and its obvious injustices.' [1] In so far as this was not simply the literary flourish of an excitable activist far from home, and momentarily forgetful of his family's dependence on the Rothschilds and Sir Ernest Cassels, it suggested how frightened he was of the proletarian *Demos*, now that it seemed to be rousing from slumber. His sympathy with its sufferings went hand-in-hand with a resolve that *Demos* should not get the better of him. At the same time, as a practical politician, he glimpsed the possibility that democracy could be enlisted in support of the Liberals, if they were to play their reforming cards right.

It certainly was not fright alone that moved him. The hardships of the poor, so far as and whenever he became aware of them, genuinely affected him, though they never again became the pressing preoccupation they were during these few years. The passage about Mrs Everest in *My Early Life* concludes on a note of self-congratulation that the Liberal government's legislation had done something to make less tragic 'the fate of poor old women, so many of whom have no one to look after them and nothing to live on at the end of their lives'.² His mind ran readily to collectivist conclusions. Not just the meanness of public provision for the poor but the haphazard inefficiency of it irked him. He had only been in office for a few weeks when a run of shipbuilders' strikes made him aware of the conditions of working-class life on the Tyne, Clyde and Mersey. Seeking the backing of Lloyd George, now Chancellor of the Exchequer, the colleague whom he most admired (and copied, and slightly feared in a way he feared no one else), to persuade the Admiralty to place some orders in advance of the timetable, he wrote: 'It does seem to me clumsy to let these people starve and have their homes broken up all winter, and then some time in June or July when things are beginning to revive to crack on a lot of new construction and have everybody working overtime ...' Lloyd George's intervention proved fruitless but Churchill persisted with it; he came back to the idea in September 1908 (while on his honeymoon in Italy) and this time succeeded.³

He threw himself into his new role with the same ruthless energy and bold appropriation of useful ideas from any quarter that he displayed on all such occasions throughout his life. He adopted the position commonly held among the socially concerned and well-informed: that Germany's comprehensive system of social security was the one to emulate. 'Germany with a harder climate and far less accumulated wealth has managed to establish tolerable basic conditions for her people', he instructed Asquith in a typically long and reflective letter. 'She is organized not only for war, but for peace. We are organized for nothing except party politics.'⁴ The Board of Trade suited him much better than the Colonial Office. Besides being his own master, he found that its excellent Permanent Secretary, Hubert Llewellyn Smith, was a man he could work with happily. Over the twenty months of his overlordship he successfully introduced and saw through the Commons legislation to establish labour exchanges, unemployment insurance and trade (wages) boards. These were small and limited measures in themselves, mere particles in the radiant beams of his grand vision of a Britain that would out-Germany Germany in the compulsory comprehensiveness of its 'defence of this country against poverty and unemployment', but they were none the less pioneering pieces of the structure which, forty years later, would become the British welfare state. There is wonderful appropriateness in the fact that the young William Beveridge was among his advisers.[5]

Churchill and Lloyd George were not the only ministers and politicians pressing this reformist programme, but they were the most forceful fighters for it, in all three of the arenas where the battle went on: Cabinet, Parliament, and the great halls up and down the country where the speeches of such political celebrities were regarded as first-rate entertainment and could be relied on to fill the house. Lloyd George would in the end acquire the greater notoriety but Churchill ran him a close second. It was no wonder that the Conservatives thought him dangerous and demagogic, as well as untrustworthy. The Liberals and their Labour allies could not, however, get enough of him. Their intellectuals admired the clarity as well as the eloquence of his speeches, made widely available later that year in book form under the title *Liberalism and the Social Problem*. Another batch came out the following year, provocatively titled *The People's Rights*. Commenting on the speech delivered in the Victoria Opera House, Burnley on 17 December 1909, David Cannadine points out 'how resourcefully and successfully Churchill learned to adapt his formal and ornate House of Commons manner to the more robust demands of the hustings'.[6] It still makes good reading, for example, these passages about the House of Lords:

> When I began my campaign in Lancashire I challenged any Conservative speaker to come down and say why the House of Lords ... should have the right to rule over us, and why the children of that House of Lords should have the right to rule over our children [cheers]. My challenge has been taken up with great courage [laughter] by Lord Curzon [groans]. No, the House of Lords could not have found any more able and, I will add, any more arrogant defender ... [His] claim resolves itself into this, that we should maintain in our country a superior class, with law-giving functions inherent in their blood, transmissible by them to their remotest posterity, and that these functions should be exercised irrespective of the character, the intelligence or the experience of the tenant for the time being [laughter] and utterly independent of the public need and the public will ... Now I come to the third great argument of Lord Curzon ... 'All civilization has been the work of aristocracies.' Why, it would be much more true to say the upkeep of the aristocracy has been the hard work of all civilizations [loud cheers and 'Say it again'].[7]

The Liberals' popular following relished the inventiveness with which, along with Lloyd George, he elaborated the core themes of the campaign: 'the peers against the people' and 'the industrious classes against the idle rich'. His excited reference at Edinburgh in July to the possibility of a dissolution drew a mild rebuke from the Prime Minister. There was so strong a whiff of class warfare in a speech he made at Leicester in September 1909 that the King's secretary wrote complainingly to *The Times* about it.

By this time the ordinary war between the parties had acquired an unusual constitutional dimension. The House of Lords, dominated by Conservatives as it has always been, broke with the constitutional convention that it did not meddle with money matters. Bills from the Commons of course had often been rejected before – the Liberals were painfully used to it, and the rejection of their Licensing Bill in 1908 still rankled – but this was something else. Lloyd George's 1909 budget, containing much to vex Conservatives in general and great landowners in particular, was not just an innovative and hefty budget designed to meet the deficit created by old-age pensions and the cost of new battleships. It was also the throwing down of a gage to political battle; a gage which the Conservatives boldly (or recklessly) picked up. The Lords' rejection of this budget at the end of November 1909 detonated the particularly turbulent and violent quinquennium which, on its Irish side, had reached the brink of civil war when another kind of war put domestic strife on hold for the duration.

Clementine, when she accepted his proposal of marriage, knew that life with Winston was bound to be strenuous. She cannot have known just how strenuous it would be, and how soon. Their first home was in his little rented house in Bolton Street, just north of Green Park. She had to do most of the work, finding a more suitable place for them to live. Having settled on 33 Eccleston Square in Pimlico, just south of Victoria Station, she had to supervise its preparation and furnishing. It was ready for entry early in May. Their first child, Diana, was born two months later. Already Clementine was having to worry about money. Winston, she discovered, was extravagant in his personal tastes, careless about bills and given to gambling. His official posts and public commitments left him little time for journalism. His salary at the Board of Trade was £2000, only £500 more than he had received in the junior post at the Colonial Office. In fact, writes her daughter, they were 'by no means well off'. Their Eccleston Square 'household of five … was not, by any contemporary yardstick, a lavish establishment for their peculiar station in life; and they lived in a world of people who were, in the main, much better off than themselves'.[8]

Financial embarrassment was to haunt their private life for many years to come. Meanwhile the demands of public life had to be met. Winston liked to have Clementine with him while he was going around the country delivering his speeches and in defiance of the persecution remoselessly (and unreasonably, since he was not outspokenly hostile to their cause) directed at him by Suffragettes. She liked to be with him, especially when he was in his constituency, protecting his seat; at this time, and until 1922, Dundee. The year 1910 was exceptionally demanding in this respect, the constitutional crisis prompting the Prime Minister twice to dissolve Parliament. These elections, which saw the Liberals' majority virtually disappear, failed to make the government's life any easier. Dependent now on the support of the Irish Members, and having dealt with the House of Lords by the Parliament Act of 1911, the government then had to bite the bullet of Home Rule. The Bill introduced accordingly in 1912 gave the Conservatives a second and potentially more popular opportunity to stage a constitutional crisis. They would oppose the Bill to the latest moment – under the terms of the Parliament Act, this could not be later than 1914 – and then, as it turned out, encourage the Orangemen of Ulster to threaten civil war if the Bill actually went through. Whatever perhaps imagined fidelities to Lord Randolph may have guided his son's adoption of the Liberal creed, none was possible now. Had it not been his father who, on Home Rule's first appearance, urged his party to 'play the Orange card' against it? Winston did his share of public speaking on Home Rule's behalf, and Clementine insisted on accompanying him in February 1912 to a Belfast Liberal rally, the circumstances of which were predicted to present real dangers. The visit turned out to be genuinely dangerous. They courageously went through it together. Subsequently, she told a friend that 'she was not afraid of being killed, but feared she might be disfigured for life by the glass of the motor being broken or by some other means ...'9 To this horrible experience, or perhaps to some imprudence on the hunting field, was attributed a miscarriage and a convalescence which lasted through much of the year 1912.

By the time of that Belfast adventure, Churchill was First Lord of the Admiralty, having done an arduous stint in the Home Office. He was evidently one of the most able and versatile men in government, but not yet the specialist in international and military affairs which history was best to know him as. Until his move to the Admiralty, towards the end of 1911, he was indeed best characterised as a Liberal reformer at home and, in regard to current international relations, a man of peace. Even when at the Admiralty, and in his newly bristling defensive posture, he was not bellicose; his reforming work was aimed primarily to improve the navy's defensive and deterrent capabilities, his speeches on foreign policy were infrequent and were no more tough than those of his non-pacifist colleagues (Asquith's Cabinet contained both sorts). Meanwhile, his twenty months at the Home Office, from February 1910 to October the following year, showed that, although he was still keen on social reform and a protector of the rights of trade unions (he played a major part in framing and promoting the 1913 Trade Union Act), he was equally keen on protecting the public, employers and the state against what he viewed as dangerous excesses of working-class activism.

The best authority on this aspect of Churchill's life entitles his chapter on these months, 'Two Faces of a Home Secretary'. This is because, while Churchill's ideas about prisons and punishments were as liberal and even as progressive as you could then find, his attitude towards non-peaceful strikers and civil disturbance showed him to be thoroughly whiggish and even conservative in respect of law and order. Never again in Churchill's long career in government did he show as much interest in social concerns, or so often use the language of social justice, as in the years 1907 to 1911. The explanation of this mental shift can only be guessed at. The man himself appears not to have found it necessary to offer any clues. It is impossible to suppose that Churchill was in any sense insincere in his enthusiastically reforming phase. He was sincere while he was in it. But it certainly was only a phase. It was in his character – the persisting boyish side to it – to take things up with enthusiasm and to put them down when something else turned up. The likeliest explanations of his apparently abrupt loss of interest in it may simply be that he found himself gripped by new consuming interests in the Admiralty and the darkening scene of foreign relations. This, after all, was when Churchill the international statesman began to materialise. It is also relevant that his liberalism, despite the characteristically extreme language he had used in the battle against the Lords' veto in 1909–11, contained no particle of socialism and therefore had no reserves of sympathy for anything that looked like class warfare. For all his ability to take on new ideas and to make improvements, and his liability to overdo the rhetoric, he was an old-fashioned paternalist at heart: a forward-looking Tory whose restless ambition and gut preference for centrist government, at least in troubled times, had put him into Liberal company and collectivist clothing.

The Home Office in those days was what it has always been, the jack of all trades department which, on top of its primary responsibility for the peace and security of the realm, was accustomed to taking on newly-discovered matters of domestic concern. Some of these novelties were better fitted for other departments or for departments of their own, and sooner or later would be moved to other ministries: workmen's compensation, for example, which Churchill's precursor had made more satisfactory, and the working hours of shop assistants, which Churchill unsuccessfully sought to get reduced. The Home Office's primary work, however, was to do with prisons and police: all the arrangements for dealing with offenders once they had been sentenced, a diffused responsibility for the policing of England and Wales, and direct responsibility for the police of the metropolis and the internal security of the British Isles.

Churchill threw himself into the business of prison reform, which he found already progressing under the head of the Prisons Commission, Sir Evelyn Ruggles-Brise, and the man who had been Home Secretary since 1905, W. E. Gladstone's youngest son, Herbert. Churchill had no doubt that too many people were being sent to prison and he was on the side of those, vocal then as now, who argued that, with regard to some types of criminal, prison doesn't work. He was not at the Home Office for long enough to make a major mark, only twenty months, but he can be credited with several humanising reforms; his energetic prosecution of which entailed, as usual, a good deal of irritation among his officials and (given the particular context) allegations by Conservatives that he was 'soft on crime'. He was not at all soft on serious crime. He shared the common belief in the possible efficacy of corporal punishment; and, far from disliking the death penalty, argued that it might be more merciful than imprisonment for life. But, like all Home Secretaries, he found the reviewing of death sentences a most upsetting part of the job; he granted reprieves in twenty-one of the forty-three cases he decided upon.

As for imprisonment itself, he felt that the many months of separate (solitary) confinement with which prisoners had to begin their terms were needlessly harsh, and insisted on their reduction, for the majority of prisoners, to one month. He was highly critical of the practice of 'preventive detention' which enabled courts to order habitual offenders to be kept in prison for extra long periods, simply to keep them out of the public's way. When the habitual offences were serious ones, he had no objection; but when the offences were trivial, as he found they often were, he objected vigorously, and insisted that, in such cases, preventive detention should not be used. He had no power to prescribe to magistrates and judges what sentences they should impose (though he would have liked to have had it) but he had a right to review sentences which might be thought excessive, and he made good use of that right, not just waiting for sad cases to be called to his attention but actively looking for them and making known what he was doing.

His principal battle was to do what, ninety years later, no Home Secretary has found a way of doing better: to keep out of prison offenders to whom it did absolutely no good, and upon whom its effects might be disastrous; and to establish more suitable forms of punishment and reformation in such cases. For Churchill in his day these were persons – in practice, working-class men – who had not paid fines imposed by courts, and young offenders. He made sure that the former were given more time to pay, and thus set in train a humanising process which by the end of the Great War reduced the annual average from an astounding figure of between 50,000 and 100,000 to less than 2000. His plans for more sensible treatment of the thousands of youths who were regularly sent to prison for various minor forms of rowdyism and otherwise lawless behaviour were shipwrecked in the political storms of 1911, but they were interesting. They displayed the belief, several times paraded in *My Early Life*, that it was natural for lively young persons to be adventurous and thereby troublesome, and they show him again in his most unaristocratically classless vein. Explaining his policy to the Commons, and after insisting that the effect of gaol on young men was usually disastrous, he said that moreover

> It is an evil which falls only on the sons of the working classes. The sons of other classes may commit many of the same kinds of offences and in boisterous and exuberant moments, whether at Oxford or anywhere else, may do things for which the working classes are committed to prison, although injury may not be inflicted on anyone. In my opinion no boy should go to prison unless he is incorrigible or committed some serious offence.[10]

A kind of prisoner posing novel and awkward problems was the Suffragette convicted for one or other of the many forms of damage, assault and obstruction to which the more violent members of the sisterhood were, at this time, increasingly given. The extension of suffrage to women was not the straightforward human rights issue simplistically imagined by the unhistorical. While many men still had no vote, it was a tricky question as to which women should have one; the two questions, suffrage in general and women's suffrage in particular, could not logically be dealt with separately; and Liberal Party managers felt it their duty to point out that the probable outcomes of some of the proposed schemes put forward would be to increase the Conservative vote.

Churchill to begin with was in favour of women's suffrage in principle, but he was not among its ardent promoters and his attitude hardened as the months went by; perhaps because he specialised in keeping calm in face of the activists' aggression. The issue caused him, in mid July, to make one of those 'over-the-top' speeches which continued to damage his public reputation until the Nazis provided a target against which no rhetoric could be overdone. In his early weeks at the Home Office he made it possible for Suffragettes to be treated as 'political prisoners'. This met many of their complaints about the way they had previously been handled in prison. He made no concession, however, on their most clamorous grievance, merely ordering that forcible feeding should not be begun until thorough medical inspection had ascertained that it would not be dangerous. Otherwise his encounters with Suffragettes and their cause were increasingly uncomfortable and controversial, and he continued to be one of their primary targets for verbal and physical assault. The Metropolitan Police had to cope with two large and very militant demonstrations in November 1910: one outside Parliament, the other in Downing Street. The Suffragettes, their political supporters and a press now equipped with cameras alleged police brutality and bad planning. Churchill was quick and firm to defend his officials and the police. He may have had good cause to do so – the story of what happened, and why, is difficult to untangle – but, so far as the women's movement was concerned, from then on he was one of the enemies, strangely wedded to a woman who was known to be a friend to women's suffrage.

The heat was to go out of the women's suffrage movement in 1919 and Churchill thereafter ceased to be dogged by tales of his hostility to it. From two other events of these years, however, tales would pass into legend. The more singular and melodramatic of these events did him little harm in the long run. At the very beginning of 1911, three supposed East European anarchists led by 'Peter the Painter' shot and killed three policemen who surprised them when they were robbing an East End jeweller's shop. They were then themselves 'besieged' in a house in Sidney Street (running south from Mile End Road, just east of London Hospital) by the police, by a detachment of armed soldiers whom the Home Secretary had allowed to join them, and (to the mixed amusement and astonishment of all newspaper readers) by the Home Secretary himself, whose attendance there had not been necessary and who perhaps ought to have stayed at his desk, but who, by his own admission, simply could not keep away.

From the other event or, to put it more accurately, train of events, much bitterness and bad blood ensued. These events pass, with questionable fairness, under the name of 'Tonypandy'. Tonypandy was, and is, in the Rhondda Valley a few miles east of Pontypridd. Relations between coal-owners and workers had become embittered, and by November 1910 most mines in that famous valley were on strike. Early that month, Tonypandy was the scene of a lot of window-breaking and looting of shops, and of a fatality in the aftermath of violent confrontations between strikers and police at neighbouring coal-mining sites. Order was then restored with the aid of detachments of police from London and of soldiers of the Lancashire Fusiliers; both of them, at the behest of the Home Secretary, under the command of a military man – which was something new. Welsh labour legend, inflamed no doubt by the troops' continued presence through many subsequent months, was soon alleging that Churchill had sent the soldiers and that they had caused such deaths as occurred. But this was not what happened. Careful scrutiny shows that Churchill sought to avoid sending soldiers at all and then, when he judged that some show of military force was unavoidable, instructed General Macready not to act, or to seem to be acting, other than in support of the civil power.[11]

If the legend of the valleys was wrong in one direction, the wholly unmilitary legend subsequently endorsed by Churchill himself (and his biographer son after him) was wrong in another. He did in the end send soldiers, and he was to do the same again and again (whether the civil authority asked for them or not) in the summer of 1911, when strikes by dock-workers, by miners again, and then by railway workers throughout the land, brought to British consciousness for the first time the possibility that revolutionary action by workers' organisations could overthrow the state. Not all of Churchill's Cabinet colleagues became as worked up as he did. Lloyd George was one of those more ready to sit things out and seek settlements by negotiation. As for the unions themselves, the weightier union leaders believed their efforts to see off the syndicalists and other militants (who were as much of a threat to them as to the liberal state) were hampered by the provocative presence of soldiers. Churchill did not see himself as an 'enemy of the people'. He perceived himself as a benevolent friend to the working class, a promoter of social welfare, and the protector of unions' rights and of everybody's civil rights; and indeed the record shows that he was all those things. But the record also shows how little he was prepared to see everybody's civil rights and the security of the state endangered by civil disorder and revolutionary activism. The legend of 'Tonypandy' after all had some justice in it, though for the wrong reason.

5

First Lord of the Admiral

'the type of retired naval officers who think that politicians should only
be in the Admiralty in time of war to take the blame for naval failures,
and provide the naval officers with rewards in cases of their successes,
if any.'

Letter to Clementine, 25 May 1954

Churchill enormously enjoyed his time at the Admiralty. (How much
Clementine enjoyed it is another matter.) His pages about it in *The World
Crisis* fizz with hyperactivity vividly recalled, giving the impression while
you read them that he can have had no time for anything else – and also
giving the impression that the senior admirals liked him more than most of
them actually did. In fact the Royal Navy was by no means the only political
problem he had to cope with at that time, and his work at the Admiralty
was not as widely appreciated at the time as he thought it ought to be.

These were great days. From dawn to midnight, day after day, one's whole mind
was absorbed by the fascination and novelty of the problems which came crowding
forward. And all the time there was a sense of power to act, to form, to organize:
all the ablest officers in the Navy standing ready, loyal and eager, with argument,
guidance, information ... Saturdays, Sundays and any other spare day I spent
always with the Fleets [of battleships] at Portsmouth or at Portland or Devonport,
or with the Flotillas [of destroyers and such] at Harwich. Officers of every rank
came on board to lunch or dine and discussion proceeded without ceasing on
every aspect of naval war and administration.
  The Admiralty yacht *Enchantress* was now to become largely my office, almost
my home; and my work my sole occupation and amusement. [Clementine fortunately was sometimes able to accompany him.] In all, I spent eight months
afloat in the three years before the war ... I got to know what everything looked
like and where everything was, and how one thing fitted into another. In the end
I could put my hand on anything that was wanted and knew thoroughly the
current state of our naval affairs.[1]

There was indeed a very great deal to do, and Churchill had been put
there to do it. The largest navy in the world was no longer quite the best,

world had become a riskier place for it since the years of Churchill's boyhood. France had then been the principal rival, and so it remained until the end of the century; about which time there occurred revolutionary shifts in both foreign policy and military organisation. The top echelons in government and foreign affairs reluctantly and creakily came to realise that imperial defence policy would have to be revised, and foreign policy with it. Countries whose navies once used not to matter were becoming big and modern enough to outmatch, in their own waters, any fleet that Britain could maintain there. Japan and the United States were both attaining such strength by 1900. Japan was therefore taken into treaty partnership in 1902, and a seal set on the conviction which had been long maturing, that the United States could never possibly become an enemy in war. That disposed of the furthest away problems. Nearer home was the problem which proved to be insoluble. Germany, not content with its unrivalled army, began to build itself a brand-new navy as well, while its alliance partners Italy and Austria-Hungary (the latter still, it must be remembered, with ports on the Adriatic) were less expensively doing the same to the south.

The foreign policy revolution which came with all this brought about the substitution of Germany for France in the minds of the defence community (to use a later expression); the settlement of colonial quarrels with France, and France's ally Russia, to make way for mutual defence discussions; and the recall of most of the big ships to home waters as a counterweight to Germany's seemingly inexhaustible naval expansionism, which quite openly had no other purpose than to frighten Britain into quiescence while Germany's army assured it of continental hegemony. Churchill was slower than some to take the measure of the German menace, but his awakening was completed by the Agadir crisis in mid 1911, when the German gunboat *Panther*'s provocative appearance in an insignificant Moroccan port ignited a major crisis which lasted through most of the summer. By the end of it Churchill had become acutely security conscious, soliciting reading-lists from experts in his usual way, and ready – as he had not been last time round – to go into the front line of national defence.

The new German navy, like other new navies sprouting up all round the world, was everything modern science and technology could make it. Much of the old British navy inevitably was obsolete and, for the new century's purposes, useless. Bringing the navy up to date had begun well before Churchill arrived at the Admiralty in late October 1911. Without having had any serious fighting to do for half a century, and with commanders trained in an authoritarian and hierarchical tradition which encouraged mental rigidity in most of them, it had drifted into ways which set more store on appearance than fighting efficiency and which were resistant to change. It was moreover governed by a Board of Admiralty on which the civilian First Lord, unless he was an especially tough character, found it difficult to do anything which the assembled Sea Lords did not want. Captain Blimp was just as familiar on the waters as was Colonel Blimp on land. In most respects which mattered for combat with a thoroughly modern foe, the Royal Navy by the early twentieth century needed reform.

This modernising process happened *pari passu* with the rise through the hierarchy of one of the officers whose intellects had *not* been atrophied, the famously reforming, outspoken, choleric and thoroughly autocratic Admiral Sir John Fisher, Second Sea Lord from 1902, and First Sea Lord from 1904 until his retirement in 1910. Churchill had been entranced when he bumped into Fisher in 1907 at Biarritz, for many years a favourite watering place.

> He told me wonderful stories of the Navy and of his plans – all about Dreadnoughts, all about submarines, all about the new education scheme for every branch of the Navy, all about big guns, and splendid Admirals and foolish miserable ones, and Nelson and the Bible, and finally the island of Borkum.[2]

The impression made was lasting, and Churchill was tempted, when he took his new broom into Admiralty House, to recall Fisher to help him wield it. Wisely (on this occasion; he would not be so wise next time he was tempted), he concluded that to bring Fisher back into the community he had so recently, however necessarily and beneficially, set at odds with itself was not worth the risk. But within the limits set by the non-war-minded elements in Cabinet and party and by the Treasury, then as ever penny-pinching on defence preparedness, he carried on much of Fisher's programmes for improving equipment and performance: bigger and better battleships with the largest calibre guns yet carried on the waters, realistic gunnery practice, accelerated promotion for the brightest of the rising men, and more attractive conditions of service and pay for the lower decks. He took a lively and, so far as regarded himself, dangerous interest in the military uses of aeroplanes, instituting the Royal Naval Air Service, which by 1914 was uniquely cultivating the skills of aerial bombing. He established a War Staff (something the autocratic Fisher had not been keen on). Finally, he joyously shared credit for a coup which, by bringing the Anglo-Persian Oil Company (in due course to become British Petroleum) into public ownership, made possible the beginning of the change from coal to oil as the navy's normal fuel; a change which, besides improving the performance of warships, made sailors' lives less burdensome.

He was from the very first day an energetic and intrusive First Lord as no holder of that office had ever been before. He got rid of the Sea Lords he thought little of and surrounded himself with officers he approved of. The former and their friends alleged that the latter had to dance to his tune; which was no great matter if the tune happened to be a good one. To the annoyance and amazement of many, he literally took command. Making himself familiar with everything that went on, investigating every shady corner he came across, and correcting whatever he considered wrong, he appeared to some of the professionals and permanent staff (but not to all of them) as intrusive, impertinent and rude. This aspect of his years at the Admiralty – indeed, of his record in every office he ever held – is generally noticed by his biographers and, of course, by service historians, as somewhat to his discredit. One can in fact distinguish between occasions when he was offensive and didn't mind being so, and occasions when he might appear offensive but didn't mean to be so at all. In the former category must come, for example, the rebuke he addressed to Admiral Limpus, naval adviser to the Turkish government, for not presenting his report from Constantinople in a clearer form and better English. Setting both letters side by side, it has to be said that Limpus's letter seems perfectly acceptable and Churchill's response pompous and unreasonable. (The admiral, however, appears to have borne no grudges; when Churchill was sacked from the Admiralty in 1915, Limpus wrote him a generous and sympathetic letter.)[3] Mary Soames prints a letter of Clementine's in which she begs him, with every resource of psychological insight and political prescience, to be very careful in the manner of 'retiring' Admiral Sir George Callaghan (commander of the Home Fleets) a couple of months early in order to make way for the more battleworthy Admiral Sir John Jellicoe.[4] Already by 1914 she was well aware of how offensive he could be or seem to be.

In the latter category of unintended offensiveness come occasions, not just in these years before 1914 but throughout the whole of his official life, when he engaged in rough arguments and said strong things in course of them, without feeling hostility to interlocutors who, for their part, if they did not understand his style, might well be surprised to find him offering them a drink and genial chit-chat after the storm was over. It was undeniably characteristic of the man that he was impatient with some types of subordinate and quick, sometimes too quick, to write them off; just as, per contra, he was given to trusting some associates and subordinates more than they deserved. His record from 1930 to 1945 contains a good many instances of that. He was ever given to enthusiasms and extremes. His infatuation with Sir John Fisher apart, it is not clear that he made any obvious errors of judgement in these years at the Admiralty. Admirals were political creatures in those days, accustomed to leak information to congenial politicians, to engage if they could on their behalf the interest of the monarch (influential still in naval matters), and in easy contact with the fleet of imperfectly mothballed admirals in the London clubs. A First Lord who wasn't worried whether or not he hurt feelings in a good cause stood in a most exposed position. The senior men he got rid of were of course held up as martyrs and victims by colleagues peering through telescopes of professional loyalty and by politicians grasping any stick with which to beat Churchill. The men he brought in – Battenberg, Beatty, Jellicoe and others – although in time he came to have reservations about most of them, were at any rate improvements on those he sacked. Together, this civilian-led 'band of brothers' made the Royal Navy as ready for war in 1914 as Churchill proudly claimed it to be.

What drew him to such sustained and successful exertion was the possibility of war with Germany. It was its possibility, not its prospect. Until the very last hours in those early days of August 1914, it remained possible that war could be avoided. Like the rest of his colleagues in the government, Churchill hoped, against diminishing hope, that it wouldn't happen. His work at the Admiralty had exactly matched and balanced that of von Tirpitz on the other side of the North Sea, then known on maps as the German Ocean. The British battle fleet, just as much as the German one, was meant to act as a deterrent. Tirpitz built battleships to deter Britain from joining in on the French side when Germany fought France, as he and his caste believed their country sooner or later would do. Churchill built battleships to deter Germany from thinking that Britain, in that event, would be too frightened to join in. Every defence-minded Briton understood that Britain's vital interests would be directly engaged if a German attack on France were to violate the neutrality of Belgium or to threaten German occupation of the French coast facing England. The pacifistic members of the Liberal government (who in the last months of peace were almost as much of a thorn in Churchill's flesh as the Conservative opposition) didn't believe, or claimed not to believe, that Germany would invade Belgium, but they were wrong. Churchill was among those who, believing that it would, were right. Churchill's unabashed enjoyment of the business of preparation for war, and his pride in being well-prepared for it when it came, contributed to the impression held by persons with conscientious or ideological objections to war, and by Liberals with minds set on more peaceful matters, that he was a warmonger. This was inaccurate and unfair. There is no evidence that he was seeking war with Germany or hoping that the Foreign Secretary would miss any chance of avoiding war. But when the war which had for several years seemed possible, and whose opening phases he had with brilliant insight predicted, actually began, he threw himself into it with zest, and was franker than most in admitting the inevitability of casualties; the more vitally important the operation, the heavier they were likely to be. That characteristic did not improve his reputation among war-fearers; but, rather than qualifying him as a warmonger, it should rather have marked him as an unusually honest 'war-fighter'.

The warmonger charge picked up another article in these years, relating to one of Churchill's actions in support of the Home Rule Bill. Preoccupied with the navy though he was in these years, he also took a leading part in the current phase of the Irish question, which between 1912 and the outbreak of the war had risen to a very high level of political tension. A third Home Rule Bill, the latest and last of a sad series, had passed through the Commons in 1912 but been blocked by the Lords. It had gone through the same process again in 1913. The terms of the Parliament Act of 1912 ensured that the Lords would not be able to block it for a third time in 1914. Home Rule for Ireland, something Conservatives and Unionists had professed to fear and had denounced for thirty years, seemed to be about to happen. It is difficult for us, in times so different, to understand how the chieftains of the Conservative Party, many of them of the highest respectability, allowed themselves to play with fire as recklessly as they then did; threatening civil war, no less. It is, sadly, not at all difficult for us to recognise some of the problems Churchill remarked upon when (once again in the political front line) he was introducing the Irish Free State Bill to the Commons in 1922. He recalled all the changes that had happened in the world since the crisis of July 1914 and the cause of his mentioning, in a famous passage of *The World Crisis*, 'the parishes of Fermanagh and Tyrone'. 'Then came the Great War', universal upheaval and transformation everywhere,

> but as the deluge subsides and the waters fall we see the dreary steeples of Fermanagh and Tyrone emerging once again. The integrity of their quarrel is one of the few institutions that have been unaltered in the cataclysm which has swept the world. That says a lot for the persistence with which Irishmen on the one side or the other are able to pursue their controversies. It says a good deal for the power which Ireland has, both Nationalist and Orange, to lay her hands upon the vital strings of British life and politics and to hold, dominate and convulse, year after year, generation after generation, the politics of this powerful country.[5]

Churchill had in his bones too much of his Unionist father ('Ulster will fight, and Ulster will be right') and too much Empire for him to become a Home Ruler before he had to, but by 1910 he was ready to make the best of the inevitable. The prospect was eased for him by a characteristic illusion and an objectively good idea. The illusion was the sentimental one that the nationalists of Ireland, once in enjoyment of the self-government which evidently mattered so much to them, would become as pleased to remain within the great British Empire as the Boers of South Africa. The good idea was one he had produced in a different context a few years earlier: the idea of administrative devolution. Might not Ireland become, he suggested, one of ten regional governments with powers for self-government under the continuing and overarching authority of the Imperial Parliament at Westminster? This advanced notion found few takers. His support for Home Rule, however, remained absolute. As we have seen, he allowed his courageous and likeminded wife to accompany him when, against a good deal of local advice, he honoured an engagement to give a public speech in support of it in Belfast in February 1912. The unchangingness of that city's political life comes home powerfully to the reader and listener who, ninety years later, reads how, on that occasion, menacing Unionist crowds gave way to cheering ones directly the Churchills' car moved into the Falls Road district.

Churchill was, however, not so doctrinaire a Home Ruler as to be blind to the desirability of a compromise over Ulster, if one could be reached. The Home Rule Amending Bill, introduced by Asquith in March 1914, enabled the government to argue that it had tried to reach one, but it had pleased neither of the Irish parties. For the Nationalists, no special arrangements for Ulster were acceptable except under a Dublin Parliament, while the Ulster Unionists saw the temporary special arrangement proposed for them as no more than a hiccup on the road to Dublin rule. The Irish situation began to deteriorate even further. The Ulster Volunteers looked more and more like an insurrectionary force. To the eyes of foreigners and in many British minds as well, civil war seemed probable. The government prepared for the worst. Among its dominant concerns were the security of the arms and ammunition depots in the North, the loyalty of the troops who might be required in support of the civil power, and the means of getting troops to Ulster from the Curragh barracks west of Dublin and elsewhere in the south, in the event that the railwaymen went on a politically motivated strike. Churchill had no share in the so-called 'Mutiny at the Curragh', a discreditable display of disloyalty by certain elements of the army, but he became much abused for ordering a naval squadron to Lamlash, on the Isle of Bute, to be near at hand if needed to transport troops to Belfast. The Conservative Unionists, who in these years found themselves infuriated by Churchill more than by any other Cabinet minister, accused him of provocation and of wanting to instigate a 'pogrom'; a word familiar at that time from the shocking mass killings of Jews in the Russian Empire. Both charges were calumnious and absurd, but they had this small kernel of reasonable suspicion in them: that Churchill would surely have supported the use of armed force to suppress insurrection in Ulster, if it had come to that. In later July 1914 it looked as if it might. Just at that time, recalled the novelist Compton Mackenzie, 'my wife and I were hurrying back from Capri, partly because the European situation looked unpropitious [for finishing the second part of *Sinister Street*], but chiefly because I hoped that the Serbian crisis would be solved and that ... I should be able to volunteer for service against Ulster'.[6] An unprecedented all-party conference at Buckingham Palace had ended without agreement, and on 24 July the Cabinet was agonising for the umpteenth time over how to resolve the problems made for the Irish parties and their respective British champions by the mixed populations of Ulster's southernmost counties,

> when the quiet grave tones of Sir Edward Grey's voice were heard reading a document which had just been brought to him from the Foreign Office. It was the Austrian note to Serbia. He had been reading or speaking for several minutes before I could disengage my mind from the tedious and bewildering debate which had just closed ... The parishes of Fermanagh and Tyrone faded back into the mists and squalls of Ireland, and a strange light began immediately, but by perceptible gradations, to fall and grow upon the map of Europe.[7]

Through the ten days of tense and momentous diplomacy which followed, the Irish question did indeed cease to head the political agenda, and Churchill was able to give the whole of his attention to preparing the navy. He admired and supported the Foreign Minister's endeavours to discourage the expansion of a Balkan war into a general European one; to persuade Germany not to do anything which was likely to drive Britain to participate in it; and to persuade the pacifistic members of the government, and ultimately the Liberal Party in the House of Commons, that Germany's violation of Belgium made Britain's participation unavoidable. Not seeking war but ready for it when it came, he was in the Admiralty with the windows open when, at midnight on 4 August the British ultimatum to Germany to get out of Belgium, expired.

> Along the Mall from the direction of the Palace the sound of an immense concourse singing 'God Save the King' floated in. On this deep wave there broke the chimes of Big Ben; and, as the first stroke of the hour boomed out, a rustle of movement swept across the room. The war telegram, which meant 'Commence hostilities against Germany', was flashed to the ships and establishments under the White Ensign all over the world.[8]

Churchill was proud to have made sure that, when war with Germany began, Britain's first line of defence was in good order. He was also able to make sure that it was ready for action more promptly than might have been expected. A fortunate coincidence had brought all three battle fleets together for a test mobilisation, less expensive than the usual grand man-oeuvres and intended as an economy measure, in the middle of July. The First and Second Fleets were still there, at Portland, on Friday 24 July – the day when that 'strange light began ... to fall and grow upon the map of Europe' – but in the ordinary course of events they would have dispersed on Monday 27 July. (The ships of the reservist-manned Third Fleet had already gone to their home ports.) Churchill was at Cromer, Norfolk, with his family on the Sunday. Clementine had to put up with his preoccupation, and with his recurrent absences to telephone the First Sea Lord, Battenberg, to find out how the drama was developing. The passing hours bringing no diminution of tension, Churchill and Battenberg determined to order the fleets to stay in being. Churchill received the Cabinet's approval of this bold initiative the next morning. As the situation worsened, so his preparations advanced. By Tuesday the 28th it seemed desirable to move the First Fleet to its war stations at Scapa Flow, the Firth of Cromarty and (for the battle-cruisers) Rosyth, and to do it stealthily lest Tirpitz launch the pre-emptive torpedo attack which had become one of the Admiralty's nightmares. Its movement through the night of the 29th gave Churchill opportunity for one of the most poetic passages in *The World Crisis*:

> We may now picture this great Fleet, with its flotillas and cruisers, steaming slowly out of Portland Harbour, squadron by squadron, scores of gigantic castles of steel wending their way across the misty, shining sea, like giants bowed in anxious thought. We may picture them again as darkness fell, eighteen miles of warships running at high speed and in absolute darkness through the narrow Straits, bearing with them into the broad waters of the North the safeguard of considerable affairs.[9]

The fleets were in place, and their crews ready to do their duty in the best Nelsonian tradition; but as a war machine, notwithstanding the reforms and improvements already made, the mentality and the equipment of the Royal Navy still left a lot to be desired. Its planning for war was cranky and defective. Fisher's legacy included an obsession with the impractical notion (never seriously discussed with the War Office) of attacking Ger-many's northern seaboards, including those in the Baltic. So strong was this obsession, and so persuasive had Fisher been in its advocacy, that it gripped Churchill too. Apart from that and from its unrealistic expectation of a Nelsonian pitched battle which the Germans would offer and lose, the navy was ready for its historic role in blockade. Distasteful awareness of the defensive uses of mines and submarines had led to the substitution of distant blockade for the traditional close kind, but what the submarine might do to commercial traffic was totally beyond imagination (as indeed it was, to begin with, for the German navy too). On the material side, Scapa Flow, where most of the big ships had to lie, was uncomfortable due to the weather, inconvenient in that it was accessible only by water, and ill-protected because no serious money had been spent on it.

The German navy was in fact superior in several respects. Its biggest ships were better protected, their armour-piercing shells more penetrative. German gunnery was always superior, German torpedoes had not the British ones' tendency to go beneath their targets, and German mines were more certain to go off. And the German navy had this singular factor working to its advantage: while the British navy had to attend to British interests in many seas, the German navy had only the North Sea to think about, once their commerce-raiders had done what they could. The Naval War Staff, which Churchill had insisted on inaugurating in 1912, was too new and inexperienced to be of much use. Its fumbling hand can be traced in most of the navy's early disasters and mishaps. Churchill naturally concentrated all possible authority around himself at the earliest opportunity (the constitution of the Board of Admiralty kept him from concentrating it entirely in himself). From this was born the Admiralty War Group, which met at least once a day and consisted of Churchill, the First Sea Lord, the Chief of the War Staff and the Secretary of the Admiralty.

This system was as efficient an instrument for directing worldwide naval operations as could have been devised in the circumstances, and Churchill was certainly the most likely of twentieth-century First Lords to direct the navy to good effect. Inevitably, however, such a concentration of novel civilian authority at top level was liable to cause offence lower down, and provoked the criticism that (as usual) he took too much on himself. (To make matters worse, he also engaged spectacularly in what might be described as extra-mural activities, soon to be described.) When things went wrong, he was in an exposed position and attracted bad publicity. When the war at sea went well – which, given that the navy's chief tasks were to maintain an invisibly distant blockade of the German coast and to keep the world's seaways open, meant when nothing spectacular was happening – the British public found little to catch its attention.

The Royal Navy in the long run proved invincible; which was what really mattered. It was not, however, invulnerable. In the short run disasters outnumbered successes. The powerful battle-cruiser *Goeben* and its smaller attendant were allowed to get unscathed to Constantinople, a great escape which was to have weighty political consequences. Three elderly cruisers made themselves sitting ducks for a U-boat off the Dutch coast. The fine new battleship *Audacious* hit a mine and sank off the north of Ireland.

German commerce raiders were at work in every ocean. And on 1 November 1914 Admiral Cradock's woefully inadequate South Atlantic squadron was destroyed by Admiral von Spee off the coast of Chile.

Responsibility for these early disasters was, and still is, hotly debated. Faulty planning in the Admiralty, ineptly worded instructions, and personal failures by feeble or over-Nelsonian commanders can all be brought into the reckoning. Churchill's many enemies naturally relished laying the blame on him. The British public mood in the First World War was more volatile and vindictive than in the Second. Party spirit shared this characteristic. It is difficult to realise, in the light of the latter war's 'party truce' which Churchill did so much to bring about, how vicious the party spirit which now and then broke through in the earlier war was. Not even in his own party was Churchill entirely popular or trusted; his Cabinet colleagues, as always, found him a mixed blessing. As for the Conservatives, they seem really to have hated him at this time. Fed with leaks from within the Admiralty, Bonar Law (the Conservative Party leader), the *Morning Post* (their party newspaper) and Lord Charles Beresford MP (their prize retired admiral) let partisanship outweigh patriotism in their allegations of Churchill's ineptitudes: allegations which in some cases could only be disposed of by disclosing the very details of naval dispositions and plans which the enemy would have liked to know, and which therefore made Churchill's defence of his own role so much the harder.

In his Commons speeches, which included instructive passages spelling out the nature of war, the necessities under which it placed those who conducted it and the inevitability of losses, we hear minor anticipations of his great expository speeches in 1940 and 1941. In his performance as one of the two armed service ministers in the Cabinet, we see a trial run for the leading role he was later to play. No other minister except the army's Lord Kitchener understood war as he did, and Kitchener, who in any case was no politician, was not the man to look to for fine speeches. Lloyd George was the only other member of that Cabinet with the zeal and capability for war-making, as would appear when later he ousted Churchill from his civilian pre-eminence; but in these early months he was not as conspicuous as he later became.

For the time being, Churchill and Kitchener between them made the military running. They were an interestingly contrasted pair, representative respectively of Britain's two characteristic war-making traditions. Churchill, looking even younger than the forty he actually was, was vivacious, buoyant, eloquent, enthusiastic, happy to be embodying his island people's maritime confidence bred in long-gone years of Cromwell and Pitt (whose names the King had, to his great annoyance, forbidden him to give to new battleships),

Rodney, Howe and Nelson. Kitchener was elderly, impassive, monumental, a strong silent wrestler with the giant problem recurrently (and not always in the end successfully) faced in the years of Edward III and Henry V, Marlborough and Wellington: the problem of raising armies to go across the seas to join continental allies in battles on land. Because Kitchener was inarticulate and Churchill had English (he always said English when he might have said British) history and warfare in his bones, Churchill in effect had to speak and write for both; something he thoroughly enjoyed doing.

Churchill was indeed keenly interested in the whole management of the war. From the beginning he involved himself in it to an extraordinary extent. Kitchener did not offer ideas about what to do at sea but Churchill freely offered ideas about what to do on land; and early in the war, to everyone's astonishment, he went and implemented one of them himself. This was his adventure to the great Belgian city and port of Antwerp, in early October 1914.

Antwerp had been on the minds of both British and French war-managers since the early days of September. By then it was clear that the Schlieffen Plan had failed. Germany's armies had been brought to a halt short of Paris and even pushed back a little. How much further they could be pushed back remained to be seen. About one-tenth of France and most of Belgium were under German occupation, but to the north of the occupied zone remained, as yet intact and from the Allied point of view preservable, the fortified city of Antwerp and a thick corridor of Belgian land around the coastal towns of Zeebrugge, Ostend and, across the French border, Dunkirk. This corridor was Antwerp's lifeline, given that access to the North Sea lay along the waterway of the Scheldt, controlled on both sides by the politically unreliable Dutch. To any strategically educated person it was obvious, first, that the Allies could threaten the northern flank of the German armies by securing Antwerp and the Belgian coast; and, secondly, that as soon as the Germans found force to spare from their main battlefront, they would want to secure Antwerp and the Belgian coastline for themselves.

Through the month of September and into early October, after which nothing more could be done, the most aggressive part of Churchill's strategic mind was turned in this direction. He had the active approval of at least Kitchener (who desperately sought to find troops for it) and the Foreign Secretary, Grey, who was anxious to keep what remained of Belgium in the war. Churchill sent naval artillery and aeroplanes from his Naval Air Service, which in the course of these few weeks and under his instructions carried out Britain's first-ever military bombing operations (attacks on Zeppelins and their hangars) from bases near Dunkirk. He landed a brigade of Marines at Ostend. By the beginning of October it was clear that these supportive gestures were not enough to keep heart in the Belgian government and its field army, sheltering within the city's fortified perimeter. The German army had brought up some of its giant siege howitzers and the destruction of the forts had begun. How long Antwerp would hold out was unpredictable, but its fall threatened disaster to the British Expeditionary Force and the whole northern sector of the Allied front.

Friday 2 October 1914 was a day of drama for the inner members of the Cabinet. The news from Antwerp was confusing, but certainly not encouraging. There was no guarantee that the promised French troops would get there before it was too late. What could be done? The Prime Minister being in Wales and unrecallable, Kitchener and Grey took the initiative to summon Battenberg and Churchill to a crisis meeting that evening at Kitchener's house. The special train to Dover in which Churchill was en route for one of his repeated trips to the Front was halted and its passenger recalled. The quartet's late-night discussion ended with a decision to let Churchill go to Antwerp to assess the situation himself. Off again to Dover steamed the special train, while orders went out to assemble at Antwerp such miscellaneous contingents as could be rapidly mustered. Most numerous of them were the men from the Royal Naval Division, one of Churchill's more controversial brainchildren, established only two months earlier, developed rather in the manner of his private army, and still largely untrained and scantily armed.

Churchill, in Antwerp by the afternoon of the 3rd, was not content with just the roles of diplomat and military attaché. He sensed a need for someone to take command, and the opportunity to do so himself. His restless energy and contagious confidence filled the prevailing vacuums of policy and leadership, and the arrival of the first British contingent, the Royal Marine Brigade, lent weight to his promise that the surviving bits of 'gallant little Belgium' would not be abandoned to their fate. Rapidly he became possessed with the feeling that he should stay there, and on the morning of 5 October he sent to the Prime Minister what has been described as 'surely one of the most extraordinary communications ever made by a British Cabinet Minister to his leader'.[10]

> If it is thought by HM Government that I can be of service here, I am willing to resign my office and undertake command of relieving and defensive forces assigned to Antwerp in conjunction with Belgian Army, provided that I am given necessary military rank and authority, and full powers of a commander of a detached force in the field. I feel it my duty to offer my services because I am sure this arrangement will afford the best prospects of a victorious result to an enterprise in which I am deeply involved ... I wait your reply. Runciman would do Admiralty well.[11]

His offer was not accepted. He stayed on for the time being, de facto commander of the still arriving British forces and, one supposes, doing more than any orthodox officer could have managed to do in so discouraging a situation; but the prospect of holding out for any useful length of time was fast disappearing. Hoped for French troops never materialised, while the Belgians' confidence had sunk to the point that they did not believe the imminent arrival of General Rawlinson's British regulars could affect the issue. Churchill left Antwerp on 9 October and the city surrendered the next day.

This adventure brought upon Churchill much criticism and ridicule; more for how he had engaged in it than for what had been achieved. He naturally believed that it had been worthwhile, and argued in *The World Crisis* that the operation had saved the BEF from a great disaster.[12] British losses had been considerable and, in respect of the totally unprepared Naval Division, rather pathetic. Out of the eight thousand or so men there, a thousand were taken prisoner and half as many again, having walked into nearby Dutch territory, were interned there. About two hundred were killed or wounded. Losses might have been fewer, and efficiency greater, if the Naval Division had not made up the greater part of the whole. (They were to do much better nine months later at Gallipoli.) Then there were the criticisms of Churchill himself. Most of them were of a kind recurrent throughout his career: he was meddling in affairs not properly his own; he should not have dreamt of resigning from the Admiralty, which was where his duty lay; he was showing off; he could not be trusted; he was unbalanced.

These charges were not entirely without substance, but they take little account of the context in which the Antwerp emergency operation had been launched – Churchill after all went there with Kitchener's and Grey's anxious blessing – and they too lacked balance, highlighting only the wilder and sometimes self-damaging sides of his complicated personality. Churchill's active and wide-ranging mind was indeed rarely content with one single focus of attention. Admiralty professionals were often irritated by the amount of time he gave to thinking about amphibious and land operations, and to visiting France and Flanders; even if they had any understanding of the strategic value of what he was doing there, which is doubtful, they believed someone else should be doing it. He was indeed given to self-dramatisation and to showing off – though many friends and colleagues found that side of him attractive – and of course he would not otherwise have been the great speech-maker that he was. But when he became excited (as he often did), he could become overexcited to the point of imbalance and unpredictability. His daughter sadly records that her mother shared the common belief on this occasion 'that Winston's sense of proportion had deserted him', and that 'in after years [she] was always to speak of the Antwerp incident with a tinge of resentment'.[13]

Something unbalanced does seem to have happened on this occasion. The emergency was great. He was the man to save the day. His Cabinet colleagues, his country, were looking to him. He was in command; something he had always longed to be. Because he was a successful First Lord of the Admiralty from 1911 to 1915, and because the Royal Navy was credibly reported as pleased to have him back in 1939–40, there has been a popular impression that he was especially devoted to the navy. That is not actually the case. He was known to say sharp things about the navy and about its commanders (even reportedly putting down a reforming admiral he didn't greatly like by remarking that all that the navy's foundations boiled down to was 'Nelson, rum, buggery and the lash').[14] He was at heart an army man. Managing the defence of Antwerp, he was in his truest element. Field-Marshal Alexander recalled Churchill saying to him, during the Second World War, 'I do envy you, you've done what I always wanted to do – to command great victorious armies in battle. I thought I got very near to it once, in the First World War, when I commanded those forces at Antwerp. I thought it was going to be my great opportunity.' [15]

It cannot have seemed much of an opportunity to anyone else, yet it must be acknowledged that the situation was not, from the beginning, absolutely hopeless. Kitchener may not have been joking when he told the Cabinet that he would promote Churchill to lieutenant-general if Asquith were to let him stay there. War and the operations of war are peculiarly subject to the play of chance. There were many 'ifs' in the Antwerp situation and it was the misfortune of Churchill – not to mention the Belgians and the Allies – that they all went the wrong way. If they had gone otherwise, Churchill might have had his opportunity after all. But the Naval Division was the only body of troops immediately available, the Germans did not allow themselves to be distracted, the French could not directly help, General Rawlinson arrived a day too late, and the Belgians had had enough. Martin Gilbert devotes many careful pages to this episode and his conclusion is that Churchill's critics were more unfair than the circumstances warranted.[16] Churchill's enemies, of course, didn't worry whether they were unfair or not.

6

The Dardanelles

'the many disappointments and surprises
of which war largely consists.'

Letter to the Prime Minister, 2 September 1939

The Antwerp adventure kept Churchill away from the Admiralty for not
much over a week, but that was more than long enough for the First Sea
Lord, Admiral Prince Louis of Battenberg, left in charge for much longer
than he had expected, to feel that he had been unreasonably thrust into
the firing line. His unhappiness was the greater for a rising miasma of
rumour and allegation (a kind of thing much commoner in the First World
War than the Second) that his Germanic background rendered him unfit
to hold such a post, and that he was perhaps dangerous in it. Neither
Churchill nor anyone else who knew Prince Louis believed such rubbish,
but its persistence was demoralising; and, besides, Churchill had discovered
that the man was not strong-minded or combative enough to be the First
Sea Lord that Churchill dreamed of. Battenberg (who in order to save his
family from further embarrassments in due course changed its name to
Mountbatten) needed little persuasion to resign, his place being taken by
someone undoubtedly more aggressive: Admiral Sir John Fisher, by now
seventy-three but raring to go again.

Whether this appointment was wise has been debated ever since. Churchill
had considered Fisher's suitability for the post three years earlier and had
decided against him. Then, he was probably right; now, he was soon to be
proved wrong. Fisher, towards whom the younger man showed an unaccustomed degree of patience and consideration, takes his place in that series
of questionable attachments (amounting at their worst to a sort of infatuation) which recurred throughout Churchill's life, often causing anxiety to
his clearer-eyed wife. On this occasion, the partnership began promisingly
enough, with shock-waves of energy throughout the service and another
round of removals and appointments (many undoubtedly improvements)
in the top jobs. The war at sea continued, however, to disappoint the navy's
and the British public's aspirations. The German battle fleet persisted in

not offering itself up on a plate. In the middle of December, Hartlepool (which was a legitimate military target) and Scarborough (which was not) were savagely bombarded by two German battle-cruisers, which, along with all the other German ships out that day, got home safely. Their escape from the well-placed and superior British forces out to catch them was only in part due to bad weather. The Admiralty's decoding section, 'Room 40', had as usual done good work, but fleet signalling, as so often, was poor; individual commanders showed bad judgement; and, to crown it all, the torpedo from submarine *E11*, which might have sunk the German dreadnought *Posen*, went beneath it. Churchill's generous side showed itself in his dissuading Fisher from sacking the senior officers concerned. He had to do the same kind office again after the Dogger Bank action in late January 1915, when poor communications and the feebleness of his second-in-command kept Beatty's modest victory from being a great one. In these areas of Admiralty management, and in dealing with Commander-in-Chief Jellicoe's unceasing worries that his Grand Fleet needed to be made still grander, First Lord and First Sea Lord worked together harmoniously.

By now their relationship was beginning to go through cloudy patches as well as sunny ones. It is unclear whether incipient mental illness was involved, or whether the ageing Fisher was simply becoming unstable, crotchety and whimsical, as old people often do; especially those who have been accustomed to indulge in rages and to have their own way. The first of his series of resignations or threats to resign came on 4 January 1915, and did not show Fisher in a pleasant light. Among the Admiralty's official responsibilities was the air defence of Britain. This task had fallen into the Admiralty's lap when the War Office was obliged to consign all its frail aerial resources to France. Churchill took on this further war-waging responsibility with his customary enthusiasm and the predictable firework display of bright ideas, memoranda and orders for action. It was the German Zeppelins from which danger was apprehended. Could anything be done about them? Churchill was absolutely right in his assessment of the developing situation. Zeppelins, he was confident, had no long-term future. Aeroplanes might not yet be able to climb high enough or fast enough to be able to shoot them down reliably, but sooner or later they would be able to do so. Meanwhile Zeppelins could be attacked in their bases. His Royal Naval Air Service did as much of this as it could with its primitive machines, from airfields improvised in France and the unoccupied strip of Belgium. With just pride he wrote:

> All honour to the naval airmen, the pioneers of the aerial offensive, who planned and executed in these early months the desperate flights over hostile territory in

an element then scarcely known, which resulted in the raids on Düsseldorf and Cologne on the Rhine, Friedrichshaven on Lake Constance, and Cuxhaven in the Heligoland Bight. Altogether in the first twelve months of the war six Zeppelins were destroyed in the air or in their sheds ... and few were destroyed by any other agency except accident.[1]

If Germany were to decide to send its Zeppelins to bomb accessible parts of Britain, however, the Admiralty's chances of stopping them were for the time being slight. Late in December 1914 British Intelligence brought news that attacks on London were being planned. (They would not actually get as far as London until six months later.) Fisher's reaction was self-centred and savage. Moved mainly, it seems, by fear of being held responsible for civilian casualties he could not prevent, 'He proposed to me that we should take a large number of hostages from the German population in our hands and should declare our intention of executing one of them for every civilian killed by bombs from aircraft'. Churchill of course rejected such a shocking idea, with the consequence that on 4 January 1915 he received a letter of resignation. He contented himself with telling Fisher that such matters were for the Cabinet and not for the Admiralty, 'and certainly not for you', to decide; and begged the old man to think again. Fisher sent no reply but, somewhat to Churchill's surprise, behaved as if nothing had happened.[2] This was the first of the series of disagreements, lasting six months, which were going to have a major part in the history of the most painful episode of Churchill's life.

By the turn of the year, the western and eastern (which also meant south-eastern) war fronts, so different in most respects, had this in common: in every state there was puzzlement about what to do next. But disaster was close in the east. The Russian army, naively likened early in the war to a steam-roller and the continuing subject of credulous myths, had suffered huge losses and run out of steam. It was reported by the British military attaché that Russian arsenals were producing fewer shells per month than its armies had been using per day. The supply of rifles was likewise inadequate. Churchill would later write dramatically about it.

> The barracks of the Empire were full of lusty manhood. 800,000 trained drafts were ready for despatch to the front, but there were no weapons to place in their hands. Every Russian battery was silenced; every Russian battalion was depleted to two-thirds of its strength ... Meanwhile, the Russian armies, hamstrung and paralysed, must await and endure the vengeance of their foes ... While the deadlock continued on the Western front ... Russia with her inexhaustible resources in men and food, might collapse altogether or be forced into a separate peace.[3]

Whether any measure of relief could be hoped for from the several still neutral states lying to the south of Russia's vast war zone was as yet uncertain. Russia's protégé Serbia had been of course involved since the beginning, and the pro-German party had not been long in coming out on top in Turkey. Each of the other Balkan States – Greece torn between the two camps, Rumania presumed to be Francophile, Bulgaria the opposite – was waiting to see which side was the more advantageous to join. To put it bluntly, they were waiting for offers.

The Foreign Office from the start had been intensely interested in these Balkan possibilities, but it took several months before the Admiralty and War Office minds could be prised from preoccupations nearer home. Kitchener's understandable priority was to train his host of volunteers and to get them across the Channel to strengthen Sir John French's still tiny sector of what was beginning to take dreadful reality in people's minds as the Western Front. Kitchener had never expected it to be a short war but was as appalled as everyone else to discover the shape the war was taking. Churchill early formed the opinion, and on 29 December conveyed it to the Prime Minister, that neither side was likely to be able to make much impression on the other, 'although no doubt several hundred thousand men will be spent to satisfy the military mind on the point ...' Memorably he inquired, 'Are there not other alternatives than sending our armies to chew barbed wire in Flanders?' He believed there were – and proceeded to describe them.[4]

Long before the Western Front had been thought of, and very soon after Germany had come into view as the British navy's likeliest opponent, Admiralty planning had included the possibility of attacking Germany's northern coast, in both the North Sea and the Baltic. Churchill had fallen in happily with this line of thinking, and now he pressed it on Asquith and, at its next meeting, the War Council. There were several variants within this strategic aspiration, which at its most ambitious supposed the incorporation of Denmark on the Allied side whether the Danes liked it or not, and the use of British and Russian troops to seize Schleswig-Holstein and invade Pomerania, although joint planning with the War Office had never been possible. Indispensable to this grand venture (which to some seemed as fantastic then as it must seem now) was the bottling up of the German fleet in its North Sea havens, and that, it was argued, required the preliminary seizure of a strategically-placed island. Old Admiral Sir Arthur Wilson, whom Churchill had got rid of in 1911 as too hidebound but whose voluntary return to the colours he had welcomed in 1914, never ceased to believe that Heligoland was the island to aim for. Churchill and Fisher favoured somewhere nearer land, and persuaded themselves that it should be Borkum, off the mouth of the Ems. One of the weightier arguments urged against this plan was that, if it was thought possible to seize and hold an island 250 miles from the nearest bit of Britain, why should it be thought impossible for Germany to retain possession of an island only fifteen miles from its coast – not to mention only thirty miles from the great naval base of Emden. The War Council on 7 January 1915 was nevertheless persuaded that it was worth looking into, and authorised Churchill, 'with his two septuagenarian Sea Dogs', as Asquith privately put it, to proceed with detailed planning.[5]

By now, however, the focus had begun to fall upon the Dardanelles, the southern stretch of the narrow channel joining the Mediterranean and the Black Sea, with Constantinople the Turkish capital not far to the north, beyond the Sea of Marmara. The Dardanelles idea was not new. It had been around ever since Turkey's entry into the war in early November, long before the plight of Russia gave it a new urgency. Churchill had pressed it upon the War Council on 25 November (its first meeting) as the most convenient way to thwart Turkey's anticipated attack on Egypt. On that occasion, he had assumed that the seizure of the Dardanelles and Constantinople (so temptingly close on the maps) would require the deployment of a substantial body of troops. The necessity for considerable numbers of men was never doubted by the members of the War Council, who took the idea up at its repeated meetings in early January. Kitchener had suddenly (but temporarily) become enthusiastic about it. So had Lloyd George, once he had been persuaded that an attack up the Adriatic on Austria's southern flank was not practicable. So had the council's thoughtful and increasingly influential Secretary, Maurice Hankey. Troops would be needed, but need they all be British or imperial? Soldiers from India's large army had already landed in Mesopotamia, and the Anzacs were on their way. French cooperation was to be solicited, and the hope was not entirely abandoned that, if the pro-British party in Greece prevailed, a Greek army would be able to do much of the job on its own.

Translation of this bold strategic idea into realistic planning thenceforth proceeded not by leaps and bounds but by shifts and starts. Navy and army were unaccustomed to work together and the Prime Minister, the only person in a position to compel them to collaborate in service of a grand strategic decision, was not the man to rise to the occasion and make them do so. Churchill, to whose ardent spirit the need for commanding leadership was apparent from the start, would provide it himself when his chance came twenty-five years later. Lloyd George would try to provide it only two years later, by when the need for some such strong-minded method of war-management had already become clear to everybody. But Asquith, who can be blamed neither for being the man he was nor for having become by chance Prime Minister of a nation at war, found himself in a job the specifications for which were not yet properly understood. The two great military panjandrums were left to respond to the War Council's decisions as they saw fit, except in so far as Churchill had any success in chivvying and coordinating them. Churchill chose to do this partly because he realised that it needed doing (Asquith, who more or less saw what was happening, was amusedly content to let him try), and partly because it was his nature to take command; but he had to be careful how he did it and, in the event, couldn't do much.

With Kitchener, understandably preoccupied and enigmatic, Churchill's relations were businesslike and rather distant. (Kitchener was one of the very few men of whom Churchill stood in some degree of awe.) With Fisher, who was by now volcanic with feelings of resentment, his relations were close and seemingly friendly but full of difficulties. The field marshal and the admiral blew hot and cold regarding the Dardanelles, according to their fluctuating sense of how their commitments to it would detract from what they still regarded as their main theatres of operations: respectively, the Western Front and the North Sea. Planning for the provision of troops and their transportation to convenient and safe bases for the projected landings on the western side of the Dardanelles therefore went ahead unsteadily, without the power and urgency which might have brought the peninsula (though one can hardly share the planners' early optimism about Constantinople) under Allied control. Churchill's initial vision, and Kitchener's, had been of a combined army and navy operation. Churchill only tried the exclusively naval one after Kitchener, for the first of several times, put the army's contribution on hold.

The Dardanelles story is so complicated in itself (and set within diplomatic, political and military contexts very complicated again) that historians find it impossible to come to the brisk and decisive judgements on it made by partisans at the time and ever since. In no other major operation of the war were there so many imponderables. Their extent and force is well recognised in the course of Vice-Admiral Peter Gretton's excellent attempt at a summary.

> Churchill's words – 'Those terrible "ifs" accumulate' – are only too true. There were numbers of moments when, if events had taken another turn, if advice had been accepted or rejected, or if decisions had been made instead of shelved, history would have been written altogether differently. But one of the most striking features of the many accounts of the campaign is that each authority seems to choose his own turning-points, and hardly any two are the same.[6]

It has to be said at the outset that the grand Dardanelles plan, which worked out so badly, was by no means damned from the start. The ifs all went against it. It might have met with some measure of success if three requirements, at least, had been met. First, a force had to be landed sufficient to make headway against the defenders; some of the more promising moments during the fighting suggest that this was not impossible. Secondly, the sooner they could have got there, the less time would the German general in charge have had to toughen the defences and rearm the Turkish defenders; this factor had its effect as the weeks passed, but even in the later stages the defences were not absolutely insuperable. Thirdly, there had to be good commanders. The performance of some of them, as the Anzacs have never forgotten, was wretched, and the Commander-in-Chief, General Sir Ian Hamilton, was not the man ruthlessly to sack and replace them; something which the culture of the British army at that time in any case made almost unthinkable.

To this point, Churchill's role presented little opportunity for justifiable complaint or criticism. The 'amphibious' plan which he was enthusiastically seeking to assist was not his but the War Council's, and the sooner and more forcefully it was implemented the better. It was, however, not the only plan on his agenda. Until 18 March 1915, it was not even the plan about which he was most excited. Early in the year he became possessed by, and thought he had persuaded Fisher to support, an exclusively naval operation to clear the way right up to the Sea of Marmara. Gilbert emphasises the fact that he only took up this idea under the impression of an impending disaster on the Russian front. Kitchener asked Churchill to try to do something, and expresssly pointed to the Dardanelles as being the most promising, or the least unpromising, place to do it.

> Kitchener and Churchill were the only two Ministers ... authorised to plan and conduct all acts of war. Kitchener's insistence that the War Office could undertake no immediate military action threw the burden of responsibility upon the Admiralty. Under the pressure of unforeseen events and dire possibilities Churchill took up the very plan which until then he had believed to be impossible.[7]

The Admiralty had considered the idea of forcing the Dardanelles years ago and turned it down, but now, on 3 January 1915, Churchill asked his War Group to reconsider. What about trying it with an array of some of the moth-balled pre-dreadnought battleships which were no longer safe to use in high-seas battle but which were heavily armoured and had suitably big guns? The opinion of the vice-admiral commanding in the eastern Mediterranean, Carden, was at once solicited by telegram; Churchill adding, as he often did when specially important operations were in prospect, 'Importance of results would justify severe loss'. Carden's initial brief response was that it might be possible; not in a rush, but 'by extended operations with large numbers of ships'.[8] This was enough to encourage Churchill, now with the War Council's interest aroused, to inquire further. Carden's more detailed thoughts arrived on 12 January. The Admiralty War Group went over them with care and reckoned that his requirements could be met and even exceeded. The following day Churchill brought the plan before the War Council. It was by no means the only plan to help Russia and to circumvent the Western Front before it, and several other options were still in view (including the badly ill-judged one at Salonika). For the Admiralty, however, this was the go-ahead. Plans regarding the Belgian coast, Zeebrugge, Borkum and the Baltic, which had until now been vigorously pursued, were put on hold. While Kitchener strove to conjure up soldiers for action somewhere in the region – not for many weeks yet would Gallipoli become their certain destination – and digested the disappointing news on 6 March that Russia had vetoed the idea of inviting the Greek army to participate, the Royal Navy was preparing to force the Dardanelles on its own.

Churchill's part in the history of the Dardanelles expedition from this point on may be viewed as divided into these three phases, the second and third of which marked accelerating declines in his popularity and authority. The first phase, which began with apparently encouraging bombardments of the outer forts, lasted until 18 March, when the spectacular naval assault on the first stretch of the waterway, although successful so far as it went and although its losses could, in the circumstances, hardly be judged severe ('less than thirty British lives and two or three worthless ships', he later wrote, conveniently forgetting a French battleship with most of its crew), failed to achieve its ultimate objective: clearance of the way through the Narrows and opening the way to the Sea of Marmara.[9] The Royal Navy, usefully aided by the French, had tried to do the job on its own, but had so far failed. Churchill, not without support, wanted it to try again, but majority opinion among senior officers was swinging against him, and in any case Rear-Admiral de Robeck (previously Carden's second-in-command, who had taken over after his overwrought superior suffered a breakdown) very soon advised that for the time being he couldn't take on any other task than protecting and safely landing the expeditionary force to which Kitchener had, at last, become committed; after which event, the forts along the Turkish coast must become more vulnerable, with an enemy behind them as well as before.

This relatively uneventful second phase ended with a bang on 25 April, a date remembered indelibly in Australasia as Anzac Day and in the opinion of a good judge as 'the most dramatic day of the whole World War'; the day when the British, Anzac and French spearheads of General Hamilton's expeditionary force landed around the coast of the peninsula called Gallipoli.[10] Its battle was to continue with much bravery and heavy casualties but no breakthrough until Kitchener finally called it off at the end of the year. The evacuation, a masterpiece of inter-service cooperation, was the most successful thing that had happened there and (in true British style) was hailed, just as Dunkirk was to be a quarter of a century later, as a sort of victory.

With regard to the Dardanelles, Churchill could not but feel sidelined after 19 March. The navy continued to be intimately involved in the second phase of the great Dardanelles project which he had wholeheartedly made his own, but no longer was he able to pull the strings of it as hitherto. In the War Council's view of the matter, the army was being given its chance to do what had been beyond the sole powers of the navy. Hamilton's expedition was a War Office affair: although de Robeck of course communicated constantly with the Admiralty about naval operations, it was well understood that his primary concern now had to be liaison with Hamilton, which in practice meant the protection of Hamilton's base (on a nearby island) and communications, and a great deal of artillery assistance. Churchill could only watch all this from afar, eagerly digesting letters about it from friends who, along with his brother Jack, were serving there; gratified at the navy's useful participation in the operations but still hankering after its return to a grand independent operation on its own. This frustrating phase did not last long. It came to a painful end amidst a bizarre concatenation of events in the middle of May. Elucidation of them makes a good opportunity to try to reach a balanced judgement about what he and Clementine felt to be the most painful experience of his life, and what is always brought into the debit side when reckonings are made about his overall career.

Churchill's difficulties may largely be laid at Fisher's door; but it must be remembered that he had brought this particular difficulty upon himself. Fisher was only involved because Churchill had put him there, and he was becoming increasingly difficult to work with through the early months of 1915. To begin with he concurred in the Dardanelles plan, but thereafter he wavered. Now he supported it, now he didn't. In the end Fisher exploded in the War Council and astonished everyone by saying that he had *never* supported it. He kept resigning. If one wonders why Churchill did not accept any of these resignations, the answer seems to be, first, that despite the repeated unpleasantnesses and difficulties of working alongside him, Churchill never shed the core of his long-held admiration, even a sort of sympathetic reverence, for the Nelsonic old blusterer; secondly, that Fisher retained the regard of the service; and, thirdly (it would have been a politician's natural reflection), that Fisher could be more of a nuisance outside the Admiralty than inside it. The more Fisher's dissatisfaction with his position as First Sea Lord became known (and increasingly, with questionable loyalty, he made it known), the more did Churchill's enemies on the Tory benches and in their editorial chairs use this as material for assaulting Churchill's performance as civilian First Lord. The British army was, they could point out, properly run by a great soldier, Kitchener. Why should a conceited busybody of a civilian be allowed to stand between the British navy and a great sailor, Fisher?

This argument was doubly fallacious. First, it was an extraordinary historical accident that a soldier should have been in charge of the War Office. Kitchener was only in such a position because of the nation's peculiar and, it might be hoped, non-recurrent unpreparedness for a great continental war. He had been called in to help the government in an unprecedented emergency. Constitutional propriety required that the armed forces should ultimately be under civilian control. Kitchener in this respect was an aberration, without precedent since the time of Cromwell and without repetition since. Secondly, Fisher was by now not up to it. His admirers seem not to like to admit this, but the evidence allows no other conclusion. Fisher's judgement in these months was unreliable, his temper uncertain and his behaviour unbalanced. He said something to Clementine that caused her to call him 'a silly old man' and ask him to leave the house.[11] At the War Council which he attended on 14 May his behaviour was quite alarming. It is possible that a perfectly balanced and sane Fisher might have possessed better judgement regarding naval management and operations than the admittedly excitable and sometimes impetuous Churchill; but that was not the choice on offer in early 1915. The fact that Fisher washed his hands of the Dardanelles connection by his final resignation on 15 May has no relevance to its objective merits.

Churchill cannot be criticised for sharing the general belief, until bitter Gallipoli experience taught otherwise, that the Turkish army would be easily defeated. A few early incidents in the autumn of 1914 lent colour to that belief; it was more excusable than the similar misjudgement about the Japanese which brought disaster in early 1942. He cannot be blamed more than anyone else for failure to reckon how defective the mine-sweeping efforts of the brave civilian trawlermen undertaking the task were bound to be. He might have been more sceptical about the likelihood of reducing the Turkish forts by low-trajectory naval gunfire, a very different sort of fire from that used by the Germans to reduce the Belgian fortresses. He was more enthusiastic about the navy's capabilities in the Dardanelles, and probably more interfering with its commander on the spot, than was sensible or prudent – his restless chivvying must have added to the inadequate Carden's burdens. He had no opportunity of knowing before the event how inadequate Carden would prove to be. He gloried in being more willing and able to withstand pressures and take risks than many war-makers, and he took them on this occasion. Sixteen years later he wrote:

> It seems clear now that when Lord Kitchener went back upon his undertaking to send the 29th Division to reinforce the army gathering in Egypt ... I should have been prudent then to have broken off the naval attack. It would have been quite easy to do so, and all arrangements were made upon that basis. I did not do it, and from that moment I became accountable for an operation the vital control of which had passed to other hands.[12]

He gambled, and lost, as afterwards he honestly admitted. Risk-taking is part of war. His defence of his actions, that great risks may have to be taken for great gains, and that a really great gain was within reach, was reasonable; he could also affirm that the War Council had been behind him most of the time. But in the atmosphere of that awful month of May 1915 it cut no ice. What might have been a survivable set-back for Churchill now turned into a unique disaster.

Other events at exactly this same time made Fisher's resignation on 15 May the catalyst of a great government upheaval. Two momentous things, neither of them related to the Dardanelles, had happened on the 14th. *The Times* published its military correspondent Colonel Repington's hard-hitting report on how Sir John French's army was suffering from a shortage of shells; the first time that Asquith's government's ability to manage the national war effort had been seriously questioned. At the same time, and privately momentous for the Prime Minister, Asquith learned from the late-met love of his life, Venetia Stanley, that she was going to marry Edwin Montagu, a long-time political associate of Asquith and currently a Cabinet colleague. This news upset him so much that he lost the confidence in handling political storms that he had shown earlier on.

The breaking of the shell-shortage scandal one day, followed by the most serious yet resignation of Fisher the next, were strong reasons that led towards the formation of a coalition government. In itself, the coalition of parties in face of a grave national danger made good sense, and appealed to the less partisan, the more statesman-minded of politicians, Churchill prominent among them. Now, as before and after, he liked to think of himself as more of a national politician than a party one. What he himself took a little time to realise was that one of the Conservatives' principal conditions was that Churchill should quit the Admiralty. The majority of them (not all – Churchill still had at least one friend at the Conservative court, F. E. Smith) had become convinced that he was doing no good there. Their idea of a good First Lord was a man whom Fisher could get on with – in other words, dominate.

This crisis took more than a week to reach its dénouement. By 21 May it was clear that, no matter who succeeded Churchill, Fisher would not remain at the Admiralty. The terms he laid down for coming back were quite impossible. They lent substance to the belief that he was a victim of megalomania. Asquith had broken it to Churchill that he would have to be moved, though what he might move to was still hidden. And it was clear that Kitchener was still so popular as to be irremovable, although (because the shell shortage could plausibly be laid at his door) he was not trusted as universally as he had been. By 25 May, when the storm abated, the political scene had been transformed. Asquith now presided over a coalition government. Lloyd George was to exercise his dynamism at the new Ministry of Munitions. The Conservative leader Bonar Law, Churchill's main political enemy, was Minister for the Colonies. The First Lord of the Admiralty was Arthur Balfour (who was going to harmonise pleasantly with the new First Sea Lord, Jackson). And Churchill, although still in the Cabinet, held no more prestigious an office than the semi-sinecure Chancellorship of the Duchy of Lancaster.

This was a come-down and Churchill felt it acutely. He was sure he had it in him to be a war leader. It was plain enough that leadership in modern war had to be qualitatively different from the sort of leadership that had sufficed through many decades of European peace, and he had felt able to supply something of this necessary leadership through this great war's first six months. Now he was being blamed, even scapegoated, for events for which his responsibility was shared with others upon whom blame did not similarly fall, because their parts in the drama were not publicly so visible (and would not become visible until much later). From now on, and for many years to come, the Dardanelles constituted his touchiest point. He defended his record before his Dundee constituency, and he circulated among his Cabinet colleagues statements of relevant facts they could not previously have known. He took the first opportunity to defend his record in the House, he joined with his political enemies in demanding a Commission of Inquiry into the fateful expedition after it was all over, and he devoted a huge quantity of pages to it in *The World Crisis*. As time went by, and as the generation of his wartime critics died off, more balanced assessments of his role came into circulation. What they boil down to is that Churchill's portion of the general blame or responsibility, whichever one likes to call it, was no greater than the portions of others involved in the famous failure. 'The Dardanelles' has not remained the black mark against him in military and Conservative circles that Tonypandy and the General Strike became, and may still be, in trades union ones.

These months through the summer and autumn of 1915 appear in Churchill's long and loud life as an unusually slow and quiet period. For the first time in ten years, he had not enough to do, which, coupled with his sense of grievance and disappointment, brought on a bad attack of depression, what he called his 'black dog'. The absence from his daughter's collection of her parents' letters of any from these months speaks volumes. He was at home and with the family much more than usual. There were three children by now: Diana, born in 1909; Randolph in 1911; and Sarah in 1914. Clementine always took some time to recover from having babies, but there were to be no more additions to the family until 1918, and she was to that extent the freer for the voluntary war work which was expected of all women in her position; her speciality became the establishment and management of canteens for munitions workers in the London area. With the loss of his post at the Admiralty, they had of course to move out of Admiralty House. Arthur Balfour kindly let them stay there until they had made a suitable arrangement. Money was tight because the change of jobs had halved Winston's salary and the cost of living was going up. They decided to pool resources with Winston's brother and his wife Lady Gwendeline (sic), engagingly known within the family circle as Goonie and a good friend of Clementine's, who had a house too big for them at 41 Cromwell Road.

Churchill still attended the House of Commons when it was sitting. But he had nothing else of an official kind to do, and it was equally depressing and upsetting for him – being the man he was and feeling the military situation as he did – to sit with his hands tied, watching the conduct of the war being inefficiently managed by less qualified persons. Clementine lovingly empathised with him in his frustration and boredom. She believed in him as much as he believed in himself. When during the May crisis her husband's tenure at the Admiralty seemed doomed, she was moved to write privately to Asquith a plea so passionate, albeit so imprudent, that one cannot read it without thinking that any man would rejoice to have a wife believe in him to that extent.[13] Entering into his state of mind as perfectly as she did, Clementine must have shared her sister-in-law's surprise and relief when Goonie persuaded him to try his hand at painting, and he found that he could do it and enjoy it.

The discovery of this talent happened at a farm near Godalming, where both families were accustomed to go to get away from London. Churchill later described this singular event in articles for the *Strand* magazine which subsequently became printed separately as *Painting as a Pastime*. It must be the only treatise on painting to describe it in terms of a military operation and a release of aggression. In the early summer of 1915 he was, he wrote, intensely frustrated.

> In [my] position I knew everything and could do nothing. The change from the intense executive activities of each day's work at the Admiralty to the narrowly-measured duties of a counsellor left me gasping. Like a sea-beast fished up from the depths, or a diver too suddenly hoisted, my veins threatened to burst from the fall in pressure ... I had to watch the unhappy casting-away of great opportunities, and the feeble execution of plans which I had launched and in which I heartily believed ... I had long hours of utterly unwonted leisure in which to contemplate the frightful unfolding of the War ... And then it was that the Muse of Painting came to my rescue ... Some experiments one Sunday in the country with the children's paint-box led me to procure the next morning a complete outfit for painting in oils.[14]

More practical help than the Muse of Painting could offer came from the experienced artists Sir John Lavery and his wife, who lived near by. From this strange start flowed two distinct benefits: to Churchill himself, in that for the rest of his life he could find in his painting an unrivalled source of relaxation and calm amidst no matter what a sea of troubles; and to his family and his entourage, in that it usually absorbed him so much that he stopped talking.

These six months were for Churchill a period of relative idleness and absolute frustration. The idleness of which he complained was not idleness by any ordinary person's standards. He continued to go to his office, such as it was, and to attend the Cabinet, the Dardanelles Committee (which amounted to much the same thing) and any other committee he was on. Nor was he a passive member of those bodies. He went on producing the thoughtful and wide-ranging papers on the military and political states of affairs which had already become and would remain one of his hallmarks. No other member of the Cabinet had so many good ideas about so many aspects of the conduct of the war. Lloyd George was his rival in energy and enterprise, not to mention his superior in politics, but his many strengths did not include military experience and that fascination with military technology (aeroplanes, tanks and guns) which was one of Churchill's specialities. Churchill was right in thinking he had a lot to offer. Even Bonar Law and Carson, who had joined the team with no predisposition to admire him, were impressed. It was unfortunate for the United Kingdom and its empire that the most war-minded member of the government had become the one whom, because he had no firm backing in party or public opinion, it was safe for the other members of the Cabinet to ignore. It was a strange paradox of parliamentary politics that such a man became the member of the Cabinet least listened to when the war was going badly.

Churchill was not, however, the only member of the Cabinet to feel frustrated with the way the war was going. Asquith's coalition government was no nearer successful management of the war than his first, Liberal government had been. Churchill and the other energetic spirits, Lloyd George, Curzon, Carson, became increasingly concerned about their collective failure to do better. The more they talked about it, the more inevitably they took on the appearance of conspirators plotting against the Prime Minister. The substantive merits of their criticisms became inseparable from the manoeuvres of ordinary political power play. Asquith was not to be replaced as Premier until the end of 1916 but through 1915, while Churchill was still more or less in the government, its two main shortcomings were its habitual indecisiveness, for which Asquith was most responsible, and its lack of information about the military situation, for which Kitchener was entirely responsible. Lord Kitchener was still a demigod to the nation at large and was consequently irremovable from office, but in the Cabinet and the top echelons of the War Office it was more and more clear that his removal was much to be desired. He was overburdened yet unable to devolve responsibilities; reluctant to share information with Cabinet members when they requested it; and evidently unreliable in what he could be persuaded to disclose. He persisted in blocking the approach to conscription, which Churchill (who served on the sub-committee to review the matter) correctly considered inevitable. And instead of committing to the Dardanelles the further reinforcement which Hamilton (not, alas, for the first time) believed likely to facilitate a victorious final push, the major British effort of the autumn was dedicated again to taking pressure off the Russians by an offensive on the Western Front. The battle of Loos, in the last days of September, was a bloody failure at least as bad as any registered in Gallipoli.

By this date, the future of the Dardanelles enterprise was poised on a knife-edge. The military breakthrough originally hoped for had still not come and so the political advantages consequent upon that presumed breakthrough had not come either. The Balkan states had reacted to the failure in much the same way as the peoples of South-East Asia would later react to the fall of Singapore: they saw which way the wind was blowing and trimmed accordingly. Italy indeed had committed itself to the Allied side earlier in the year, when the outlook was brighter. But Greece remained non-committal, until the Entente allies forced their embrace upon it, and Bulgaria, having opted for the other side, was by the end of October helping it to finish off Serbia. It was in hope of saving something of Serbia and of bringing its fancied ally Rumania into the war that France in late

September opened a bridgehead at Salonika, insisting that the British join them. The opening of this new front, together with the approach of winter, put an end to the possibility of continued action at Gallipoli. Churchill, unsurprisingly, was the last member of the government to abandon belief in it. The Dardanelles expedition having come to such a bad end, there was no longer any point in a Dardanelles Committee. Asquith gave notice that it would be closed down and replaced, as Churchill and the other activists had been urging, by a small War Committee or Council. Churchill was not on it.

This was the last straw. For several weeks already, Churchill had been entertaining thoughts of getting away from Westminster. Convinced that he could no longer do any good there, he resigned. His letters of resignation (there were actually two), besides reiterating his confidence that his reputation would rise again when the whole story of the Dardanelles came out, specified his dissatisfaction with the way the war had so far been managed. But he had not been able to do anything about it.

> Nor do I feel in times like these able to remain in well-paid inactivity. I therefore ask you to submit my resignation to the King. I am an officer, and I place myself unreservedly at the disposal of the military authorities, observing that my regiment is in France.[15]

7

Recovery

'Not allowed to make the plans, I was allowed to make the munitions.'

The World Crisis, iii, chapter 12

Equipping himself for going to the war was done with the same brisk decisiveness and disregard of cost shown in fitting himself up as a painter, but with a lot more fuss. He was transformed from civilian into soldier within forty-eight hours. 41 Cromwell Road throbbed and hummed with excitement and activity, as his family decked him out and friends called to wish him luck. He left for France on 18 November and was to be in France or just over the Belgian border (except when he was on leave in London) for twenty-three weeks.

This was not much of a stint of active service, but one of its points of interest is in showing several of Churchill's better features and a few of his worse. It is in any case an extraordinary episode. This new eccentricity by so unique a celebrity attracted public attention, amusingly chronicled by E. V. Lucas in his satirical column in the *Star*: 'Mr Winston Churchill announces his intention of returning to the army ... Reiteration by Mr Winston Churchill of his desperate military purpose ... Mr Winston Churchill leaves for the front. Panic among the enemy ... Mr Winston Churchill, having sufficiently changed the trend of events, relinquishes his commission.'[1] The reality was this. The first thing he did on reaching France was sensibly to arrange to get some first-hand experience of trench life; this was done with the Grenadier Guards, from 20 to 30 November. From 1 to 11 December, he was at Sir John French's HQ at St-Omer, awaiting a posting and socialising with its influential inmates and hangers on. (Several were to remain important to him in later years: Archibald Sinclair, Edward Spiers and Max Aitken, the future Lord Beaverbrook.) 11–14 December, he was back with the Guards. 14–22 December, at St-Omer again, swallowing his disappointment at having to become a colonel in charge of a battalion instead of brigadier-general with a brigade. 22–27 December, in London. 27 December to 4 January 1916, again at St-Omer (where Haig had replaced French), waiting for a battalion. From 5 January to 3 May, Churchill was in command of the 6th Battalion of the Royal Scots Fusiliers and he was with them for most of the time at Ploegsteert (anglicised as Plug Street) just across the Belgian border and a couple of miles north of Armentières. This brief period of active service was twice broken by weeks of leave: 2–13 March and 19–27 April, both spent politicking in London. On 3 May, his battalion left 'Plug Street' and on 6 May he was given permission to return to his parliamentary duties.

When, with some pride, he told Herbert Asquith that 'he was a soldier', it was the Oxfordshire Yeomanry/Hussars he had in mind. In that regiment he had long held the rank of major and, until seduced by the attractions of the Admiralty yacht, he had been wont to go on its annual summer camp. It is pretty clear that he hoped for a superior placement, and he was not surprised when destiny intervened in the shape of the Commander-in-Chief. Sir John French, with whom he had long been friendly, caused him to be met at Boulogne and spirited to GHQ, where it was proposed to him that he should either stay there as an ADC or await an opening with a brigade. This offer (as it seemed to be) was irresistible. He accepted it as to the manner born, promptly instructed his wife to order the proper bits of brigadier-general's uniform, and remained confidently expectant – until, three weeks later, came the crushing news that his appointment had been vetoed by the Prime Minister. His friends generally were relieved that he was not again going to be thrown under the spotlight of criticism. Clementine herself had thought such instant promotion imprudent until, love vanquishing misgivings, she had come over to his more sanguine view of the matter. Churchill as usual had no doubts about his ability to hold high office in any sphere of action, and failed to understand what a handle the job would have given to his enemies and critics.

Disappointment, however, made no difference to his resolve to learn the business of Western Front soldiering and to do it well. His battalion, when he got to it on 5 January 1916, was with the Royal Scots Fusiliers, who were 'resting' some miles behind the line at Meteren, trying to recover strength and morale after suffering terrible losses at Loos the previous autumn. It was due to return to the front in two to three weeks. Although Churchill had not much time to make it efficient and confident again, he succeeded. At all times and in every respect true to his unique self, his methods were a mixture of control and kindness. Control he asserted at once and frighteningly. A long-retired officer recalled how intensely the mess had disliked the prospect of coming under so strange a commander, and how their fears were confirmed by their first meeting with him. Their first parade under his instructions was a shambles. He was probably too optimistic in reporting, after a couple of days, that 'Everyone is filled with the desire to obey and assist'.[2] The evidence, however, is that the battalion did again become an efficient unit in good time for its return to the line. Churchill's methods were eccentric (including apparently spending his own money) but successful. He was appreciated perhaps more by the Other Ranks than by the NCOs and officers. His interference with the workings of the normal chain of command was felt to weaken the latters' authority. Here was a recurrence of behaviour which had marked each of his pre-war ministries. It is difficult to explain it except as the efflorescence of a sort of autocratic sentimental paternalism.

The battalion marched (while its colonel rode) to Ploegsteert at the end of January: a muddy, wet, dismal, bleak landscape dotted with low little farm buildings and, as you approached the front line, obscurely ribbed and criss-crossed with supply-line duck-boards and trenches and diversified by several military cemeteries. Gilbert provides a good summary of the situation:

> Men whom the Army considered fresh were replacing those who were in every way exhausted ... Holding the line at Ploegsteert was not easy or safe work, but it was not 'going over the top'; during the hundred days in which the Battalion was in the trenches under Churchill's command only fifteen men were killed and a hundred and twenty-three wounded. After the horrors of Loos, with its swift, brutal losses, the men accepted Ploegsteert with equanimity, and became attached to it.[3]

Churchill himself escaped injury at Plug Street but not because he took good care of himself; rather the opposite. He unconcernedly did things that others considered reckless, and practised his preaching that it was pointless to duck when you heard a shell or bullet passing because, if it hadn't already done so, it couldn't hit you. He cut his hands badly showing others how to get over barbed wire without hurting yourself. As ever, he showed no fear of death, attributing his continuing survival to that vague destiny which he believed was working through all the changes and chances of his mortal life to preserve him for higher roles and bigger things. Clementine was naturally in a state of perpetual anxiety about him. After an extraordinary experience when an irritating bungle turned out to be the salvation of his life, he comforted her by writing:

> Now see from this how vain it is to worry about things. It is all chance or destiny and our wayward footsteps are best planted without too much calculation. One must yield oneself simply and naturally to the mood of the game and trust in God which is another way of saying the same thing ...[4]

They wrote to each other almost daily, longish letters, which often included (on his part) requests for 'tuck', brandy and cigars, extra clothing and other items, and instructions for promoting his political interests. They also disclosed, more than his writings at any other stages of his life, his most serious and quasi-religious feelings. It is interesting and, one might think, admirable that he didn't seek to clothe the possibility of his death in conventional colours of patriotism but placed it rather in a stoic philosophy of life and death. What this was, he had already outlined in a beautiful letter 'To be sent to Mrs Churchill in the event of my death'.

> Do not grieve for me too much. I am a spirit confident of my rights. Death is only an incident, and not the most important which happens to us in this state of being. On the whole, especially since I met you my darling one I have been happy, and you have taught me how noble a woman's heart can be. If there is anywhere else I shall be on the look out for you. Meanwhile look forward, feel free, rejoice in Life, cherish the children, guard my memory. God bless you. – Good bye. W.[5]

All the same, anyone reading their letters to one another (no less than one hundred between 18 November 1915 and 2 May 1916 are printed in their daughter's collection) is driven to realise that their respective ways of loving were quite different. Her love and commitment was total and filled the whole of her capacity for loving; his love and commitment to her was total only within the space left for love after his compulsive commitment to public life had pre-empted its share. It is clear that he was sometimes aware of this conflict of loyalties. It is not clear whether he ever understood what a measure of pain it imposed on her. In her letters to him, the pre-eminence in her heart of concern for his safety and success is constant and undiluted. In his letters to her, his love and longing for her is counterpointed almost all the time by concerns about his standing and prospects at Westminster. This does not make any less affecting this exchange in March 1916. After her usual endeavour to deal with his political queries and worries, this sad little paragraph:

> My Darling, these grave public anxieties are very wearing. When next I see you I hope there will be a little time for us both alone. We are still young, but Time flies stealing love away and leaving only friendship which is very peaceful but not stimulating or warming. Clemmie.[6]

This 'heartfelt outburst', writes their daughter, 'drew from Winston a declaration of the depth of his feelings for her, and a rare (very rare) admission that he too knew a longing for tranquillity'.[7]

> Oh my darling do not write of 'friendship' to me – I love you more each month that passes and feel the need of you and all your beauty. My precious charming Clemmie – I too feel sometimes the longing for rest and peace. So much effort, so many years of ceaseless fighting and worry, so much excitement and now this

rough fierce life here under the hammer of Thor, makes my older mind turn –
for the first time I think – to other things than action ... But would it not be
delicious to go for a few weeks together to some lovely spot, in Italy or Spain
and just paint and wander about together ... far from the clash of arms or bray
of Parliaments?[8]

But Parliament obsessed him, whether he willed it or not. For the first
few days in France, he tried to convince himself that he had cut himself
off from politics in order to give himself wholly to the military life, but he
simply couldn't do it. Clementine had to act as his political agent on top
of her war work (which, like so many women thus liberated from home,
she found thoroughly satisfying) and acting as head of the family. She was
privy to all his worries and suspicions with regard to political associates,
his plannings and plottings about when and how he should return to the
fray at Westminster. As ever, she lovingly understood what was going on
in his mind; as ever, she tactfully offered excellent advice and patiently put
up with his frequent neglect of it. The root and rationale of his restlessness
was Asquith's inadequacy as a Prime Minister and the consequent ineffec-
tiveness of his administration; an opinion held by plenty of good judges
besides Churchill himself. He could not resist planning parliamentary demonstrations of the government's deficiencies and imagining its replacement
by a better and brighter coalition – with himself, of course, prominent
within it.

'Party' had no place in his lucubrations. A coalition of parties in a national
government was evidently the natural and right way to go; a grouping he
particularly liked the idea of – Lloyd George, F. E. Smith, Bonar Law, Carson,
Curzon – was much more Tory than Liberal. How far Bonar Law trusted
him he was not sure. How far he could trust Lloyd George was also matter
for speculation. But that he would have to act along with Lloyd George he
never doubted; the totally distrustful Clementine could do no more than to
reinforce his instincts for caution. For her part, she couldn't warm either
to Lloyd George or to any of these Tories. Still less could she warm to the
'friends' her husband valued in the newspaper world. Churchill wrote re-
gretfully in *My Early Life* of the rising power of the press, but he was not
so silly or impractical as to disregard it. Suffering as he did from the vigilant
enmity of the *Morning Post,* and the recurrent malice of *The Times* and the
Daily Mail, it was not surprising that he sought the approval of Lord
Northcliffe's better-natured younger brother Lord Rothermere (*Daily Mirror*
and *Sunday Pictorial*) and welcomed the interest and backing of C. P. Scott
of the *Manchester Guardian* and J. L. Garvin of the *Observer*. These men,
like Max Aitken, figured in Clementine's list of undesirables: 'good time
men and personal friends, but often wrong-headed'.[9] Considering how

their counsel was partly responsible for the débâcle of his reappearance in Parliament on 7 March 1916, who can say she was wrong?

For this débâcle, another of her 'undesirables' shared responsibility: old Admiral Lord Fisher. So long as he was alive and physically well, firing off his eccentric letters and making his outrageous remarks about the alleged failings of the government in general and the Admiralty in particular, he continued to magnetise the admiration of some of the politicians and journalists who felt the same way, and shared with Kitchener the worship of the uncritical and ill-informed public at large. We can now clearly see, what many then could accurately reckon, that neither of them was worth it; that it was desirable to get rid of Kitchener (though it was very difficult to see how) and that Fisher, having been got rid of, ought not have been brought back. Clementine was of the latter school of thought and it was a matter of some distress and perplexity to her that her husband, despite the difficulties Fisher had made for him while they were in office together, continued to see only the good side of him and, when he was home on leave, was pleased to be in touch with him again. It was this infatuation that turned what would otherwise have been an estimable and successful speech on 7 March into a risible and disastrous one.

Taking advantage of a debate on the navy estimates, Churchill rose from the front of the Opposition benches and embarked on a well-informed, well-argued and not intemperate criticism of the management of the navy since he had left it. So far, so good. He was listened to with respect and it was possible for all but the most hostile to feel that he was beginning to make a political come-back. Then he astounded everyone by concluding with a 'practical proposal': that Fisher should return to the Admiralty. In the gallery were Asquith's daughter, Violet Bonham Carter, and Churchill's devoted secretary over many years, Eddie Marsh. She records that the latter had tears in his eyes, that her husband (Asquith's secretary) was speechless, and that she herself wondered whether her friend had become de-ranged.[10] They did not stay to hear the beginning of his destruction, which was finished off by Balfour the following day.

Defeat had been snatched from the jaws of victory, and it seems that Churchill never really understood why. He was sometimes so full of himself that he had difficulty in seeing himself as others saw him. Generous towards opponents, he was surprised by spitefulness towards himself. But even his friends had to admit that, on this occasion, he had asked for it. This was only one of the several similarly ill-judged speeches which marked his long career. They were like the snakes in the game of snakes-and-ladders. If there had not sometimes been great need and welcome for him at the top of some ladders, these parliamentary snakes would have been his political death. He avoided further mistakes through the remainder of 1916 and his next two big speeches after returning to civilian life were full of sound sense and valuable wide-ranging commentary: 17 May, on defence against aerial attack and making the case for an Air Ministry; and 23 May, on the many ways in which the nation's limited manpower was used inefficiently, wastefully (including Western Front massacres) and inequitably (including staff officers' avoidance of front-line dangers). These speeches, widely reported, brought him some popularity among the common people but none in the higher levels of the services and administration. They might have cut more ice had they not also contained strains of what were near obsessions through these later months of 1916: the justification of his role in the Dardanelles affair (continually being brought up by his enemies in press and politics); and resentment that his services were being dispensed with by the men at the top.

The former of these two unhappinesses was the first to be relieved. Churchill was not the only man with a reputation to rescue from the mess. Fisher believed he could benefit from a full and proper inquiry, and so did Sir Ian Hamilton. After hedging and havering for some weeks, the government announced at the beginning of June that there would be a disclosure of as many relevant papers as national security permitted. Each principal player began to look forward to his vindication; which, in the cases of Churchill and Hamilton, would involve some degree of inculpation of Kitchener, who had not dealt fairly with either of them or with the War Council itself. Great was that pair's disappointment when, only a few days later, Kitchener was spared from giving evidence by going down with the warship taking him to Russia when it struck a mine and sank. Not until later July were the form and scope of the inquiry finally determined: a Commission of Inquiry chaired by the retired proconsul Lord Cromer. Preparing his own evidence for it and dealing with the commission's questions became Churchill's main occupation through most of the rest of the year. The Fisher spell was still so strong that he worked with the former First Sea Lord to present a harmonious version of events, obscuring the facts about the old man's mental disturbance in the crisis month of May 1915.

Churchill could not hope to return to regain his proper authority in the House of Commons until and unless its report vindicated him, at least to the extent of a fair distribution of responsibility among the several besides Churchill who were responsible; but this did not happen until the commission reported early in 1917. Lloyd George, who became Prime Minister early in December 1916 at the head of a reconstituted coalition, would have liked to be able to include Churchill, but he was black-balled by some of the Conservatives. This was mortifying, but all the same the worst period of his life was coming to an end. His views on the conduct of the war could no longer be cavalierly brushed aside by his enemies and their newspapers. His friends indeed had never brushed his views aside, and it was a good thing they owned newspapers too, for loss of ministerial office in November 1915 had meant loss of all income save the ordinary MP's yearly £400, a negligible sum for anyone in Churchill's station in life. Soon after his return from France, he had been glad to resume his earlier trade as journalist, and a very well-paid one too. The powerfully expressed and exceptionally well-informed misgivings about the management of the war effort which appeared in articles in Rothermere's *Sunday Pictorial* and elsewhere were followed up in speeches (as usual, carefully prepared and on the lengthy side) which he began to make again to good effect in the Commons in early 1917. So impressive was his contribution to one of the House's rare secret sessions, on 19 May, that Lloyd George was persuaded that the time had come when he could be brought back into office, whatever might be said by 'those who at that time had accustomed themselves to regard me with hostility'.[11] Northcliffe (because of his papers, the most dangerous critic) having been sent on a special mission to the United States, the Prime Minister staged a general ministerial reshuffle and under its smoke-screen brought Churchill into office again, as Minister of Munitions.

Churchill was glad to be back in high office and made the most of it. His ministry was one of the many new ones established since 1915 to cope with the demands of a war without limit or visible end. By the time he took it over (its head office was a requisitioned hotel in Northumberland Avenue), it had a huge bureaucracy purporting to control the supplies and outputs of a vast network of privately- and publicly-owned factories. After several months there, Churchill enthused about it:

An extraordinary improvisation without parallel in any country in the world took place in our industrial system. Thousands of persons who knew nothing at all about public business or public departments, thousands of firms which had never been used for warlike manufacture, were amalgamated together ... and out of this ever-growing and enormous organisation that great flow of material of all kinds which raised our army to the very forefront of the combatant armies was almost immediately produced.[12]

He was proud to be in charge of it, and, having begun his term of office with bold strokes of rationalisation and the import of senior officials whom he had come to like and trust in his Admiralty days, he remained there with credit for the rest of the war. His term of office was by no means trouble free, least of all where wages and working practices were concerned, but the consensus is that no one else was likely to have managed any better.

One of the attractive aspects of the post was that it made a good base for involving himself in many aspects of the management of the war beyond the one for which he was directly responsible, besides giving him time for those visits to the Front he loved so much. The memoranda about the conduct of the war which continued to flow from his pen could now begin flying around Whitehall from within the magic circle. His post was not of Cabinet status, but he was invited to attend the Cabinet when his ministry's business was under discussion, and he used these occasions to join in the discussion of other ministers' business as well. These interventions, and the letters of advice or inquiry he freely wrote to other ministers, caused some annoyance to the hostile and touchy. Besides being engagingly characteristic, however, they provide continuing testimony to the unquenchable zeal for rational, scientific, efficient and energetic management which he had shown since the war began – and which he was to show again, with astonishingly undiminished force, next time round. Many of the lessons learned in the First World War, and many of the ideas it bred in him, would help prepare him for the tougher tests of the Second.

Some of his reflections about how to fight a war, and how not to, are plain to read in his book about the war, *The World Crisis*, which came out volume by volume through the 1920s. Arthur Balfour, for more than a score of years a detachedly amused but not unappreciative observer of Winston's ways, characterised it as 'an autobiography disguised as an history of the universe'. That neatly hit off the egocentric and self-justificatory elements of the work, but left out of sight its scholarly accomplishment and its many literary merits. There is good history in *The World Crisis* as well as autobiography, and the autobiographical element has a particular interest, in that it charts the development of the biggest lesson he learned from the war: the importance of preventing the admirals and generals (and budding air marshals) from running their own shows beyond Cabinet control.

Churchill didn't coin the aphorism that 'war is too serious a business to be entrusted to soldiers' (it gets into *The Oxford Dictionary of Quotations* from Aristide Briand via Lloyd George) but he thoroughly agreed with it and believed that the history of the war proved it. The men in charge of armed services might be good at their job, they might not; it was essential, and well within the powers of capable civilian statesmen placed in national authority by democratic process, to be able to distinguish the one from the other, and to extract the bad from their protective webs of professional routine, ritual, mystification and mutual protection. Automatic promotion and command according to seniority, norms of the Victorian army and still to some extent operative, served the interest of the military profession more than that of the nation the military profession existed to serve. This was no new discovery for Churchill. His earliest writings as a war correspondent and campaign historian had been cheeky about the top brass. In *My Early Life* he recalled the military grandee Sir Redvers Buller, whom he had plenty of opportunity to observe at close quarters when they were on the same ship going to South Africa in 1899.

> Buller was a characteristic British personality. He looked stolid. He said little, and what he said was obscure. He was not the kind of man who could explain things, and he never tried to do so. He usually grunted, or nodded, or shook his head, in serious discussions; and shop of all kinds was sedulously excluded from his ordinary conversation ... His name had long been before the public; and ... their belief in him was unbounded ... He plodded on from blunder to blunder and from one disaster to another, without losing either the regard of his country or the trust of his troops.[13]

Men like Buller were still common in the armed services in 1914, and Churchill had long had them in his sights. His parliamentary career began with criticising the army estimates, and proceeded by way of criticising the navy estimates to shaking up the navy. Apart from his blind spot regarding Fisher, and notwithstanding his likeable habit of recognising the better side of people before going on to illuminate the worse, he viewed the admirals and generals of 1914–18 with critical detachment; finding fault with the former especially for their collective stupidity about convoys in 1917, and with the two most important of the latter, Haig and Robertson, for their obtuseness in the management of the Western Front in 1916 and 1917.

Kitchener too had some responsibility for errors on the Western Front (for example the battle of Loos, which Churchill correctly anticipated would be a 'vast, futile and disastrous slaughter'), but the principal lesson Churchill learned from his observations of Kitchener was not military but political and constitutional. Given virtually plenary powers as Minister for War in 1914, and with a tremendous reputation behind him, this military colossus progressively lost the Cabinet's confidence through the latter months of 1915, but so high did he continue to stand in the public's estimation that he became unsackable. The hieratic grandeur which successfully beckoned hundreds of thousands to volunteer to fight for King, Country and Kitchener made his removal impossible for those who, close up, saw the flaws in the man. Churchill was no longer in the Cabinet when similar problems arose vis-à-vis Sir Douglas Haig, Commander-in-Chief in France from the end of 1915 until the end of the war, and Sir William Robertson, Chief of the

Imperial General Staff, who, so long as he had a complaisantly impression-able War Minister in Lord Derby, was found to out-Kitchener Kitchener. The Prime Minister and others both in and out of government entertained growing misgivings about these men's management of the military effort but were kept in too great ignorance of facts and alternatives to be able to assert corrective authority. Haig, who had the advantage of royal favour and who in any case showed improved form as the war neared its end, proved irremovable. Lloyd George had lost confidence in Robertson and would have liked to remove him months before he at last found strength to do so early in 1918. Churchill followed these events with intense interest, and drew the obvious liberal and democratic conclusion. 'A Government is entitled to know the facts from its servants', he wrote apropos of the War Office's exaggerated figures of German losses during the battle of the Somme.[14] If ever destiny should place him in charge of a British Government at war, he would make sure that it did know.

Churchill's complaint (representative, of course, of many others) about the generals in charge of the operations of the British and imperial armies was that they remained fixated on the Western Front, persisting in losing men fruitlessly there by failing to understand the improbability of achieving worthwhile victories, and by failing to take note of either innovatory means of doing better or alternative possibilities of action in other places. But it was not just that. Churchill does not fit easily into the dominant pattern of historical thinking which divides Great War leaders into either 'Wester-ners' or 'Easterners' because, although Churchill was the Dardanelles man par excellence in 1915 and retained a lively interest in 'back-door' possibilities and East Mediterranean operations, what most interested him from 1916 onwards was working out how the German defences in the west could be cracked. That they could not be cracked by operations not very different from the Somme, which were all that Haig and Robertson could think of, was clear to him. Nor would he accept either the dreadful bloodletting argument, advanced *faute de mieux*, that Germany could less well afford the human losses than the Allies, or the figures presented by the War Office which purported to show that German losses in these pitched slaughters were higher than British. He did not believe these figures when they were first advanced – apart from anything else, it seemed contrary to reason that defenders (especially German ones) should suffer more casualties than attackers – and the more he went into the matter, the more cause did he find to believe the facts to be otherwise. The many pages given to the casualty figures in *The World Crisis* supported his conclusion that the War Office and Lord Haig's admirers were wrong. One of the best contemporary historians of the war sums up in the same sense: 'there seems no firm ground for doubting that the Allies lost more heavily than the Germans'. This is what Churchill believed from the start.[15]

Not only did Churchill find defective the very conception of such battles, he considered it wrong and almost incredible that the plans included no timetable by which success or failure could be reckoned, and no resolve to call it off in the event of failure. In so far as it was the objective of the long drawn out battles of the Somme and Passchendaele to make great breakthroughs, there should he insisted have been no difficulty in recognising quite early on in both cases that they had failed. He could think of no good reasons, only bad ones, for continuing to throw further thousands of lives into the furnace. His language on these points was very strong. From many possible passages, I select this about the continuation of the battle of Passchendaele after the Prime Minister had done everything he could to stop it:

> Accordingly in Flanders the struggle went on. New divisions continued to replace those that were shattered. The rain descended and the mud sea spread. Still the will power of the Commander and the discipline of the Army remained invincible. By measureless sacrifices Passchendaele was won. But beyond, far beyond, still rose intact and unapproachable the fortifications of Klercken. August had passed away; September was gone; October was far spent. The full severity of a Flanders winter gripped the ghastly battlefield. Ceaselessly the Menin gate of Ypres disgorged its streams of manhood. Fast as the cannons fired, the ammunition behind them flowed in faster. Even in October, the British Staff were planning and launching offensives and were confident of reaching the goal of decisive results. It was not until the end of November that final failure was accepted ...
>
> It cannot be said that 'the soldiers', that is to say the Staff, did not have their way. They tried their sombre experiment to its conclusion. They took all they required from Britain. They wore down alike the manhood and the guns of the British Army almost to destruction. They did it in the face of the plainest warnings, and of arguments which they could not answer.[16]

Churchill did not let himself be so explicit about what was done badly without stating how it could have been done better. From the earliest weeks of the war his busy mind had been at work on schemes and devices for overcoming the particular difficulties of the Western Front and for conducting hostilities in other ways as well as other places. No other prominent person in Britain (indeed, no one else at all, so far as I know) had at that time so many or so good ideas about the management of the war. Some (but not all) of these ideas were impractical, if only in the sense that they suggested the implementation, as a matter of urgency, of changes which ordinary mortals needed time to take in and of measures which went beyond the normal imaginations of liberal democracy and free market capitalism.

That they were not forever impractical is proved by the fact of their general resurrection when even more urgently needed, twenty-five years later.

His ideas concerned the whole as well as details. Britain had entered the war hoping for 'business as usual' but found it difficult to adjust to the evolving realities of a war wherein the stakes rose higher with each passing month until national survival itself became an issue. The government liked to believe, or at least to tell the people that it believed, that the war was going well and that there was no need for striking violations of the familiar amenities of national life, but the fact was that for most of the time the war was not going as well as it could have done, and the nation needed to get organised in radically new ways. 'War socialism', was A. J. P. Taylor's description of what Churchill urged in one of his big speeches in the summer of 1916.[17] The state, he argued, should take control of every element of the economy which worked to less than maximum war-effort advantage (anticipating this, the railway system had been nationalised at the very beginning of the war), or caused fellow Britons to fall out of trust with one another, as did the rising cost of foodstuffs and the too easy profits of ship owners.

> Everything in the State ought now to be devised and regulated with a view to the development and maintenance of our war power at the absolute maximum for an indefinite period. If you want to shorten the war, do this. If you want to discourage the enemy, let them see that you are doing it. If you want to cheer our own people, let them feel that you are doing it.[18]

Let the Germans know, he said, that we 'are coldly, scientifically and systematically arranging [our] national life for the one supreme business in hand', He never again publicly expressed himself in such total terms, but he hardly needed to, given that the nation did bit by bit become geared up for an all-out war effort, and that the Ministry of Munitions, one of the institutions crucial to that process, grew and grew following its establishment under his fellow war-organiser David Lloyd George until it was, as Churchill grandly reflected, the biggest purchasing business and industrial employer in the world.

To maximise the nation's relevant material resources (while minimising demand for its irrelevant ones) was one thing. To decide how to distribute them to the best advantage was another. At Munitions Churchill's nose was well rubbed in the practical difficulties of doing this. One conspicuous example must serve for all the rest. His ministry was born out of the shortage of shells for the army. The navy was not short of shells, having quite enough of them besides whatever else it thought it needed. The Admiralty therefore was left outside the scope of the new ministry's operations and was even given priority in procurement of materials and workers for handling the threat posed to vital commerce by U-boats from early 1917. Churchill, poacher turned gamekeeper, could see not only that the Admiralty was not using these privileged resources intelligently (for example, it was 'strengthening the Battle Fleet and increasing its already overflowing resources of stores, guns and ammunition'), but that the needs of the navy in any case should not be given automatic priority over those of other parts of the nation's war machine (for instance, tanks and aeroplanes). The War Cabinet was the proper place for thrashing out these questions. It naturally irked him that, having only an occasional foot in the Cabinet, he was at a disadvantage in dealing with the First Lord at the time, Sir Eric Geddes, a hard man who 'reinforced the Admiralty's particularism with an ability and domineering vigour all his own'.[19]

The navy problem apart, he learned at once that material resources could not be dealt with on their own. Human resources, manpower (plus the novel phenomenon of womanpower), were the other side of the same coin, and were dealt with from later 1917 by the Ministry of National Service, with whose capable director Sir Auckland Geddes (the more genial brother of Sir Eric) he established good relations. They agreed that, ideally, materials and manpower ought to be under unitary management. Both of them, however, found that they had little control over organised labour, within whose territory lay minefields: touchy trade unionists, costs of living, complaints about profiteering, conscription and exemptions from conscription. Sensitive to the feelings of unfairness and injustice so easily aroused at a time when the national ethos invited common sacrifice in a common cause, Churchill showed more patience than might have been expected in dealing with the strikes which recurrently disturbed industrial peace. He had been one of the earliest proponents of conscription for military service, and might have shown similar interest in industrial conscription had not the ever-bubbling cauldron of labour relations made anything of the sort quite unthinkable. But the question of using all resources to best advantage in total war never ceased to exercise him, attaining striking form in the attempts he once made to give mathematical form to the analysis of war-making efficiency. Groping for appropriate terminology, he posited each belligerent's possession of a limited quantity of 'national life-energy' and offered as an example the differential between the amounts of it expended by Germany and Britain in their warfare at and under the sea. 'Would it be an exaggeration to say that for one war-power unit Germany has applied to the submarine attack, we have been forced to assign fifteen or twenty?'

This passage comes in the most impressive of his many war memoranda, composed originally at Lloyd George's request in November 1916, when the disappointments of the Somme were freshly painful. It was circulated to the Committee of Imperial Defence as well as the Cabinet, apparently without intelligent notice being taken of it. Its full title was 'The Greater Application of Mechanical Power to the Prosecution of an Offensive on Land'. In it Churchill went beyond the immediate question of the Western Front to the whole matter of the uses of science and technology. He pinpointed a problem which would continue to exercise him through the next thirty years:

> A hiatus exists between inventors who know what they could invent, if they only knew what was wanted, and the soldiers who know, or ought to know, what they want, and would ask for it if they only knew how much science could do for them.

By professional standards Churchill was scientifically illiterate, but he had great curiosity and intuitive intelligence about the workings of mechanical things, and a wonderful faculty of imagining how they might be used to expedite victories and (incidentally) avoid human casualties. Hence the great survey summarily titled, in the appendices to *The World Crisis*, 'Mechanical Power in the Offensive'.[20] It includes most of the inventions he had already helped to promote and the revolutionary strategies that might take advantage of them: aeroplanes, for what would in due course be called command of the air and, consequent upon that, strategic bombing; gas, which he didn't like when the Germans began using it but which he saw no reason for his own side not to use in return; trench mortars, in the possession and use of which the Germans were unaccountably far superior; railway artillery, in which the French were showing the way; and, above all, tanks.

There was so much of lasting value in this memorandum that he placed a shorter version of it before the Cabinet a year later. When he first circulated it, it had the particular point of suggesting to the Army Staff how repetitions of the battle of the Somme might be avoided by the use of tanks and other caterpillar-tracked vehicles. That such vehicles must take time to produce and prepare was for him no argument against them. Resources devoted to them would be better used than anywhere else. Until enough tanks and appropriate aerial formations were ready, the Allied armies ought to do no more than stand sturdily on the defensive. He detested the Haig and Robertson philosophy of doing something very risky and murderous 'because it was better than doing nothing'. Training and preparing for offensive operations with a good prospect of being successful was not the same as 'doing nothing'. Months spent in not attacking ineffectively should be used to train and prepare for attacking effectively. Thus ran his argument throughout the war (of course he was not alone in making it, but he was the only one with direct access to the governing heights), and by 1918 some of these innovations were in use, though not necessarily in ways or under direction he thought suitable. Tanks indeed were allowed to demonstrate their value at Cambrai in November 1917 but, as would happen again the following year, without optimal integration in an overall strategy which might have made the victory greater. Through 1916 and most of 1917 the possibilities of these technological advances were ignored.

That Churchill should have lamented this neglect was only to be expected. His opinion was of course contested by interested parties and their partisans, but it was supported by C. R. M. F. Cruttwell, whose *History of the Great War, 1914–1918* (1934) is still well regarded on its military and political sides.[21] After noticing how difficult it was for civilian statesmen (including Lloyd George before the disaster of Passchendaele, and Painlevé before that of Chemin des Dames) to argue with military chieftains about their plans when, without providing evidence to support an objective assessment, the generals insisted that their plans were excellent ones, Cruttwell went on:

> Less easily explicable was the violent hostility often aroused, particularly in the British military hierarchy, by the strenuous and beneficent efforts of ministers to improve the weapons at the disposal of the army. The indispensable instruments of victory so eagerly offered by civilian hands were angrily rebuffed ... The history of the tanks is a classic example of the dogged determination with which GHQ fought against the most fruitful of all modern improvements in the art of war.[22]

It was not just stupidity, insensitivity and political non-responsibility that caused the British 'brass hats' to embark on battles reckoned even by themselves to be unlikely to achieve much. In a war fought alongside allies, there was often the factor of alliance politics to be considered. Even without allies to be taken account of, generals cannot always choose the time and place where they give battle; it is part of the art of war that the clever general picks the time and place *he* wants and makes his opponent accept it. From allies too can come pleas, pressures and threats tending to the same disadvantageous end. As a good historian and man of war, Churchill naturally understood all this. His own arguments in the winter of 1914–15 for the Dardanelles operation included support for Britain's ally Russia. He acknowledged that Haig and Robertson were under an obligation to support France. It can be argued that in *The World Crisis* he made too little allowance for the pressures of the alliance factor. It would have been in character for him to assume that, if he had been doing the negotiations with the French, the result would have been different. Twenty-five years later, he found himself negotiating with the French at a time of supreme crisis; and then with the Americans and Russians in the Grand Alliance. He was to show how good he was at it.

With munitions issuing in a torrent from all the factories controlled by his ministry, and with the tanks and aeroplanes he had for so long been interested in ready for the kill in 1919 (not until quite late in 1918 did it become clear that the war might not go on into the following year), the last weeks of the war found Churchill in better spirits than he been since he was at the Admiralty. He had got back to almost the top level of war-making – now, war-winning – responsibility; his contribution to the war effort was again generally admired; he was on good terms with the Prime Minister; and he could look forward to further high office after the general election which must quickly follow victory. His wife was about to have a fourth baby (Marigold, born on 15 November 1918), and he was happy in his home life, much of which was spent at a rented country place near East Grinstead in Sussex. In celebration of the tenth anniversary of their marriage, he ended a cheerful letter from Paris to Clementine:

> Do you think we have been less happy or more happy than the average married couple? I reproach myself very much for not having been more to you. But at any rate in these ten years the sun has never yet gone down on our wrath ... My dearest sweet I hope and pray that future years may bring you serene and smiling days, and full and fruitful occupation. I think that you will find real scope in the new world opening out to women, and find interests which will enrich your life. And always at your side in true and tender friendship as long as he breathes will be your ever devoted, if only partially satisfactory, W.[23]

8

Bolsheviks and Irishmen

'The failure to strangle Bolshevism at birth ... lies heavily on us today.'

Speech at the Massachusetts Institute
of Technology, 31 March 1949

The return of peace marked for Churchill the beginning of ten years of considerable celebrity and achievement. He was as prominent in public office as anyone can be who is not actually Prime Minister. He did good work in relation to a variety of really important national and imperial issues, not all of them directly his departmental responsibility. He was at the top of his oratorical form and was one of the most effective parliamentarians. His capacity for persisting in what most of his colleagues considered an untenable proposition (that Britain and France should not rest until the Russian Bolsheviks were destroyed) displayed itself in only that one connection and, in fact, did him little harm other than with the British Left, which had anyway long been wary of him. That Churchillian quirk apart, his political performance though the 1920s was first class.

Perhaps it was the very turbulence and novelty of the post-war climate of politics both British and foreign that drew the best out of him. He excelled at handling emergencies and meeting new challenges. British politics after the war would not be as they had been before it, and could not be. They would not be, because the Prime Minister plumped for an immediate general election and gained the country's approval for maintaining in power his war-winning coalition. It was an endorsement of those Liberals who had stuck with Lloyd George rather than Asquith after the latter's deposition in December 1916, plus the (numerically superior) Conservatives who were content, for the time being, to go along with a national leader so provenly potent and popular. Beyond that, the pattern of British politics could no longer be as it had been, for two reasons: Britain had at last become a recognisable democracy, virtually all men over twenty-one and all women over thirty being enfranchised in 1918; and the Labour movement, for whose support both Liberals and Tories had previously angled, was now confident and weighty enough to support a Labour Party which, having decided to withdraw from the coalition and go to the polls on its own, attracted nearly half the votes cast and, as the largest of the Opposition parties and with so large a national following, might begin to aspire to occupying the government benches.

Coalition governments never seemed to Churchill the unnatural things they did to party managers and constituency zealots. He thoroughly approved of Lloyd George's bid to protract the life of the wartime coalition, and would even have liked it to project itself boldly as the 'National Government'; not long after, he had a go at promoting a 'fusion' of middle-minded moderates from both non-socialist parties. As for the Labour Party and the trade unions, which had come out of the war with the huge total membership of eight million, double what it had been in 1914, Churchill's wariness differed from that of his class in general in two respects: he was well known to have a very short fuse when confronted by strikes affecting the public interest; and his dislike of socialism was founded on articulate liberal principle, not just selfish class interest. On the other hand, he remained true to the collectivist paternalism which had guided him through the pre-war years, and he was sentimentally vulnerable to the arguments of human decency and social justice. At the same time he felt himself to be true also to the Free Trade principles which had drawn him in 1904 across the floor of the House to join the Liberals. He was also, in the words of the Psalmist, 'fearfully and wonderfully made', still causing friends and politicians to speculate on what he would do next, and to wonder how he would end up.

Churchill's office in the re-formed coalition was as Secretary of State for War and for Air. This proved to be too large an assignment for one minister; not least because 'Air' meant civil aviation as well as military. (To his all-embracing military mind, the idea of bringing all three services and their supply, each with its own minister, under the umbrella of a single Ministry of Defence greatly appealed; but that was an idea whose time was not to come for a long time yet.) The Air part of his post-war work can be quickly dealt with. We have seen how he had already given fruitful thought to the development and military uses of air power. Now he was enthused enough to go through a repetition of the pre-war cycle: lessons in flying (aircraft, as he always called them, had developed a lot since 1914); a near-death disaster when taking off from Croydon; and pressure from wife and friends to drop it. He got on well with Sir Hugh Trenchard, the Chief of Air Staff, and supported his campaign to make the RAF an independent service. He identified for the airmen a congenial new role in colonial policing. But he was so busy with his army responsibilities, and with the many items of British and world affairs that caught his attention, that he simply had not the time to fight the Treasury on behalf of the airmen as doughtily as he

otherwise might have done. It seems, moreover, that what fighting he did
do tended to benefit only the military side. He showed no interest in the
work of the small staff labouring under Sir Frederick Sykes to establish
good foundations for civil aviation. 'Civil aviation must fly by itself', he
said.[1] Sykes had in view the development not just of an addition to Britain's
domestic communications network but a strong new bond of empire. For
Britain's lamentable falling behind in the development of civil air transport,
Churchill has to carry his share of government responsibility. This was one
of the many post-war might-have-beens stunted by Treasury insistence that
wartime extravagance must be compensated by post-war retrenchment – a
principle with which this Secretary of State (on the Liberal side of his mind)
did not actually disagree.

Post-war is hardly what it felt like on the other, the much larger side of
his official responsibilities. War against Germany, the Habsburg and Ottoman Empires and Bulgaria might be over, but peace had not yet broken
out. A large force was going to be needed for the British zone of occupation
in Germany; forces of some size would be needed for Constantinople and
the Dardanelles. Armies of British imperial and commonwealth troops were
already in occupation of Palestine and Mesopotamia (the modern Iraq).
Apart from these troops in or about to go into former enemy lands, others
were still in the lands of former allies: the rescued ally Italy, the reluctant
ally Greece – and the deserter ally Russia. There was no problem about
bringing the troops home from the two former, but Russia was a different
matter. Along with France, the United States and Japan, Britain had sought
to prevent Russia's withdrawal from the war (and possible German acquisition of all the munitions the Allies had provided) by landing troops all
round the accessible pieces of the perimeter of that vast state after the
October Revolution. Most of them were still there a year later. What to do
about Russia would soon become Churchill's preoccupation; but before that
could happen, he had to deal with the demobilisation crisis.

The United Kingdom of Great Britain and Ireland (as it still was) ended
the war with about 3,250,000 men under arms. Of those, only a nucleus of
regulars did not expect to be rapidly demobilised and sent home. This
presented Churchill with his first big problem. He found the army, as he
vividly put it, in a state of 'liquefaction'. The demobilisation plan in place
and beginning to be implemented was felt by conscripts and volunteers
alike to lack natural justice and, besides that, to be working too slowly.
Discontent was ubiquitous and noisy, mutiny might not be far off. (In fact
disturbances and disobediences which struck martinets as mutinous *did*
begin before January 1919 was out.) Churchill grappled with the problem
decisively and successfully. He worked out that the men who had survived

the war could be rapidly demobilised, and the needs of occupying forces and maintaining imperial security at the same time be met, by the device of a Bill to continue conscription for one year and one year only. He persuaded his Cabinet colleagues to drop the existing industrial-needs priority criteria and to accept instead criteria of wounds, age and length of service. 'Let three men out of four go, and pay the fourth double' was how he put it to the Commons.[2] Once the terms of his plan had become understood, it went ahead without serious trouble. Churchill was justifiably proud of it. By the end of October 1919 this 'work of immense magnitude and difficulty' had been completed, and the Treasury was relieved to learn that the cost of maintaining the British army had dropped from about £4,000,000 a day to no more than £1,250,000.[3]

We come now to the episode which more than any other has lent colour to the charge that he was a warmonger. Churchill was passionate about wanting the United Kingdom to commit itself to supporting the counter-revolutionary 'White' Russian armed forces in the mixture of civil war and secessionist wars that ravaged Russia from 1918 well into 1920. He was not playing to an unsympathetic audience. It hardly needs saying that the October Revolution and the consequent ascendancy of the Bolsheviks was regarded with loathing by the propertied elites of the victorious Allies. That Russia should become a source of revolutionary contagion not long after it had, militarily speaking, left the Allies in the lurch, was felt to have added insult to injury. In Germany and in Hungary, Communist revolution even seemed for short periods within reach of success. In every country where there was a working-class movement, revolutionary enthusiasts were active and the Russian happenings were admired. Britain was as much affected as everywhere else. Even before the launch of the British Communist Party in 1920, the stoutly non-Communist trade unions and Labour Party committed themselves to the slogan, 'Hands Off Russia'.

No Tories or Liberals (of either adhesion) liked Bolshevism, which is what Churchill insisted on calling it; but no other person of highest political stature publicised and went on about his dislike of it as much as he did. He became worked up and histrionic in much the same way as Edmund Burke had become worked up about the French Revolution. For example, in the chapter about Poland in *The Aftermath*, his conclusion to *The World Crisis*, he wrote of Poland's neighbour to the east,

> the huge mass of Russia – not a wounded Russia only, but a poisoned Russia, an infected Russia, a plague-bearing Russia; a Russia of armed hordes not only smiting with bayonet and with cannon, but accompanied and preceded by swarms of typhus-bearing vermin which slew the bodies of men, and political doctrines which destroyed the health and even the soul of nations.[4]

Why it became such an obsession puzzled his colleagues then and has puzzled his biographers since. He made much of Bolshevism's callousness with regard to individual human beings generally, but it was the Revolution's impact on the aristocracy that upset him most. Colleagues put this down to his ducal background and connections, but Paul Addison points out its profounder source: the rootedness of his affections and principles in the nobly-led, many-tiered, property-owning society he had been brought up in; and his well thought out conviction that only in such a society could individual freedom and social progress coexist.[5] Besides that, the fate of the Russian royal family really distressed him. All through his life he showed a principled respect for the institution of monarchy and a sensitive sympathy for living kings and queens. He also felt with regard to the embattled Tsarist officers a chivalrous obligation not to let them down, now that the tide of history had swung against them. Much of what he said was sensible. He correctly intuited the miseries which Bolshevism would bring upon the Russian people, and he correctly predicted (as indeed did others) that the Communist regime would evolve into a dictatorship. In speeches up and down the country and in newspaper articles, as well as in Cabinet and committee, he plugged this theme and spent much of 1919 and early 1920 trying to persuade his colleagues that Britain should militarily aid and abet the 'Whites' in their widespread struggle with the 'Reds'. He also advocated, at any rate through the first half of 1919, that British foreign policy should include sustaining an anti-Soviet alliance into which a reconciliated and rearmed Germany could be introduced (an interesting anticipation here of his next round of post-war planning).

Eighty years later, with the horrific story of Communist Russia behind us, the reader may conclude that Churchill was not so silly after all. But statesmen have to work with the practicalities of the present, not the practicalities as a later generation may wish them to have been. There always are limits to what a nation can do for even the most attractive of foreign causes, and it is a measure of Churchill's passion that he could not see them. His colleagues remained unenthused. They were sure that the British people would not support such an intervention. Britain had not ended one unexpectedly long war only to embark on another of indeterminate length. Even if such a war was to be fought by volunteers, they would still need to be supplied and supported; and would it not be risky to place part of the national interest in the hands of a bunch of foreign generals of whom most Britons knew nothing? In any case, was it not for the Russians themselves to determine their own destiny? Nothing makes squabbling parties find common cause more quickly than foreign interference. Churchill's historical mind produced the precedent of Britain's belligerent reaction to the French Revolution, but the answer to that was that Revolutionary France (and *a fortiori* the Napoleonic France which followed) challenged and menaced our national and imperial interests much more directly than could be believed of international Communism based in a wrecked homeland. Russia needed reconstruction and could become again a trading partner. Only if the new-style Russia began to interfere with the post-war order beyond its own boundaries need it be considered dangerous.

What exactly the Soviet Union's borders were to be remained uncertain until the new states to Russia's westward – Finland, the three Baltic Republics and Poland – had established themselves and won Soviet recognition. British foreign policy supported all of them, and Churchill found himself for once in harmony with his colleagues in stiffening the sinews when Poland, having sought to appropriate more of the Ukraine than it could manage, found the Red Army close to the outskirts of Warsaw in mid 1920. British military involvement (which Lloyd George was covertly working to avoid) was averted by two remarkable events. The Red Army was unexpectedly defeated in the battle of the Vistula. And the British Labour movement, which had long disliked Churchill's belligerence, threatened direct political action to prevent military aid going to Poland – thus fulfilling Churchill's worst fears about the effect of the Russian example. (Nothing so extreme ever happened again.) Once Poland and the other new states were for the time being secure, the Foreign Office could relax and return to the serious business of negotiating Russia's return to membership of the society of nations. Churchill's unremitting hostility to his foreign *bête noire* served to delay but could not deny that diplomatic necessity for ever. The abrupt and total turnabout he made in June 1941 remains amazing, but seems less so when one realises that he meant what he said about the Devil.

Churchill was moved from the War Office to the Colonies in the middle of February 1921, and there he stayed until the fall of Lloyd George's government in October 1922. The work to be done was still mostly concerned with clearing up after the war and cementing the peace supposed to follow it. Throughout the regions for which he now bore responsibility, peace was still a long way off. In his handling of these difficult and at times infuriating matters, Churchill usually appeared in his more reasonable, pacific and humane aspect.

Ireland, the whole of which was then still part of the United Kingdom, was the region where those aspects were most tested. Most of the inhabitants of what is now the United Kingdom of Great Britain and Northern Ireland supposed or hoped the larger Union would remain intact when the project of Home Rule, which had got so far just before the war, was defrozen; but the inhabitants of what is now the Republic of Ireland indicated at the general election of December 1918 a different state of mind by voting solidly for Sinn Fein, the nationalist republican party which sought independence and which established a national assembly of its own, the Dail. Early in 1919 the militants of that persuasion, under the title of the Irish Republican Army, began to use violence (intimidation, arson, bombs, ambushes, kidnappings and killings – the familiar repertoire) against the Royal Irish Constabulary and the British military forces in support of it.

During 1919, when Churchill did not have much to do with Ireland, the Irish Office and the military commanders on the spot continued to handle it and to hope that they were getting on top of the troubles. By the early months of 1920 it was clear that they weren't. None of the choices open to the government was attractive. Simply to maximise the military presence, declare martial law and in effect subject Ireland, or at any rate the nationalist bulk of it, to military occupation did not commend itself as a good way to improve the prospects of the latest version of Home Rule or a dignified way to govern the part of the British Empire nearest to home. Massive reinforcement of the Royal Irish Constabulary plus allowing reprisals in response to IRA terrorism was the option taken. That reinforcement took the form of the volunteers known as 'Black-and-Tans' and 'Auxiliaries', who either through bad management or their own bad behaviour, and because of the escalation of terror and counter-terror that came with them, made the troubles worse. Churchill's soldierly soul didn't like being driven in this direction, but from the middle of 1920, and despite Clementine's gentle remonstrances ('It always makes me unhappy and disappointed when I see you *inclined* to take for granted that the rough iron-fisted "hunnish" way will prevail …'),[6] he accepted it and did his political duty by defending it in Parliament.

By the end of the year, however, when it became no longer possible to refuse the generals' demand for a declaration of martial law in the worst-affected counties, he was one of the ministers persuaded that it was impossible to continue along so mutually damaging a road. Churchill began to advocate calling a truce and trying to open negotiations. For a few more months, the tough policy continued, but by April it was becoming arguable that the authorities were doing no better with martial law than without it. In May 1921 the elections for separate Southern and Northern Irish Parliaments promised by the latest version of Home Rule which had been going through Parliament while all this was going on were held. King George V's speech on opening the Northern one was used to invite the Southerners to reconsider their position. Responses which might perhaps be favourable having been received from Dublin, a truce was proclaimed early in July.

From this time on, Churchill moved into a position of prominence and influence in the handling of the Irish question. He was one of the group of ministers selected by the Cabinet to meet the Sinn Fein delegates (led by Arthur Griffith and Michael Collins) when the series of meetings began at Number Ten Downing Street on 11 October 1921. The task was to persuade them that it was not worth their while to persist in self-ruinous fighting to get out of the British Empire, when by staying within it – the more cynical might say, by the mere gesture of staying within it – they could have the same sort and degree of self-government as, for example, Canada. Such an offer proved to be less irresistible to hard-bitten republican minds than Lloyd George and Churchill had expected. The logic by which some of them were guided (including the absent de Valera, who considered himself to be president of an already existing independent Irish state) was that they could not be within the Empire because they had already seceded from it. To pragmatic British minds, this was not sensible. For Churchill, moreover, his mind always alert to strategic considerations, the big problem was that British security still depended, as it had been thought to do for four hundred years, on the existence of a reliably non-hostile Ireland and the use of the Atlantic ports. The Irishmen scouted this with assurances that Ireland would always stay neutral, and that it would acquire means to defend its neutrality. Churchill was not persuaded that they would or could do this; a matter that would return to haunt him twenty years later.

The meetings went on, week after week, with Churchill remaining rather more patient than Lloyd George, the Prime Minister. Griffith and Collins won from him some degree of understanding and even grudging admiration. He was much better at fighting than at hating. Like the Boers, with whom he had always been able to sympathise, the Sinn Feiners were fighting for a homeland against a perceived foreigner. (Clementine told him that, if he had been Irish, he would have been on their side.) They were fighting by nasty means, indeed, but there was some justice in Collins's argument that they could do no other; Churchill later related how Collins had actually said he had regretted that the IRA could not 'conform to the status of belligerents. We had not got even a county in which we could organise a uniformed force.'[7] In the same article where he recalled that remark, Churchill actually acknowledged that Ireland should have been given Home Rule when Gladstone first tried it – an interesting departure from his usual line of maintaining that Lord Randolph was always right. It also mattered that, the more Churchill encountered Ulster Protestants, the less inclined he became to give their brand of bigotry a deciding vote over the fate of the whole of Ireland. Thus he was able to play a leading and helpful part in the long series of meetings which culminated in what has been called Lloyd

George's ultimatum (though it was recognised by all present that further talks would get them nowhere) on the afternoon of 5 December 1921. Churchill's descriptive powers later rose to the occasion.

> The Irishmen gulped down the ultimatum phlegmatically. Mr Griffith said, speaking in his soft voice and with his modest manner, 'I will give the answer of the Irish Delegates at nine tonight; but, Mr Prime Minister, I personally will sign this agreement and will recommend it to my countrymen.' ... Michael Collins rose looking as if he was going to shoot someone, preferably himself. In all my life I have never seen so much passion and suffering in restraint. [Nine o'clock came, but no Irishmen.] It was not until long after midnight that the Irish Delegation appeared. As before, they were superficially calm and very quiet. There was a long pause, or there seemed to be. Then Mr Griffith said [that they would accept it subject to a few 'points of drafting']. Thus, by the easiest of gestures, he carried the whole matter into the region of minor detail, and everyone concentrated upon these points with overstrained interest so as to drive the main issue into the background for ever ... It was nearly three o'clock in the morning before we separated. But the agreement was signed by all. As the Irish men rose to leave, the British ministers upon a strong impulse walked round and for the first time shook hands.[8]

The negotiators had signed a treaty but now it had to be put to their respective assemblies. What happened in Ireland was tragic. Civil war broke out between those willing to go along with the treaty and those, led by de Valera, who were not. (De Valera, for this and many other reasons, understandably became one of Churchill's *bêtes noires*.) The border between the Irish Free State and Northern Ireland became more of a standing irritant than it might have been had there been fewer aggressive extremists on both sides of it. Arthur Griffith and General Collins, which is how Churchill liked to name him after their London encounters, were both dead by August 1922 (a heart-attack and assassination, respectively) before the last British troops sailed for home in December, a year later than the Cabinet had hoped.

That the story of its acceptance by the British Parliament and people was altogether different was in part Churchill's work. He was given the honourable but risk-fraught task of explaining the treaty to the House of Commons with its Conservative majority, and he did so with complete and much-admired success; reminding the nation incidentally that he had it in him to be a conciliator as well as a conqueror. His introductory oration on 16 December was planned with so much art and replete with so much statesmanlike wisdom and humane sentiment that it deserves a place in any collection of great political speeches.[9] Like everyone else, he was distressed that the Irish couldn't agree about the treaty, and when their quarrelling turned to civil war he shared the general fear that, if the treaty party lost and a republic was proclaimed, Britain would have to resort to armed force in the interest of national security. He had difficulty, as did most Englishmen, in understanding why decent Irishmen were ready to kill one another (let alone those whom they perceived as oppressors) for what seemed to be of little *practical* importance. After two nationalist gunmen had assassinated Field-Marshal Sir Henry Wilson on the steps of his London home, Churchill himself for a while had to be on his guard. But he never lost faith in Griffith, Collins and their Provisional Government, and in the end he was justified. The faith that Griffith and Collins and their successors kept in him was equally important in bringing this bloody chapter in the history of Anglo-Irish relations to a more or less happy ending.

9

Eastern Questions

'There ought to be room for many different kinds of culture in the British Commonwealth and Empire.'

Letter to the High Commissioner for South Africa, 1941

Any attempt to understand Winston Churchill is faced with a need to locate his deep-down principles and passions – indeed his principles-cum-passions – which alone explain or help to explain the sometimes contradictory attitudes and actions which appear on the surface. On the one hand, he was held up by some as unreliable, unpredictable and unprincipled. On the other, he could boldly present himself as 'more truly consistent than almost any other public man', and he closed a 1927 essay on 'Consistency in Politics' with these 'charitable lines of Crabbe':

> Minutely trace man's life; year after year,
> Through all his days let all his deeds appear,
> And then, though some may in that life be strange,
> Yet there appears no vast nor sudden change;
> The links that bind those various deeds are seen,
> And no mysterious void is left between.[1]

He certainly did not feel mysterious to himself.

Two of his deep-down passions and principles were, first, the rule of law as protector of civil and religious liberty, and of the standards of civilisation; and, secondly, the place and prestige in the world of Great Britain and its Empire, as necessary both for the security of the English-speaking people and for the welfare of its other subjects. In the gap which sometimes opened between them may be glimpsed, not at all surprisingly, prejudices and assumptions which he shared with other men of his age, race, nation and class.

The former of these principles came out strong in his handling – again, as the government's anchorman – of the affair of General Dyer, unforgotten in the Punjab and indeed much of India as the butcher of Amritsar. Brigadier-General Reginald Dyer had spent all his adult life, except for a year each at Sandhurst and Camberley, in and around India. The Indian Congress Party, after many years of relative docility, became rather suddenly active and aggressive about the time the war ended, and had picked on the Punjab (subject since before the war to the rule of a particularly unsympathetic Governor, Sir Michael O'Dwyer) for the launch early in 1919 of what its new leader M. K. Gandhi advertised as non-violent resistance. Rioting and mayhem ensued. Dyer had the tough task of trying to restore order in Amritsar and its neighbourhood. A succession of alarming incidents – the usual killings, burnings, lootings, attacks on policemen and other representatives of government, plus the killings of four European men and a more unusual attack (which she survived) on an English missionary lady Miss Sherwood – was followed by a defiant call to a public meeting in the Jallianwalla Bagh, an open space with a wall round it and, as it happened, only a few narrow exits. Not everyone there may have heard Dyer's proclamations the previous evening that all processions and gatherings were banned, but the leaders and many others must have done. A huge crowd of men and boys were enjoying the speeches when Dyer and a squad of Indian sepoys marched in and opened fire. By the time he called a halt, over three hundred were dead and at least a thousand injured. Then he marched his squad away, satisfied that he had 'taught the Punjab a moral lesson'.[2] The lesson was emphasised by summary floggings of suspected persons and by the order that Indians, if they wished to traverse the street where Miss Sherwood had been attacked, must do so on their hands and knees.

The Amritsar Massacre at once became a *cause célèbre*. Dyer's immediate military superiors promptly backed him. The mills of the civil authorities ground more slowly and to the opposite effect, but by the time the case reached the Army Council there was nothing else it could do, in face of Dyer's superiors' support, than simply to decline to allow him any further employment. Military men in Britain as well as India were predictably outraged, and the Conservative Party perceived an opportunity to needle the India Office and its Secretary of State, Edwin Montagu, for whom they had a peculiar dislike. Hence the debate in the House of Commons on 8 July 1920.[3]

Montagu opened the debate and was badly received. Whether this was because he was, perhaps tactlessly, provocative in what he said or because he said it in a way that excited prejudice against his Jewishness is unclear. What is clear is that Sir Edward Carson's presentation of the pro-Dyer arguments concluded with the snide insinuation that Montagu had got overexcited because he wasn't a properly self-controlled English gentleman. With the debate seeming to be going badly, Churchill (who had a speech prepared) was asked to speak next. He did so magnificently, not just by clever debating tactics but through the deployment of arguments and the drawing of crucial distinctions rooted in his essential rule of law liberalism. It is possible also that his resolve was stiffened by his dislike of the anti-semitism showing itself in the House.

He did not deny the difficulties of Dyer's situation, but demonstrated with a wealth of arguments that Dyer had inexcusably gone too far. His indictment had the interesting feature that it came from a man not known for sympathy with the political aspirations of Indians but well known for toughness in face of civil disorders. Dyer, he said, was only one of many officers in the Punjab at that time who were having to make difficult decisions: whether to order their men to fire or not; and, if to fire, how much. In each case, and sometimes admittedly with not much time for consideration, delicate judgements had to be made. Soldiers acting in support of the civil power must be particularly careful to use the minimum of force required in the particular circumstances, and must take the advice of the civil authorities whenever possible. The crowd penned up within those Amritsar walls was not armed in any significant sense (they only had whatever sticks they had brought in with them and stones picked up on the spot); and, from the point of view of the necessity to support the civil power, those could not be considered lethal weapons. It was a revolutionary mob, perhaps, but not the 'revolutionary army' which Dyer alleged. The distinction was absolutely crucial in the context of so delicate a matter as preserving British authority in India.

> Men who take up arms against the State must expect at any moment to be fired upon ... Men who take up arms unlawfully cannot expect that the troops will wait until they are quite ready to begin the conflict ... Armed men are in a category absolutely different from unarmed men ... I carefully said that when I used the word 'armed' I meant armed with lethal weapons or with firearms ... This crowd was unarmed. These are simple tests which it is not too much to expect officers in these difficult situations to apply.

The soldier's job was to stop the revolutionaries, or whatever you liked to call them, from doing whatever violence they were evidently and imme-diately intending. It was the civil authorities' job to take care of what might happen on all other occasions. What Dyer had engaged in, Churchill went so far as to say, was in fact 'terrorism' or 'frightfulness'. This was strong language indeed, 'frightfulness' being the English translation of *Schrecklich-keit*, what the Germans at their worst had been accused of during the recent war. This was not how the British should want their rule in India to be characterised. 'We have to make it absolutely clear, some way or other, that this is not the British way of doing business.'

He ended with warm personal support for Edwin Montagu. The debate went on till late at night, but Churchill's exemplary performance determined its conclusion. Brigadier-General Dyer remained disowned, and the world was invited to notice the fact. Eighty years later, one has to admit that India did not notice the fact at all. The Jallianwalla Bagh at Amritsar at once became a focus for nationalism and a seed-bed of anti-British legends. But that was largely because of circumstances and global movements of ideas over which Churchill and his imperial kind had no control.

The Dyer affair landed on Churchill's desk while he was Secretary of State for War and Air. However momentous its long-term effects were to be (experienced India hands correctly reckoned they would be), it seemed small beer by comparison with the great imperial concern that awaited him when he moved to the Colonial Office in February 1921. He had to super-intend the dismantling and redistribution of the territories of the Ottoman Empire, a business which had not yet proceeded far under the ageing and ailing Lord Milner. One of the conditions of his taking the office was the creation of a Middle East Department to handle the affairs of what was now, apart from India, the most concentrated and economically significant block of territories within the Empire, because of all the oil exploration and exploitation in the area. It naturally took most of the time that could be spared from the other duties laid upon him: continued responsibility for Air until it had a ministry of its own; and then, from the middle of December 1921, the chair of a Cabinet committee to manage the withdrawal of British military presence from Ireland, a movement which took many months longer than was hoped or expected.

He had insufficient time, and the Treasury allowed him insufficient money, to take up his earlier visions of development in Kenya and the adjacent East African colonies. Of the West African colonies, and the bits and bobs of Empire scattered all around the seas and seacoasts of the world, he appears to have known little. The grandest items of Empire were of course beyond his official ken. India had its own Whitehall ministry and, in the subcontinent, its own government. The Dominions enjoyed complete Home Rule, and were beginning to question whether 'the old country' should continue to manage their foreign affairs. Egypt behind the veil was a protectorate run by the Foreign Office. Churchill's situation at the Colonial Office may be summed up as having charge of those parts of the British Empire which were not looking after themselves or being looked after by someone else. Those parts, however, included the Middle East, which he found interesting and congenial. Churchill was in fact superintending the extension of his beloved British Empire to its greatest ever extent. There was more red on the map between 1919 and 1955 than ever before or since.

The easily-drawn inference is, of course, misleading. Britain's ability to defend such widespread interests in so fast changing a world was already a topic for grave consideration in the inner sancta of imperial power. So far as Australia and New Zealand in particular were concerned, they were right to worry. If Japan were ever to become an enemy, Britain could only offer defence to those Dominions on condition that it had no major enemies to deal with nearer home. Churchill seems never properly to have understood the risks and difficulties of the antipodean pieces of the imperial puzzle; those two Dominions never had the same reality in his imagination as did the others, and he actually revealed a certain prejudice regarding ordinary Australians, remarking after the parting of the ways in 1942 that they came of 'bad stock'.

There was no doubt, however, about his sense of the reality of the Middle East. He had known it as a traveller and soldier in earlier years, and its strategic importance had been at the front of his mind since 1914. He was prepared to take advice from his new friend T. E. Lawrence about how to handle the aspirations of the Arab peoples, and now, in 1921, he had the benevolent conqueror's task of incorporating its newly acquired lands into that Empire which he sincerely believed to be a blessing to all peoples living within it. There were, however, limits to his freedom of action. Those lands had not been acquired by absolute right of conquest. They had been 'mandated' under the terms of article 22 of the Covenant of the League of Nations to one of the victors to be looked after 'until such time as they were able to stand alone'. Moreover, they came encumbered with a variety of conditions. An agreement had been made during the war with France as to the disposition of Ottoman possessions outside the Turkish heartland. The Zionists had been promised a Jewish Homeland in Palestine. And throughout the Arab world there was a rising spirit of nationalism, similar to and so far as Moslems were concerned akin to what had risen in India. Lawrence himself had encouraged the Arab chieftains to expect to be rewarded for assisting the British victory.

The centrepiece of this post-war settlement was the Cairo Conference in March 1921. Something of this sort was already being planned before Churchill arrived at the Colonial Office, but he made sure it would be a grand event. Clementine was able to accompany him; and, after it was over, they proceeded in state to Palestine before coming home via Naples. The flavour of the occasion and the realities of power are plain to see in a revealing group-portrait of the participants: Churchill of course sits mid-centre, flanked by the High Commissioners of Palestine and Mesopotamia, respectively Sir Herbert Samuel and Sir Percy Cox; also in the front row are the generals commanding the forces of occupation, while on the steps behind them stand equal numbers of military men and civilians, two of whom are identifiable as Gertrude Bell, the Arabist and archaeologist who had become Sir Percy's secretary, and the famous T. E. Lawrence himself. There are also two lion cubs 'on their way from Somaliland to the London Zoo', but not a soul in Arab dress, and no one who even looks indigenous unless it is a fez-topped greybeard in dark suit and stiff collar.[4] Churchill positively wished not to have any more to do with Arabs than he had to, and he did not have to meet many until he got to Jerusalem.

The principles governing British policy in respect of the mandates was that, however these territories were governed, their government should work for and not against the imperial interest, and that Britain need pay no more than was minimally necessary to keep them on side. Conquering and holding Mesopotamia had so far been especially expensive. The scheme eventually implemented, with the aid of Lawrence, was to establish Feisal and Abdullah, sons of King Hussein, the current ruler in the Hejaz, as emirs (quasi-kings) respectively of Iraq, the former Mesopotamia; and Transjordan, the larger and more arid part of Palestine east of the river. Apart only from the necessity of Parliament's approval, which it received after a first-rate Churchill performance giving, said Lord Winterton with equal admiration and amusement, 'an impression of power and grandeur which is possessed by few persons and institutions with the possible exception of the Pyramids or Lord Northcliffe', Churchill had the rare experience of acting as king-maker.[5] Security in Iraq, the more extensive and troublesome country, was to be achieved by a novel means which Churchill and the air barons had conceived while he was still at the War and Air Office, and which had already been successfully tried out in Somaliland. The civil authority, instead of having to send expensive columns of troops over great distances to bring rebellious villages to heel, would simply summon the RAF to bomb them. Transjordan was made secure by more traditional methods: a financial subsidy and the secondment of British officers to manage the (very efficient) military force which became known as the Arab Legion.

Churchill's party then went on from Cairo to Jerusalem where, an Arabic-speaking member of it recorded, the Arabs whom he assumed to be shouting greetings to him were actually demonstrating against the Jews.[6] The borders of Palestine and the security of the Jewish settlements within it were his main business here, and he devoted most of his working time to laying down the law impartially to Jews and Arabs alike; the latter in the person of Abdullah, whom he respected as having been recently a military ally. To Arab representatives, he insisted that the Jews would enrich Palestine and would never become so numerous as to swamp them. To Jewish representatives, he insisted that their area of settlement could not go beyond the

River Jordan, and urged them to tone down their propaganda about the Homeland which understandably worried the Arabs. Being generally ready to believe the best of people, and having no time for religious dogmas anyway, he was perhaps too optimistic in both directions; but what else could a British statesman be after so many promises had been given and so many passes sold? In any case, he had long been a supporter of the Zionist movement and sincerely believed that the Jewish presence in Palestine would improve the land. This was not an ungenerous attitude. Reflecting on everything that has happened since then and happens still, one's conception of Churchill cannot be lowered by learning that another of his ideas during these post-war settlement weeks was for an autonomous region for the Kurds in the northern part of Iraq.

Thus was settled, for better or worse, the destiny of the last pieces of Turkey's empire in Asia. What remained to be settled, and what was in fact becoming more unsettled by the month, was the destiny of metropolitan Turkey itself. Like all the defeated states, Turkey experienced both military occupation by its conquerors and revolution by proponents of a new political order. Conqueror in this context is a technical rather than a literal term, in as much as two of them, Greece and Italy, had achieved nothing of military significance in the Turkish theatre of war, and the third, France, relatively little; but all three of them descended as vultures on the corpse of old Turkey, put troops into the areas they wanted to seize or to hold hostage, and signed the Treaty of Sèvres in August 1920 with the Constantinople-based remnants of the wartime government. Meanwhile a nationalist movement under the military hero Mustafa Kemal Pasha, well-organised in central Turkey and with a rival capital in Ankara, denounced that treaty and undertook to push the Italians out of southern Turkey and the Greeks out of everywhere they had seized in western Turkey and eastern Thrace, and also to recover control of the Dardanelles and Constantinople from the French and British, who were still in control of them. During 1921 the Italians and the French tactfully withdrew, leaving the cautious British and the ambitious Greeks increasingly exposed.

The British Cabinet found itself divided over what to do. What happened to Greece on its own was no great matter; but what happened to the Straits mattered considerably, as did Turkey's prospective relations with Russia. Through 1921 and early 1922 Lloyd George was leader of the pro-Greek group in the government, Churchill chief of the pro-Turks. Churchill respected the Turks as fighters and was as usual ready to be magnanimous towards former foes. He also did not wish his Middle East settlement to be upset by a hostile Turkish regime, and he believed Kemal would make a stronger Turkey into a better bulwark against the Bolshevik monster looming over its north-eastern border. Only when Kemal's troops, having expelled the Greeks, entered into the neutral zone established by Sèvres, and came face to face with the British contingent in the occupied zone along the eastern side of the Dardanelles and the Bosphorus, did Churchill feel affronted. His quick change of policies is interesting as evidence of – one might even say, as an eruption from the depths of – his primal British imperial principles.

The British contingent's base, the coastal town of Chanak, gave its name to the political crisis which suddenly blew up in September 1922. Faced with the possibility of having to fight Kemal's nationalist army and, worse, of actually being pushed off the mainland by it, the majority of the Cabinet (Foreign Secretary Curzon was the principal exception) swung behind Lloyd George's opinion that Britain must show fight. Churchill became characteristically enthusiastic, even extreme; Sir Maurice Hankey's diary for 27 September noted that 'Winston ... has swung round to the threat to his beloved Dardanelles and become violently Turko-phobe and even Phil-Hellene'.[7] His earlier respect for Kemal yielded to alarm lest damage should be done to British prestige, that essential ingredient of imperial survival in the Middle East and in India, where the Moslem millions were keenly interested in what was happening to their co-religionists nearer Europe. In this way, facing down Kemal was necessary for prestige as well as security. Kemal had to be taught a lesson. France and Italy having by now moved onto the sidelines of the imbroglio, it was felt to be up to Britain and its Dominions alone. But the Dominions declined to cooperate, and there was no enthusiasm for war in Britain itself. The Cabinet had got the country into an awkward situation, threatening to go to war for what the world appeared to consider no very good reason. That hostilities did not break out was due principally to the good sense and calmness of the general commanding at Chanak, Sir Charles Harington, who turned a Nelsonian blind eye to what was confusing or provocative in the instructions which deluged him, and in his relations with the Turks proved himself a born diplomat. By the first day of October the worst of the Chanak crisis was over. Churchill remained in an excitable and belligerent mood for a few days more, and continued to feel that Britain had been humiliated, but found solace in the belief that Kemal would not have been brought to the agreement which soon followed had not Britain stood so firm. There was no easy return, however, to political calm. The crisis on the Dardanelles was directly followed by a crisis at Westminster. There were signs that Conservative support, upon which the coalition depended, was slipping away. The Prime Minister decided that it was time for a general election.

Tory Chancellor

'The biggest blunder of my life was the return to the gold standard.'

Lord Moran, *Winston Churchill: The Struggle for Survival*,
10 September 1945

The two years which followed were the most unsettled and among the most uncomfortable of Churchill's life. He lost his seat at the November 1922 general election. Only at the third attempt to get back to Parliament did he succeed, at the end of November 1924. The nervous strain was heightened by his feeling obliged to change parties again. He left the House of Commons as a Liberal and returned as a Constitutionalist: a Conservative who didn't want to be taken as dyed-in-the-wool. That took a good deal of planning and explaining. To complete the tale of this accumulation of discomforts, they began with a serious operation and a prolonged convalescence.

The operation was for appendicitis. When stomach pains began on 16 October, they were at first set down to gastroenteritis, but on the 17th appendicitis was diagnosed. Moved into a nursing home, he was operated upon on the evening of the 18th. Appendicitis then was a much more dangerous and painful matter than it has since become. Sulfphonamides and antibiotics were yet to be invented, anaesthetics were cruder, painkillers more primitive; the patient was expected to be incapacitated and at risk for many days, and frail for a long time thereafter. Churchill was therefore *hors de combat* through the high political drama of Lloyd George's resignation, Bonar Law's hasty formation of a Conservative administration ('this government of duds and pip-squeaks', Churchill called it when he had come to),[1] and the dissolution of Parliament on 26 October. By then he knew that his campaign for re-election at Dundee would have to be begun from his sickbed in London, and that, whether he won or lost, it would need to be followed by a sustained and possibly lengthy campaign to recover a place on the political heights.

Even without his severe handicap, the two Member seat of Dundee was a tough proposition. A Victorian industrial city, which had been quite prosperous when he first went there in 1908, it was suffering badly by 1922 from the current depression and was just the kind of constituency which the recent Representation of the People Act had made a 'natural' for the Labour Party and the far Left, the latter aggressively present in the person of the Communist William Gallacher. Churchill's candidature as a National (that is, coalition) Liberal was promoted as best it could by his Liberal allies and by Clementine, who went north with the newborn Mary to see what charm and loyalty could do. It turned out that they couldn't do much. Her public appearances beyond the middle-class enclaves were made unpleasant by rowdyism and heckling, and by the hostility of working women who inevitably took against her cultivated manners and well-dressed appearance more than did their menfolk. Churchill himself, his stitches still in place and feeling groggy, managed to get there for the last four days, but had to sit for most of the time, looked ill, and was driven by the prevalent rudeness and intolerance to lose his temper. Of his two big speeches, that to a 'ticket meeting' of not unfriendly Liberals in the Caird Hall was successful enough, but the mainly hostile audience in the public Drill Hall gave him a terrible time.

> I felt desperately weak and ill. As I was carried through the yelling crowd of Socialists to the platform I was struck by looks of passionate hatred on the faces of some of the younger men and women. Indeed but for my helpless condition I am sure they would have attacked me. Although I had enjoyed for the previous eight years the whole-hearted support of the Dundee Conservatives, both Conservatives and Liberals together were swept away before the onslaught of the new electorate. Enormous masses of people hitherto disfranchised through not paying the rates, and great numbers of very poor women and mill-girls, streamed to the poll during the last two hours of the voting, besieging the polling-stations in solid queues. My majority at the 'victory' election of fifteen thousand was swept away and I was beaten by over ten thousand votes.[2]

On an 80 per cent turn-out, the winners were the official Labour candidate, E. D. Morel, and Edwin Scrymgeour, a local social-reformer and (standing for something Dundee surely needed) prohibitionist who had been trying for as long as Churchill could remember. With his sensitivity to poverty and his gift for respecting virtue even in opponents, Churchill had no difficulty in putting some praise for the latter into his farewell speech at the Liberal Club: 'a man who stood for endurance, and also for moral orderly conceptions of democratic reform and action', a useful representative of a city 'where there was such fearful misery and distress and such awful contrast between one class and another'.[3] Morel he did not like; the man was a socialist and during the war he had been no patriot. And his detestation of Bolshevism was heartily confirmed by what he experienced at the hands of the Gallacher gangs. All in all, it was a disappointing, distressing and literally painful experience, leaving him, as he neatly remarked some years later, 'without an office, without a seat, without a party, and without an appendix'.[4]

He still had his stitches in when he returned to London and his election-eering efforts had set back his convalescence. His wife and friends seized the opportunity, made by the loss of all his accustomed political activities, to propose a long holiday in one of his favourite places. Clementine and Winston let their London house and rented for six months a villa at Cannes, where he devoted most of his time to painting and – a necessary source of income as it had been before and would be again – writing. The first volume of *The World Crisis*, which astonishingly he had managed to write while still in office, was published early that year, 1923; at Cannes he worked on the second volume, which appeared in October. Serialised in the *Times* and published overseas as well as at home, this great book was to make a lot of money.

Throughout the year 1923 he was, as his daughter Mary well puts it, a 'political wanderer'.[5] The political structure within which he had flourished for the past five years had now dissolved. Coalition was 'out' and party was again 'in'. But to which party did he belong? We have seen how his idiosyncrasies made him equally at home, or equally not at home, in classic Liberal or Conservative company. Finding his way in the new circumstances was made the more puzzling by the disarray of the classic parties. Labour for a little while had the greater appearance of unity and promise. Coalition had deranged the others. There were two brands of Liberals and two of Conservatives – in each case, the division being between those who had stuck with Lloyd George and those who hadn't.

Towards the end of the year the 'normal' party pattern of British politics began to reappear. The Conservative Prime Minister Stanley Baldwin (suc-cessor to Bonar Law, who had retired due to ill health in May) reckoned that he could reunite the party by going to the country with a programme of tariff reform, presented as a means of bringing work back to the depressed areas of industrial Britain. This unexpected turn of events made up Chur-chill's mind for him. He discovered that he was still enough of a Free Trader to have to cast his lot with the Liberals, who, like the Conservatives, felt threatened by the onward march of Labour and were also recovering some sense of togetherness. When the Prime Minister sprung his surprise in mid-November and the curtain suddenly opened on a general election, Churchill went into action as an old-style Liberal ready for battle under the restored old-style Liberal leadership of H. H. Asquith. Lancashire was the natural region for such a man with such a doctrine. He could have contested a seat in that county but calculated that his chances would be better in Leicester West. His calculation was wrong and the Labour candidate won handsomely. Churchill was wandering again.

His wandering now was burdened with a new load of worries. The Labour Party's share of the vote had gone up again and it had more Members in Parliament than the Liberals. The Conservatives still had more Members than either of the others, but Labour and Liberal votes together could command a majority. Asquith, with King George V's approval, came to the conclusion that it would be better for the country to let Labour have its chance, on the Liberal leash, rather than to bestow the Liberals' political favour on the Conservatives. To Churchill, with his somewhat irrational phobia of socialism, this seemed terrible. The Labour Party not only professed socialism, it was committed to improving relations with the Soviet Union. His predictable first thought after the announcement of the election results had been that an anti-socialist coalition was called for. When he found that Asquith would not consider any such thing, he was driven to wonder whether he was a Liberal after all. Nor can it have been immaterial to his thinking that, if the traditional two-party pattern of politics was going to reassert itself, the polarity was more likely to be Conservative versus Labour than Conservative versus Liberal. How long might have elapsed before he made the jump we cannot tell. In the event it (or he) was precipitated by Baldwin's abandonment of tariff reform in February 1924. Churchill's way back towards the Conservatives was made so much the smoother. If they wanted a scourge of socialism, he was their man.

An opportunity soon offered. The Conservative Member for Westminster had no sooner been elected than he died. Churchill could not hope, and indeed did not want, to come forward under the straight Conservative banner, but there was another possibility. Would the party stand in the way of his contesting the seat as an Anti-Socialist? The party oracles intimated that it would not. The constituency association decided, however, not without dissension, to back its late Member's nephew. Churchill therefore launched himself as an Independent Anti-Socialist. The Westminster by-election of March 1924 at once became the political sensation of the season. To anyone of sophistication it was clear that beneath the stagey title of Churchill contra Lenin (the latter unconvincingly played by the mild figure of Fenner Brockway), the real fight was Churchill (playing his Tory Democrat father's son for all he was worth) versus diehard stick-in-the-mud Conservatism. Only one Cabinet minister came out openly in support of the commonplace official candidate. The Prime Minister was known to be privately sympathetic. The Churchill camp's extemporised organisation enjoyed the services of a number of Conservative MPs (many of whom had homes there) and of Winston's new admirer and business adviser, the go-getting man from nowhere Brendan Bracken, who from this time on was installed in what would soon be described as Churchill's court. Churchill himself hugely enjoyed the campaign and later wrote about the novelty and glamour of it all:

> As the campaign progressed I began to receive all kinds of support. Dukes, jockeys, prize-fighters, courtiers, actors and businessmen, all developed a keen partisanship. The chorus girls of Daly's Theatre sat up all night addressing the envelopes and dispatching the election address. It was most cheering and refreshing to see so many young and beautiful women of every rank in life ardently working in a purely disinterested cause not unconnected with myself.[6]

But he lost by a narrow margin, just forty-three votes. The constituency managers' man beat him. Fenner Brockway, whose share of the votes benefited from the excitement following the celebrity's intervention, did better than expected. The Liberal was nowhere. But neither, politically speaking, was Churchill. Working his way back to Parliament was going to be a long haul.

Clementine, by no means overjoyed that the Liberal she had married was undergoing another party change, warned him not to rush it. She was afraid that, in his desperation to get back into Parliament, he would sell himself cheap. The other voices to which her husband listened were more impatient and less principled. The support of the press-lords Rothermere and Beaverbrook had been important to him in the Westminster campaign, and the importance of having the press on his side had been rubbed into him by the hostility at Dundee of all three local newspapers, like many others in Scotland the property of D. C. Thomson of the *Beano*. In some moods now and later he would say he deplored the power of the press, but he preferred to have it with him rather than against. His relationship with Beaverbrook was curious and important. On one level they were chums, lads together, early-risers who had made it, talking big of power and money and empire; on another level, they were national politicians with programmes to push and parties to think about, professionals in the political jungle, equally ready to go for one another's throats or to scratch one another's backs, with no hard feelings afterwards. Stolid Stanley Baldwin and his bourgeois kind couldn't stomach that degree of worldliness and frivolity, while it appeared positively shocking to the puritans of Labour. Churchill, however, took it in his stride and turned his relationship with Beaverbrook to good advantage whenever he could. The nation would benefit in 1940. Churchill benefited in 1924.

He benefited also from the encouragement of Stanley Baldwin and other weighty Conservatives, who knew what strength he could bring to the government they would sooner or later be asked to form. For the party managers, the problem was that he had long been too controversial and upsetting a figure to be producible as the 'Conservative' candidate. Since Churchill himself preferred to sail under the colours of Constitutionalist and Anti-Socialist, there was no great problem. He sought, and began to receive, invitations to address Conservative gatherings; he began to be asked whether he would consider contesting this or that constituency; and the happy conclusion of these manoeuvres was his adoption by the Epping Conservative Association as their 'Constitutionalist' candidate at the next general election – whenever that might be. As things turned out, he had not long to wait. Ramsay MacDonald's government muddled its way into an appearance of softness towards Communism by dropping a prosecution of a newspaper editor who, following a familiar Communist line, had urged soldiers not to fire on strikers, proletarians like themselves. The ensuing trouble in the House of Commons led to the dissolution of Parliament on 9 October 1924. Churchill made the most of such a gift of an opportunity. His speeches were reported in the national press as well as admired in Epping, he worked tirelessly in the constituency (as did Clementine), and the result was his election at the end of October 1924 by a majority of nearly ten thousand over his Liberal opponent. He was to remain Epping's cherished MP (the constituency's name changing to Woodford in 1945) for the next forty years.

Churchill was back on course. What had begun by looking as if it might be a disaster for his political life came to seem merely a hiatus. But the episode had long-term consequences. His political position and status were not quite what they had been. It took many years and the traumas of a world war to restore him to the bosom of the party to which he was now rewedded, without possibility of a second divorce. His motives for returning to the Conservative fold – a return completed by formally rejoining the party and the Carlton Club in 1925 – were of course mixed. It is difficult not to believe that some (perhaps unconscious) measure of opportunism was not mixed into his decision: he wanted to get back into government; his extreme confidence in himself made him believe that he ought to be in government; and the Tory way was the only one open. But there was principle in the mixture too. The Liberals whom he had been happy to work with, especially in his ideal form of government, a coalition, now disgusted him by their softness towards the first Labour administration; and the bee in his bonnet about socialism was an absolutely sincere bee.

This was actually one of the things about him which Stanley Baldwin, back in Number Ten, brought into the balance when considering the question of what to do with Winston. Socialism wasn't so much of a bugbear to Baldwin and other senior Tories. They could see that, no matter how socialist the theory and programme of the Labour Party might be, the prospects of any of it being turned into practice were, for the foreseeable future, remote; and they refused to shiver at the spectre of Communism when its only avowed representatives in Parliament were a cultivated ex-Quaker and a rich Parsee. Meanwhile they relied on the influence of common bonds of shared religion, ethics, constitutionalism, nationhood and patriotism to keep the forces of Labour within hailing distance. On the other hand, Baldwin, who in any case rather liked Churchill, knew what an effective head of department he could be and what debating strength he would bring to the front bench. Regardless of what the Tory diehards were sure to think, he took the risk, and invited Churchill to fill the very important office – second in prestige only to that of the Prime Minister – of Chancellor of the Exchequer. Churchill was thrilled. He was to hold the high office his father had once held. Given his peculiar political career to date, he knew he was unlikely ever to rise higher.

So began a relatively tranquil and satisfying phase of Churchill's life. He was happy at home, in the house and estate he acquired at Chartwell in north-eastern Kent in September 1922, and he was happy in his work as Chancellor of the Exchequer throughout Stanley Baldwin's second administration, which came to an end in May 1929. The two men got on well together through these years, each discovering qualities in the other that impressed and amused. The Chancellor's official home was Number Eleven Downing Street and the two men saw quite a lot of one another informally; Baldwin might look in for a chat while Churchill was still going through his first batch of business in bed, and Churchill might stop for a chat with Baldwin on his way to the Treasury (going through the back of Number Ten) later in the morning. He managed to work harmoniously with his Cabinet colleagues for most of the time and, although he remained suspect to many back-bench Conservatives and at least one on the front bench, he felt comfortable in an administration which intended to exhibit what Conservatives, he told the doubtful Clementine, had never really shown before: 'a moderate and even progressive leadership'.[7] Of course there were the usual arguments in the Cabinet (some of them because Churchill as usual could not help minding other ministers' business as well as his own) and battles over budgets; there was also in May 1926 the spectacular and unique event of the General Strike which Churchill considerably enjoyed. But overall it was a peaceful time for the government, with the economy performing better than earlier in the decade or at its close.

In his office as Chancellor of the Exchequer Churchill had special responsibility for the health of the British economy. Many of its features are familiar to anyone who has lived through the second half of the twentieth century. Old staple industries were stuck with out-of-date machinery, uneconomic methods and stick-in-the-mud management, and were declining or beginning to decline in face of foreign competition. New industries of promise located themselves mainly in the midlands and the south. The case for nationalisation of railways and coal was powerfully put (the former, not least by Churchill himself) but rejected as politically unacceptable. Unemployment never fell as much as hoped for between the years when it was high, and never below a million. Labour relations were very bad in the coal industry, merely bad on the railways and in the heavier industries of northern England and Clydeside. Skilled men's unions (a vast variety of them) were embattled in defence of their members' 'differentials', although wartime industrial experience had shown that their skills were not in every case difficult to acquire. Women's chances and wages were much inferior to men's, their bright hopes of wartime almost entirely dashed. The socio-economic divide between north and south was as marked as it long had been and would continue to be. 'The City' was pre-eminent in such fiscal and economic planning as there was – but even more out of gear with 'Industry' than it is still accused of being. The Bank of England and the Treasury were two minds with but the single thought of at all costs avoiding inflation, therefore keeping interests rates high, while weeping crocodile tears over the consequent unemployment. Their common aspiration was summed up in the expression 'Return to Gold' (which some then, including the great John Maynard Keynes, and many since have characterised as of more mystical than material significance); an attempt to recover for the City the global supremacy in international finance which it had possessed before the war when all major currencies were pegged to a fixed rate of exchange, expressed in their value in terms of gold.

Chancellors of the Exchequer come and go; the Treasury stays forever. Churchill was glad to find himself in so prestigious a post, but he entered the post with no mature plan of action and no more ideas concerning fiscal management than came with his belief in the general virtue of Free Trade, learned during his ministerial apprenticeship before 1910. When Churchill arrived at the office he found awaiting him the 'Return to Gold' plan of action which had been several years preparing and for which, said his advisers and the supposed financial wizard Montague Norman, Governor of the Bank of England, the circumstances were right.

As usual on taking up a new job, Churchill busily set about mastering its basics and essentials. He had a lot to learn and not much time to do it, with Budget Day in April one of the fixed points in the parliamentary calendar. 'Return to Gold' was not the only problem that had to be dealt with directly – there were also the naval estimates, which to his practised eye seemed excessive. He familiarised himself with both sides of the argument concerning gold, put up with the batterings he received from their respective protagonists, and found powerful support for his misgivings in an article by Keynes. To the Treasury mandarin Sir Otto Niemeyer he returned this heartfelt answer (which incidentally sounds as relevant to more recent history as to the 1920s):

> The Treasury has never, it seems to me, faced the profound significance of what Mr Keynes calls 'the paradox of unemployment amidst dearth'. The Governor shows himself perfectly happy in the spectacle of Britain possessing the finest credit in the world simultaneously with a million and a quarter unemployed ... This is the only country in the world where this condition exists, [this] unique British phenomenon of chronic unemployment and the long, resolute consistency of a particular financial policy ... It may be of course that you will argue that unemployment would have been much greater but for the financial policy pursued [and] that there is nothing for them [the unemployed] but to hang like a millstone round the neck of industry and on the public revenue until they become permanently demoralised. You may be right, but if so, it is one of the most sombre conclusions ever reached ...

Churchill admitted he could not see his way confidently to any alternative but still found the Treasury policy a bitter pill to swallow. Nor would he believe that no one outside the Treasury and the Bank was competent to offer an opinion.

> I would rather see Finance less proud and Industry more content. [The] fact that this island with its enormous extraneous resources is unable to maintain its population is surely a cause for the deepest heart-searching.[8]

In the end and not surprisingly Churchill came down on the side of the Treasury plan, announcing in his budget speech of 28 April 1925 that Britain would return to the Gold Standard at the pre-war parity. He would have to have been an even more confident man than he was to have gone against such massive departmental advice, while the majority of Conservatives would have been furious had he done otherwise. His decision was not surprising. Nor was it surprising that Keynes should at once have put pen to paper and within three months denounced the decision in his book, its title only slightly adapted from his famous critique of the Treaty of Versailles, *The Economic Consequences of Mr Churchill*. A Chancellor of the Exchequer has to expect to carry the can for what the Governor of the Bank of England and the majority of his advisers persuade him to do. Keynes and other critics were sure that return at the pre-war rate was overambitious and that it greatly overvalued the pound. Within two years Churchill was beginning to suspect he had done the wrong thing; by 1931 he was sure he had. Economic historians, going over the ground again and again ever since, have concluded generally that indeed it was the wrong thing but that doing the right thing – or what we may now see to have been the right thing – would hardly then have been politically practicable.

The return to gold was the most momentous item in his first budget but there were three other items of note, each of which had importance for him: a bit of Imperial Preference and a few modest tariffs, marking his move away from the doctrinaire liberalism of his earlier years; a state-backed contributory pensions scheme, affirming the concern for social welfare he had retained undamaged from that time; and a reduction of income tax by sixpence to four shillings in the pound, which he made out to be beneficial to the worse off as well as the prosperous, but which pleased the latter most. He reduced super tax but correspondingly raised death duties. Imperial Preference went down well with the Conservative rank and file, and would come into its own in the 1930s. Churchill's modest gesture was in respect of sugar (West Indies), tobacco (Kenya and Rhodesia), wines (South Africa and Australia) and dried fruits (Middle East). The fixed tariffs did not amount to much, just import duties on a few luxury imports (such as silk both natural and artificial, motor cars, watches) and films (United States); but there was also an extension of the existing provision for 'safeguarding' British producers by the imposition of duties on imported goods which could be shown to be made unfairly cheap because of subsidies, 'dumping', and 'inferior conditions of employment abroad', by which was inferred Japan.[9]

As one who had been prominent in helping to lay the early foundations of the 'Welfare State' before the war, Churchill had particular pleasure in introducing the contributory pensions proposals, which however were equally the brainchild of Neville Chamberlain, the efficiently reforming Minister of Health. Their two departments had worked together, and the Prime Minister had given them his blessing. The beneficiaries were widows (of any age), their children and orphans (to the age of fourteen and a half) and everybody at the age of sixty-five (instead of seventy). The contributions were to come from persons in work (4d. per week, women paying half as much) and in equal sums from their employers. To Churchill and Chamberlain, that made it a 'tax on industry' but, however indirectly, a form of self-help. To Labour, it looked more like a 'tax on the worker' and a stingy hand-out. But Labour liked its guiding principle: that these benefits, however minimal, were guaranteed as of right, sweeping away the long accumulation of conditions and qualifications, 'means tests' as Churchill himself called them, to which charitable hand-outs had customarily been attached.

Although the sums involved were quite small, this nevertheless constituted 'a landmark ... the first contributory scheme of state pensions, covering more than fifteen million people', freeing many of them 'from dependence on the poor law'.[10]

To the government and its supporters, this was a very acceptable and ingenious budget, and the way the Chancellor put it over had to be admired by everyone in the House who was not already determined to dislike him, as most Labour Members by now were. The Prime Minister was delighted that his gamble had paid off. The relatively cloistered atmosphere of the Treasury had not chilled the energy and enthusiasm which Churchill had previously brought to his tenure of other offices. Baldwin's report to the King is worth quoting, not just for what it says about the budget but for what it shrewdly says about Churchill:

> His speech ... was a first-rate example of Mr Churchill's characteristic style. At one point he would be expounding quietly and lucidly ... At another moment ... he indulged in witty levity and humour which come as a refreshing relief in the dry atmosphere of a Budget speech. At another moment, when announcing the introduction of a scheme for widows' and mothers' pensions, he soared into emotional flights of rhetoric in which he has few equals; and throughout his speech he showed that he is not only possessed of consummate ability as a parliamentarian, but also all the versatility of an actor.[11]

His next four budget speeches were no less entertaining, but none of them had the substantive importance of the first. In 1926 and 1927 he did for the first time what motoring organisations and motorists have not ceased to consider a wicked thing; he 'raided the Road Tax', insisting that road users were wrong to believe that its profits were hypothecated exclusively to road purposes. In 1928, again in collaboration with the tirelessly reforming Neville Chamberlain, though after some brisk Cabinet battles with him, he announced a radical change in the arrangements of local taxation, designed to relieve the burdens (apt to be heaviest in the less prosperous areas of the country) on industry and agriculture. Grants from the Exchequer were to make up to local authorities what they would lose by the total exemption of farmers from local taxes ('rates') and by their reduction in respect of industry to the tune of 75 per cent. Here was, however unintendedly, the distant source of the 'block grant' element of local government finance and of the power which central government has acquired over it.

There was one proviso to Churchill's satisfaction with his first year as Chancellor of the Exchequer. The calculations upon which his budget was based included the assumption that, through at the least the forthcoming year, the economy would undergo no change for the worse. In specific terms, this meant hoping that the bad weather which had long overcast the coal industry would not blow up into a storm. But it did. Put off for nine months by the appointment of a Royal Commission of Inquiry and by a subsidy of many millions (the first of the several coal-holes in Churchill's budget), the storm burst towards the end of April 1926. The coal-owners and the miners simply could not find a way to agree, and the government simply could not find a way to bring them to an agreement. The cost of failure was known to be high. The General Council of the Trade Union Congress had been ready to call a general strike in solidarity with the Miners' Federation the previous summer. That crisis had then been averted. This time it wasn't. By 1 May the miners all over the kingdom were locked out. The General Council instructed its 'first line', vanguard unions to begin the strike at one minute before midnight on 3 May.

Despite the devotion of a huge amount of effort by government and union representatives through the first three days of May to seeking a way back from the cliff edge, no way was found. Whether a way could have been found, and where the blame lies for its not being found, has been vigorously debated ever since. There were settlement seekers and confrontation seekers on both sides. Baldwin for most of the time was among the former, Churchill – once the universality of the strike was clear, as it was by the early hours of 4 May – among the latter. The difference between them was largely tactical. No one could have put more strongly than Baldwin the argument that the general strike was a political one and in principle destructive of the constitution, but Baldwin shrewdly understood that some members of the Trade Unions' General Council must be unhappy about what they had become involved in, and that plenty of trade unionists in other industries than coal would be happy to get back to work; he preferred to let their solidarity crumble rather than to cement it with threatening or abusive language, and the majority of the Cabinet was with him. Churchill, on the other hand, was all for making displays of force and for rubbing into the strikers the lesson that they could not take on the state. He only became magnanimous to opponents after he had beaten them. His language in private became intemperate and warlike. He would have liked soldiers to appear more conspicuously than the Cabinet thought prudent. He was not so far beside himself as to seek to provoke a civil war, but he did talk as if the government had been pushed towards a state of war by the 'revolutionaries' (and indeed there were some on the other side), and he wanted them to be under no illusions as to what would happen if the civil power, the regular police and the numerous 'specials' rapidly enrolled had to call on the military to help keep the peace.

The government had made good use of the nine months' warning it had

had that it might have to deal with a general or, as the TUC preferred to call it, national strike. Its plans were put inconspicuously into operation, and the Home Secretary Sir William Joynson-Hicks (who had been Churchill's Unionist opponent at Manchester twenty years ago) convened a committee of the Cabinet, innocuously titled the Supply and Transport Committee, to supervise the maintenance of essential services. Among these was deemed to be the dissemination of news or, at any rate, such news as the government thought good to disseminate; a proposal all the more reasonable in face of the TUC's *British Worker*, issuing from the works of its *Daily Herald*. Newspaper owners were sounded out and Churchill was set to draft an overall plan of action. It very quickly appeared that the newspaper owners would prefer the government to produce its envisaged news sheet or whatever on its own. Several ministers and many top officials were involved in these brisk comings and goings. Churchill being one of them, he took on the role of impresario. In the course of 3 May an arrangement was made with the editor of the *Morning Post* (another of Churchill's former foes) for the government's paper, the *British Gazette*, to be printed on the *Morning Post*'s press on paper boldly requisitioned from wherever it could be found. The first issue came out on 5 May, the last on the 13th. Churchill enjoyed playing the newspaper mogul; the higher the *British Gazette*'s circulation, the more he strove to hold off the demands of Beaverbrook, Rothermere and other newspaper proprietors to be allowed to resume publication of (shrunken versions of) their own products. He wrote a lot of the paper himself and submitted with an ill grace to the softenings of tone sometimes demanded by John Davidson, the junior minister and Conservative Party stalwart who also had a title to be regarded as editor. Davidson was more of Baldwin's way of thinking than Churchill's, and with Cabinet support overrode Churchill's objection to printing the story about the famous football match between strikers and police in Plymouth.

The ending of the general strike was much more messy than its beginning. The *British Gazette*'s last issue carried the triumphalist headlines 'Unconditional Withdrawal of Notices by TUC' and 'Surrender Received by Premier', but the *British Worker* on the same day implied that the strike had ended because of understandings or undertakings to the miners' advantage, which was by no means the case. There ensued for a few days what has been called the 'Second General Strike', when workers returning to their workplaces and finding conditions imposed and penalties threatened, went on strike again until Baldwin had again made it clear that the government neither wanted nor would tolerate victimisation. So ended Britain's first and only general strike. Everyone went back to work, except the miners.

True to type, now that his side had won hands down, Churchill reverted to his normal mood of Tory-Democratic paternalist benevolence, and moved to the more conciliatory side of the Cabinet table. Throughout the summer and autumn efforts continued to be made to seek a formula which would bring together the miners and the mine-owners, collectively two of the most obstinate bodies of men with whom any conflict-resolving government can ever have had to deal. When the exhausted Baldwin went for relief to his favourite spa, Aix-les-Bains, Churchill was left in charge of negotiations for a month. His change of attitude was such that, to his colleagues' astonishment, he began to make proposals for putting as much pressure on the owners as on the workers. The back-benchers and the business world in general were disquieted, and at the beginning of November Churchill's coal-owning cousin, the Tory grandee Lord Londonderry, reproached him for turning on a group of industrialists who were his allies in the fight against socialism. Churchill's reply included the making of one of those distinctions which showed how firmly his thinking was grounded in rule of law constitutionalism.

> Both sides are represented by their worst and most unreasonable elements and by people selected for their obstinacy and combative qualities ... With those parts of your letter which deal with the necessity for combating Bolshevism I am in entire accord. But there could be no worse way of combating Bolshevism than to identify the Conservative Party and His Majesty's Ministers with the employers ... The duty of the Government is to occupy an impartial position in the interests of the State and of the whole community ... You say that the Owners are fighting Socialism. It is not the business of Coal Owners as Coal Owners to fight Socialism. If they declare it their duty, how can they blame the Miners' Federation for pursuing political ends? [12]

He had not gone soft on the miners, upon whom – at least, upon whose leaders – he never ceased to place the primary blame for the national disaster of the general strike and the damage it did to his Treasury calculations; but neither did he, once the strike was over, abandon the effort to come upon a formula the miners would accept, nor would he slip into the character of a mere class warrior for whom there was virtue on only one side of the argument.

It remains to consider Churchill's Chancellorship in relation to questions of defence and security. His state of mind through the later 1920s was quite different from what it had been between 1912 and 1922. The making of war and readiness for war had then been at the front of his mind. Economy was ensconced there now, while disarmament was being strongly promoted at the League of Nations, which meant that the armed services were deprived of their best argument for spending money. The last embers of the Great War having been extinguished at Chanak, active hostilities were off the agenda. Notwithstanding Churchill's deep-down concerns about the future, as a practical politician he was content to accept – and in 1928 even to institutionalise – the 'rule' laid down as early as the summer of 1919, and renewed annually since, that the armed forces in their planning could rely on being involved in no major conflict for the next ten years. Stout patriots and service chiefs who had admired the wartime Churchill, and who recalled the free hand with which he had spent taxpayers' money as Minister of Munitions, were surprised, even indignant, that he was now a cost-cutting Chancellor more willing to spend on social welfare and debt repayment than on battleships.

How much need there was for battleships and other, perhaps alternative, types of warship continues to be debated by historians, especially military ones, who have looked back from the later 1930s with the shared perception that the nazification and rearmament of Germany and, on the other side of the world, the deterioration of relations with Japan found Britain painfully unprepared. The fact is unquestioned, but it is not relevant to an appraisal of the situation in the 1920s. The Germany of that time posed no threat. Although critics of the Treaty of Versailles, Churchill among them, had predicted that Germany would be so embittered by it that it would become again a public danger at the earliest opportunity, events in 1925 gave them cause to wonder whether they had misjudged after all. The Treaty of Locarno marked, in general, Germany's re-entry into the mainstream of European economic and political life and, in particular, the dawn of hope that its relations with France, upon which the prospects of future peace depended, would gradually become less edgy. And if Germany presented no immediate problem, what European country did? The semi-European Soviet Union was a disagreeable presence to all its neighbours westwards, but militarily threatening only on the Afghanistan side of India, which was something to be worried about more in New Delhi than in London. Italy and France were counted as more or less friendly powers, each presenting problems (the novel fascist style of Mussolini, the seemingly incurable French neurosis about Germany), but neither was thought of as a military menace. Where else might danger lie?

The answer was in the Pacific. A curious triangular rivalry had developed in that vast region. Japan had become a considerable military power, considerable enough to have made a useful ally for Britain during the war. The United States, more recently an ally also, was likewise a very considerable military power, and Japan was its natural rival in the ocean where geography destined the two of them to compete. Complicating their rivalry as a potential ally of either or neither was the British imperial presence, stretching from India and Burma round the Malay States (as they were then known) and the naval base of Singapore up to Hong Kong. The economic value of this region and of the sea-routes to Australasia that ran through it was immense. But there was more to it than trade. The British government and people were conscious of a huge debt of gratitude owed for blood unsparingly shed on the Empire's behalf by the brave men of Australia and New Zealand. Having sent their soldiers to far-off Europe, when Britain called for them, those Dominions looked to Britain for defence against what they perceived as the potential menace of Japan. (They did not see the United States as a prospective menace, but neither did they yet think of the USA as any sort of alternative protector; imperial sentiment was still very strong.) The facts of geography being what they were, most of that defence would have to be provided by the Royal Navy. Singapore was acknowledged to be the only place where British naval power could concentrate in safety. It needed to be turned into an impregnable fortress and military base. But was Japan bound to become a menace, even if the termination of the twenty-year treaty in 1922 meant that it was no longer an ally? Here were defence problems entirely different from the traditional European ones to which the policy-makers in London were well accustomed.

As to the United States, Churchill shared the common conviction (common, that is, among the ruling classes and the ordinarily patriotic citizenry) that the British navy should not allow any other maritime power to outbuild it – the so-called 'single-power standard'. This was admittedly a come-down from the 'two-power standard' observed when Britannia had no rival on the waves, but it was felt to be essential to the maintenance of British prestige. So important was the power of prestige – reduced to its lowest terms, the effect of uncalled bluff – that this meant maintaining at least equality with the American navy, itself now aspiring to head the league, although there was scant cause for believing that Britain and America would ever find themselves at war with one another. Since America and Japan *might* be believed capable of finding themselves at war with one another, Britain could hardly look forward to being on good terms forever with both of them. Japan being therefore the one more likely to threaten the security of those precious Dominions and Colonies, it followed logically that Singapore, often referred to in naval and imperial discourse as the Gibraltar of the Far East, should be strongly fortified.

There was no lack of Admiralty planning to this end, and rudimentary combined services planning also; but the money to pay for it was never forthcoming, and proper planning was repeatedly wrecked on the rocks of inter-service rivalry and jealousy. Churchill has to carry some of the blame for the lack of money, in as much as he was the longest-serving Chancellor of the Exchequer in the 1920s and moreover might have been expected to share the services' view of the situation. The topic of Singapore came before him repeatedly but never rated more than a low priority. One wonders why. Churchill himself wondered why, when it was too late. In *The Second World War*, and with direct reference to the disastrous events of early 1942 but incidentally revealing something about his state of mind in these earlier years, he wrote:

> It had never entered my head that no circle of detached forts of a permanent character protected the rear of the famous fortress. I cannot understand how it was I did not know this ... I had put my faith in the enemy being compelled to use artillery on a very large scale in order to pulverise our strong points at Singapore, and in the almost prohibitive difficulties and long delays which would impede such an artillery concentration. I do not write this in any way to excuse myself. I ought to have known and I ought to have been told, and I ought to have asked ... [13]

Part of the explanation of his unmindfulness was something Churchill shared with plenty of others in Britain's governing and military classes: undervaluation of the Japanese, amounting sometimes to actual contempt for them. This explanation itself needs some explaining, since it had been universally recognised before the Great War that Japan had become a first-rate modern military power, and very clear by 1920 that it was a territorially acquisitive one, of whose southwards expansion Australia, and not Australia alone, might reasonably be wary. The more frankly this uncomfortable prospect was taken on board, the more undeniable it must have become that imperial security required from Britain the capability to put powerful air and sea forces in South-East Asia and the construction of a reliable defensible base from which they could operate. But many men in the relevant sectors of British government were unwilling to understand this, and Churchill was one of them. Outwardly, they talked down the Japanese military potential and in any case pooh-poohed the likelihood of Japan's becoming a menace. Was there inwardly a wish, a yearning, not to have to face up to this ultimate challenge to imperial security because of some sense that the problems looming in the mists of the future were going to be, in the last resort and the worst case, insoluble?

11

Empire and India

'India is a geographical term. It is no more
a united nation than the Equator.'

Speech in the Royal Albert Hall, 18 March 1931

The general election of May 1929, and the ensuing entry into office of the Labour government, marked an epoch in Churchill's life. At the time, neither he nor anyone else could tell what economic and political hurricanes were soon going to hit them. Labour with 288 seats had become the biggest party in the House and the Liberals, reunited under Lloyd George but numbering no more than fifty-nine, were going to keep it in office instead of helping the Conservatives to keep it out. This was enough to signal to Churchill the opportunity to embark on two new ventures: the beginning of a grand-scale biography of his warrior ancestor, the Duke of Marlborough; and a North-American trip that would agreeably combine business with pleasure. American newspaper proprietors and book publishers were as eager as the British ones to sign contracts for his articles and books; and, what for the moment was even more exciting, money apparently could easily be made on the New York Stock Exchange. Bernard Baruch and his other rich American friends would be glad to help him make it. The need to generate income was pressing. His salary had been reduced to the meagre level of an ordinary MP, but his quality-of-living expectations remained high, and Chartwell continued to eat up money. To speed and solidify his work on the biography, he engaged the services of a bright young Oxford historian, Maurice Ashley. To enlarge the pleasures of his tour – his first crossing of the Atlantic since 1900 – he took with him Randolph, now a wilful and hard-drinking Oxford undergraduate, his brother Jack, and Jack's undergraduate son Johnnie.

They set off for Quebec on 3 August 1929 and, journeying royally in the steel magnate Charles Schwab's private railway carriage, went by way of Montreal, Ottawa, Toronto, the Rockies, Vancouver, Victoria, Seattle, California and Chicago to Washington DC and New York. In California he was entertained by William Randolph Hearst at San Simeon, in Hollywood he partied with Charlie Chaplin; from Washington he made expeditions to the battlefields of the Civil War. His letters home included thrilled estimates of how much money he was making or, once he got to New York in October, would make. Alas for the Churchills, his circle of friends included none of the very few men in the United States who sensed that the fabulous investment boom was just about to burst. He was in fact there through the climactic days of what has ever since been known as the Great Crash. On the Friday following 26 October, 'Black Thursday', he witnessed on the sidewalk outside where he was staying the results of a suicide's leap from the fifteenth floor above. His last letter from New York, written perhaps before he was fully aware how much his friends had lost on his account, referred to the Crash philosophically as

> only a passing episode in the march of valiant and serviceable people who by fierce endeavour are hewing new paths for men, and showing to all nations much that they should attempt and much that they should avoid.[1]

Homecoming was not the happy event he had been telling Clementine to look forward to. Much of the money he had made, or relied on making, had disappeared. His daughter Mary, seven at the time, recalls how, that winter, 'Chartwell was run down to a low ebb: the big house was dust-sheeted, only the study being left open so that Winston could work there'.[2] She and her governess stayed in a cosy little cottage on the estate, while her parents spent their London weeks in short-term lets or hotels. This sadly reduced existence came to an end after a second lecture and journalism trip in the winter of 1931–32, which was financially successful but marred by an accident in New York which left him with a scar on his forehead. Searching in the dark for Baruch's Fifth Avenue house, he had forgotten that American traffic moved on the other side of the road to Britain, was knocked down, and hospitalised or otherwise bedridden for three weeks. With characteristic decency, he made no attempt to blame anyone but himself.

Home from the first trip in early November 1929, with his 'Impressions of America' coming out weekly in Lord Camrose's *Daily Telegraph*, and with a place in Stanley Baldwin's Shadow Cabinet, Churchill resumed his parliamentary duties and political career. He found the look of things not at all to his liking. The Empire Free Trade campaign begun by the press-lords Beaverbrook and Rothermere directly after the election was still going on and was arousing a sympathetic response among the Conservative grass-roots. How long could the leadership withstand the pressure? Churchill, still a Free Trader at heart, feared that Baldwin might cave in. But on another great issue, and without such close-to-home pressure to account for it,

1. Churchill at the age of seven. Mrs Everest's darling already knew how to look cool and masterful. (*Imperial War Museum*)

2. Lord Randolph Churchill, the father who denied Winston the interest and affection he longed for. His memories of an emotionally deprived childhood helped make Winston an affectionate father, when his turn came. (*National Portrait Gallery*)

3. Lady Randolph Churchill. To little Winston, she 'always seemed a fairy princess'. Here seen after she had lost the sleek slimness of her early married years. (*National Portrait Gallery*)

4. Second Lieutenant Churchill of the 4th Hussars. With Britain at peace with the world, he soon found military life dull and boring. (*Imperial War Museum*)

5. Clementine Churchill with the year old Diana, 1910. Clementine's sharp and delicate profile suggests the refinement and intelligence which made her socially formidable. (*Baroness Spencer-Churchill Photograph Album, Churchill College, Cambridge*)

6. Randolph Churchill, who found his father an impossible act to follow. Plentifully endowed in heart and brain, his extraordinary family nickname was 'the Chumbolly'. (*National Portrait Gallery*)

7. Sarah Churchill. A red-head, her determination to make a career on the stage upset her parents. Her father called her 'the Mule', because, he said, she was very obstinate and she wouldn't breed. (*National Portrait Gallery*)

8. Mary Soames and her husband Christopher at the christening of their fourth daughter, Charlotte, in November 1954; with Winston and Clementine. (*Conservative Party Archive and Bodleian Library*)

Baldwin had already committed himself and those who would stay with him to a policy which bothered Churchill much more: movement towards Dominion status for India.

Resisting this movement was going to become Churchill's principal political activity through the next five years. His enormous capacity for work, together with his pressing need for income, enabled him also to write, in 1930 alone, forty articles for magazines and newspapers. He began an 'Eastern Front' sequel to *The World Crisis*. What began as a serial in the *News Chronicle* became the most attractive and admired of all his books, *My Early Life*, published in October. The years 1931 and 1932 would be even more productive. Such an output, which would not have disgraced a full-time professional writer, went on alongside Churchill's political life, which now came to one of its several crises. His Indian concerns became intense and troublesome enough to cause, in January 1931, a breach between him and his party's leadership. That breach has generally appeared as the formal beginning of the period of 'political isolation', the 'years in the wilderness' which are noted under these and similar descriptions in every book about him. This period of his life was so strange an interlude in his political life, and so unsatisfactory in his own estimation of it, that such a judgement is not unreasonable. But to present the India issue as its source is to take too limited a view of it. His overt concern was indeed with India, but India was only part, admittedly a very large part, of his concern about the Empire as a whole; and even the Empire was not the whole of what he was concerned about. Beneath his often buoyant exterior, and apart from his chronic recurrent depressions, he entertained profound anxieties about the future of the world, the state of the Empire and – what was to constitute the other and more easily intelligible of his two grand preoccupations through these years – the condition of Europe.

His anxieties and fears existed on several levels, one of them personal and subjective. A fellow Conservative, Leo Amery, who was also aboard the liner heading for Quebec, recorded Churchill saying, in the course of a conversation, that he had been all he ever wanted to be, short of the highest post which now seemed unattainable, and anyhow politics were not what they had been. The level was lower; there no longer were great men like Gladstone or Salisbury.[3] Innocent of false modesty, he felt himself to be a survivor from an age of giants, an old-fashioned 'great man' in a world increasingly shaped by the commonplace. Politics was not what it had been in the age when, as a youngster, he had sometimes met the giants at his parents' and relations' houses, and when, evidently, his oratorical style was formed (which by now sounded old-fashioned to younger parliamentarians). In a well-known passage of *The World Crisis* he recalls how, when he was twenty-one, he was privileged to lunch with the great Sir William Harcourt.

> In the course of a conversation in which I took, I fear, none too modest a share, I asked the question, 'What will happen then?' 'My dear Winston', replied the old Victorian statesman, 'the experiences of a long life have convinced me that nothing ever happens.' Since that moment, as it seems to me, nothing has ever ceased happening ... The scale on which events have shaped themselves has dwarfed the episodes of the Victorian era ... The smooth river with its eddies and ripples along which we then sailed, seems inconceivably remote from the cataract down which we have been hurled and the rapids in whose turbulence we are now struggling.[4]

That some changes were for the better he gladly acknowledged – indeed, he was proud of having had a good deal to do with changes for the better in his own country's social and penal administration – but many changes were for the worse. Prominent among these latter was the popular press, corrupter-in-chief of politics, and the changing nature of war, which in the future could only become even nastier than it had recently become, which was bad enough. Settlement of disputes between states being, in his view, inconceivable without last-resort threat or use of armed force, he had little faith in the pacific endeavours of the League of Nations. As of 1930, more obviously aggressive ideologies not yet having made much of a mark, he rated 'Bolshevism' as the principal new wellspring of violence and oppression in the world. He did not believe in guaranteed progress. Retrogression seemed to him to be equally possible, and one of the forces at work in the world to check it was the British Empire.

What he deeply felt about the Empire and Commonwealth (as it had officially become in 1926) more often surfaced in these inter-war years than before the war, because there was now something to worry about. Before the war, the Empire was a great fact that could be taken for granted. The 'mother country', the 'white Dominions' (as Canada, Australia, New Zealand and South Africa were commonly known), and the gigantic white-controlled territory of India, together presented an unprecedented spectacle of extended racial and linguistic solidarity; a phenomenon from which Churchill's project to write a *History of the English-Speaking Peoples* naturally derived. This vast Empire stood solid through the war and came out of it victorious and even enlarged. Expressive of its apparent weight in the world and of its singular constitution was the presence at Versailles of the Prime Ministers of the Dominions, insisting that President Wilson (who thought their presence improper) should know exactly what their countries expected to get out of the treaty.[5]

Beneath the show of power and solidarity, however, a number of problems and difficulties were developing. The anxiety about maintaining imperial prestige and power which marked Churchill's response to the Chanak crisis had roots in his feeling that the Empire was not so secure in the world as it had been. We have already glimpsed the development of problems regarding defence and commerce. Now they were becoming political also. They were apparent in both 'white' and 'non-white' sectors. With regard to the former, it might be said that the Dominions were growing up. Assertions of independence and questionings of parental wisdom were bound to happen sooner or later. That these movements of thought and feeling have not detached the Dominions from the Commonwealth (as it became known *tout court* in 1949) more considerably than they have testifies to the genuineness of its cultural and moral heritage, and the seriousness with which that has been valued. It had two weak spots, but Churchill like everyone else within British imperial circles was blind to them. The revered stature in Britain of Churchill's friend Jan Smuts obscured the fact of the primordial disaffection of the Afrikaners in South Africa, and the possibility that the francophone Canadians of Quebec might turn secessionist had as yet occurred to no one. The great white core of the Empire appeared to be solidly founded. Churchill on the whole correctly sensed that he had no need to worry about the Dominions; their response to Britain's need in the next great war was to prove him right.

India was what he came to worry about most. He was not alone in this. What was happening in India puzzled and worried almost everybody. It was the part of the Empire where indigenous nationalism (already questioning British authority in Egypt before the war) became most troublesome; and, since it was also the most glamorous, populous and (for occupational as well as commercial reasons) valued part of the Empire, the room for worry was very great. British rule in India had felt secure before the war and remained so to its end. India made an enormous contribution to imperial triumph, its British-officered regiments valuably supporting the home raised armies, just as its African regiments did the French. No sooner was the war over, however, than nationalist disturbances began with unprecedented vigour. They took on many different forms. Some disturbances were, or became, violent and internecine, and therefore counterproductive in their impact on a Raj dedicated to preventing Hindus and Moslems from killing each other. But the Indian nationalist movement also produced something quite original, unprecedented and difficult to deal with: varieties of principled non-violent mass action popularised and on some notable great occasions led by M. K. 'Mahatma' Gandhi, a personage not only difficult but also, for all but truly philosophic Britons, infuriating to deal with, not least because his own non-violence often served as a signal for the violence of others. Promoting and orchestrating the bulk of the demonstrations and resistances, and with Gandhi as its most celebrated and influential leader, was the Indian Congress Party, to whose typically middle-class and educated (what is more, English-style educated) members it seemed reasonable to demand a measure of Home Rule, Dominion status preferred.

To most of the British government's policies vis-à-vis India Churchill took emphatic exception. Even to sketch what they were is perilous, Indian history being a field of study of its own and 'government policies' themselves having two sources, the India Office and Cabinet in London and the Viceroy and his Council in India. The gist of British policy from 1917 to 1935 was a halting but never reversed succession of gestures in the direction of self-government, persisting in face of repeated rejection by Congress and against backgrounds of cyclical disturbance and repression in India – and, from 1930, the sniping of Churchill's posse of diehards in London. The main landmarks of these 'years of failed strategies and dashed hopes' were the viceroyalty of Lord Irwin (better known under his later title of Lord Halifax) of 1925–31, the three Round Table Conferences in London in 1930–32 (Gandhi, released from prison by Irwin in order to help represent Congress, spectacularly appeared in his usual scanty coverings at the second of them), and finally the Government of India Act in 1935.[6] So slow and in some respects grudging was this progress that Indians found it difficult to believe that the British really meant ever to go away, for all that it became increasingly common as the 1930s wore on for Britons in India to express such sentiments as 'This can't go on forever' and 'We'll have to go soon'. There was also the structural problem of the social gulf fixed (by the British) between the two communities; so much the more galling for Indians when, as was often the case, they were better educated and more cultivated than the British who snubbed them.

The plan put forward by Ramsay MacDonald and Stanley Baldwin's National Government enjoyed the backing of some of the Labour Party, all the Liberals, and (in the long run) all but about eighty Conservatives. It proceeded from the basis that British imperial theory, notwithstanding the gibes of Leninists and indigenous nationalists, was sincere in its declared principle that overseas territories were held by the British for the benefit of their inhabitants (besides whatever the British themselves got out of it, which sometimes wasn't much), and for only so long as it took those inhabitants to acquire the capacities and capabilities to govern themselves. The Congress Party had begun staking India's claim to be on the road to Dominion status well before the war. The first tentative British recognition of the justice of the claim had been in 1917. In a famous announcement, the liberal-minded Secretary of State for India, Edwin Montagu, said that 'for the first time something like colonial self-government was envisaged, however remotely, for a non-white colony'.[7] By the close of the 1920s it was clear to the governments in both London and Delhi (the grand New Delhi was not inaugurated until 1931) that something more attractive and more like Dominion status had to be offered. On the last day of October 1929 Lord Irwin, the Conservative Viceroy, momentously declared that 'the natural issue of India's constitutional progress ... is the attainment of Dominion status'. Churchill just then was on the way home from New York. When he heard of it, he was electrified. Already by 16 November he was setting out the grounds of his hostility to the project in a long article in the *Daily Mail*. From that time onwards he was one of the Conservatives who would find it ultimately impossible to follow their leader's liberal line on India.

Declining to follow his leader also meant rejecting the judgement of the man on the spot, the Viceroy. Lord Irwin, an unusually conscientious and culturally sensitive Christian man, believed it was necessary to take risks to find a peaceful solution to the endless round of arguments and repression into which the nationalist movement and its canny, cussed leadership was locking his administration. Responding to Churchill's congratulations on his survival of an attempted assassination, he mildly remarked:

Half the problem here is psychological and a case of hurt feelings. I don't overrate the politicians, but I do think once Edwin Montagu had set our feet upon the present road and unless we are prepared indefinitely to pursue methods that I don't think British opinion would long tolerate, you are bound to do your utmost to carry some public opinion with you in your task of government.[8]

Again, a few months later Churchill made shocking comments – words that have never been forgotten in India – on Irwin's having officially received Gandhi ('a seditious Middle Temple lawyer now posing as a fakir of a type well-known in the East, striding half-naked up the steps of the Vice-regal palace ... to parley with the representative of the King-Emperor'). Irwin expressed himself in a letter to Baldwin's right-hand man John Davidson:

Winston's attitude ... seems to me completely and utterly hopeless ... The day is past when you can make nations live in vacuums. The day is also past in my humble opinion when Winston's possessive instinct can be applied to Empires and the like. That conception of Empire is finished.[9]

That was a private expression of disapproval. A very public one, similar in principle but more rugged, came in a letter to the *Times* from the Prime Minister, Ramsay MacDonald, after one of Churchill's fire-eating speeches to the Indian Empire Society, a blimpish organisation set up expressly to oppose the consensual policy. He dismissed Churchill as a mischief-maker, whose mind encompassed

> nothing except an antiquated relationship between Imperial authority and the people who come under its sway, blind to every modern movement in politics, stiff-necked regarding the handling of people whom we ourselves have enlightened in political affairs and aspirations.[10]

Almost all of us now, I suppose, would consider that the Viceroy and Prime Minister had reason on their side, and that the majority of parliamentarians at that time did well to follow their lead. Why did Churchill throw himself into such a reactionary posture and keep it up for nearly five years? For neither the first nor the last time, though for longer than on any other occasion, he became extraordinarily worked up; so much so that he distanced himself from Baldwin in the last days of 1931 in order to be free to try to shoot down the government's slowly but steadily maturing India policy. His 'courtiers' and 'the Winston crowd', as Sir Samuel Hoare called them,[11] now and then talked as if he was en route to a political coup, and something of that sort may have been in his mind, but it was a high-risk strategy. Much of what he did simply annoyed the leaders, wise men and managers of his party, and ultimately many of its constituency activists. A peak of annoyance came when Randolph Churchill put himself forward as an Independent anti-India Bill Conservative candidate at a by-election at Wavertree, a suburb of Liverpool, in January 1935. He had not previously consulted his father, who was a good deal embarrassed but, loyal as always to the members of his family, went to Wavertree and spoke on his son's behalf. All that Randolph achieved was to split the Conservative vote and give Labour an easy victory. His father's reputation for intemperate eccentricity and illiberal extremism seemed to be confirmed. To the charges of Churchill the warmonger (true enough in respect of Bolshevism) and Churchill the enemy of socialism (true also) and enemy of the workers (not true) was now added the charge of Churchill the diehard white-supremacy imperialist. How much truth was there in it?

His hostility to the Government of India Bill (as it was when at last passed in mid 1935) deployed a variety of arguments; some more remote-seeming to our post-imperial minds than others. Not at all remote now, and most widely persuasive then, was his belief that what mattered to the great majority of the inhabitants of the subcontinent was not self-government but good government. Good government meant the rule of law and the reliable administration of impartial justice; the preservation of peace between religious and racial communities notoriously liable to flare up against one another; and the spread of 'western' standards of public services of sanitation and health. These were matters that the Raj took seriously. Churchill believed that without the impartial authority which only an externally-based Raj could provide, justice would be corrupted, religious and racial animosities would be let loose, and progress towards 'western' levels of public health would be bogged down. He did not believe that Indians would be able to govern their country as well as the British were governing it. He also believed that, as soon as the British began to leave, the Hindus and Moslems would begin to slaughter one another. The reader must make up his and her own mind to what extent Churchill's beliefs were absurd.

With those rule of law concerns went what our age might recognise as certain proto-human rights concerns. In respect of India, as formerly in respect of Africa, he believed in protecting minorities from oppression and exploitation. He had the interests of the 'untouchables' particularly at heart. (It was ironic that Gandhi, an unorthodox Hindu, had them at heart too.) The caste system as a whole he found unattractive and inexplicable, but he was not so presumptuous as to suppose that it was any non-Hindu's business to try to demolish it. What it meant for the untouchables at the bottom of the scale, however, he found repulsive, and he believed that Hinduism left to itself would never redress what he viewed as a fundamental denial of human rights (the words were not yet in his vocabulary, but they are in ours). The plight of the untouchables was not the only feature of Hindu Indian culture that he deprecated, as we may be sure from the appreciation with which he read Katherine Mayo's book *Mother India* (1927). Mayo was a sociologically and medically minded American whose travels and inquiries in India led her to write a powerful demonstration of how appallingly different the standards of common Indian life were from those of her own East Coast America. India did not come well out of the comparison. Her chapters on indigenous medicine, child-brides, the treatment of animals and what passed as midwifery indeed make horrifying reading. Such descriptions, perfectly accurate as far as they went, were not calculated to dent Churchill's conviction that the Indian masses needed to be shielded by Britain's superior science and superior law.[12]

His paternalist concern for the welfare of the apolitical masses (not the less real for his knowing of them only through what he was told and what he read in books), and his disdainful distrust of the politically-active middle classes (hardly any of whom can he ever have met), was accompanied by a sympathetic fellow-feeling for the Indian princes, with whose kind he did have some slight familiarity from the polo fields and high social occasions, in Britain as well as in India, where they might be encountered. The princes, some with a good deal of British advice and some with as little as they could get away with, still ruled over more than 70,000,000 of the subcontinent's 300,000,000 souls. It was part of the plan of the Government of India Act to give the princes representation in an All India Federation, a part to which Churchill was not especially hostile – although he hoped the princes would decline to participate (as, in the event, they did). To the part of the plan which aimed to establish very substantial measures of self-government and virtually total indigenous recruitment of officials in the provinces, he was prepared to give a trial, although he believed that the removal of British controls would open the door to nepotism, corruption, inefficiency and other evils. What he absolutely could not stomach was the part of the Bill that admitted an Indian element to the central government. This would, he declared, sooner or later lead inevitably to its wholesale Indianisation, for which he used such hyperbolic language as 'a crime against civilisation' (1930) and 'a catastrophe which will shake the world' (1935).[13]

What affections, fears or hatreds produced this apocalyptic talk? Indians of course were likely to consider him a racist or (if there is any difference) racialist; and so long as the term is understood in a fairly loose sense, they had ample justification. Without any serious knowledge about Indians or any other non-white peoples, he believed they were 'less civilised' or 'less advanced' than whites. He shared the growing concern about immigration from the coloured countries of the Commonwealth when it began in the early 1950s, remarking that if it went on unabated Britain would become 'a magpie society', but he didn't make a big issue of it. He hardly ever met non-white men and women except at the highest-class sporting or diplomatic occasions. Never very fond of new faces even if they were white, he absolutely disliked, and tried so far as possible to avoid, coloured ones, justifying this as a matter of choice, not prejudice. His language in private about coloured and foreign people generally was of the casual, unthinkingly demeaning character commonplace in his class and kind, let alone the British people at large: 'blackamoors', 'niggers', 'wogs', 'chinks', 'eyeties' and so on (but not, in his unusual case, 'jewboys' or 'yids'). But he would not have referred to any of the princes known to him in this manner, and it is impossible to believe that in an emergency he would have objected to being operated on by an Indian surgeon, advised by an Indian scientist or counselled by an Indian lawyer. He stopped objecting to Indian independence once it had become a *fait accompli*, and defended against diehard critics the acceptance of a republican India within the Commonwealth. He had no difficulty in chatting amiably with the Indian Prime Minister Pandit Nehru when Clement Attlee brought them together at a Commonwealth Conference in the late 1940s.[14] There is no denying that racial difference did matter to him and that he remained totally 'unreconstructed' in this respect until the end of his days. But good governance and Empire always mattered a great deal more.

Churchill's grand idea of the British Empire absolutely excluded the possibility of any of its major elements being controlled by non-Britons or persons of non-white European stock. The Conservative leader Stanley Baldwin and Sir Samuel Hoare, the minister who put the Government of India Bill through the Commons, and Lord Irwin and his successors in the viceroyalty, these and all such men did not feel that the Empire and Commonwealth was done for if the unique and wonderful Indian part of it was allowed, because of its historic and cultural singularities, to become in due course a non-white Dominion within it. Churchill did feel that. Those others had some understanding of the moral force of the idea of national self-determination, though they might doubt whether the practice of it would turn out well for the country that pursued it, and even whether in the long run it would turn out well for the Empire that permitted it. Churchill had little sympathy for it (except in Ireland) and thought the chances of it turning out badly for all concerned were so great that it shouldn't be encouraged.

He also felt, in what was perhaps an even deeper level of his being, that Britain had a right to be there because of its right by conquest. Empires were acquired by conquest, solidified by commerce, homogenised by habit and custom. That was the way the world was, and there was nothing wrong with it; a self-respecting power did not willingly give away what it had conquered unless superior force or strong self-interest (unimaginable in this case) made it do so. Prestige was a precious attribute, hard to acquire and easy to throw away; he told the electors of Wavertree that the choice before them was whether or not Britain had the 'will to survive as a great nation among men'.[15] Churchill was unmoved by his opponents' reminders that in earlier years, and particularly in the well-remembered business of General Dyer, he had refused to believe that British rule had to be maintained by brute force. They also reminded him of his prominent part in abandoning the policy of force to maintain British control of Ireland. These and other such *ad hominem* arguments were of no effect. In the Government of India Act of 1935 he sensed the beginning of the end of Empire, and it is arguable that he was correct to do so. He fought on to the end, complaining about the sharp tactics adopted by the government (to counter the equally sharp tactics used by himself and his band of supporters), only to find the final vote in the Commons going against him to the tune of 386 against 122; that minority being made up of his eighty or so dissentient Conservatives plus about forty Labour MPs who opposed the Bill because it didn't go far enough.

The final battle of that long campaign being over, Churchill extraordinarily supposed that his relations with the leaders of his party could at once return to normal. Always ready to be magnanimous to the defeated, now that he was himself defeated he expected magnanimity to be shown towards him, and publicised his readiness to return to high office in an open letter to the electors of Epping which recalled Lord Salisbury's dictum after losing the fight against the 1867 Reform Bill: 'It is the duty of every Englishman and of every English party to accept a political defeat cordially, and to lend their best endeavours to secure the success, or to neutralise the evil, of the principles to which they have been forced to succumb.'[16] That he was sincere in this expression of constitutional propriety cannot be questioned. What has to be questioned, on this as on other occasions, was his awareness of political realities and personal relations. He had revived all the earlier suspicions of his excitability, unpredictability and lack of judgement. Less regular in attendance at Westminster than he used to be, and than straighter-laced colleagues thought proper, he had missed no opportunity to obstruct the government's legislative programme. He had allowed himself to become the flag-bearer of a phalanx of reactionaries and backwoodsmen, and he had done so in collaboration with one of the most powerful of the press lords (Rothermere) at the very time when the leader of his party, Stanley Baldwin, won lasting acclaim for standing up to them and their misused power in his often-quoted Queen's Hall speech of 17 March 1931.[17] He had advertised to world public opinion, and especially to the vigilant Indian and American parts of it, that a significant segment of British imperialism was unreconstructable. Closer to home, he had made fun of the Prime Minister Ramsay Macdonald – of whom his own party leader was a close colleague in the National Government – as a 'boneless wonder' and a 'Don Quixote, with Sir John Simon as his Sancho Panza'; and he said in private (but such privacies never last long in the Westminster hothouse) very rude things about Sir Samuel Hoare and the other ministers struggling to get the Bill through. If Churchill really thought that he was going to be taken back into Baldwin's bosom, he was very much mistaken.

12

Chartwell and Hitler

'All the black swans are mating, not only the father and mother but both
brothers and both sisters have paired off. The Ptolemys always did this
and Cleopatra was the result. At any rate I have not thought it my duty
to interfere.'

Chartwell Bulletin, no. 3, to Clementine, 21 January 1935

If his India campaign was what Churchill was best known for through the
early 1930s, his campaign to arouse Parliament and people to the dangers
of Hitler's Germany took over as the earlier campaign petered out. But his
private life at the same time was very important to him. He was continuously
busy as a writer and had to be so because it was his only source of serious
income and therefore the necessary means of caring for his wife, his children
and his home. This is a good place for standing back to look at Churchill
in mid-career.

He was not yet the great man he would soon become. Everyone recognised
that he was an important man and a most uncommon man, the most
uncommon man to have attained a high political office apart from David
Lloyd George, who was at least as uncommon and who had attained the
highest office of all. Like Lloyd George, he had made many enemies on his
way to the top and, like him again, he was regarded by sound party men
and political moralists as untrustworthy, though in an entirely different
way. Lloyd George could never be anything but a Liberal, Churchill had
been Conservative, Liberal and Constitutionalist, and it was not clear what
he might be in ten years' time.

He still held to the belief that he was destined to do great things for the
nation he loved, but when, if or how he would ever be able to do them
seemed doubtful even to him. War was what especially excited him and
brought out what was most original and powerful within him. Aware of
the dangers of such a temperament, he was not the bad sort of man who
would wish to start a war in order to shine in it, but his early scepticism
about the Treaty of Versailles had been borne out by subsequent events,
and by now, the early 1930s, he felt more and more sure that what was still

universally known as the Great War would sooner or later become called the *First* World War. Recollection of his own experiences between 1914 and 1918 continued to pain him. At its beginning, he had been the only member of the Cabinet who was cheerful and optimistic. His career had then still been on the upward path and, if only the Dardanelles expedition had turned out better, it might have led even to his overtaking his political colleague, mentor and rival, David Lloyd George, to become the Prime Minister who led his people to victory.

His experiences in the Great War stayed with Churchill for the rest of his life. We have seen how badly he had been hit and hurt by the Dardanelles failure and how he had been unfairly made the scapegoat for it. For about two years, from the middle of 1915 to the middle of 1917, he toiled under this shadow and strove to rise from beneath it. Only through the last eighteen months of the war had he been once again in a seat of power. He had filled it creditably; but at the armistice he was just one of the many ministers of a broad coalition government, not one of its inner circle and certainly not its star. The ten years that followed had seen him back in the political front line and back on the Conservative side of it, but he did not think much of the party's leader, he was viewed as vulgar and untrustworthy by the respectable society of conventional Christian gentlemen who composed its parliamentary strength, and he was openly hostile to its main policies from the turn of the 1930s. Would he ever appear at the political top again? Churchill thought it doubtful, and so did everyone else.

In personal terms, he was now well into his fifties and had acquired a more impressive presence than when he was younger. His body was a bit bulkier, the rather large balding head on top of it less disproportionate than it once had been; his face was fatter, readily delivering the chubby, saucy looks which encouraged the impression that he was always good-humoured and nice to everybody. In fact, he was not always nice to everybody. He could put on a good show of benevolence in public, but the truth is that he didn't enjoy mixing with people he didn't already know and, unless embarking on a well-prepared for public occasion or in the House of Commons, he much preferred being in private with familiar faces around him. Without thinking about it, he had grown into the style of taking servants for granted. (Some biographers define this as typically aristocratic, but it was just as characteristic of the late-Victorian upper middle class.) He had and he would retain a way of looking at subordinates and inconsequential strangers described by them variously as staring, scowling or glowering; sometimes, if there was a group of them, facing them down one by one. He was bossy and demanding, good-humoured and genial so long as he wasn't thwarted. He couldn't cope without a manservant or valet and he was unselfconsciously accustomed to having himself fussed over and looked after, and to living well. Winston, said his bosom friend F. E. Smith, 'is a man of simple tastes. He is always prepared to put up with the best of everything.' He took exercise as often as he could: a practised rider, he had gone on playing polo until at last giving it up in 1925; he would still go out with the hounds when at Blenheim or with rich friends on their estates, and he was a keen and good swimmer.

His lifestyle did not appear to be a healthy one, but appearances were deceptive. Clementine, herself relatively abstemious, worried about his love of whisky, brandy and champagne. On festive occasions and in tense times he drank more copiously than on working days, and it is impossible not to believe that some of the people who said they had witnessed him drinking too much had really done so, but overall there was justice in his remark, later in life, that he had taken more out of alcohol than alcohol had taken out of him. As for the huge cigars (the older he became, the more often were they gifts from admirers and friends), it was observed that he mumbled and played with them rather than seriously smoked them, and they seem not to have been held responsible for his occasional chest troubles. His most evident recurrent affliction was not physical but psychological: depression. He was familiar enough with it to call it familiarly his 'black dog', a bout of gloom and despair that came over him directly after big disappointments and when he had no challenge to meet. Much has been written about this since it became public knowledge in the book his personal physician Lord Moran published very soon after he died, but its importance has been exaggerated. It never stopped him doing anything he wanted to do.

He was immensely fortunate in his wife, an intelligent, capable, fine-looking woman, by 1930 entering her later forties. She believed in him and understood him, was proud of him and continued to love him despite his dark moods, self-centredness and frequent absences, usually holidaying at rich friends' places in the south of France. One of the reasons she disliked those trips was that he enjoyed gambling and tended to lose more in the casinos than he could afford; another was that she didn't like most of those friends and simply didn't enjoy or, in her heart of hearts, approve of ostentatious luxury, whereas, with a sort of self-indulgent innocence, he did.

Of the four surviving young Churchills (the fifth, little Marigold, had died in 1921), the elder three were becoming in their different ways troublesome. Randolph, handsome and impressive, had all of his father's boldness, energy and appetite for good living, but not much of his father's seriousness, power of application and ability to hold his liquor. Recalling his own unappreciated adolescence, Winston indulged the boy's self-indulgent spoilt behaviour and allowed him – with such a formidable act to follow, one cannot but feel some compassion for the lad – to grow up with a sense that he too was someone special, capable of cutting an early dash in the world. Having found Oxford boring and restrictive, Randolph took himself away from it in the middle of his second year and launched himself as a journalist, lecturer (he went down particularly well in America) and man about town. His rudeness and intemperance in print as well as person became notorious, while his unsolicited political interventions on his father's behalf (the Wavertree by-election early in 1935 and another in Scotland twelve months later) served only to confirm the widespread impression that the Churchills were a rackety lot.

Daughters mattered less than sons in that pre-war world, but sharp notice was taken of daughters who transgressed the standards of respectability. Diana and Sarah both confirmed the impression given by their brother, Diana by divorcing in 1926 the husband her parents had not wished her to marry in the first place (John Bailey), and Sarah by going onto the stage, falling in love with an Austrian-born Jewish comedian nearly twice her age, Vic Oliver, and running away to marry him in New York in 1936. Only the exemplary Mary, by eight years the youngest of the children, gave no trouble; a happy, horse-loving and hard-working schoolgirl, she would celebrate the last summer of peace by passing her school certificate.

Chartwell, three miles south of Westerham in Kent, was exclusively the Churchill family home through the 1930s, and Winston loved it. Clementine didn't. Her relationship with the place got off on a bad footing when her husband purchased it in the autumn of 1922 without consulting her. He showed it to his three elder children and got them on his side before he told his wife what he had done. It took her no time at all to realise that, whatever the natural beauty of the site, it would prove a difficult and expensive establishment to run for whoever had the responsibility for running it, in other words herself. Her daughter says that his buying it without telling her 'was the only issue over which Clementine felt Winston had acted with less than candour towards her'.[1] The thousands who go there as pilgrims to a shrine are unlikely to realise that it is the monument par excellence to the great man's ineffable egotism.

Today's Chartwell, handsomely maintained by the National Trust, is almost entirely a Churchillian creation. The house was an unattractive semi-derelict mess when he bought it, the gardens and grounds nothing like as interesting or extensive as they are now. Only the magnificent southern view was already there: down the little valley and over miles and miles of spreading woodland. Churchill surveyed the scene with the eye of an eighteenth-century aristocrat, noting at once its capabilities and determining to realise them regardless of expense; perhaps there was also in his vision something of the general scanning a battlefield and planning how to gain his victory. That he was victorious nobody who goes there now can doubt; but the battle went on for nearly twenty years and proved every bit as expensive as Clementine feared.

To make the house habitable and attractive was of course the first task. The building faced north and stood close to the Edenbridge road. Churchill wanted its principal rooms to face the other way, which meant that a mighty extension had to be constructed on that side of the house. Since he interfered as much with his architect Philip Tilden as he was accustomed to do with colleagues and subordinates generally, their relations became sadly strained. Much additional expense came from the unforeseen defects: dangerous wiring, leaking roofs and that particular terror of the house-buyer, dry rot. Not until the spring of 1924 did it begin to become habitable as a home.

As for the gardens and grounds, Churchill went on improving them until the next war called him back to London. In their present shape they are not significantly different from what they were when he had finished with them. There are the lengths of brick wall he personally built around the kitchen garden, the orchard trees he planted, and the summerhouse he made for Mary. (The tree house he made for the elder children has gone.) But the great glory of the place, and Churchill's biggest achievement there, is the way its natural water supply and hillside situation were made to support a noble water garden of descending pools, a couple of lakes in the valley bottom, and halfway down a swimming pool that with millionairish extravagance was heated to about 75 degrees (Fahrenheit) in cold weather. One visitor arriving on a clear frosty winter morning was amazed to find the area of the pool shrouded in a cloud of rising steam from which came the happy voices of a family at play.

Chartwell was not only where his friends and extended family could always be sure of a welcome, it was also, until September 1939, a place of some importance in British history. It served as a sort of alternative Cliveden; a regular meeting-place for Churchill's extensive circle of political associates and admirers, with an inner circle of particular friends at its core. Some stayed for the night but most came for lunch – it was only an hour's drive from central London – and stayed until the topics of the hour were exhausted. Upon Clementine necessarily fell the hard work of providing for this endless succession of guests and keeping the establishment in good running order; no small task through the 1930s when the basic staff was about eight indoor servants, one or two secretaries, a chauffeur and three gardeners.

Three particular friends were of peculiar importance to Churchill in these, as he himself called them, Wilderness Years. (Was it significant that all three were confirmed bachelors, and thus more likely than married men to give him their entire attention?) One was Frederick Lindemann, Professor of Experimental Physics at Oxford, whom he came to know in the early 1920s. The German name was misleading. Lindemann's father had left Alsace when Germany seized it after the Franco-Prussian War. Lindemann himself was born in England and was bred to dislike Germany, but he was at home in the language and, along with many rising scientific stars at that time, he had studied in Germany. Extraordinarily unlike Churchill in many respects, not least because he was a vegetarian and total abstainer, he became specially valued for his ability to explain scientific matters in terms a layman could understand. Again and again in his later writings Churchill acknowledged his debts to Lindemann, whom he kept close to him throughout the war, referring to him familiarly as 'The Prof' and causing him to be created Lord Cherwell in 1941.

The second core member of Churchill's Chartwell coterie was just as unusual a character. Where Brendan Bracken came from, and how he made enough money by 1921 to become a Conservative MP when he was only twenty-one years old, remained for long mysterious. It was rumoured, to Clementine's vexation, that he was her husband's illegitimate son; a rumour which his reverential attachment to Churchill from 1923, and Churchill's amused acceptance of it, did nothing to scotch. Brendan Bracken came into the category of friends of Winston about whom Clementine had reservations or worse; either because she suspected their motives for seeking his company or because she distrusted his motives for seeking theirs, or simply because in her objective way she didn't reckon his life and career likely to be bettered by their influence. It took her many years to accept Bracken. Churchill, however, enjoyed the man's company from the start, found him useful in various ways, valued his loyalty, and was glad to give him important roles when war came: Parliamentary Private Secretary to begin with and then, from 1941, Minister of Information. He was so regular a presence at Chartwell that by the 1930s Sunday was known in that unchurchy household as Bracken Day.

More specialised and secretive in his Chartwell role was Desmond Morton, a military man known to Churchill since the Great War and helpfully domiciled at nearby Edenbridge. Director of the Industrial Intelligence Centre from 1930, it was his job to discover all that could be discovered about German rearmament: what sorts of rearmament, and how much of it. These discoveries he covertly revealed to his influential neighbour. Churchill later asserted that Morton did this with permission from Ramsay MacDonald while he was Prime Minister, and that Baldwin and Chamberlain successively extended it. Some mystery continues to hang over this matter. Martin Gilbert found no written evidence of Prime Ministerial connivance in such a breach of the Official Secrets Act; but the late Robert Rhodes James declined to take that as conclusive that it didn't happen. It was certainly of great importance. Churchill could not have packed his speeches and journalism with so much solid matter about the need for Britain to rearm had not Morton, not to mention many other less regular unofficial suppliers both British and foreign, fed him with relevant facts. His dependence on Morton and confidence in his judgement was such that, in May 1940, Morton was given a place in what we would now call the Prime Minister's private office, acting for a while as the confidential agent through whom highest-level Intelligence was conveyed to the chief.

Chartwell was also where the bulk of Churchill's writing was done. His literary output continued to be prodigious in both quantity and variety: punchy journalism, thoughtful essays (including those collected in *Great Contemporaries*, 1937) and the kind of history-writing at which he excelled, not unscholarly but with pronounced military interests and patriotic purposes. Inevitably a man who didn't know how to live economically and moreover didn't want to, and whose only regular income was his annual few hundred pounds as an MP (£400 till 1937, then £600), had to exploit to the utmost his literary talents.

> I earned my livelihood by dictating articles which had a wide circulation not only in Great Britain and the United States, but also, before Hitler's shadow fell upon them, in the most famous newspapers of sixteen European countries. I lived in fact from mouth to hand.[2]

He produced at Chartwell his four-volume *Marlborough: His Life and Times* – the first volume published in October 1933, the fourth and last in September 1938. Supplied with material as usual by professional scholar-assistants from Oxford, he then began to work on what would many years later become his *A History of the English-Speaking Peoples*, and with 500,000 words done by September 1939 had more or less finished it when it had to be set aside 'for the duration'. These sustained literary endeavours and serious speech-preparation required relays of secretaries. Such was the pace that in 1937 a resident secretary was engaged with a particular commitment to do night work. This was Mrs Kathleen Hill, who was to become his personal private secretary throughout the war. Martin Gilbert records her telling him that

> The idea was that I would get a rest in the afternoon. It hardly ever happened. I had never been in a house like that before ... When he was brick-laying we used to take our notebooks and mount the ladder – even there he could dictate

but not at length ... Often we would dash up to the House of Commons, he dictating as we drove, and then we would type it out in the Commons. Sometimes we would pass the sheets in as he was speaking.[3]

Back in Parliament and the arena of public affairs, Churchill continued to play a conspicuous though, in comparison with before and after, somewhat intermittent part. It was intermittent for a variety of reasons. No office demanded his presence and he had more than enough to do at home. The governments of which he was nominally a supporter had such vast majorities that they didn't need his vote, though they could certainly have done without his opposition. He didn't know as many Members as he had known in earlier years, and he felt little need or desire to get to know new ones. Except for short periods in 1935 (the India Bill) and 1938/9 (the Munich agreement), his constituents appeared to be content with having as their representative a quixotic celebrity who visited them no more often than he had to. (Conservative MPs were not usually bothered by constituency 'surgery' attendance in those days.) He was not as popular a figure in the House as he once used to be, and he felt it. His absences were noted, and his presumption when he was there was resented. Labour Members generally disliked and feared him until, about 1938, the wiser of them came to realise that, after all, he and they had a common enemy. Liberals and Conservatives acknowledged his supremacy as a speaker and crowded to hear him when he was in action; they admired the form, but often reserved judgement on the substance.

The substance, from 1933 onwards, was ever more to do with Hitler's Germany. The passage at last of the Government of India Act cleared the way for his concentration on the Hitler menace. Its force, however, was to be for a while diluted by a spectacular sideshow which can be seen as creditable to Churchill's heart but, again, suggestive that there was still something amiss with his head. This sideshow was for most of December 1936 the cynosure not just of British and imperial but of world interest and concern: the abdication of King Edward VIII.

Churchill had been on friendly terms with Edward through the many years while he was Prince of Wales, and appears never to have doubted that he had it in him to become a good monarch; in any case, Churchill was such a strong, even a romantic, believer in hereditary monarchy that he was fervently of the opinion that Edward ought to stay King. The attributes which many wrote down as defects of character – lack of seriousness of mind, liking for flashy company, irreligion, sexual adventurism – did not particularly bother Churchill, who knew how often monarchs had been like that and how little it need matter constitutionally. Besides,

Churchill was not himself a religious man and, although not personally interested in divorces or amorous adventures, he was far too familiar with them in his own extended family and social circle to think that account should be taken of them in public life. So when, in his father's last months, Edward became attached to Mrs Wallis Warfield Simpson, an American socialite who was on the way to divorcing a second husband, Churchill felt none of the disapproval and disquiet which spread throughout the members of the governing class who knew anything about it. For many months after George V's death in January 1936, the fact of Edward's attachment remained unpublicised and therefore popularly unknown to a degree, which, by our contemporary standards, is quite unbelievable. Only Britons who knew Americans or who went abroad could be aware that the affair was an international sensation. Meanwhile, Edward's intentions regarding Mrs Simpson remained conveniently obscure. They were the easier to conceal because her divorce could not become definitive until April 1937, about the time his coronation was scheduled to take place.

The crisis, when it came, came suddenly. The silence so long and so extraordinarily observed by the British political class and press was broken at the beginning of December. Egged on by Lord Beaverbrook and with the support of his 'courtiers', and mistakenly believing that he would be able to convict the Prime Minister of heartlessness and unconstitutionality, Churchill took up Edward's cause and, in the few days available, agitated in both press and Parliament to get the decision about Edward's future delayed. His brief campaign did Edward no good and did Churchill himself some harm, which, fortunately for his country, proved to be short-lived. He had excitedly underrated Edward's resolve to marry Mrs Simpson and to make her Queen – over-optimistic though Churchill was about other things, he never thought that possible – and he had overrated the degree of popular support that might be aroused on Edward's behalf. Clementine as usual held a more balanced view of the situation. She was not surprised, though of course she shared his hurt, when his last attempt to put the King's case to the House of Commons, on 7 December, was shouted down. It was the most humiliating event of his parliamentary career.

Churchill's attitudes regarding India and the abdication were of some importance in the history of the British Empire, but the great matter with which he was dramatically connected through the 1930s, the rearmament and nazification of Germany, was of importance in the history of civilisation. He was the first British statesman of any note to identify, and to call public attention to, the dangerous twist given to German national aspirations (which he well understood) by their confluence from 1933 with Nazi ideology and Hitler's leadership. He correctly sensed before evidence had accumulated to support the charge, how dangerous to the peace of the world Germany would become in Hitler's hands. He was also singular in never being taken in by the peace talk with which Hitler cleverly and calculatingly varied the war talk in his public pronouncements through the six years between achieving control of Germany and the beginning of the war. The importance of those peace offers and public pronouncements cannot be overstated. It was largely because of them that 'appeasement' had such a long life. The British public in the 1930s was curiously suggestible, and Hitler was a politician of genius and a platform orator of unusual skill whose words became listened to (literally listened to, by whole families sitting round the loudspeaker of the wireless, though few in Britain could understand him) with unparalleled attention. Many politicians and most of the publics of Britain and France, the only two countries which really mattered in this connection (since they alone had the power, if they chose to work together, to resist German pressure), were, to put it crudely, keener on hearing what Hitler said about peace than what Churchill said about war. It is necessary to understand the former before examining the latter.

Few Britons positively liked or admired the Führer. The British Fascists of course liked him, but they were never numerous and to anyone who wasn't a Jew or a Communist they could even appear as figures of fun (as in the case of P. G. Wodehouse's Roderick Spode and his Black Shorts), just as could the dictators themselves, as conflated in the great cartoonist David Low's composite dictator 'Muzzler'. There was a fashion of admiring Hitler at the dotty extremity of conservatism and in hard-headed right-wing aristocratic and business circles. Otherwise the general rule was that the more anyone knew about Hitler's ideas, and how they were being implemented in Germany, the less acceptable did the Führer and the more menacing did his Third Reich appear to be. In stark contrast, the idea of any sort of armed confrontation with Hitler, which was the logical conclusion of Churchill's arguments, was extraordinarily unpopular, nearly as unthinkable as a thought can be, and it is not difficult to understand why. The prospect was a fearful one, whether you looked forward or back. If forward, there was the widely-held (and, until the very end of the 1930s, officially endorsed) belief that London was accessible to German bombers, that it was indefensible against them and that, besides causing vast destruction, they would rain poison gas. If you looked backwards, the experience of the Great War was, to adult men and women, only fifteen years behind them; nearer, in fact, than the Falklands War is to the present day. Although plenty of 'old soldiers' (ages ranging from thirty to sixty) recalled their wartime camaraderie and ultimate victory with pride, some preferred not to remember the war and some positively hated the memory. Besides the whole-bodied survivors, there were the hundreds of thousands variously maimed and marked for the rest of their lives, and hundreds of thousands more who had never come home but whose images were present on so many domestic walls and mantelpieces and whose names shone out on the war memorials of every parish and many major buildings.*

Supporting this belief that there couldn't be another big war in Europe (Manchuria and Abyssinia were exotically remote and Spain was not part of the Europe most people in Britain were aware of) was confidence that the unprecedented measures taken to ensure that it had been 'the War to End Wars' must be worth something. Huge numbers of people in Britain and France and the smaller countries belonged to associations like the League of Nations Union, and numbers smaller but still impressive signed up under pacifist banners. Only conscientious pacifists like George Lansbury, leader of the Labour Party from 1931 to 1935, and doctrinaire Marxist-Leninists like Stafford Cripps in one of his earlier phases, made known their unwillingness to fight at all. The pacifist and internationalist mass of believers in the power of the League to prevent war and the efficacy of disarmament (hopes of it stayed high until 1933) were not in theory unwilling to fight in a good cause, but believed that two League talismans called Collective Security and Economic Sanctions would turn fighting into a last resort so remote as scarcely to require serious consideration. Such was the background of feeling and belief about peace against which Hitler performed

---

* My own memories of the Great War's continuing presence are relevant. The Bests were a conventional middle-class family in Osterley, a western suburb of London, with no recent trace of the military in their pre-1914 background. Yet evidence and legacies of the war were all around us. Upright Mr Davis next door had lost an eye in it. Giant Mr Piercy from twenty houses along our road, whose daughter was one of my occasional playmates, had lost a leg in it and thumped up to Osterley station each morning on large wooden crutches. Our dear friend Mr Draisey had served alongside my Uncle Harold on the Somme and had come out of it in one piece; poor Harold lost an eye, was shell-shocked, and never wholly recovered. Cousin Henry from Australia died of wounds at Gallipoli and lay buried at Malta. Courtesy Uncle George, who had knocked about the world a good deal before settling down in Sussex, had fought in South-West Africa in 1914–15 and at Passchendaele in 1917. My father went early in the war to an officer's training school but contracted pneumonia and pleurisy, which left him with a cardiac weakness for the rest of his life; one of my treasures was the piece of the metal skeleton of a zeppelin whose shooting-down he had witnessed over north London. He was a civil servant in the Ministry of Pensions, created during the war to administer the pensions of war-widows and war-wounded. Songs like 'It's a Long Way to Tipperary' and 'Pack Up Your Troubles' were as familiar to me as the hymns we sang in church every Sunday; but it wasn't 'Oh What a Lovely War' for us at all, it was 'Oh What a Grim War, and How Could There Ever be Another?'.

his black arts, now threatening that war would follow the rejection of Germany's 'just demands', now promising peace if those demands were met. He was much assisted, as his more ordinary predecessors Brüning and Stresemann had been, by the belief, held with varying intensity throughout the British political public, that some parts of the Treaty of Versailles had indeed been 'unjust', and that British policy towards Germany was therefore right to show understanding of the German position. From this derived an irremovable element of grit in the relations between Britain and France, the French remaining unpersuaded that the nation justly punished for its aggression had anything to complain about. Hence also the paradox that, while there was a tendency in Britain to blame France for declining to disarm to the extent that British disarmament enthusiasts suggested, there was a parallel tendency to be sympathetic towards Germany's rearmament, even when this was in breach of the military restraints set upon it by the treaty. The remilitarisation of the Rhineland, in March 1936, was excused as 'only going back into Germany's own backyard'. Hitler took much of the wind out of the sails of potential critics by justifying his ambition of integrating with all other German-speaking populations as no more than observance of the Versailles principle of self-determination. Some of his gambits became as familiar in the later 1930s as did the catch-phrases of popular radio shows. Everyone knew how each successive advance was advertised as 'positively my last territorial demand', and how every delay in meeting his demands provoked the warning that 'my patience is nearly exhausted'.

Given so crafty and unprecedented an opponent, so awkward a case to argue and so large a desire in the electorate that confrontational policies should be avoided, it is not surprising that the governments of Stanley Baldwin and, from May 1937, Neville Chamberlain (although they were in fact beginning to rearm within the modest limits considered affordable) sought to avoid all appearance of arms-backed firmness in their responses to Hitler's repeated measures of rearmament and expansionism. They told themselves, their party and the public that readjustment of the political map of Europe was reasonable in view of the justice of Germany's complaints. In this way the word 'appeasement' acquired the more modern and sinister of its meanings, adding to pure 'pacification' the taint of 'peace at any price'.

Churchill was the most prominent of the few leaders of British opinion who refused to believe that this policy of appeasement, once the British government had unmistakably adopted it, was either honourable or sensible. He understood what Hitler meant by the Versailles grievances but something, probably just brilliant intuition, told him that Hitler had much more in mind than the mere redress of them. He was never taken in by Hitler's talk of peace. It has to be said that not everyone who pursued the policy of 'appeasement' was taken in either, but even those who allowed themselves to be so – of whom the most conspicuous in the end was Neville Chamberlain when he overconfidently assumed control of foreign policy in 1938 – were finally and conclusively disabused in March 1939, when Hitler took over what remained of Czechoslovakia, the non-German-speaking part, following its partial dismemberment at Munich the previous autumn. At last Churchill could say what he pleased without meeting the frowns and hearing of the embarrassments of those who had to handle Hitler's complaints; complaints which of course included the accusation that Churchill was a warmonger. It became realised that Churchill had been right about the seriousness of German rearmament and the profound unappeasability of Germany's dictator, and the clamour became insistent for restoring Churchill to a defence-related place in the government. Chamberlain obstinately resisted these pressures until the last possible moment. Churchill only got back to office at the Admiralty on 3 September, the day the war began.

Churchill was worried about Germany long before he found cause to worry about Hitler. He had feared German military resurgence from the earliest moment it was possible to conceive of anything so unpleasant: the formulation in early 1919 of the Treaty (or, as the Germans preferred to call it, the *Diktat*) of Versailles. The opening pages of his *The Second World War* cite Marshal Foch's 'singularly accurate' comment on the treaty that it was 'not Peace [but] an Armistice for twenty years'. Churchill himself said of the economic clauses of the treaty that they were 'malignant and silly to an extent that made them obviously futile'; of the way they worked out, he said it was 'insane', 'a sad story of complicated idiocy'. And not only were parts of the treaty absurd, the treaty as a whole was totally unstatesmanlike and imprudent, because it ensured that Germany, a country that no treaty could keep from remaining the largest and potentially most powerful state in Europe, would enter the post-war period with feelings of grievance and a desire for revenge, precisely the results which a wise and (Churchill's constant passion) magnanimous peace treaty ought to have avoided. In an earlier book he took to himself a share of the blame. He recalled how, standing for re-election when the war was only just over and passions still high, 'The Prime Minister and his principal colleagues were astonished and to some extent overborne by the passions they encountered in the constituencies ... It was not from the majesty of the battlefield nor the solemnity of the council chamber, but from the scrimmage of the hustings, that the British Plenipotentiaries proceeded to the Peace Conference.'[4] Consolation of a kind was available only in the reflection that every other participant victor behaved as badly.

The harm done was irreparable. However buoyant and cheerful he normally appeared, Churchill was henceforth fundamentally pessimistic about Europe's future. The Weimar Republic he rightly characterised as a 'flimsy fabric' beneath which 'raged the passions of the mighty, defeated, but substantially uninjured German nation'.[5] He felt it impossible that a Germany so conditioned would not sooner or later seek revenge and re-establishment. In what form this renewed German menace would present itself and when, he had, of course to wait and see. The economic downturns of 1931 and 1932 were exactly calculated to precipitate the dénouement. It came in the form of that 'maniac of ferocious genius', whose accession to the Chancellorship in 1933 surprised Churchill as much as it surprised almost everyone else, but whose use of his power directly thereafter showed that the giant forces of German nationalism were going to be put to the service of a novel nationalist and racist ideology, operating by its own unpredictable rules.

Churchill was right to fear Hitler and Nazism, but he did not do so because he was an expert on German affairs. He liked to present himself as a good European, but he was an Englishman first and foremost. He had first-hand knowledge only of France, but it is questionable how well he understood what he saw even there; for example, he never glimpsed until too late how little the French army was to be relied on. Of Germany, and its history and culture, he was but patchily informed. He had an *idée fixe* about the awfulness of 'Prussians' which was unhelpful in understanding current Nazi realities, and actually inconsistent with his belief until 1938 that Hitler could be unseated by revolution in the German High Command. He couldn't read German, he knew hardly any Germans, and his trip to Bavaria in 1932 to visit the sites of Marlborough's battles was the first time he had been to Germany since his youthful attendances at the Kaiser's army manoeuvres before the deluge. On the other hand, two of his Chartwell companions kept him well informed about much that was going on in Germany. Desmond Morton knew more than almost anyone else about German rearmament and 'The Prof', as Frederick Lindemann was always known in the family, was well equipped to fill in the gaps in Churchill's general knowledge. Hitler's book *Mein Kampf*, translated as *My Struggle*, was available in Britain in a somewhat bowdlerised version by the end of 1933, so Churchill would have looked at it and learned what was in the omitted bits (not least because he would have been told by his Foreign Office friend Ralph Wigram, a Chartwell occasional) by the time he referred to it in an article about Hitler in the *Strand* magazine of November 1935.[6] His wish to reach the widest possible readership no doubt explained his sounding a note somewhat softer than usual, but readers with their wits about them cannot have got to the end of the essay without concluding that, if what Churchill reported of Hitler was true (as in fact it was), the man was very unpleasant and dangerous indeed. True to his unwavering and consistent dislike of antisemitism, Churchill included a powerful paragraph about the Nazis' persecution of the German Jews. His inability to suppress his feelings in that connection was thought to have been a major cause of Hitler's failure to turn up on the one occasion in 1932, only a few months before that fatal day of his becoming Chancellor, when the two men might have met one another in a Munich hotel. No other British politician saw into Hitler so early, or pointed out more vigorously, once Hitler had attained total power and initiated the Nazi revolution, how all the principles, apparatus and decencies of a liberal constitutional state were being overturned. Far from soft-pedalling his criticisms in the mainstream Conservative manner (because, after all, Nazism was hostile to Bolshevism), Churchill's readiness in the later 1930s to consider military alliance with Soviet Russia suggested that, although both ideologies were evil, there might not be much between them.

With German military nationalism resurgent and the dictator Hitler in charge of it, Churchill became from 1934 a keen-eyed Berlin-watcher, seeing German power and intentions as the issue which dwarfed all others, freed of any lingering doubts and hesitations by Hitler's reoccupation of the demilitarised zone of the Rhineland in May 1936. He was relatively unconcerned about what else went on in Europe. Eschewing the liberal-cum-socialist practice of bracketing together the two fascist dictators, he clung for long to a *Realpolitik* hope that Mussolini (whose regime in any case he correctly assessed as much less unpleasant than Hitler's) could be kept friendly or neutral in the forthcoming conflict. He was an anti-Nazi, not an anti-Fascist until very late in the day. He failed to give serious thought to the issues at stake in the Spanish Civil War and he did his own anti-Hitler campaign no good by appearing at that time to be pro-Franco. Germany was his constant theme, to the point of being blinkered about other problems. In press and Parliament, in public oration and occasional broadcast, he called attention to the treaty-breaking rearmament going on in Germany and to the need for Britain to match it. Of the many examples available, here is one from his wireless broadcast on 16 November 1934. After denouncing the Nazis' maltreatment of minorities and dissenters, and dismissing disarmament as more likely to encourage Hitler than appease him, he said:

I am afraid that if you look intently at what is moving towards Great Britain, you will see that the only choice open is the old grim choice our forbears had to face, namely, whether we shall submit or whether we shall prepare. Whether we shall submit to the will of a stronger nation or whether we shall prepare to defend our rights, our liberties and indeed our lives.

The choice for Britain, he said, was between preparing to submit to 'a Teutonic domination of Europe' or to prepare to resist, which meant rearmament in collaboration with other nations of like resolve. The League of Nations might, he said (although it was not until later in the decade that he took the League seriously), become the basis for such a collective stand. If so,

> it would ... enable us to get through the next ten years without a horrible and fatal catastrophe, and in that interval, in that blessed breathing space, we might be able to reconstruct the life of Europe and reunite in justice and goodwill our sundered and quaking civilisation. May God protect us all![7]

Within his general anxiety about German military resurgence was a particular anxiety to arouse the British government and people to the rapid development of the Luftwaffe, and the consequent need for British counter-measures. The government was not as unaware of the danger as Churchill publicly alleged, nor was it as thick-headedly unresponsive. It is generally recognised that Britain began to rearm in 1934. But the rearmament (for reasons already explained, plus the Treasury's passion for 'sound finance') was grudging and, so as not to upset the Germans, untrumpeted. It was emphatically not part of that national reawakening that Churchill and his few faithful supporters believed to be necessary.

Yet Churchill was never treated as a total outsider, nor would he consent to behave like one. To be for so long excluded from office and regarded by the meaner-minded as a political pariah might have led a lesser man to give up and let the office-holders lead the state to perdition in their own obstinate way. Churchill was not someone who gave up. His political status from 1934 to 1939 became that of a privileged eccentric. He was a constant questioner and critic of the government's defence policy, but no attempt was made to stop him acquiring inside defence and intelligence information from official and covert sources to a degree unthinkable nowadays, and he was actually given membership of a secret interdepartmental committee on the all-important business of Air Defence. With him came, at his insistence, his 'scientific adviser' Frederick Lindemann, who despite his popularity at Chartwell was a man whom most other people, not least the scientists with whom he was expected to work on the technical sub-committee, found unbearable and disruptive. But Churchill's faith in 'The Prof' never wavered.

Churchill's grave warnings about Germany, and indignant German complaints about him, continued without a break until, in the last months of peace, it became unmistakably clear to all but the most prejudiced (including by now many in the Labour Party and the trade union movement whose perception of Nazi realities had no Neville Chamberlain to obscure it) that he had been right all along. This of course included being right in his condemnation of the Anglo-French sacrifice of Czechoslovakia, finalised at the third of Chamberlain's meetings with Hitler, at Munich on the last day of September 1938. His fine speech about it in a largely hostile Commons on 5 October included this great stroke of bitter humour:

> We really must not waste time after all this long debate upon the difference between the positions reached at Berchtesgaden, at Godesberg, and at Munich [the three places where Hitler met Chamberlain]. They can be very simply epitomised, if the House will permit me to vary the metaphor. £1 was demanded at the pistol's point. When it was given, £2 was demanded at the pistol's point. Finally, the Dictator consented to take £1 17s. 6d. and the rest in promises of good will for the future.

The speech contained nothing else to raise a laugh. What the Prime Minister proclaimed as a sort of victory, 'peace with honour', Churchill plainly declared a dishonourable defeat.

> All is over. Silent, mournful, abandoned, broken, Czechoslovakia recedes into the darkness ... We are in the presence of a disaster of the first magnitude which has befallen Great Britain and France. Do not let us blind ourselves to that ... What I find unendurable is the sense of our country falling into the power, into the orbit and influence of Nazi Germany, and of our existence becoming dependent upon their good will or pleasure. [The British public should know that] we have passed an awful milestone in our history, when the whole equilibrium of Europe has been deranged, and that the terrible words have for the time being been pronounced against the Western democracies: 'Thou art weighed in the balance and found wanting.' And do not suppose that this is the end. This is only the beginning of the reckoning. This is only the first sip, the first foretaste of a bitter cup which will be proffered to us year by year unless, by a supreme recovery of moral health and martial vigour, we arise again and take our stand for freedom as in the olden time.[8]

Perhaps because it was too painful to some Conservatives to admit how right he was, and certainly because Conservatives prided themselves on loyalty to their leader, Churchill's excoriation of the Prime Minister actually got him into more trouble with his party than he had encountered since the climax of his campaign against the India Act. He even had to defend himself in his own constituency. By March 1939, however, that blip in the return of his popularity was over, and he was awaiting the inevitable call to office with calm assurance.

13

'Winston is Back!'

'In this peaceful country, governed by public opinion, democracy and Parliament, we were not as thoroughly prepared at the outbreak as this Dictator State whose whole thought was bent upon preparation for war.'

Broadcast to the nation on 20 January 1940

Hitler's armed forces launched their assault on Poland at first light on Friday 1 September 1939. Through the next forty-eight hours the Prime Minister and his Foreign Secretary, Lord Halifax, prepared for the worst but retained some sparks of hope that it wouldn't happen. Neville Chamberlain decided to form a small War Cabinet of non-departmental ministers and invited Churchill to be one of them, while Halifax juggled with a last-minute attempt to get Hitler to pull back, at the same time dealing with the French government's prudent wish not to let it seem that Britain was dragging it into war. Through Saturday the 2nd the moods of Parliament and people hardened against further postponement of the inevitable. Churchill was restless and impatient. At last an ultimatum was sent to Berlin. It remained unanswered. At 11.15 on the morning of Sunday 3 September Chamberlain glumly broadcast his declaration that a state of war had come to exist between Britain and Germany. After the serio-comic interlude of a false air-raid alarm, Churchill went to the House to hear Chamberlain say much the same thing again. Labour's Arthur Greenwood having affirmed his party's support, Churchill made the short speech he had prepared for the occasion. (Had he taken it for granted that he would be called? Probably.) Then Chamberlain told him that the War Cabinet was to be enlarged to include the three services ministers, and asked whether Churchill would take the Admiralty. He would. He sent word to the Admiralty to be ready for him at 6 p.m. In the words of the signal flashed to the Royal Navy's ships and stations worldwide, 'Winston is Back!'

What he did with the navy through the eight months that followed was interesting enough, as we shall soon see; but more interesting and in the long run more important were his activities outside the Admiralty. He was as active a First Lord as could have been wished – indeed, a good deal more active than suited the admirals – but it was temperamentally impossible for him to confine his activity within even the ample sphere of the world's biggest navy and his country's first line of defence. His country was now engaged in the war he had long foreseen, its armed forces were imperfectly prepared for it, and its people scarcely prepared at all; he therefore felt obliged to do what needed to be done and what no one else in the government was likely to do. That at any rate was his opinion; and neither a detached observer then nor an historian now can find grounds for disagreement.

In taking upon himself this agreeable burden, Churchill had to move carefully. His arrival in the Cabinet was not in response to a warm and pressing invitation by colleagues who had been yearning for his company or because their party demanded it, it was because circumstances forced him on them. It signified, on the part of the Prime Minister and his close associates in appeasement, an admission of failure. Churchill was on the way to becoming 'the people's Winston', but the dominant political party and the self-selecting governing elite felt differently. For his part, Churchill understood the situation very well and was content to let it develop naturally. To what extent he felt that he must sooner or later move into the highest office of all is unclear. Superintendence of 'the mighty machine of the Navy, on which fell in this phase the sole burden of active fighting', gave him plenty to get on with. Luckily, common standards of gentlemanly conduct and the conventions of parliamentary life enabled erstwhile opponents to work quite harmoniously together. It early struck him that a War Cabinet whose average age (in its first version) was sixty-four was hardly likely to encourage popular confidence. He suggested some infusion of younger blood, for example his protégé Anthony Eden, whom Chamberlain had let go from the Foreign Office early in 1938. Churchill himself, being nearly sixty-five, saw that he would 'have to strive my utmost to keep pace with the generation now in power and with fresh young giants who might at any time appear'.

The last pre-war chapter of Churchill's *The Second World War* describes how he geared up to meet the challenge of these humorously imagined rivals, and the extraordinary daily (and nightly) routine to which everyone connected with him would have to accommodate themselves through the years that followed. The flood of books about his earlier life not yet having begun to flow, readers would not have known that his home life through the 1930s had already been rather similar.

> I always went to bed at least for one hour as early as possible in the afternoon and exploited to the full my happy gift of falling almost immediately into deep sleep. By this means I was able to press a day and a half's work into one ... I regretted having to send myself to bed like a child every afternoon, but I was rewarded by being able to work through the night until two or even later –

sometimes much later – in the morning, and begin the new day between eight and nine o'clock. This routine I observed throughout the war, and I commend it to others if and when they find it necessary for a long spell to get the last scrap out of the human structure.[1]

He was to go on getting the last scrap out of his for the next six years, with no other breaks than came with illness or long trips, and he would wear out younger and fitter-looking men and women in the process.

He would not have been his usual self if he had not at once taken the general conduct of the war into consideration and given the Prime Minister and his colleagues the benefit of his advice. No other civilian at this level had his depth of understanding of how war should be conducted or his capacity for strategic planning. His advice and queries seem to have been generally well received. Chamberlain indeed found Churchill's bombardment tiresome and in mid September wrote, a little testily,

All your letters are carefully read and considered by me, and if I have not replied to them, it is only because I am seeing you every day, and moreover, because as far as I have been able to observe, your views and mine have very closely coincided [2]

Either because he didn't take the hint or didn't choose to take it, Churchill replied (at great length) by return of post, and another long letter followed three days later. He was not easily put off.

But cranking up the war effort was, after all, what Churchill had been brought in to do, and there was for the moment the peculiar problem that no one else knew what to do. The ostensible purpose of the war was to save Poland, but Poland had always been unsavable. Before the war started, there had been some cautious and qualified hope that the Soviet Union might be drawn into a military alliance against Germany; but after the Molotov-Ribbentrop Pact of 23 August 1939 Russia looked more likely to be Germany's ally. The French army, expected to do most of the fighting on land while the British navy dominated the war at sea, was evidently not going to budge from its fortified defences. Hitler, for his part, was happy to hold back from doing great violence to the Allies. He expected them to be having second thoughts about the wisdom of the war and cherished for many months yet the hope that Britain would retire into friendly neutrality. Chamberlain and Halifax had had enough of Hitler's duplicities to convince them that no deal was likely, but the question remained as to how the war was to be prosecuted.

The army could do nothing to help. The modest British Expeditionary Force was stuck in north-eastern France waiting for a German move, and the only other substantial body of British troops was in the Middle East. The contingents expected from India and the Dominions were still many months distant. The Royal Air Force was ready to try to drop bombs anywhere it was told to, but inland Germany was for the time being ruled out lest it provoked the much-feared Luftwaffe to retaliate. Could the Royal Navy help out? Churchill believed it could. He had only been at the Admiralty four days when he launched upon its astonished staff his idea of 'forcing a passage into the Baltic' by means of some heavily re-armoured old battleships (floating fortresses) and fleets of minesweepers and destroyers; its purpose being to cut Germany off from the valuable war materials of Sweden.

This was only the first of Churchill's several bright ideas for aggressive action in northern Europe. Others were for seizing the Norwegian port of Narvik, through which Sweden's high-grade iron ore was shipped to Germany when the Baltic was frozen; for mining Norway's territorial waters to block that sea route; for sending troops through Norway and Sweden to aid Finland when it got into a war with the Soviet Union (not Churchill's own idea, but one he gladly went along with); and for dropping mines in the River Rhine. Some of these ideas were practicable, some were not; some sensible, some not. The most interesting aspect of them is what they tell about the furnishings of Churchill's mind. In them, as in plans and projects he would put forward throughout the war (many will appear in their proper places), can be seen one or more of these principles of action. He could not forget the Dardanelles: what might have been achieved if his plan had worked; how it had been frustrated by the unenthusiastic and the hidebound; and how admirable were the officers, some of them still around, who had backed him then. He showed impatient disregard for the feelings of neutrals who, if they would not do the sensible thing and plainly align themselves with the side of Right and Freedom, ought not to mind being inconvenienced in a good cause. He was resigned to the fact that war always brought surprises, disappointments and disasters as well as successes, glories and victories. For too long he shared the belief, almost universal throughout the navy, that modern warships could protect themselves against attack from the air. He was slow to realise how badly handicapped ground forces were if they lacked their own air force's protection against attack by the enemy's. Alongside a hearty desire to avoid bloodletting *en masse*, he was ready to risk heavy loss of life in particular dashing exploits, and assumed that the British people and armed forces would understand that this was the right and necessary way to wage war. Unable not to think big, his mind set every operational idea in a grand strategic context. His mode of thinking was always offensive. When one plan failed to work out, he turned at once to another.

Churchill's ideas about denying German sea traffic the shelter of neutral

Norway's coastline, whether by mining or by seizure of key ports or both, were batted about between the Chiefs of Staff and the Cabinet for many weeks before the Cabinet decided at last to do something. In February 1940 serious planning was ordered. In March, it was put into abeyance. In early April, it was revived. The mining was to go ahead and certain land and sea forces were stood ready for whatever seizure of key Norwegian ports might be necessary to ward off the anticipated German response. The mines were duly laid early on the morning of 8 April. By then, however, Germany had jumped the gun. Having made plans with much more speed and a lot more unscrupulousness, and combining the operations of land, sea and air forces in an effective manner that the British were to take painfully long to learn, Hitler was not going merely to respond to the British moves on the coastline. He determined to take over the whole of Norway, and Denmark as well. By nightfall on 9 April German soldiers, landing from sea and air, had seized all their primary objectives, and their invasion had made a good start.

The Royal Navy could probably have prevented it going much further had it been better positioned to attack the mass of German shipping, warships and troop-carriers committed to this daring operation. While almost the whole of the German surface fleet was involved, the quantity of British warships theoretically available was overwhelming. But not many were at once available where they were immediately wanted. Admiralty orthodoxy, to which Churchill at this time subscribed, held that the Royal Navy ruled the North Sea and that Germany simply could not conduct major operations in it without being caught; furthermore, that if German warships did appear in the North Sea, their purpose must be to break into the Atlantic for the purpose – very much on naval minds in this early phase of the war – of commerce-raiding. Beyond those blinkerings were failures of Intelligence, which Churchill noted and determined in due course to correct. A variety of intimations had in fact been coming in from one source or another, to the effect that some serious operation was afoot. The trouble was that the messages had not been collated and digested by a body competent to convey reliable Intelligence to one single decision-making authority. In consequence of these accumulated failures of intelligence and Intelligence, the British and Allied warships were often a move behind. Royal Navy professional officers were rather liable to have fixed ideas, but the Intelligence failure was less predictable, and this was very damaging; in the opinion of a good judge, comparable even to the American failure before Pearl Harbor in December 1941.[3]

When the Allies did get going, their combined navies sank or damaged so many German warships that the German surface fleet became for some months non-existent in operational terms; months that were to include Hitler's hopes of a cross-channel invasion of England. But British (and French and Polish) losses were heavy, and to no avail. From everywhere except the Narvik region, troops had been withdrawn before the end of May, and Narvik itself, taken at last on 28 May, was abandoned two weeks later.

The campaign's many incidents of expertise and heroism could not conceal the fact that overall it was a disaster. If the times had been normal, Churchill's responsibility (to what degree it was actual or nominal continues to be debated) would have got him into trouble. Not only was he responsible as First Lord of the Admiralty, but since 8 April he had at the Prime Minister's request been chairing the Ministerial Co-Ordination Committee, the supposed control-panel of what General Hastings Ismay called 'Mr Chamberlain's machinery of war direction'.[4] It was not good machinery. Within it, Churchill later wrote,

> the Chiefs of Staff worked as a separate and largely independent body without guidance or direction from the Prime Minister or any effective representative of the supreme executive power. Moreover, the leaders of the three Services had not yet got the conception of war as a whole, and were influenced unduly by the departmental outlook of their own Services ... Here was the fatal weakness of our system of conducting war at this time.[5]

Such was his account of the matter, which understandably placed Churchill on the side of the angels. Paul Addison's account shows that, whatever war-fighting sense and strategic wisdom may have been on Churchill's side, he made so much trouble that at one stage the official world mutinied against him and Ismay had to 'implore the service chiefs to keep their tempers' lest 'a first-class political crisis' be provoked.[6] Churchill's brief and unhappy experience of this war-directing machinery had at least the advantage of clarifying his mind as to how it should be reconstituted. But for the meantime he had to make the best of it. He was more obviously involved than any other minister; and, when the House of Commons came to debate the way the Norway campaign was going, Churchill did not try to dodge his personal responsibility.

By then what had happened in Norway was suddenly lost to sight in the glare of what was happening nearer home. By a paradoxical turn of fortune which Churchill took in his stride as an agreeable manifestation of his destiny, a debate which could have added another to the long list of Churchillian embarrassments instead set going the train of events which made him Prime Minister.

The Norway debate filled two days, 7 and 8 May 1940. It was exciting and passionate. The question in everyone's mind was whether Neville Chamberlain's government could go on in its present state. The debate ended late on the 8th with a majority for Chamberlain, but so many of the government's usual supporters voted against him or abstained that he got the message and began sounding out the Labour Party as to the idea of joining a coalition. The Labour leaders said they would consider it, but doubted whether their national executive, just then assembling in Bournemouth, would accept him as its leader. They would be able to give him a firm answer on the 10th. Chamberlain had no wish to resign but became persuaded in the course of the 9th that he would have to. It was not his job but the King's to appoint a successor, although if the King sought his advice he could of course give it. His Cabinet included many nonentities. The only ministers self-evidently of real stature were Lord Halifax, whom the bulk of the party, King George VI and the Whitehall mandarins preferred, and some Labour dignitaries would have accepted, and Winston Churchill, the more popular and charismatic figure. Halifax settled that question by standing down. At daybreak on the 10th, pending only the Labour executive's decision, it looked like Churchill without further delay. But once again Hitler sprang a surprise. That morning, very early, German forces began to move into the Netherlands and Belgium. The Phoney War (or, as Churchill himself called it, the Twilight War) was ending with a bang. Chamberlain had a sudden recurrence of confidence, and wondered whether after all he should soldier on. Wiser colleagues told him he shouldn't, and the Labour leaders told him he couldn't. He went to Buckingham Palace at teatime and, in answer to the King's hopeful question, said that Halifax was 'not enthusiastic'.

> Then [recorded the monarch] I knew that there was only one person I could send for to form a Government who had the confidence of the country, and that was Winston. I asked Chamberlain his advice and he told me Winston was the man to send for.[7]

Winston Churchill became Prime Minister soon after six.

It was a terrible time to become Prime Minister, on the first day of the Blitzkrieg, but Churchill was remarkably unruffled. The famous words with which he closed the first volume of his *The Second World War*, the volume titled *The Gathering Storm*, recall the historic moment:

> During these last crowded days of the political crisis my pulse had not quickened at any moment. I took it all as it came. But I cannot conceal from the reader of this truthful account that as I went to bed at about 3 a.m., I was conscious of a profound sense of relief. At last I had the authority to give directions over the whole scene. I felt as if I were walking with destiny, and that all my past life had

been but a preparation for this hour and for this trial ... I thought I knew a good deal about it all, and I was sure I should not fail. Therefore, although impatient for the morning, I slept soundly and had no need for cheering dreams. Facts are better than dreams.[8]

His calm confidence was the more remarkable for his knowledge that the majority of Conservative MPs, those who had sustained Chamberlain in the vote of confidence on 8 May, would rather have had someone else. Nor did hostility and fears end at the gates of the Palace of Westminster. Snide remarks about Churchill and pessimistic estimates of how he would behave were also common among the Whitehall mandarins, and in the clubs and country houses where the socio-political elite congregated. His splendid leader-like performance, in circumstances of great national peril, would soon silence most of those high-level doubters. But the middle and lower levels of English society (whether also British, it is less clear) were to some extent won over already. The later 1930s may have been 'wilderness years' from his political point of view, but they had made him a very well known and distinctive figure in public life. The Labour Party and trade union movement had come to admire the courage and foresight of his stand against Nazism; many were prepared to set Tonypandy and the General Strike aside in the presence of Munich and *Kristallnacht*. Newspaper cartoonists had presented him as a tough John Bull figure for years. Churchill had astonishingly begun to reappear as 'a man of the people'. The appearance (in which of course there was always some make-believe on both sides) would not become complete until the dark days of later 1940, when also the King and Queen earned popular acclaim and affection by refusing to allow their daughters to be evacuated to Canada and by sharing with other Londoners the terrors of the Blitz. A. J. P. Taylor summarised how Churchill did it.

He was an eccentric, which exactly suited the mood of the British people. They welcomed his romantic utterances, though themselves still speaking in more prosaic tones. [His speeches] were rhetorical and cheeky at the same time, Macaulay and contemporary slang mixed together, much as Churchill sometimes wore a Victorian frock-coat and more often an extremely practical siren-suit reminiscent of a child's 'rompers'.[9]

It was not until the Blitz that the world became amusedly familiar with those 'siren-suits' which his wife caused to be made up for him. They came in a variety of colours and materials but looked much the same as the boiler-suit he had long been seen to wear while bricklaying. His love of unusual hats was another well-established and homely trait; the costumes room at Chartwell shows eight of those most often worn. His journalism had been more for middle-brow and popular newspapers than for what we now call 'broadsheets'. But there is no doubt it was the public speeches and, above all, the wireless broadcasts (he never used the word 'radio') for which, even before May 1940, he was most popularly known.

Neville Chamberlain and other ministers were also to be heard over the airwaves, but none of them could sound the same note of comradely and heroic optimism. Nor had any of them the same ability to attract attention in the United States, which he was also obviously doing. As First Lord of the Admiralty he had been the one minister who actually had some spectacular events to report, including the destruction of the *Graf Spee* in mid December and British infringement of Norwegian neutrality to release prisoners from the *Altmark* two months later. The Royal Navy's main business, however, its ceaseless struggle with insufficient and unsuitable ships to keep the sea-ways open against commerce-raiders, U-boats and mines, had been more difficult to paint in bright colours. Regarding the sinking of U-Boats (as he insisted they should be called), he showed a readiness to tell encouraging fibs which thankfully vanished once his mood had become more wholly serious. In other ways too these broadcasts before he became Prime Minister had an overconfident, even boastful air which displeased the fastidious. But he was fulfilling an immensely important function. No other public figure had come forward with a convincing explanation of why the war was being fought, through these months when nothing seemed to be happening and the Poles were in danger of falling into the same memory hole as the Czechs. It was in this period that there circulated in Whitehall this excellent limerick about Chamberlain.

> An elderly statesman with gout,
> When asked what the war was about,
>   In a Written Reply
>   Said, 'My colleagues and I
> Are doing our best to find out'.[10]

Churchill understood from the outset what a huge, as yet unimaginable change of mentality and habits had to be made by 'a peaceful democracy ... suddenly made to fight for its life'.[11] It was not defeatism he had been combating through the months of the Phoney War, it was puzzlement, boredom and slackness. He was addressing, among others, what was probably 'the first generation in European history which had been brought up to expect that there would not be another war'.[12] Therefore he fired at them both barrels of his oratory: clarion calls to arms and activity, together with *tours d'horizon* to make the British people proud of the part they were playing in world history. Of the former, the best example is how he closed a long speech (not broadcast in its entirety) in Manchester on 27 January 1940.

> Come then: let us to the task, to the battle, to the toil – each to our part, each to our station. Fill the armies, rule the air, pour out the munitions, strangle the U-boats, sweep the mines, plough the land, build the ships, guard the streets, succour the wounded, uplift the downcast, and honour the brave. Let us go forward together in all parts of the Empire, in all parts of the Island. There is not a week, nor a day, nor an hour to lose.[13]

In his panoramic surveys, he liked to encourage his fellow-islanders with the thought that, far from being alone in the island, they had helpers and well-wishers all over the world; as for instance, on 1 October:

> the vast latent powers of the British and French Empires [and specifically] the freely given ardent support of the twenty millions of British citizens in the self-governing Dominions ... the heart and moral conviction of India ... the respect and goodwill of the world, and particularly of the United States.[14]

A statesman is not on oath when delivering patriotic speeches in an hour of national peril, so we need not wonder whether Churchill knew he was exaggerating when he included within his rhetorical embrace South Africa where the Afrikaner part of the population wanted to keep out of the war, Canada where the Québecois might lack enthusiasm, and India whose political leaders seethed with resentment at the Viceroy's committing them to fighting a war on behalf of their oppressor (as they saw it). It was Churchill's business to be encouraging and optimistic. And even in these earliest days, before 1939 was out, he was sounding the ultimate theme of encouragement which was to become obsessive by the middle of the following year – the prediction that 'the great English-speaking Republic across the Atlantic Ocean' would sooner or later wake up to the fact that in this war against Germany, as in the last, its interests and Great Britain's were one. Better make up your mind and join in soon was his message to the Americans, rather than wait until, to suppose the worst possible case, 'the United States will be left single-handed to guard the rights of man'.[15] Such was the Churchillian vision, grandiose and not entirely reasonable but hopeful and heartening, marking him out in May 1940 as a man acceptable to the people as their leader when their nation's situation suddenly became most perilous.

14

His Finest Hour

'I displayed the smiling confidence and confident air which are thought
suitable when things are very bad.'

The Second World War, ii, chapter 7

Churchill understood that the military situation was not good when he
became Prime Minister, but no more than anyone else had he an inkling
of how very bad it was going to become within six weeks, or how bad it
was going to stay through the next twelve months. The title often and justly
conferred on him as the Saviour of the Nation rests above all on how he
managed the war and kept the country going and its people united through
this period from May 1940 until June 1941. Britain had only ever once before
been in as dangerous a situation, and that was in the spring of 1917 when
German unrestricted submarine warfare brought the country to within a
few weeks of starvation. The dangers that threatened now were invasion
and, that failing to materialise, destruction of its cities and factories and
demoralisation of its people. Looking back on the summer and autumn
days of 1940, his daughter (who was closer to the centre of the storm than
most) wrote that although later times were often anxious and painful, 'never
again, I think, did one feel one could scarcely breathe. We got through the
days almost automatically, living from news bulletin to news bulletin, and
dreading what each would bring'.[1]

Bad news came thick and fast. Three days after Hitler's forces attacked
the Netherlands and Belgium, they began to penetrate France by way of
the Ardennes, which the French high command had assumed would be
impassable for them; by 19 May their spearhead had reached the Channel
near Abbeville. Sensing that all was not well in France, on 15 May Churchill
made the first of five flying visits to find out what was going on. As did
other like-purposed visitors in those darkening days, he got a gloomy
impression. Even before the full extent of the danger to the BEF was clear,
the possibility of its evacuation began to be quietly considered. With every
passing day, even hour, the danger became worse. By relentless pressure
on every front except the one where the French had been best prepared

for them, the Maginot Line, the German panzers (the German word for tanks was promptly adopted) driving towards the Channel succeeded in dividing the French and British armies north of their advance from the larger French ones south of it, and threatened to squeeze the northwards ones to death. Churchill and the Chiefs of Staff began to go through agonies of debate whether to commit more forces to France or to keep them safe at home; and, worse than that, the Chiefs of Staff were instructed to report on the defensibility of Britain 'in a Certain Eventuality', which meant, if France collapsed.

The eventuality which the Chiefs of Staff were instructed to consider as possible had become probable enough by the time their report came into the War Cabinet's hands, on 26 May, for Churchill and his War Cabinet partners to feel obliged to consider whether Britain (with, presumably, the continued backing of the Empire) should carry on alone. Now began a brief and tense episode which Churchill and Halifax, the persons chiefly concerned, were happy to obscure from their contemporaries, though a less patriotically inflamed later generation might think they need not have done so. To Churchill the question was distasteful. He nevertheless felt obliged to go along with the discussion for several reasons. The French government urgently wished to stop Italy from joining in the war and also wondered whether Hitler could be persuaded to stop it. The fate of the BEF was hanging in the balance, and Churchill himself was still a new, untried and (so far as the Chamberlainite majority in the Commons was concerned) unwelcome Premier. There was at any rate the useful by-product that it enabled him to bring into his rather desperate correspondence with President Roosevelt the grim prospect of British surrender and of the Churchill government giving way to a pro-German one. (To his great disappointment and annoyance, the President remained unmoved, as anyone with less exalted ideas of the Special Relationship could have predicted.)

Churchill was willing enough to say that he would consider coming to acceptable terms with Hitler because he felt sure that no terms offered by Hitler would be acceptable. Halifax and to a lesser degree Chamberlain were not so sure, and in any case shared the hope of Reynaud, the French Prime Minister, that something might come of an approach to Mussolini. It may be unjust to their memories to say that they were defeatists, but Halifax was certainly ready to use every diplomatic trick in the book to find out whether Mussolini could, by the offer of French and British possessions in Africa and along the Mediterranean, be bribed to stay neutral and (a separate matter) to act as an intermediary between the Allies and Hitler. The question was batted back and forth within the War Cabinet (twice with Reynaud there) at no less than five meetings, some of which went on for as long as four hours.[2] By the last of these five occasions, at 4 p.m. on 28 May, Attlee and Greenwood were still on Churchill's side of the argument and Chamberlain had come round to it. Churchill deftly chose the moment to 'consult' the rest of the Cabinet, who had been summoned to a room nearby. A Churchill consultation in such circumstances being a Churchill oration of the most exalting and blood-stirring character, he could naturally report back to the members of the War Cabinet that all the others were firm for continuance of the struggle. So too from this time on was Halifax, although Churchill never thereafter felt entirely happy about him (could a former appeaser entirely change his spots?) and seized the opportunity to send him as Ambassador to Washington when the opportunity occurred at the end of the year.

Some people at this juncture thought it time for Britain to get out of the war. The nearer they were to the apex of power, the more information they possessed about the nation's predicament, and the more aware they were that Hitler – still not despairing of Britain coming to like the prospect of a privileged place in his projected new world order – was offering peace on easy terms, the likelier were they to think this way. The British public at large knew nothing of all this. Churchill's rousing calls to courage and confidence, backed by intensive use of the media to keep spirits high, kept the idea out of popular sight. Churchill subsequently kept it obscure in his memoir-history of the war which, notwithstanding that it was admittedly *his* version, became the generally accepted one for so long as he was alive, with the heroics of 1940 as its finest episode. The fact that there was such unheroic talk in the middle and later months of that year was, however, never hidden from the more searching of political historians. Becoming common historical property in the course of the years since his death, it has encouraged a few historians and political writers to wonder whether the negotiated peace-seekers of mid 1940 may not, after all, have been right.

The most prominent and powerful proponent of this revisionist tendency is John Charmley, who argued in his 1993 biography, *Churchill: The End of Glory*, that Churchill's greatness at that time did not do his country nearly as much good as we have been accustomed to think. Britain's victorious though exhausted emergence from the war, which Churchill himself in quieter moments admitted to have been no more than an avoidance of defeat, is presented by Charmley as having left the nation in a state of decline: its Empire 'on the skids'; its independence 'dependent on America'; and Churchill's '"anti-Socialist" vision of Britain vanished in a Labour election victory'.[3] Charmley's determined iconoclasm has won him few admirers. What makes it intellectually unconvincing is the conjectural leap which takes him to the negative conclusion just quoted. That Britain would

have been better off in the long run, with its Empire still in being, if it had
negotiated the sort of terms that seemed to be on offer in the early summer
of 1940, rests on two unreasonable suppositions: first, that the British Empire
would not have gone on crumbling along the fault-lines already apparent;
secondly, and more important, that Britain could have remained an independent nation fit for decent and freedom-loving people to live in once it
was tethered within easy reach of a Europe dominated by Nazi Germany,
gigantic in power and ambition as it would have become after defeating or
at any rate neutralising the Soviet Union, the probable outcome of a straight
war between those two powers.

These suppositions are simply not believable by anyone who has taken
the measure of the mentality of Adolf Hitler, the principles of National
Socialism, and the directions in which military technology was developing.
Churchill was right to believe that Hitler and Nazism had to be fought to
the end, no matter what the cost; and the British people did well to sense
that it was better for them and their posterity to follow his lead, even
though the road promised to be hard and rough. The war indeed did not
work out to Britain's material advantage (which was not in fact aimed at
or expected), but Britain remained free, civilised and with a clear collective
conscience. As for continental Europe, it was saved from the beastliness
of racist oppression, the western side of it soon becoming a thriving community of states which Britain was free to join or not to join – its relationship
with the United States notwithstanding. No rationally conceivable course
of events following a British treaty of peace with Germany in 1940 was
likely to have worked out tolerably for Britain – even leaving out of account
old-fashioned considerations such as national self-respect and sense of
honour.

In settling for war to the end, however, Churchill and the War Cabinet
were certainly placing national survival in hazard. The Chiefs of Staffs'
report on the chances of national survival was that it was possible, but only
just; the crucial thing being that the Royal Air Force must be able to keep
the Luftwaffe from destroying it and the factories which supported it; and
taking it for granted that Britain's supply line to the United States would
remain open. So unpromising was the military situation by the time the
War Cabinet digested this grim assessment that it was decided to complete
the already begun evacuation of British forces within reach of Dunkirk, the
only place still open to most of them; but how many could actually be
evacuated remained to be seen. Churchill did not know until much later
how lucky Britain was going to be. Hitler had become convinced that his
panzers needed a break for maintenance and repair. Their inactivity between
24 and 26 May proved crucial. Against all expectations, and by prodigies

of valour, more than 338,000 troops (roughly half of them British, half French and others) were evacuated from Dunkirk before 3 June, necessarily leaving behind them everything they could not carry. Ten days later, the French government sued for an armistice. The eventuality whose name no one had dared to speak, but everyone had expected, had actually happened.

As Churchill on 18 June told the Commons, and then by broadcast the British people, the Battle of France was over, and the Battle of Britain about to begin. Beginning in early July, an aerial battle went on until it petered out in late September, the battle of which Churchill memorably remarked, while its outcome was still uncertain (20 August), 'Never in the field of human conflict was so much owed by so many to so few'. British victory did not mean more than that the RAF had, just, managed to retain command of the airspace over the island in daylight, but it did ensure that invasion, if it came, would come with a severe handicap. Now a new danger appeared – what was called and has ever since been called the Blitz. From 7 September 1940 until May 1941 the cities of Britain were subjected to aerial bombardment with the purpose of destroying docks and factories, and demoralising their workers and the population generally. Despite the destruction and damage done, war production was not greatly interrupted and only in its early stages and here and there was popular morale significantly depressed. The Luftwaffe did not have the heavy bombers necessary for such work (nor, yet, did the British, though they were on the way), and in any case by the spring of 1941 Hitler needed most of his bombers for the coming assault on Russia. Invasion was by then no longer a credible threat. The pressure on Britain was lifted. By the time the next phase of mortal danger occurred, the crisis of the Battle of the Atlantic in early 1943, Britain was no longer fighting alone.

Such were the great events of Churchill's first year in office. They tested him to the utmost and showed him at his best; not only that, they also showed him as more acceptable a Prime Minister than the doubters in May 1940 had expected, and more nationally popular a leader than anyone could have predicted. He memorably told his compatriots, at the close of the 18 June broadcast, that 'This was their finest hour'. It had also been his. His had begun five weeks before when he took charge of the government and picked his team. At such a desperate hour no one wanted to make difficulties, and everyone understood that it was going to be a coalition – the very kind of government that Churchill had always preferred. The Labour Party leader Clement Attlee recalled:

> We were all united in the great task of ensuring our national survival. Labour and Conservative Members worked wholeheartedly together and differences on

Party lines did not arise. There was also unity between military and civilians ...
We had a Prime Minister who understood war and a high proportion of Ministers
had served in the First World War, and this made for greater understanding.[4]

The ministerial appointments were in fair proportion to the numbers in
the parliamentary parties, themselves (it must not be forgotten) unchanged
since the general election of 1935 and with the Conservatives therefore more
numerous than experts believe they would have been if the election due in
1939 had not been held over. Churchill's War Cabinet to begin with was
smaller than Chamberlain's, a mere five – three Conservative and two
Labour. The Labour men were the two at the top of the parliamentary
party: Clement Attlee, a good man of business, who as time went by became
de facto Deputy Prime Minister, and Arthur Greenwood, not a good man
of business, who would soon be dropped. The two other Conservatives
besides Churchill were Lord Halifax (in the circumstances self-selecting)
and Neville Chamberlain, surprising to many but undiminishedly popular
with the Conservative majority – more popular by far, indeed, than Churchill
himself – and, apart from that, a human being for whose feelings after so
dramatic a dismissal Churchill felt sympathy. Only Halifax and Churchill
himself, doubling the roles of Prime Minister and (his own invention)
Minister of Defence, were 'departmental' ministers. This was a War Cabinet
of civilians free to give the whole of their minds to the highest questions
of strategy and foreign policy, and to the overseeing of war management
in general. Its membership changed from time to time, according to the
master's ideas of who was specially needed or of who he wanted to have
near him, but he never tried to pack it with sycophants as some men in
his position might have done. The one about whom there was most gossip
was his old-time friend and sparring partner Lord Beaverbrook, who, holding a variety of offices, was in the War Cabinet from August 1940 to February
1942. Everyone else who got there was of more conventional cut and a
commoner to boot. The most effective were the Minister of Labour Ernest
Bevin, who was in the War Cabinet from October 1940 and upon whom
Churchill came greatly to rely, Anthony Eden from December 1940 when
he replaced Halifax in the Foreign Office, and the Home Secretary Herbert
Morrison from October 1942.

The 'ordinary' Cabinet met less often than the War Cabinet, but that
was not surprising. Its ministers managed the more 'civilian' side of the
war effort and, once it became possible to look confidently ahead, the
planning for post-war reconstruction. The War Cabinet's primary responsibility was to win the war, which above all meant receiving and adjudicating
on business sent up from the Defence Committee, the Chiefs of Staff

Committee and so on. Whatever business therefore appeared to be of 'civilian' or civil character had to some extent a life of its own beyond the Prime Minister's normal war-winning range of vision. To this Premier, however, unless he was totally preoccupied with a pressing war problem, nothing that went on in any department of state was alien, whether it was of 'civilian' character or not. He took an intermittent interest in even the most remote and petty matters, once they caught his attention, and he was liable to interfere with any minister's business at the shortest notice. None of them much minded what he did during the early months of peril, but his obsessions and restlessness became resented later on when there was less urgency in the atmosphere and when the end of the war was in sight. The most substantial disagreements that came to disturb the wartime harmony of the Cabinet were precisely those to do with that most 'civilian', but also most gigantic of topics: planning for the peace that was to come, and for reconstructing the country when at last it emerged from its exhausting, impoverishing and debilitating ordeal.

The 'machinery of war direction' which Churchill inherited was already good enough to need only a few adjustments before it exactly suited his needs, prominent among which was his determination to chair, or at any rate to know what went on in, every committee where serious business was being discussed. Since even he could not be everywhere at once, he used the eyes and ears of trusted colleagues: conspicuous among these were, first, and to the annoyance of the administratively orthodox, Professor Lindemann and, in more orthodox vein, General Hastings Ismay, Chief of Staff to the Minister of Defence, and, by Churchill's particular desire, a permanent member of the Chiefs of Staff Committee. This very capable and good-tempered officer's role as manager of Churchill's 'handling machine' was of exceptional importance, and his account of it in his 1960 *Memoirs* became essential reading for understanding of Churchill as warlord. It was fortunate for his country that Hastings Ismay, universally known as 'Pug', was a man of unfailing tact and good sense, because Churchill's appointment of him to the Chiefs of Staff Committee, as he later recorded,

> gave rise to not a little suspicion and resentment. My duties were never specifically defined, and it was left to me to interpret them as best I could. First and foremost, I made it my business to express, and if necessary to explain, Churchill's views to the Chiefs of Staff Committee, and to inform him of their reactions. Now and then a certain amount of tactful expurgation was necessary ... I had to be not only an interpreter, but a mediator.[5]

As to the Chiefs of Staff themselves, respectively heads of the three armed services, there was little change among them once Churchill was in charge.

After Field-Marshal Sir John Dill's departure to Washington as the Chiefs of Staff's special representative to their American counterparts in December 1941, the Chief of the Imperial General Staff was General Sir Alan Brooke. From October 1940 to the end of the war, the Chief of Air Staff was Air Chief Marshal Sir Charles Portal. Admiral Sir Dudley Pound was the First Sea Lord until he was succeeded in October 1943 by Admiral Sir Andrew Cunningham. Churchill met the 'Chiefs' almost daily when he was in Britain and sometimes took them abroad with him. How he and they got on together was of the highest importance. If there was any forum outside the War Cabinet that mattered supremely, this was it.

Ismay constituted a human link between the Chiefs of Staff and the supreme direction of the war. The other link was an institutional one, a Churchillian invention, the Defence Committee (Operations), through which the concerns and recommendations of the Chiefs of Staff Committee were funnelled on their way to the War Cabinet. The normal composition of the Defence Committee (Operations) was the de facto Deputy Prime Minister or sometimes the Prime Minister himself, the three service ministers, the Foreign Secretary (from December 1940 Anthony Eden), with the three Chiefs of Staff always in attendance and whatever ministers happened to be involved in the business of the day. Here again, it will be noticed, the civilian membership was absolutely in control. The military element was always on tap, never on top. Churchill was not going to have more Kitcheners, Robertsons or Haigs.

Such was the backbone of the national war-waging organisation over which Churchill presided. Military history experts have compared it favourably with the other notable war organisations of the age. It differed utterly from Hitler's system of divide and rule, and avoidance of argument. The USA had nothing like it and America's Combined Chiefs of Staff, as established in 1942, 'was modelled on British foundations'.[6] While the United States was still an observer, the British method of arriving at decisions greatly impressed Averell Harriman, one of the several weighty Washingtonians inspecting their ally-presumptive. His 1941 observations, related by his biographer, have special value as coming from a shrewd and well-informed outsider:

All important decisions were made in Churchill's War Cabinet, a coalition of the Conservative and Labour parties. This assured both tight coordination and parliamentary approval when necessary, a far cry from the Battle of Washington, where agencies fought one another for scarce materials and appropriations. In Britain, he soon discovered, the Chiefs of Staff had no direct access to Parliament, nor did they enjoy the mighty influence that America's military leaders could exert on Capitol Hill. The British Chiefs of Staff were simply advisers to the War

Cabinet, which in turn represented the political leadership of the country. It was the politicians who ran the war ... not the generals or admirals. In Washington, Harriman had seen interagency meetings degenerate into bitter conflict where little action could be taken at the end of long, heated and wearying discussions. In London, he found decisions being taken promptly, above all when Churchill was presiding.[7]

'For the first time in their history', Ismay admiringly noted, 'the Chiefs of Staff were in direct and continuous communication with the Head of the Government, and were able to act as a combined Battle Headquarters.' In this way efficient management was attained and assured at the summit of the military half of Britain at war. The other half was no less well served by Ismay's civilian counterpart, Sir Edward Bridges, the Secretary to the Cabinet, upon whom Churchill came increasingly to depend for guidance about those Home Front matters on which he was, inevitably, less well informed.

Churchill was not the man to let this great machine run without constant inspection and interference. His style of management was striking and peculiar, the most remarkable no doubt of any Prime Minister's, and although it undoubtedly had abrasive and time-wasting aspects, overall and in the long run it did much more good than harm. Inevitably Churchill was determined to make sure that his special interests were attended to, and he was insistent on making provision for the Chartwell faithfuls. Brendan Bracken stayed on as Parliamentary Private Secretary until Churchill, for once in his life adopting a high tone with his reluctant monarch, insisted on his being made Minister for Information in 1941. But where should 'The Prof' and Desmond Morton fit in? Having attained the summit of power, Churchill expected to be able to bring with him advisers with whom he felt comfortable, and it was natural that they should be eager to oblige. It was also natural that the officials whose functions would thereby be usurped should view the prospect with misgivings. It was the admirable Ismay who had to cope with this most awkward set of relationships.

Churchill's chance finally came while he was still First Lord of the Admiralty, in the last days of April 1940. Amidst the mounting public and parliamentary unease about the conduct of the Norway campaign, and after the great row that it caused, he 'persuaded' Chamberlain to give him such powers in relation to the Chiefs of Staff Committee that he would become a sort of Minister of Defence, with a staff headed by a senior officer. Chamberlain agreed, noting that of course the said senior officer should be General Ismay, who, after many years ascending the staircases of power, was now head of the military wing of the War Cabinet Secretariat. But who were to be his staff? Ismay was dismayed to discover that Churchill had in mind not Ismay's professionals but the Chartwell coterie.[8] A parallel at once came to Ismay's mind: the private corps of congenial counsellors whom Lloyd George had gathered in the grounds of Number Ten, earning the sobriquet of 'the Garden Suburb'. According to the wisdom of Whitehall, that innovation or intrusion had not worked out well. His attempts to dissuade Churchill having failed, Ismay was left wondering what his own future might be; but, before the pending dénouement, there then burst the political storms of early May. Churchill's first (probably bad) idea gave way to the (undoubtedly good) one of keeping Ismay and his experienced staff intact while installing the most valued of his Chartwell companions, Lindemann, as his personal assistant with an office of his own.

The King's Government, as Churchill was careful to call it when his mind was running on constitutional lines, would of course have been carried on by someone else if Churchill had not providentially been there at the right time. It is, however, unlikely that any one of the other 'possibles' could have filled the position so successfully. One may speculate indefinitely as to what the system of government would have been, and its degree of popular acceptance, had Lord Halifax headed it to begin with; or Sir Stafford Cripps, who astonishingly was the choice of a strange mish-mash of malcontents in the downcast days of 1942; or Anthony Eden or Ernest Bevin who would both have had a chance if any of Churchill's illnesses had proved fatal, or if he had happened to come to grief on one of his many overseas travels. (Determined never to be taken alive, when travelling by ship he insisted there should be a machine-gun in his designated lifeboat.) One may enjoy imagining such alternatives. But one cannot imagine that any of the others would have run the national war machine the way Churchill did, and to such good effect. It was an experience no one involved in it could ever forget.

His entry into office had the usual effect of electrifying the atmosphere within it, differing from precedent only in this respect, that the effect now spread well beyond his own department.

> Government Departments which under Neville Chamberlain had continued to work at much the same speed as in peacetime awoke to the realities of war. A sense of urgency was created in the course of a very few days and respectable civil servants were actually to be seen running along the corridors. No delays were condoned; telephone switchboards quadrupled their efficiency; the Chiefs of Staff and the Joint Planning Staff were in almost constant session; regular office hours ceased to exist and weekends disappeared with them.[9]

Churchill did not spare himself and he did not spare anyone else. He might well have spared himself more, and, if he had done so, people would have understood because after all he was in his later sixties with a mixed health record and habits of late hours and smoking and drinking which could not but seem unhealthy. Yet he went on working as hard and usually even harder than the people working for him, and his manner of driving them was remarkable.

He remained faithful to the routine of alternating (maximal) work and (minimal) sleep whenever circumstances did not disrupt it, and everyone else except royalty and distinguished foreigners was expected to fit in with it. He would telephone aides at two in the morning as readily as at two in the afternoon. He took it for granted that someone would be around to take his dictation at any hour of day or night. He convened the War Cabinet on a bank holiday; he caused his Deputy to convene it at 1.45 a.m. Holidays he denounced as a peacetime concept, telling people who wanted to have them that a change of work did them just as much good. The Chiefs of Staff might be summoned to drive out of town to Chequers, the Prime Ministerial house in the country, for a meeting after dinner. He rarely considered the convenience or comfort of other people. Indeed, he often seemed not to think about their feelings at all; anyone familiar with George Bernard Shaw's play *Pygmalion* may well find Professor Higgins coming to mind.

And yet – such is the mystery of greatness – his servants and staff were glad to work for him, and subsequently looked back on the experience with pride, and on him with affection. It seems significant that some of the high officials who worked closely with him, and who were in good positions to arrive at a balanced judgement about him, disapproved when others went into print with undigested spur-of-the-moment impressions and notes of unguarded private conversation. One of the purposes of *Action This Day: Working with Churchill* (1968), by six men who had worked with him close-up, was to correct wrong impressions liable to be gained from two books of 'revelations': General Sir Alan Brooke's (Lord Alanbrooke's) diaries as used by Arthur Bryant in *The Turn of the Tide* (1957) and *Triumph in the West* (1959), and his personal physician Lord Moran's reflections on his experiences from 1942 onwards published under the title *Churchill: The Struggle for Survival* (1966). General Ismay, than whom no one worked closer with Churchill, thought saying too little more gentlemanly than saying too much. He was upset by Bryant's rendering verbatim of the rages which the choleric CIGS instantly recorded for private consumption. Similarly the officials who came together to write *Action This Day* were upset not only by Moran's betrayal of his patient's trust and by his variety of misunderstandings (he was after all politically an outsider) but also by the presentation of so much casual, unconsidered and sometimes unattractive chit-chat as if it was of equal weight with what his patient said on duty and in public. No matter how irritating, bullying and wearing people found Churchill at times, their negative reactions were in the end outweighed by the long-term positive one: the man was after all a marvel, and his own moods changed so rapidly and completely that the bad impressions of one day's storms were recurrently banished by the rays of next day's sunshine.

Understandably enough, he approached his most nearly insupportable and unreasonable at the time of the most acute peril and therefore, for him, of the greatest strain. This strain he never showed in public. Self-respect, courage, self-control, the classic qualities he had learned in study of great commanders like Marlborough, Wellington and Nelson, ensured that his public face would always be resolute and optimistic; and he demanded that everyone else's public face should be the same. On 28 May 1940, the day when he clinched his victory over the fainthearts in the Cabinet (and while the upper strata of Conservatism were still relishing their resentments against 'Winston and his gang'), he issued a 'general injunction' to everyone in high office:

> In these dark days the Prime Minister would be grateful if all his colleagues ... would maintain a high morale in their circles; not minimising the gravity of events, but showing confidence in our ability and inflexible resolve to continue the war till we have broken the will of the enemy to bring all Europe under his domination.[10]

But the strain showed in private and prompted, four weeks later, what must be the most remarkable admonition ever addressed to a Prime Minister. Coming from Clementine, of course it was loving and sympathetic, but there was steel in the message.

> My Darling, I hope you will forgive me if I tell you something that I feel you ought to know. One of the men in your entourage (a devoted friend) has been to me and told me that there is a danger of your being generally disliked by your colleagues and subordinates because of your rough sarcastic and overbearing manner – It seems your Private Secretaries have agreed to behave like schoolboys and 'take what's coming to them' and then escape out of your presence shrugging their shoulders – Higher up, if an idea is suggested (say at a conference) you are supposed to be so contemptuous that presently no ideas, good or bad, will be forthcoming ...

> My darling Winston – I must confess that I have noticed a deterioration in your manner; and you are not as kind as you used to be ... You used to quote:- 'on ne règne sur les âmes que par le calme' – I cannot bear that those who serve the Country and yourself should not love you as well as admire and respect you ... Please forgive your loving devoted and watchful. Clemmie

[At the foot there was a postscript following her little drawing of a Pussycat, the playful role in which, from earliest days, she had matched his role of Pug.]

I wrote this at Chequers' last Sunday, tore it up, but here it is now.[11]

Her daughter presumes that her remonstrance worked. So it probably did in the longer run, but her magic perhaps had not had time to work by 27 July 1940, when Lieutenant-General Marshall-Cornwall recorded in some detail the events of a long evening at Chequers under the heading, 'The Mad Hatter's Dinner Party'.[12] (Similar experiences may be sensed behind the more guarded accounts of other military visitors.) It included remarkable rudeness (if extreme abruptness and throwing papers towards him may be so described) to the Chief of the Imperial General Staff, General Sir John Dill; and an ostentatious display of confidence in the judgement of the civilians present – none other than his familiars Lindemann and Beaverbrook – the purpose of which could only have been to humiliate the professional soldiers. The latters' sympathetic understanding of the strain Churchill was under at the time, their acceptance of the eccentricity of genius, and the British officer's principled deference to the civil power must have done much to persuade such cultivated and intelligent men as Dill and Marshall-Cornwall to put up with it. Colleagues both military and civil went on putting up with it. Indeed it was only intermittent. Once the first desperate and perilous months were past, meetings were less often unpleasant until the last nine months or so, by when Churchill himself was visibly older and tireder, the Americans and Russians had clearly become dominant partners, and Germany continued to spring nasty surprises. Brooke's diary was not the only one to record room-shaking rows. The diary of Anthony Eden for 6 July 1944 reads:

After dinner a really ghastly Defence Committee ... Winston hadn't read the paper and was perhaps rather tight. Anyway we opened with a reference from Winston to American criticism of Monty for over-caution which Winston appeared to endorse. This brought explosion from CIGS, 'If you would keep your confidence in your generals for even a few days I think we should do much better.' [Winston puzzled or feigns to be so. Brooke spells it out.] 'You asked me questions, I gave you answers. You didn't accept them and telegraphed to Alexander who gave the same answers', and more in the same vein ... I tried to pour oil.[13]

Eden, Brooke and everyone else in these last months of the war found that Churchill's management of meetings was liable to be maddeningly self-indulgent and time-wasting. Not Clementine this time but Clement Attlee (a chairman universally admired for brisk efficiency) told him the truth about himself. One of the private secretaries recalled what happened.

Outraged ... Churchill [in bed with a cold] sought a denial of the distasteful thesis first from Lord Beaverbrook and then from Brendan Bracken. Both said they thought Attlee was quite right. He had then turned to Mrs Churchill ... only to be met with the reply that she admired Mr Attlee for having the courage to put into writing what everybody else was thinking. [Churchill disconsolate.] Suddenly, at about 4 p. m., he threw back the bedclothes, [smiled and said]: 'Let us think no more of Hitlee or of Attler; let us go and see a film.' And for the rest of the weekend the sun shone.[14]

15

Democratic Warlord

'It was a nation and race dwelling all round the globe that had the lion heart. I had the luck to be called upon to give the roar.'

Speech of thanks to the House of Commons
on his eightieth birthday, 30 November 1954

It will have become clear by now how wide the range of Churchill's managerial vigilance was, over and above being master within the British war machine. Yet what exactly was the nature of his mastery, and what if any were its limits? Its nature was peculiar, just as he was peculiar. He was dominant and he liked to have his way but he was not a dictator, nor in principle did he want to be. He knew that, for so long as a state of national emergency lasted, even the most democratic democracy had to have a single responsible leader. Summing up the critical debates which produced some Cabinet changes early in 1942, he wrote 'All I wanted was compliance with my wishes after reasonable discussion'.[1] (This must have provoked hollow laughter among the senior officers who had had to do the discussing with him.) His understanding of his position was strictly constitutional. He was Prime Minister because the King had appointed him and because Parliament supported him; he was also Minister of Defence because the King (with mild reluctance, being mindful of how the service chiefs would dislike it) had allowed him to be so. King George VI would have preferred Halifax as his Prime Minister, but he very soon came to respect and like Churchill; and Churchill, for his part, was punctilious in maintaining the convention of weekly visits to the Palace: the King and his Prime Minister lunched together most Tuesdays.

The constitution indeed allowed the King little actual control over him, though the King's word was apparently decisive in dissuading him from accompanying the D-Day armada. Parliament's controls, however, were real enough. He could only do on his own what his Cabinet and what the House of Commons were happy to let him do on his own. The Cabinet (whether the War Cabinet or the ordinary one is immaterial) was in the end his master, and now and then showed it, though his means for getting his way in it and his drive to do so meant that for most of the time it did what he wanted. Of course a Prime Minister could, in war as in peace, change the composition of his Cabinet to suit the temper of the Commons, and that is exactly what happened in the bad times of 1942.

Behind the Cabinet stood Parliament, the ultimate control, meeting more or less as usual throughout the war, its major proceedings reported in a free press still functioning, and its numbers kept up by by-elections which, in the circumstances of an all-out war and an agreement to hold off the overdue general election until the war was over, had significance as indicators of shifts in public opinion. MPs continued to put questions about anything they liked and ministers went on answering them or declining to answer them in the usual parliamentary way. Churchill, unless he was away from London on war duties (as he was more frequently from 1942), took his place in the Commons as Prime Minister in the forefront of the parliamentary battle, developing a theatrical deftness in the handling of questions which delighted his admirers and surprised everybody, for he had not always been like that. 'I am first of all a Parliamentarian and House of Commons man', he assured the House on 17 September 1940 when proposing that in the circumstances – invasion threatening, Battle of Britain still going on and the Blitz beginning – they need not meet so often or at the traditional late hour.[2]

Because of his deep-rooted constitutionalism, and because the House of Commons was the altar of his mystic communion with the British people, he took pains to keep Members informed of the major events and developments of the war, grim ones no less than grand. On relatively few occasions were there secret sessions, not to keep particularly bad or perturbing bits of news secret (for that was generally impossible) but to make possible a fuller explanation of facts and background than would have been prudent to reveal to the enemy in a normal open session. Several times there were votes of confidence on the continuing acceptability of his administration, and each time he won by a colossal majority; some, perhaps sometimes many, of that majority must have doubted whether everything that his administration was doing was sensible or right, but it appeared to be the best administration Britain could get, and there was no point in not supporting it. Five of Churchill's secret session speeches are preserved. The three most substantial were all occasioned by crises. On 25 June 1941 his sombre theme was the Battle of the Atlantic, then going through one of its worst patches. He wanted the House to understand why the government, reluctantly, was going to cease publishing figures of shipping losses:

> We cannot afford to give any advantages to the enemy in naval information nor can we afford to paint our affairs in their darkest colours before the eyes of neutrals and to discourage our friends and encourage our foes all over the world.[3]

The worst disaster of all was the theme of the secret session on 23 April 1942 – the fall of Singapore and Japan's run of victories, which led him to 'frankly admit that the violence, fury, skill and might of Japan has far exceeded anything that we had been led to expect'. The third major secret session, on 10 December 1942, was for a different sort of purpose. It was to explain the small print and hidden agendas in North African events, on the face of them difficult to understand and moreover of immense diplomatic delicacy, capable of upsetting the awkward quadrangular relationship between Britain which supported the Free French; the Free French who detested the Vichy French still governing Tunisia and Algeria; the Vichy French whom the British public had learned to detest; and the United States which much preferred the Vichy French to de Gaulle and the Free French.

Churchill was therefore a war leader exercising authority within a constitutional frame which war conditions did nothing much to alter. He could not do anything the House of Commons would surely disapprove of, he always laid before it matters that might cause it concern, and he had to do a lot of explaining to it at times when the war seemed to be going inexplicably badly, as it did through much of 1942. He could not do anything the War Cabinet or, in the last resort, the King would not let him do. His bright ideas for military operations would not get anywhere unless the Chiefs of Staff went along with them. His authority nevertheless was very great, exercised with extraordinary vigour; and if we wonder how he got away with so much, the answer is simply that the men who worked with him close at hand, the MPs who were in a position to know a good deal of what went on, and the British people who were aware of it from a greater distance, wanted it that way.

That sense of participating in a great drama was shared to some immeasurable degree by the people at large. It was of course necessary that the people's spirits and a collective will to persist should be sustained through five years of hardship, injury, loss, anxiety, destruction and impoverishment. An example was very close to hand, just across the Channel in fact, of what could happen to a nation with a proud military past and no evident military inferiority if it lacked optimistic spirit and collective will. We have seen more recently, in Vietnam and Afghanistan, what can happen even to a military superpower when its people become divided about the merits of a war and begin to think the costs of it too high. It is well known that wars put nations and their systems of government to the test. The British people stood the test of 1939–45 pretty well. In so far as this was because the government made satisfactory arrangements for alleviating hardships and making possible a continuing way of living, Churchill had no more responsibility than as *primus inter pares* of his competent ministerial team. But in so far as it was because the people felt that the war was worth fighting, and its costs worth bearing, Churchill had unique responsibility, for his was the voice that persuaded them.

It may not be easy in the dawn of the twenty-first century to understand how it was that Churchill's speeches could matter so much sixty years ago. The explanation begins with the nature of the media then: film, press and wireless. Film was by no means equivalent to what television is now. Every cinema programme included a 'newsreel' but, sandwiched between the feature films, scrappy in itself and mostly out of date, it was not a medium for serious political communication. Newspapers, however, were more serious in that respect than they are now. The proceedings of Parliament were still considered interesting and important; even the most popular papers paid them a little attention, the quality ones a good deal. Important speeches delivered by famous figures in the House of Commons would receive good newspaper coverage, and Churchill's received most of all. His speeches continued to be the events they always had been. *The Times* reported them in full, some were issued separately by the Ministry of Information as pamphlets, and all were collected into a series of six volumes, from *Into Battle* (February 1941 and in its seventh edition by July) to the final one, happily titled *Victory* (1946). Statesmen and political heavyweights set great store on the ministry of the word, confident in the importance of Parliament and knowing that their words would be noticed outside, not least in their constituencies, the provincial press retaining a vigour and intelligence now unimaginable.

What the press could deliver only at second hand, the BBC delivered fresh. Ministers made the most of the opportunity. The listening public was ready for them. Talks had always been one of the BBC's staples and some of the regular talk-givers were very good at it. Ministers would not retain much of an audience if they could not be good too. Churchill was good, in a unique, sonorous, portentous way (not to mention a very imitable one), and he had working for him the gravity of the matters he was talking about. An historian too young to have experienced his wartime broadcasts has ventured to cast doubt on their significance, on the ground that most of Churchill's famous speeches were delivered in the House of Commons, and that he only broadcast on five occasions in the summer of 1940.[4] It has to be rembered that Churchill's speeches in that House or elsewhere in Britain, together with the big ones delivered later in North America, very soon became known in print. As for what he calls 'the myth of Churchill inspiring the nation huddled round its crackling wireless sets', it has to be said, first, that wirelesses did not necessarily crackle when receiving the BBC Home Service; and, secondly, that people listened in pubs, clubs, factories and air-raid shelters too, work and talk stopping for the occasion. The evenings when word went round that 'Winston's going to be on' became almost religious occasions, massively attended: 64 per cent of the adult population, for example, listened on 14 July 1940. The figure rose to over 70 per cent in 1941.[5]

What was it that made those 1940–41 speeches unlike any others that have been read or heard in Britain? Churchill made the British feel proud and strong. His speeches set them on a world stage, somewhere few had dreamed of ever finding themselves, defending values important for the world at large. Their survival was to mean more than the survival of their insular selves, it meant the survival of civilisation and freedom. In his very brief broadcast on 17 June 1940, about the French surrender (less than two minutes long, and all the more effective for that), he said for example: 'We have become the sole champions now in arms to defend the world cause ... we shall fight on until the curse of Hitler is lifted from the brows of mankind.'[6] His listeners came to feel important and responsible. They were fighting for more than just themselves. Far from being sorry for themselves, they were to rejoice at living in an hour that let them play so dignified a role. Under bombardment, they were all on the battlefield. They could all acquire honour. He did not quote Henry V – in fact, he made far fewer historical and literary references than a more commonplace performer might have done – but the effect was to reproduce the congratulations addressed by Shakespeare's hero to the Englishmen lucky enough to be with him at Agincourt. It became possible for Britons to believe in themselves as he portrayed them: a valiant and valuable people and nation (and, as the word was used then, but cannot be used now, race).

Here was a strange but happy conjuncture between Churchill's imagination and reality.

> At some point between May 1940 and the London blitz of September, the career of Winston Churchill merged with the history of the British people and he was transformed into a popular hero ... The threat of invasion, and the knowledge that Britain now stood 'alone' against Hitler, produced a wave of tribal feeling that converged with Churchill's own fighting spirit.[7]

Direct evidence of the same came in Isaiah Berlin's essay *Mr Churchill in 1940*. The description of his quasi-magical impact has deservedly become famous.

> The Prime Minister was able to impose his imagination and his will upon his countrymen ... precisely because he appeared to them larger and nobler than life and lifted them to an abnormal height in a moment of crisis. It was a climate in which men do not usually like – nor ought to like – living ... But, in the

event, it did turn a large number of inhabitants of the British Isles out of their normal selves and, by dramatising their lives and making them seem to themselves and to each other clad in the fabulous garments appropriate to a great historic moment, transformed cowards into brave men, and so fulfilled the purpose of shining armour.[8]

At a later date, when asked about his part in rousing his compatriots, Churchill said they had the lion's heart and all he provided was the roar.[9] That was surely to do himself an injustice. The inhabitants of Britain at the end of the 1930s did not look much like the lions Churchill said they were; but there must have been something in it. Isaiah Berlin went on to say in his essay:

So hypnotic was the force of his words, so strong his faith, that by the sheer intensity of his eloquence he bound his spell upon them until it seemed to them that he was indeed speaking what was in their hearts and minds. Doubtless it was there; but largely dormant until he had awoken it within them.[10]

It was important that those speeches contained such contrasts of darkness and light. He did not conceal or brush away the dangers. The exemplary offer of 'blood, toil, tears and sweat' came in his first speech as Prime Minister. It was followed at once by the prospect of 'many, many long months of struggle and suffering' – and that was while France was still in the battle. In his 'Dunkirk' speech, on 4 June, he said we must not be blinded 'to the fact that what has happened in France and Belgium is a colossal military disaster'. 'Our people do not mind being told the worst', he told the House of Commons on 8 October. The Battle of Britain seemed to be over and won, but what would follow? This was his peroration:

Because we feel easier in ourselves and see our way more clearly through our difficulties and dangers than we did some months ago, because foreign countries, friends and foes, recognise the giant, enduring, resilient strength of Britain and the British Empire, do not let us dull for one moment the sense of the awful hazards in which we stand. Do not let us lose the conviction that it is only by supreme and superb exertions, unwearying and indomitable, that we shall save our souls alive. No one can predict, no one can even imagine, how this terrible war against German and Nazi aggression will run its course or how far it will spread or how long it will last ... Death and sorrow will be the companions of our journey; hardship our garment; constancy and valour our only shield ... Our qualities and deeds must burn and glow through the gloom of Europe until they become the veritable beacon of its salvation.[11]

Part of the force and shock of such language rested of course in the fact of its absolute singularity, its monumentality. It was perhaps less of a shock to the ear then than it would be now, because the people he was addressing had a large familiarity with the rich language of the Authorised Version of the Bible and the works of Shakespeare, still staples of school work, besides being encountered at church, chapel and theatre. Unusual language after all suited unusual circumstance. That his delivery was to some degree theatrical, and his voice temptingly imitable, only made him more impressive and accessible. And the darker, painful passages were stylishly balanced by lighter, optimistic ones. The latter predictably became more prominent as the war passed its climacteric, but they were part of the early scene-painting too. The 'Dunkirk' speech ended with an expression of confidence (incidentally flattering to the Americans) that 'in God's good time, the new world, with power and might, [will] step forth to the rescue and the liberation of the old'. The 'Finest Hour' speech on 18 June, awaiting the onslaught by 'the whole fury and might of the enemy', opened also a heavenly vista: 'If we can stand up to him [Hitler], all Europe may be free and the life of the world may move forward into broad, sunlit uplands.' And the conclusion to his 20 August speech, in the middle of the Battle of Britain but with the beginning of a glimmer of hope that the USA ('But westward, look, the land is bright') would turn helpful, was cheerful as well as stoical:

I do not view the process [the future] with any misgivings. I could not stop it if I wished; no one can stop it. Like the Mississippi, it just keeps rolling along. Let it roll. Let it roll on full flood, inexorable, irresistible, benignant, to broader lands and better days.[12]

The words and the voice must have been how he became best known to the people, but he was known also in person and as a character. He made visits and went on tours, at home and abroad. He liked to see for himself, and was happy to be seen, though he did not usually pause to talk. The contrast with his arch enemy could not be greater. Once the war had begun, Hitler became virtually invisible to *das Deutsche Volk* and left the business of speechmaking to Goebbels. Not Stalin but the Communist Party kept the Russian people at it. Churchill, going places with newsreel cameramen and press-photographers often in attendance, became more visible than he ever had been before. During the Blitz and the months of threatened invasion these outings contributed to sustaining popular morale, but that was not his only reason for making them. He would have toured the gun-emplacements on the Channel cliffs and the fortifications along the beaches whether the press had been there or not. Whether visiting the armed forces at their work or the common people bearing the brunt of the Blitz, he was impelled to taste something of their experience. When the raids were on London, he often went to where the damage was and talked with the survivors. Ismay went with him to Dockland after its first heavy raid.

Our first stop was at an air-raid shelter in which about forty persons had been killed and many more wounded by a direct hit, and we found a big crowd ... all seemingly very poor. One might have expected them to be resentful ... but, as Churchill got out of his car, they literally mobbed him. 'Good old Winnie', they cried. [Churchill moved to tears]. Having pulled himself together, he proceeded to march through dockland at breakneck speed. I could never understand how he managed it. He was no longer a young man, and normally he never took any exercise at all ... And yet, on his inspection visits, he would cover miles of ground at a remarkable pace.

On and on we went until darkness began to fall ... he was in one of his most obstinate moods and insisted that he wanted to see everything. Consequently, we were still within the brightly-lit target when the Luftwaffe arrived on the scene ... [13]

Many roads by then being blocked by bomb-damage and fire-engines, it was 'very late' when they got back to Downing Street and Ismay found himself 'rebuked by all and sundry for having allowed the PM to take such risks'. But he could not be stopped; and when the Blitz switched to provincial cities, he visited several of them: Coventry, Birmingham and Liverpool in late September 1940, Bristol and Plymouth the following April and May, other places further north in due course. It is an interesting paradox that although, as 'ordinary' persons close to him quickly realised, he had no idea how ordinary people lived, he imaginatively empathised with ordinary people's sufferings and was at least sentimentally moved by them. Feudal, patriarchal, paternalistic, call his concern what you will, it was real enough to upset him, and for them to perceive it.

The Churchill people saw on these occasions was usually the civilian Churchill, in black jacket and striped trousers or pin-striped suit, overcoat according to the weather, spotted bow tie, walking stick, cigar, and one of his distinctive black hats. For military occasions, he had a variety of military or quasi-military uniforms, but he would not always wear them. He liked to wear what was comfortable; most of all his 'siren suits'. He was liable to appear in them on any occasion, at home or abroad; for instance, under an Australian bush-hat in the Western Desert, and (at least for the photographers) in Washington. The black 'civvies' were often worn when reviewing troops, imperial or American. In top-hat and morning-suit on formal occasions, he looked the same as he had done for forty years. And no matter what he was wearing, he would acknowledge cheers with that V-sign which he gave to the world and which the uninitiated may unfortunately copy with the hand the wrong way round. His more gentlemanly minders to begin with didn't like it, thought it vulgar and liable to misinterpretation, but he went on doing it all the same.

He was often on the move. To begin with it was only in Great Britain, which was in the front line and where he wished to be, and indeed there was nowhere else to go (other than Egypt, not yet of dramatic significance). He had a special train which could carry his secretaries and closest staff and a miniature 'map room', a Lilliputian version of the big one in Whitehall where he kept an eye on all military movements. His first crossing of the Atlantic was in August 1941, to meet President Roosevelt at Placentia Bay, Newfoundland. He went there on the new battleship *Prince of Wales* and in the course of his subsequent four crossings managed to sample her sister-ships *Duke of York* and *King George V*. Very rough seas apart, those ships were relatively comfortable. So was the *Queen Mary* (converted to a troopship), on which he travelled twice. Quite comfortable also were the larger American aeroplanes: the 'enormous Boeing flying-boat' which flew him home in January 1942, for example, and the Skymaster, which the chief of the US Army Air Force had given him for Christmas 1944. At other times the planes were not so good: ordinary bombers, perhaps not much adapted to diplomatic use. The journey to Moscow and back in August 1942 was the most arduous. From Lyneham in Wiltshire he flew in an unheated Liberator bomber ('razor-edged draughts cut in through many chinks … no beds, but two shelves in the after cabin …') to Gibraltar,[14] and then, dodging as much neutral and enemy territory as possible, to Cairo; after a stop-over of some moment, on to Moscow via Tehran; and then, after the first of his meetings with Stalin, home by the same route, stopping off for some time in the desert with Montgomery. Mary Soames justly quotes General MacArthur's comment on this epic trip:

A flight of 10,000 miles through hostile and foreign skies may be the duty of young pilots, but for a Statesman burdened with the world's cares [and nearly sixty-eight years old] it is an act of inspiring gallantry and valour.[15]

His health indeed was not the better for these adventures. Clementine persuaded him never to go without his personal physician, and Sarah and Mary sometimes kept a family eye on him, alternating as his personal aides-de-camp on the grander diplomatic occasions. But there was a series of anxious episodes: a minor heart attack during his first visit to Washington, pneumonia after Casablanca and again, more seriously, when he was in Tunisia in December 1943 on his way home from the Teheran summit. Sarah was the daughter on guard on that occasion; she to some extent succeeded in keeping him quiet with readings of *Pride and Prejudice* until the dramatic arrival of Clementine, who stayed with him through his convalescence at Marrakesh until he was able to return to England (plane to Gibraltar, *King George V* for the rest of the way) in mid January. There was pneumonia again in the summer of 1944, directly after a hectic visit to the Mediterranean taking in the Pope, Marshal Tito, the Greek Prime Minister and the British army in Italy, and alarmingly close to the scheduled starting date for a meeting with Roosevelt and the Canadian Prime Minister in Quebec. He managed it.

He went on managing his demanding official schedule to the end, and even added impromptu items such as the dash to Athens on Christmas Eve 1944 to thwart the Communists and to save the Greek monarchy, opting out of the splendid family party which Clementine had arranged and reducing her, when he announced it, to 'floods of tears'. 'It was rare for Clementine to give way', remarks their daughter; 'she was accustomed to sudden changes of plan, and had, in these last years especially, developed a strict sense of priorities. Somehow this sudden departure of Winston laid her low; but not for long.' 16 She understood that what mattered to him more even than his love for her and the family was winning the war and (with Greece in view in late 1944) 'winning the peace' after the war was over. Their love for each other remained deep and constant. The Christmas party at Chequers received a 'Love and many thoughts for you all' telegram from his stopping-off place near Naples. Thereafter he sent her a telegram daily, and on the 28th she sent one back, congratulating him on good work done in Athens and concluding, 'I am so grateful that you are well and long for your return. All my love, Clemmie.' There is eloquent testimony to his love, need and, despite everything, dependence in the handwritten conclusion to a long letter from Malta in early February 1945: 'Tender Love my darling. I miss you much. I am lonely amid this throng. Your ever loving husband W.' 17

Keeping Winston going should certainly be counted as Clementine's main contribution to the war effort. So far as it included any home life, once their early brief tenancy of Admiralty House was over, most of it took place either in 'the Annexe', a strengthened part of the Storey's Gate buildings at the Westminster end of Whitehall and just over the Cabinet War Rooms in the air-raid shelter basement, or at Chequers, the Prime Minister's country house on the north edge of the Chilterns, not far from Aylesbury. Parts of Number Ten went in and out of use according to demand and the chance of air raids. Week-ends were no let-up from the strain of the working week. Mary Soames reckons that, from January to September 1944, 'out of a total of thirty-three week-ends, twenty-four … were all, or partly, taken up with entertaining …', there being not merely one 'shift' of guests per week-end but often two or three.18 Clementine's husband never let up, nor would she. When not with him, she was heavily engaged with three philanthropic activities: the Fulmer Chase Maternity Home for the wives of junior officers, often impoverished and usually away from home; the Young Women's Christian Association's Wartime Fund, to help look after servicewomen and women workers, also often away from home, friendless and comfortless; and, from October 1941, the Red Cross Aid to Russia Fund, which swelled to mighty proportions and earned her in 1945 a six-week visit to the Soviet Union, a meeting with Stalin and the Order of the Red Banner of Labour.

The others of the family were all in war service too. Randolph joined his father's regiment, the 4th Hussars, directly after war began, went to Egypt, transferred to the Special Air Service in 1942, and was parachuted into Tito's part of Yugoslavia early in 1944; he was lucky to leave it alive, though injured, six months later. By the time he came home, the marriage he had contracted with Pamela Digby just after joining up had come to its predictable end. Sarah, bravely reconciling herself to the dissolution of her marriage, entered the ranks of the Women's Auxiliary Air Force (the WAAF) in 1941, was commissioned, and became an expert in the interpretation of aerial photographs – a skill useful for the assessment of bombing damage and essential for mapping coastal defences and identifying V1 and V2 sites. Mary joined the Auxiliary Territorial Service, the ATS, also in 1941, trained for work in anti-aircraft batteries, was a subaltern by 1943, and after participating in the defence of southern England against Hitler's V1 secret weapon, the 'flying bombs', ended the war with her battery in Belgium, part of the defence of Brussels. Diana, the eldest, who had married (as her second husband) the young Conservative politician Duncan Sandys in 1935, had too much to do as a wife and mother to be capable of full-time service, but did voluntary things, not least as an air raid warden. Thus was the Churchill family, like most other families in Britain, wholly absorbed in the national war-effort, a social molecule of that total mobilisation of the population over which its paterfamilias and patriarch presided.

16

'Action This Day'

'All I wanted was compliance with my wishes after reasonable discussion.'

The Second World War, iv, chapter 5

Several veterans of Churchillian service recorded descriptions of what a normal working day was like. Apart from the fact that no day was normal when he was around (an entry in a secretary's diary begins, 'The PM being away, an unnatural calm reigns'), some regular items and features can be discerned.[1] He had to be awake by eight because that was when the daily report from the Map Room arrived. He stayed in bed and worked from there, attended by secretaries and assistants, unless or until he had to get up for the War Cabinet, which met daily or even more often through the early perilous months, usually twice a week thereafter, or for any other unavoidable committee. (Neville Chamberlain to begin with, then Sir John Anderson, and finally Clement Attlee chaired the Lord President's Committee which relieved him of much routine work and almost everything to do with the Home Front.) Ismay would always be there, walking his tightrope between the Prime Minister and the Chiefs of Staff; also one or more of his Private Secretaries, and often the Secretary to the Cabinet would look in. After a hot bath the great man himself would get up for lunch, an interlude regularly used for discussion of war business with persons he wanted to talk to. After lunch, there might be a Cabinet meeting or one of the ad hoc committees which brought together all interested parties for consideration of specially important business, perhaps the 'Tank Parliament' (which never succeeded in doing much good) or the Anti-U-Boat Committee (which did). 'But whatever his arrangements, he invariably got between the sheets [in the afternoon or early evening] for an hour or so. His capacity for dropping off into a sound sleep the moment his head touched the pillow had to be seen to be believed.' 'He reappeared', says Grigg, 'as a giant refreshed ... and with stores of energy which carried him on to the small hours of the morning.'[2] Upon this siesta, and if possible another bath after it, he was insistent, and since the timing of it could not always be fixed, it meant that people scheduled to see him between lunch and dinner were often kept waiting. Dinner was a big meal at about eight o'clock, with a moderate quantity of good wine (champagne for preference), usually with visitors and more war talk. Then at ten o'clock or thereabouts (or even later, if there was a film showing, which often happened at Chequers week-ends), he would go to work again; perhaps chairing one of the committees kept under his own hand, notably that for Defence (Operations), otherwise doing as he pleased – which of course meant being in company with such officers, ministers, civil servants and secretaries as he chose to have with him. The accomplished and steel-nerved women who typed his dictation straight onto the typewriter had to take it in turns to do 'Night Duty'. One of them christened these sessions 'the Midnight Follies', and the name stuck. He would go to bed at last usually between one and three in the morning.

Such was a 'normal' day at the court of King Winston. For everyone in attendance it was of course abnormal, tiring and demanding; and, on occasions when his manner was particularly peremptory and his saving graces of humour and *gaminerie* absent, it could be unpleasant and even embarrassing. The late nights were wearing for persons who had to be up early next morning and who couldn't look forward to a siesta. Even the equable Ismay, who felt it his duty to keep the old man company when there was no one else around, admits that he often wondered what good was being achieved by labouring on so long when so tired. But even when Churchill seemed groggy with fatigue at two a.m., he might suddenly get one of his bright ideas, spring into action, summon a secretary and dictate, for example, a minute to the CIGS, or the draft of a broadcast to the French people, or a letter to the President of the United States. His reserves of energy and will were fathomless, his power of total concentration (until the closing phase of the war) undiminished. Grumbling was endemic in his entourage but, after all, serving him was a form of war service; and service to such a leader could be regarded after all not as a burden but as a privilege. Submission to his will was a tribute paid to genius.

His bright ideas and his minutes were so marked a feature of his managerial style that they justify special mention. All through his official life, colleagues and subordinates had observed with mixed feelings the fecundity of his mind in the production of ideas, suggestions and questions relative not just to his work but also to theirs; which is why his copious supply of ideas and his energy in pressing them was felt to be in varying degrees insensitive and time-wasting. The ambiguous term 'bright ideas' seems right for them, because of their notoriously mixed quality. Alan Brooke wrote later: 'Winston had ten ideas every day, only one of which was good, and he did not know which it was.' Ismay's estimates were more generous: twenty a day, of which five were good.[3] One of the commonest complaints made by the high-level officers, officials and politicians who shared in the making of policy was that so much time was wasted in arguing him out of his impractical ideas, time which might have been better spent on the good ones or on business elsewhere. While this peculiar defect in him has to be admitted, it should be noted, first, that sometimes his view, even when the Chiefs of Staff at first opposed it, was later adopted by them and found to have been right, and secondly, that even his persistence in the end yielded to the opposition of those he constitutionally had to work with. He was not an autocrat.

Along with the ideas came the daily barrage of minutes and messages that marked his unique style of management. Minutes had long been Whitehall's preferred mode of communication within departments and from one department to another; in normal times they circulated without indecent haste, gathering additional papers and marginal annotations along the way. Churchill converted the minute into a rocket. Within hours of his entry into office, he had caused to be supplied a limitless quantity of red labels bearing in capital letters the words, 'ACTION THIS DAY'. There were also labels for 'REPORT PROGRESS IN A WEEK' or 'IN THREE DAYS'. The more peremptory of his minutes became known as his 'Prayers' because he liked to begin the order with the genteel imperative 'Pray': for instance, 'Pray cause inquiries to be made ...', 'Pray let me have by tomorrow ...' The ferocity of his war against the Axis was matched by the ferocity of his war against dilatoriness, prolixity and muddle. He maintained that any matter, no matter how complicated, could have its essentials summed up on a single sheet, even only half a sheet, of quarto paper; only thus might an extremely busy Prime Minister hope to be possessed of all the information needed for well-informed decision-making. It was an uncomfortable discipline for officials used to spreading themselves and covering their tracks in stylish prose, but it worked. The paper work whizzed from office to office as never before or, probably, since.

A selection of minutes, ones he considered especially important or illustrative, appears among the appendices to each of the six volumes of *The Second World War*. They are indispensable for understanding how he projected the power of his personality, although the reader must bear in mind that he does not print the recipients' responses and that the substance of some of them was subsequently the subject of aggrieved criticism. Here is a random selection of minutes from volumes two to six.[4]

> 29 August 1940, to Secretary of State for Air, Chief of Air Staff, and Ismay: 'I was much concerned on visiting Manston Aerodrome yesterday to find that although more than four clear days have passed since it was last raided the greater

part of the craters on the landing ground remained unfilled and the aerodrome was barely serviceable.' [The Germans do much better than this. Here are some suggestions].

22 November 1940, to Dominions Secretary (following earlier correspondence about Ireland, whose neutrality Churchill much resented): 'I think it would be better to let de Valera stew in his own juice for a while. Sir John Maffey [British Ambassador] should be made aware of the rising anger in England and Scotland ... and he should not be encouraged to think that his only task is to mollify de Valera and make everything, including our ruin, pass off pleasantly ...'

17 July 1941, to Ismay, for departments concerned: 'What is the cause of the failure to produce containers [for gas] in June? A fall from 1500 to 500 tons is shocking and absolutely contrary to the express instruction of the Cabinet over many months ... Let me know exactly who is responsible for this failure.'

6 December 1941, to Minister of Food (Woolton), by all accounts a fine minister whom Churchill for some reason or other enjoyed badgering: 'Among your many successes ... the egg distribution scheme seems to be an exception. I hear many complaints from many quarters ... Will you please give me very short statement of your plans and policy.'

12 December 1942, to Minister of Aircraft Production (Cripps), whose fecundity in good ideas Churchill rather resented. It may be summarised thus: No, I *don't* think your idea for improving anti-U-Boat operations is a good one. The present system is working well enough and the Americans and Canadians would not be more impressed by Admiral Somerville than they are by Admiral Pound.

2 March 1943, to Secretary of State for War: 'I agree with the Deputy PM's minute about the expenses of military funerals', all of which 'whether of soldiers or officers' should be placed 'on a satisfactory dignified and honourable basis. Pray let me have amended proposals ...'

16 July 43, to Chief of Air Staff: 'I still do not understand why it is necessary to have 2946 crews on effective strength [in Fighter Command] in order to man 1732 serviceable aircraft ... See how different are the figures of Bomber Command ...' [What is the explanation?]

27 September 1943, to First Lord of the Admiralty: 'Please see that Lord Cherwell is kept informed about the German glider bomb and also about the foxing devices so that he can keep me in touch with all developments.'

1 September 1944, to Colonial Secretary: 'The establishment [official number] of the apes on Gibraltar should be twenty-four, and every effort should be made to reach this number as soon as possible and maintain it thereafter.'

20 November 1944, to War Secretary (following his discovery that American troops received four bottles of beer a week and British rarely one): 'Good. Press

on. Make sure that the beer – four pints a week – goes to the troops under fire ...
before any of the parties in the rear get a drop.'

18 March 1945, to Ismay, for COS Committee, Secretary of State for Air, and
Chief of Air Staff. [The Netherlands government's complaint is justified and
reflects upon us in two ways.] 'First, it shows how feeble have been our efforts
to interfere with the rockets [V2 sites], and secondly the extraordinarily bad
aiming which has led to this slaughter of Dutchmen. The matter requires a
thorough explanation ...'

The minutes showed how the range of Churchill's interests was without
limit. Some interests, however, were much more intense than others. No
other conceivable Prime Minister would have paid so much personal attention to the military uses of science and technology, and no other could
have had the same earlier experience of inventing, making and using munitions of war. He had an instinctive 'feel' for the qualities of weaponry. Since
early in life he had been impatient with the traditionalism in attachment
to familiar weapons and methods which reigned in the armed services. His
pioneering interest in aircraft, in submarines, chemical weapons and, above
all, caterpillar-tracked vehicles taught him that admirals and generals could
be slow to grasp their potentialities, and that he could understand the
applications of science better than most of them. In fact he had virtually
no scientific education, just a bit of chemistry and mathematics to help
him enter Sandhurst; but, as he explained in *My Early Life*, he enjoyed
popular scientific lectures and from his first ministerial appointment onwards it was his practice to master the rudiments of the relevant expertise;
thus continuing the self-education which had begun in the cantonments of
India. He enjoyed the company of experts so long as they could be lucid
and terse like Frederick Lindemann. A disastrous meeting in 1944 with the
great Danish nuclear scientist Niels Bohr, who wanted to turn Churchill's
mind to the problems of controlling nuclear power *after* the war, showed
what could happen when they weren't.

One of the reasons why Lindemann was the earliest regular member of
the Chartwell set was that he brought with him news from the otherwise
impenetrable scientific world; besides being a lucid expositor, he was
enthusiastic about helping Churchill explore the uses of science in war. On
one level of their connection, Churchill converted some of Lindemann's
news items into the readable journalism gathered in his book, *Thoughts
and Adventures*; on another, Churchill took Lindemann with him into
the air defence preparations, and became a keen follower of what was
going on there. When war began, this personal scientific adviser acquired
official status as the First Lord of the Admiralty's personal assistant and

head of his Statistical Section; then, less than a year later, as head of the same for the Prime Minister and Minister of Defence. It was not long again before he was in the House of Lords as Lord Cherwell. While he was always just 'The Prof' to people who liked him, or could at any rate stand him, he was less affectionately referred to by the majority of those who came across him; he was regarded in the corridors of power as Churchill's snooper. His manner was found by most people to be disagreeable, he conducted vendettas against individuals and departments he disliked, and there was some ground for wondering whether the high degree of confidence Churchill placed in him was deserved. A different scientific adviser and helpmate might have done as much good with less offence, and might not have pushed Churchill towards certain decisions regarding, for instance, the uses of Bomber Command and the conduct of the Battle of the Atlantic which were unfortunate. But Lindemann, like Brendan Bracken and Desmond Morton, was one of Churchill's faithful companions from his 'wilderness years', and his affection for him and confidence in him were unshakable.

There is no questioning the usefulness of the Statistical Section. To some extent its strange title meant exactly what it said. Churchill found it helpful that complicated questions could be resolved as far as possible into quantitative terms; and, besides that, he was justly suspicious of the statistics produced by departments in explanation of their own activities. He wanted to have his own statistical materials, he wanted others' statistics to be subjected to independent appraisal (that is, *his* appraisal), and very sensibly he wanted everyone's statistics to be brought into a common frame. Hence this minute of 8 November 1940 to the Cabinet Secretary Sir Edward Bridges, who shared with General Ismay control of the clutch and gears of the war machine:

> it is essential to consolidate and make sure that agreed figures only are used. The utmost confusion is caused when people argue on different statistical data. I wish all statistics to be concentrated in my own branch as Prime Minister and Minister of Defence, from which alone the final authoritative working statistics will issue. The various departmental statistical branches will of course continue as at present, but agreement must be reached between them and the Central Statistical Office.
>
> Pray look into this, and advise me how my wish can most speedily and effectively be achieved.[5]

But better management of statistics was only part, and perhaps not the most significant part, of Lindemann's section's usefulness. Holding an office which only Churchill understood in a ministry (the Ministry of Defence) which existed only on paper and in Churchill's head, Lindemann became the means by which science and technology reached parts of the war-machine impenetrable to other scientists, bypassing the leisureliness of departmental routines and ignoring the scepticism of unimaginative officers. Lindemann himself was a copious contributor to innovation, for example convincing Churchill of the possibility of atomic bombs, arranging for Bomber Command's impressionistic early accounts of the success of its operations to be subjected to something like scientific evaluation, and participating in the exploitation of radar and the other electronically-based inventions engaged in what Churchill called the 'Wizard War' and R. V. Jones, one of the chief wizards, the 'Battle of the Beams', culminating in the very effective aerial navigation system known as H2S.

Then there was the regular work of the Statistical Section. It was quite small – there were usually only six or seven persons in it at any one time, mostly economists – but the spread and range of its influence was very considerable. 'Every week Lindemann produced charts showing clearly and accurately the state of aircraft production, the losses and new building of ships, the output of tanks and guns, the availability of coal stocks and other statistics which saved the reading of long and complex documents.'[6] Besides that, it was the main channel through which Churchill's zeal in support of invention and ingenuity was diffused throughout the system; a zeal which transformed the careers of two men whose unusual talents might have remained unused but for Lindemann's organisation and Churchill's protection: Millis Jefferis and Percy Hobart.

Millis Jefferis was a modest Royal Engineers officer whom Churchill came across when he was tinkering with the project of mining the Rhine: a 'brilliant officer' with an 'ingenious, inventive mind' over whom Churchill and Lindemann cast a protective mantle. Jefferis needed such protection because his less inventive colleagues regarded him as a bit of a crank, sneering when his inventions flopped, as their first versions in early experiments, naturally enough, often did. In June 1940 he was trying to make a 'sticky bomb' meant to adhere to a German tank when thrown at it from nearby by a valiant Home Guard. It took some time to get it right and Churchill watched the trials with intense interest, minuting Ismay on the 24th: 'Any chortling by officials who have been slothful in pushing this bomb over the fact that at present it has not succeeded will be viewed with great disfavour by me.'[7]

The 'sticky bomb' did work in the end. Jefferis and his small band of assistants went on to invent and plan the production of many ingenious and surprising weapons, including the limpet mine and the 'Projector, Infantry, Anti-Tank', to become blessed by footsloggers under the title of the PIAT. Their organisation, officially known as MD1 (Ministry of Defence 1) and often referred to outside the Prime Minister's hearing as 'Churchill's Toyshop', was answerable directly to Lindemann, who kept Churchill in touch with it. It could not have existed without his particular interest and patronage.

MD1 from 1943 was kept busy working on inventions to assist the invasion and liberation of the Continent. One of the most important projects in that giant enterprise was the floating harbour, codenamed 'Mulberry', for whose conception Churchill himself was largely responsible. As early as May 1942 he foresaw the need for it and even put his finger on the crucial desiderata: first, that the whole huge thing must be prefabricated and towed across the Channel in pieces; and, secondly, that its pierheads must be floating ones, able to go up and down with the tide. Ten months later, impatient and irritated that the hoped for progress was not being made, it was natural that he should inquire, 'Was Brigadier Jefferis consulted?'[8] It was just about that time that the 'Toymakers' were brought into contact with the other odd character whose peculiar talents would have remained unused had not Churchill taken him up.

This was Percy Hobart, known as 'Patrick' or 'Hobo'. He was a tank expert whom Churchill had known and respected for years, from the time when their common interest in mechanisation brought them together in the Great War. In the autumn of 1940 Churchill heard how Hobart, having recently incurred the wrath of the Commander-in-Chief Egypt, was back in England and serving his country as a corporal in the Home Guard. Hobart's reputation among the brass hats was not high: an innovating tank commander and theorist of exceptional energy and abrasive originality, a difficult man with a record of disobeying orders he considered stupid, and an improper man who had attracted to himself a brother officer's wife. In its struggle to reconstitute and enlarge itself, the army in the summer of 1940 made plans for adding five armoured divisions to its existing three. At such a time, should a senior officer of Hobart's experience be left on the shelf? Churchill made his wishes known. The War Office swallowed its distaste and Hobart was persuaded, with difficulty, to swallow his pride and resentment. Churchill's consequent minute to the CIGS included some sharp remarks:

> I think very highly of this officer, and I am not at all impressed by the prejudices against him in certain quarters. Such prejudices attach frequently to persons of strong personality and original views. In this case General Hobart's original views have been only too tragically borne out [about tank design and tactics] ...
>
> We are now fighting for our lives, and we cannot afford to confine Army appointments to persons who have excited no hostile comment in their career.

[Your] catalogue of General Hobart's qualities and defects might almost exactly have been attributed to most of the great commanders of British history ... This is a time to try men of force and vision and not to be exclusively confined to those who are judged thoroughly safe by conventional standards ...[9]

The more Churchill saw and heard of Hobart in his new role as commander and trainer of the 11th Armoured Division, the more he admired him. Montgomery (another unclubbable general) admired him too. The War Office hoped to see the last of him when medical factors were judged to prevent him from leading the 11th overseas, but Churchill dressed it down in a minute of contemptuous severity:

He is a man of quite exceptional mental attainments, with great strength of character, and although he does not work easily with others it is a great pity we have not more of his like in the Service ...

The High Commands of the Army are not a club. It is my duty and that of HMG to make sure that exceptionally able men, even though not popular with their military contemporaries, should not be prevented from giving their service to the Crown.

'Hobo' was put on to creating the specialised 79th Armoured Division, which is where his work made connection with MD1's. The 79th was to be equipped with tanks specially designed for the Normandy landings and whatever obstacles geography and German ingenuity might present thereafter: in effect, a twentieth-century siege train. Brooke took Eisenhower to Hobart's headquarters early in 1944 to see what was cooking. They found

the Sherman tank for destroying tank mines with chains on a drum driven by the engine, various methods of climbing walls with tanks, blowing-up of minefields and walls, flame-throwing Churchill tanks ... floating tanks, teaching men how to escape from sunken tanks etc.[10]

Brooke could also have added tanks with searchlights and dazzler attachments, and tanks that could carry bridges and ditch-fillers on their backs. Hobart would have liked to add a 'jumping tank', having an idea that rockets beneath the four corners would do the trick, but it was not thought practical. His creations were known in the Tank Corps as 'the Funnies'. Constructed and tested under Hobart's eagle eye, most of them proved to be successful when put to the grim test of leading the assault on Fortress Europe and then on Germany itself. Their losses were heavy but, medical opinion notwithstanding, Hobart went with them all the way to Lüneberg Heath. Dad's Army's loss was the Grand Alliance's gain.

Another of Churchill's particular interests was Intelligence: the word with a capital, otherwise 'Sigint', meaning what could be learned from listening in

to the enemy's communications. He had long been convinced that professional service officers were disinclined to take it seriously enough, and as a
younger man he had been excitingly close to one of the few places where it
was taken seriously, the famous Room 40 in the Admiralty. Signals Intelligence
had not been neglected in the general process of rearmament through the
second half of the 1930s. From 1936, responsibility for collating and making
sense of military Intelligence had been concentrated in the Joint Intelligence
Committee of the Chiefs of Staff. The numbers employed were still small,
however, and those banes of effective national endeavour, interservice rivalry
and departmental particularism, were still rife. Among the consequences was
the failure of the various units (both between themselves and with the
supposedly collating machinery above them) correctly to assess German
intentions regarding Norway in April 1940 and France four weeks later.

By that year, however, the Intelligence collection apparatus was progressing by giant strides, thanks principally to the brilliant brains assembled
in the Government Communications HQ at Bletchley Park. May 1940 was
the very month when they made their first breakthrough into the 'Enigma'
code, the version used by the Luftwaffe. It was also the month when
Churchill became Premier and Minister of Defence. His enthusiasm for
Bletchley knew no bounds. He called it 'the goose that laid golden eggs'.
He followed developments eagerly, and once he had become apprised of
its shortage of personnel and equipment thundered like Jove on its behalf:
'Make sure they have all they want extreme priority and report to me that
this has been done – Action This Day.'[11] As for his use of the Intelligence,
it is difficult to make out exactly what happened and when – Churchill of
course could say nothing about a matter still so secret when he wrote his
The Second World War – but it seems that, quickly becoming fed up with
(what he regarded as) the fumbling and mumbling of the Joint Intelligence
Committee, he insisted on being sent the Bletchley decrypts direct; thus
setting himself up, as F. H. Hinsley, the senior historian of Intelligence put
it, as 'a one-man Intelligence service.'[12]

The quantity of 'Ultra' material coming before him however was soon
so great, and its substance so mixed, that he wanted to have its wheat sorted
out from the chaff before he opened his daily delivery of what now had to
be called Special Intelligence. This task, at first entrusted to one of the
closest of the personal assistants drawn from the Chartwell court, Desmond
Morton, was gradually taken over by the head of MI6. By the middle of
1941 the ever-growing host of men and women at Bletchley was producing
such a quantity of decrypts that Churchill had to reconcile himself to
receiving only a summary of the more interesting items, plus the occasional
treat of a thought-to-be sensational decrypt in the raw. His daily dose of

Intelligence became a sort of addiction. It had to be sent to him wherever he was, which posed problems later when he was in North Africa or the Soviet Union. From the very beginning, his passion for Ultra decrypts added to the tensions already felt by the Chiefs of Staff in their relationship with him. He was receiving the stuff straight from Bletchley while they, waiting to have it digested by the painstaking Joint Intelligence Committee, were at a disadvantage. The remedy was in their own hands. They gave the JIC a strong enough staff to produce assessments more quickly; and this was done by mid 1941.

It was not only against the Chiefs of Staff that the impatient and anxious Churchill deployed his Ultra information. Through 1941 and into early 1942 he now and then called upon it to thicken his advice and urgings to commanders in the field; Generals Wavell and Auchinleck being the principal beneficiaries or, as they saw it, sufferers from these attentions. The decrypts being no more than parts of a puzzle, other parts of which remained out of sight, they were not the infallible magic Churchill would have liked them to be. His deductions might have been no more than intuitions prompted by them and thus as liable to be wrong as right. But the Chiefs of Staff too could make mistakes in their use of them. The difference between his readings and theirs – which is to say between the War Cabinet's and that of the Chiefs – was of course that he and the War Cabinet brought to their reading political considerations as well as military ones; which for example mattered much in 1941 in the shaping of policy towards Yugoslavia, Greece and Turkey. That difference of emphasis apart, what was militarily risky or insignificant might be politically so promising that the War Cabinet would feel justified in telling reluctant senior officers to stop raising objections and just get on with it. The evidence is complicated and shares of responsibility are so difficult to separate that it seems impossible to decide whether Churchill made better use of the Ultra material than the Chiefs of Staff, or vice-versa. It is clear that mistakes were made on both sides; a commonplace conclusion worth stating only because of the tendency of some writers to believe that Churchill could do no wrong.

That Ultra from 1942 was making a substantial contribution towards winning the war is undeniable; just how substantial historians continue to debate. Churchill's share in that contribution was the important one of taking it seriously and supporting it vigorously from the very beginning, hastening the days when it was taken as a matter of course. Referring to the time following the winter of 1942/43, Ronald Lewin wrote:

Ultra now seeped through many branches of what had become a highly articulated politico-military system of war administration. The volume of intercepts had greatly increased. Britain was now involved in an alliance strategy, and Churchill was no longer the monolith of 1940.[13]

The story of Ultra has become very well known since the truth about it began to be told in the mid 1970s. F.H. Hinsley's five-volumes on *British Intelligence in the Second World War* only began to appear in 1979. Churchill kept the secret as did everyone else. The fact of this long-maintained silence is the more remarkable for Bletchley Park's having employed, at its peak of activity, more than ten thousand men and women, of several nationalities besides British and American, all of whom knew something and some of whom knew everything that was done there. Yet, until the declaration of open season in the mid 1970s, not one of them broke his or her undertaking not to talk about it. Historians, facing the tantalising occupational problem of making the ethics and mentalities of by-gone generations intelligible to a later age, must notice the contrast between 'then' and 'now', for who can believe that so huge and widely-shared a secret could be kept in our own age of leaks and sales of secret information, of breakages of faith and of promises not to talk? An outreach of imagination is needed to understand the notions of loyalty, duty, patriotism and honour which obviously flourished at Bletchley; an effort perhaps as exacting as that required for understanding the minds of Cromwell's soldiers or Charlemagne's vassals. The same sort of effort has to be made to understand how it was that Churchill, in his bearing and speech so much a man of the past (so far as he was not a timeless eccentric), succeeded in getting the ordinary people of Britain to 'brace themselves to their duties' and, more than that, to persuade them that they actually had duties to perform. Were they people of the past too? A shrewd observer thinks it possible. 'His oratory painted the British people in archaic terms as an "island race" dwelling in their "cottage homes". But perhaps, deep down, the British of 1940 were an insular people whose ambition was to live in a cottage with a garden.'[14] The rustic scene of village greens and parish churches protected by Spitfires and Ultra is a nice representation of the creative confusion, the marriage of modernism and make-believe which were among the many ways of describing the Churchillian mind.

Britain came out of the war victorious and Churchill had been at the head of affairs almost all the time. But if one seeks to calculate Churchill's share of responsibility for the victory, and for all the elements that contributed to it, one runs into a difficulty similar to that awaiting the inquirer who persists in asking whether the army, the navy or the air force did the most to help win the war. The unexciting answer is that no one of the armed services could have won the war on its own, plus the necessary reminder that neither Britain and its Empire, nor the United States, did as much to bring Nazi Germany to its knees as did the Soviet Union. As to the particular question about Churchill's share of responsibility, it may be said that, although there were strong gusts of opinion in 1942 that Churchill was attempting to do more than one man could do efficiently, it only needed some Cabinet changes to secure his continuance at the apex of the war machine, which ran on without major changes to the ultimately victorious end; which does not say that its leader was faultless, but nevertheless says a good deal.

More may be said. It was an admirable feat of Churchill's to have picked winning teams of warriors and ministers and to have presided over them and a cohesive national war-effort, despite having to work with less than ideal materials: for example, industrial obsolescence, a bankrupted economy, awkward allies, an army that had to be built up almost from scratch, and an Empire less united and enthusiastic than he liked to think. It is easy now to see that the war, notwithstanding that it ended in glorious and deserved military victory, inevitably marked a stage in Britain's long drawn out decline from global greatness, just as it marked the decisive stage in the rise to global ascendancy of the United States. That diminution of status was, however, not at once apparent, and sharing in military victory did something to conceal it. Consequently Great Britain at the end of the war walked taller in the world than it might reasonably have been expected; and although Churchill attributed this to the British people, their majority opinion attributed it to him. It was what he wanted and worked for, and the achievement may be put to his credit. That again is to say a good deal, but it is not saying anything new or illuminating. More interesting is the inquiry as to which parts of the achievement the man had most to do with, and whether his share in them worked to their advantage or disadvantage.

Churchill's first volume of what were, in effect, his war memoirs came out as early as 1948; his sixth, and last, no later than 1954. It is a fine and remarkable achievement which, apart from its other uses and merits, has had a place among the basic texts for students of the war ever since. He was only half jesting when he said, just after the war, that history would vindicate him because he would write the history. In the book itself – just as was the case with *The World Crisis* – he doesn't claim to be presenting more than a contribution to the history. It has been fairly described as a memoir history. It is avowedly his side of the story; as are also, sometimes less straightforwardly, books by other Second World War warriors of the same generation. From the strictest scholarly point of view, and forgetting about things like style and drama, it invites critical reading. One soon realises how he lays the greater stress on *his* side of the arguments and negotiations he was engaged in, and how he slides too easily round some of the more dangerous corners in the narrative. Interested parties have made much of his 'suppressions', but they cannot be considered gross. He began to write so soon after the events that the book is deficient in perspective and of course it lacks some of the materials that only became available later, 'Ultra' the most substantial of them; but was a septuagenarian to be expected to wait ten years before he started? There is more of him in it than in *The World Crisis* and its sequels, simply because he was at the centre of events all the time instead of near it for part of the time. Like all his multi–volume historical works, it has these characteristics: the world for its background, a good cause to be fought for, and himself or (in the cases of Marlborough and Lord Randolph Churchill) someone he believed himself to resemble at the heart of the action or close to it.

The book's singularity and limitations are obvious enough and have been plentifully noticed. What has not so often been noticed is the generosity of his handling of human failure and of opponents, even enemies. Churchill's memoir-history could have been a quarrelsome book, but it isn't. Even the self-justificatory aspects of it may not be obvious to a non-specialist reader, so genially are they woven into the grand narrative. Nor is it a notably self-glorifying book. Indeed it is the history of the war from his unique standpoint – no other human being except Hitler was as advantageously placed, and as things turned out Hitler had no opportunity to dictate his version – but Churchill was writing as much on behalf of the English-Speaking Peoples as on behalf of himself. The issue at the heart of the struggle, as he repeatedly insisted while it was going on, was the survival of what those peoples stood for: civilisation, freedom, toleration and the rule of law; and the book ends not with peals of congratulatory triumph but with intimations of tragedy, the shadows of the nuclear age beginning to fall, and the frosts of the Cold War already nipping the blooms. At heart, he was no more optimistic about the future of humankind at the end of the Second World War than he had been at the end of the First; and for all his brave words repeated on public occasions, inwardly he was less optimistic about the future of his beloved British Empire. (But he never wondered, as some latter-day imperialists have done recently, whether after all the British Empire and Commonwealth would have had more life left in it for the second half of the century if it had withdrawn from the war earlier or never got into it at all.)

Throughout the years of his Premiership, he stood at the apex of both military and civil command, but his contact with the latter was necessarily slighter. For the history of the Home Front, one has to look elsewhere. His book is primarily about what he knew best, the military side of the war, its fighting fronts and the grand strategy and foreign policies that under-pinned them. It was at once a blessing and a bane to the chiefs of the armed services that he could think masterfully about war and that he took so great an interest in it. They knew that no other conceivable Prime Minister could have made a better job of being also their ministerial super-chief, as he was in his role of Minister of Defence; incidentally, and doubtless intentionally, reducing the significance of their departmental ministers. On the other hand, the military chiefs wished that he had a more sensitive nose for matters which he really didn't understand and that he had not brought into the Second World War some not always relevant ideas and impressions from the First. They also wished, as has already been intimated, that he was not so much given to interfering with commanders in the field. The latter should, they thought, be left to follow the directives and execute the commands handed down to them by the Prime Minister and Ministry of Defence on behalf of the War Cabinet, without the complication of conti-nuing responsibility to any civilian authority. Churchill's persistence in chivvying and prodding them (to use their terms for it) was rarely ill-meant, and in the critical months from the summer of 1940 to the spring of 1941 it was not inexcusable, in as much as survival itself sometimes seemed to turn on the success of a battle or the safe arrival of a convoy, and he had political burdens on his mind – principally, relations with the United States and the British people's confidence in themselves – as well as military ones. He supposed commanders would be glad to understand how much he cared about what they were doing, and grateful for the bits of advice and infor-mation (often about what was going on elsewhere) he was wont to enclose. He sought their confidence. All of them, when in London, were welcome to find out about the progress of the war generally at the 'Secret Intelligence Office' he caused to be established expressly for their benefit. They were likely to be invited to lunch or dinner too. He liked to think of the senior officers and himself as one big happy band of brothers, they communicating as freely with him as he with them, with no offence taken.

Of course the relationship could never be as easy and trouble free as that. Men trained to the courtesies and prejudices of the officer class were bound to be uneasy in the verbal rough-house which the veteran parliamentarian brought to their discussions. Churchill in any case was a man of prejudices and fancies. He liked ready talkers and clear expositors, and favoured perfect-gentleman types so long as they were good as their job. The rather inarticulate but militarily very capable Archibald Wavell was subjected to much chivvying he could have done without, and received little sympathy when things went badly wrong, while the urbane and easy-going Harold Alexander, whom some of his peers thought not very bright and lacking in firmness, was the recipient of more generous continuing confidence and praise than many commentators think he deserved. It is probable that Churchill's indulgence towards the showy and pretentious, though diplomatically gifted, Lord Mountbatten was partly because he cut a dashing figure in the world and was moreover a member of the royal family. On the other hand, Churchill could be smitten with enthusiasm for the eccentric and the oddball. His most obviously successful general, Bernard Montgomery, was rather of this description, although not so prickly as 'Hobo' Hobart, or so odd as the bizarre loner Orde Wingate. Then there were the 'old salts' to whom he was indulgently attached, Admirals Sir Roger Keyes and Lord Cork early on and, of much more importance, Admiral Sir Dudley Pound, the First Sea Lord, whom he found in office and kept there longer than his peers on the Chiefs of Staff Committee thought safe and the devoted old man's terminal illness justified.

The military chiefs with whom Churchill came most often and most directly in contact were the Chiefs of Staff. From the nexus between Churchill and the Chiefs of Staff derived, sometimes after much argument, most of the directives for major military operations and movements, though he sometimes issued one on his own. The Chiefs of Staff Committee's centrality and significance even increased in proportion with the decline in importance of the Defence Committee (Operations) which diagrammatic representations of the war machine show as coming between the Chiefs of Staff and the War Cabinet. Churchill could not constitutionally come to military conclusions without the Chiefs, and in fact did not do so. On the many occasions when they found themselves engaged in argument, they sometimes came round to his point of view, he sometimes came round to theirs or found his suggestions absolutely squashed – for example, his ideas for landing an expeditionary force in Norway and for using chemical weapons. He and they were bound together in indissoluble wedlock, immortalised at victory time by the celebratory lunch he gave them and Ismay on 8 May 1945, and by their appearance along with the War Cabinet on a Whitehall balcony to exchange greetings with the vast cheering crowd on VE Day, the 9th. But it must not be thought that their marriage was troublefree. There was usually argument, sometimes annoyance and anger. Churchill was not gentle in argument when determined to get his way. Sometimes he was not even gentlemanly. The men who served on that committee had to be tough, but, once the professionally defensive and overcautious Field Marshal Sir John Dill had been replaced as CIGS by General Sir Alan Brooke, they all were so.

This excellent 'professional trinity' stayed united from the beginning of 1942 until the end,[15] with only one change and (to Pound's particular disapproval) sometimes plus the young and inexperienced Mountbatten in his role as chief of Combined Operations. The essential three were Brooke, who became its regular chairman early in 1942; Air Chief Marshal Sir Charles Portal; and, after Pound's retirement in September 1943, Admiral of the Fleet Sir Andrew Cunningham. Each had his own way of coping with their extraordinary master. Portal had the easiest time of it. The Royal Air Force was the service about which Churchill knew least – and about which he was therefore least inclined to pontificate. For its part, the RAF, which was given to claiming that Bomber Command could win the war on its own (in the navy it was known as the Royal Advertising Force), was happy to be left alone. Portal himself was a silent and rather forbidding man, contributing to discussions only when invited to do so, and then in a manner which discouraged discussion. Pound had a relatively easy time too. Churchill felt warmly towards him and was more tolerant of his qualified somnolence during committee meetings ('qualified', because mention of anything naval brought him fully back to life) than he would have been of any other chief. Cunningham, on the other hand, when he replaced Pound, invited no favours. His relations with Churchill were correct, not close. He found it difficult to forget the prodding he had suffered while Commander-in-Chief in the Mediterranean. (The index of his autobiography contains, for instance, under the heading 'Churchill', such references as: 'messages concerning Mediterranean Fleet often ungracious and hasty' and 'lays down responsibility of Med. Fleet, to which no reply is sent'.) But he was a good First Sea Lord. When it was all over, he wrote that, despite their disagreements, he had 'never for a moment [lost his] profound admiration for that most remarkable and courageous Englishman who by his energy, obstinacy and sheer force of character led Britain and her people'.[16]

Brooke had the most difficult row to hoe. As Chairman of the Chiefs of Staff Committee he had to accompany Churchill to all the important inter-allied conferences. As CIGS he was head of the one of the three armed services of which Churchill was most suspicious, and with which he was most prone to interfere. And as a strong-minded, plain-speaking and testy Ulsterman, Brooke was wont to give as good as he got in the arguments in which he felt he was too often engaged and which he recorded in his detailed private diaries. Just how stormy their partnership was he let the world know by allowing Sir Arthur Bryant to make two big books out of his diaries, not many years after the war was over. The diaries and 'auto-biographical notes' are obviously and admittedly edited but how much has been omitted, and precisely why it has been omitted, is not made clear. Having to take the lead in coping with Churchill for more than four years was all the more of a tough assignment for Brooke when what he would

have liked above all else was to command in the field. By the end of the
war he was as worn out as Churchill, and a lot more fed up. One can
imagine that some of what he scribbled down in fury or frustration was,
by the refined standards of the 1950s, literally unprintable; perhaps also
offensive to other ex-Chiefs still then alive.[17] But for all the ups and downs of
Brooke's relationship with Churchill, their respect for one another remained
rock-firm to the end. When Brooke was told of a Churchillian explosion
to the effect that Brooke 'hated him', Brooke replied to the peace-making
Ismay: 'I don't hate him, I love him, but when the day comes that I tell
him he is right when I believe him to be wrong, it will be time for him to
get rid of me.' Ten years or so later, when he composed his Foreword to
Bryant's first volume, *The Turn of the Tide*, he wrote:

> My abiding impression of him remains that expressed by an entry in my diary
> made in the heat and stress of war: 'He is quite the most wonderful man I have
> ever met, and it is a source of never-ending interest studying him and getting to
> realise that occasionally such human beings make their appearance on this earth
> – human beings who stand out head and shoulders above all others.'

17

America and Roosevelt

'the United States, erect and infuriate against tyrants and aggression.'

The Second World War, iii, chapter 27

Momentous decisions about strategy and foreign relations had to be made within a few weeks of Churchill's assumption of the national leadership. Britain's military situation quickly became as unfavourable as could have been imagined. Germany's swift defeat of France, close on the heels of the occupation of Denmark, Norway and the Low Countries, meant more than the loss of Britain's only major ally; an ally moreover who had been relied on to provide the greater part of the land forces with which Germany was to be fought. It meant that the German armed forces were also far better placed for operations against the British Isles. U-boats could sail straight into the high seas from bases on the Atlantic coast of France instead of having to creep through the Straits of Dover or go the long way round between Scotland and Iceland. Bombers operating from bases in France, Belgium and Norway could reach every desirable British target and bring heavier loads of bombs with them. Warships and commerce raiders had the whole Norwegian coastline to operate from, and the French ports too if they could get there. Germany's war-making potential was increased by control of the economies of the occupied countries (Czechoslovakia's of course was already in the bag), and the traditional British idea of blockading a continental foe into submission was gone forever.

All that was catastrophic enough, yet there was even worse to come. Italy entered the war on 10 June 1940. Its incursion into south-eastern France was of little significance, but it mattered much that British security in East Africa, Egypt and the Middle East generally was now threatened. It mattered also that the Mediterranean had suddenly changed from being a safe sea into a perilous one. One of the nightmares of the pre-war imperial security planners had become a reality: the Royal Navy had to fight in the Mediterranean, on its own, as well as in the Atlantic and everywhere else. To complete the distress of the strategic planners, there were intimations that the worst nightmare of all – war simultaneously with Japan – might soon become real as well. Japan's militarists and hypernationalists had become the ultimate determinants of foreign policy, and their undeclared war of aggression against China continued, regardless of its contribution to the worsening of relations with the United States and, indeed, with all the non-Asian powers having commercial interests in the region. In September 1940 Japan signed a Tripartite Pact with Germany and Italy, which if it meant anything could only mean trouble. Japanese hunger for the rubber, minerals, oil and rice of the Dutch, French and British colonies in South-East Asia was undisguised. The Japanese government was pressing Britain and Vichy France to sever China's remaining land links with the rest of the world. Ideally, the British government's response would have been the dispatch of powerful military forces to the Far East, as it was then known; in the real world of mid 1940, Britain just had to trust to luck, and to Singapore.

Setting aside the necessities of winning the Battle of Britain and staving off invasion, Churchill in the summer of 1940 had other immediate problems to deal with. In the first place, the armed forces had to be re-equipped and built up for a war that, having begun badly, threatened to be much more extensive and demanding than had been anticipated. The expeditionary force left most of its equipment in France, the aircraft production industry was short of machine tools and many of its materials came from abroad, and the navy already felt a shortage of destroyers and smallish vessels generally for escort duties, mine-laying and mine-sweeping. Secondly, there was the question of what to do with the French General Charles de Gaulle. His arrival in England on 17 June to raise the flag of Free France was heartening; but with him came a diplomatic problem of the first water, in as much as the neutral United States adhered to normal diplomatic practice by moving its embassy from Paris to Vichy. Anything that hurt the sensibilities of the United States was therefore to be avoided at all costs, because the most acute of all necessities presenting themselves to Churchill's mind was to engage America's active sympathy and hopefully its actual alliance. President Roosevelt personally was known to be sympathetic, and there were grounds for believing that pro-British opinion, or at any rate anti-Nazi opinion, might become vigorous enough to overcome the isolationists and pro-German lobbies who did not consider that German mastery of the European continent would present such a 'clear and present danger' as to justify American intervention.

Partnership with the United States was no new idea of Churchill's in 1940, suddenly brought to the boil by the June disasters. The idea seems to have been in his head since the early 1920s, when the common interests and values of the English-Speaking Peoples became a recurrent theme in his writing and speech-making. That it stayed so despite a variety of Anglo-American diplomatic contretemps throughout that decade, in some of which as Chancellor of the Exchequer he was directly and furiously involved, must be counted as a triumph of faith over experience. Its first appearance in organised form was in his American lectures in 1931–32. The big book about the shared histories of the British and American peoples which he had in draft by 1939 was above all a history of a shared political culture, possessed in common over many centuries before the War of American Independence and not so much separated by that event as moved on to parallel tracks by it. In Churchill's journalism and broadcasts through the later 1930s, some of the latter directly to America, two themes recurred: first, that the shared values and interests of Britain and America were highlighted by comparison with the ideals and doings of the European dictatorships; and, secondly, that if the United States waited too long to help Britain stand up to them, its ultimate task of restoring the world to rights would be so much the more burdensome. All this Churchill was saying well before the war.

Supporting this ideological conviction were other props of memory and affection. America's intervention in the Great War had been decisive although tardy, as he hoped it would not be again. Churchill had some rich American friends and he had happy memories of his lecture tours in 1929 and 1931–32. He had been fond of his mother and because of her nationality he could describe himself as half-American. As a good showman he made much of this when performing in the United States and before American visitors to Britain, but it was not a significant source of the pro-Americanism which it became his pleasure to preach during the war; his mother's American relations and connections had never meant much to him and he had never been to the States except to make money and see sights. As for American politics and culture, whatever the write-up in his *A History of the English-Speaking Peoples*, his sober appraisal of America in the present was less than enthusiastic. This is how he conveyed his idea of it in a newspaper article of 4 August 1938:

a Sphinx who under the mask of loquacity, affability, sentimentality, hard business, machine-made politics, wrong-feeling, right-feeling, vigour and weakness, efficiency and muddle, still preserves the power to pronounce a solemn and formidable word.[1]

But, a few weeks later, he was hammering again at the flattering theme in a dramatic broadcast of 16 October, not long after the Munich crisis:

I avail myself with relief of the opportunity of speaking to the people of the United States. I do not know how long such liberties will be allowed. The stations of uncensored expression are closing down; the lights are going out; but there is still time for those to whom freedom and parliamentary government mean something to consult together.

Far away, happily protected by the Atlantic and Pacific Oceans, you ... are the spectators and I may add the increasingly involved spectators of these tragedies and crimes. We are left in no doubt where American conviction and sympathies lie: but will you wait until British freedom and independence have succumbed, and then take up the cause when it is three-quarters ruined, alone? [2]

That the people of Britain were happy about the direction of 'American conviction and sympathies' was wishful thinking, but it was true that the President and many educated Americans, including the chiefs of the armed forces, knew enough about Hitler and the Nazis to share Churchill's conclusions about them. Franklin D. Roosevelt himself, from 1937, was looking for ways to involve his country in the better management of world affairs, European affairs above all; but the domestic obstacles were many and the European reception, not least Neville Chamberlain's, was cool. A window of opportunity opened when the war began and Churchill re-entered the government as First Lord of the Admiralty. Churchill was surprised and delighted to receive, in mid-September 1939, a letter from the President (using as an introduction the fact that they had both been connected with navies in the last war and had even once been at the same dinner in London), emphasising his interest in the European situation and inviting Churchill to 'keep me in touch personally [and privately] with anything you want me to know about'.[3] The language was guarded and non-committal but the implications were enormous. Churchill replied at once, keeping the tone light by subscribing himself as a 'Former Naval Person'. Thus informally, almost casually, began the most important correspondence and political connection of Churchill's whole life. Nearly 2000 written exchanges took place between them,[4] and there were numerous telephone talks as well; not to mention the nine occasions when they were actually together for several days at a time.

Was the Churchill-Roosevelt connection a highwater mark of the so-called 'Special Relationship'? How trusting a 'friendship' was it? Inevitably the friendship, as friendship of some order it certainly became, was more eager on Churchill's side than Roosevelt's. Churchill set about ingratiating himself with Roosevelt while Roosevelt wondered for many months whether to become committed. The risks Roosevelt ran in 1940 were no more than political while Churchill's life and Britain's freedom were at stake. Churchill was left hanging on desperately and Britain was close to running out of cash during the interval between the disasters of June and Roosevelt's third election as President in November. That duly achieved, and the bipartisan Committee to Defend America by Aiding the Allies having evidently attracted more support than the America First Committee, Roosevelt was freed to bring his beliefs into the open. Churchill seized the opportunity. Early in December, and after prudent consultation with the British Ambassador in Washington, he wrote a long letter to the President, 'one of the most important I ever wrote', the brave tenor of which was that Great Britain and its Empire could not merely survive but might expect to win *provided* that the United States became a reliable and generous provider of armaments and materials, of shipping to carry the stuff to where it was needed in Europe and North Africa, and of assistance with the protection of that shipping while it was exposed to enemy action. It was not at that time to be expected that America would become a co-belligerent, but Hitler's presumed reluctance to add the United States to his list of enemies suggested that the Americans could safely practise 'constructive non-belligerency'. Churchill, mindful that the business of America was business, concluded by expressing the belief that the United States would not wish Great Britain

> to be divested of all saleable assets, so that after the victory was won with our blood, civilisation saved, and the time gained for the United States to be fully armed against all eventualities, we should stand stripped to the bone. [Britain, to put it bluntly, was broke.] You may be certain that we shall prove ourselves ready to suffer and sacrifice to the utmost for the Cause, and that we glory in being its champions. The rest we leave with confidence to you and to your people, being sure that ways and means will be found which future generations on both sides of the Atlantic will approve and admire.[5]

From this letter and Roosevelt's responses to it came the encouraging headlines of 1941: Lend-Lease, placing at the disposal of Britain and her allies the inexhaustible outpourings of 'the Arsenal of Democracy'; the assistance of the US Navy in convoy protection, one consequence of which was damage to the USS *Kearney* and the loss of the folk-song-famed *Reuben James*; the 'Liberty Ships' which in due course would be produced in such numbers that more tonnage was launched each month than the Germans could sink; the first meeting between the two leaders at Placentia Bay, Newfoundland, in August 1941; and the promulgation of the Atlantic Charter, a statement of principles and aims upon which the two peoples were agreed. On Britain's part, there was a restored mood of optimism summed up in Churchill's broadcast speech of 9 February 1941: 'Give us the tools, and we will finish the job.'[6]

That Britain, even a Britain plentifully armed with American equipment, could conceivably have defeated Hitler's Germany on its own seems impossible in retrospect and seemed improbable then. But Churchill had

more in mind than it was prudent to reveal. He knew that the President
and those close to him were privately talking in terms of alliance whenever
Congress could be brought round to their view of the situation. He also
knew that among the inevitable surprises of war would be mistakes made
by the enemy. A chapter in a recent book about the calm and prudent
and in every respect un-Churchill-like Lord Halifax is headed, 'Churchill
as Micawber'.[7] The point is a good one. Churchill was always ready for
something to turn up and to take advantage accordingly. It was not unreasonable to expect Hitler to make mistakes; he had already made a big
one just before Dunkirk. Nor was it unreasonable to hope that he might
become so frenzied by America's pro-British behaviour that he would regard
the United States as an open enemy. This indeed happened in 1941. Hitler
made one of the mistakes that ultimately assisted his downfall. Not many
weeks after the 'Give us the tools' speech, British Intelligence began to
detect evidence of Hitler's intention to attack the Soviet Union – as risky
an enterprise as could have been undertaken; and later in the year Germany,
with Italy in tow, and nominally in consequence of their Tripartite Pact
with Japan, did declare war on the United States, a few days after Pearl
Harbor.

By these events the shape and character of the war were utterly changed.
No more, 'we will finish the job'! Hitler had long and unpersuasively
complained about being 'encircled'. Now he had brought real encirclement
on himself. The phenomenon of the Soviet Union as an unexpected co-
belligerent produced a fresh set of problems for Churchill, to be considered
later. The transformation of the United States from a friendly neutral to a
fighting ally produced another.

Churchill's relationship with Roosevelt was such that, within a few minutes
of hearing incomplete first news of Pearl Harbor, he was at the telephone.
'"Mr President, what's this about Japan?" "It's quite true", he replied. "They
have attacked us at Pearl Harbor. We are all in the same boat now."' In
his book Churchill gladly confessed his joy and relief. 'We had won the
war.' Such a recollection says much about the anxieties which had persisted
behind the bold exterior of the preceding eighteen months. 'Being saturated
and satiated with emotion and sensation, I went to bed and slept the sleep
of the saved and thankful.'[8] Within twenty-four hours he was making plans
to go to Washington. He would take with him the Chiefs of Staff and
Beaverbrook and the usual train of aides-de-camp, secretaries and doctor;
the Foreign Secretary, Eden, could not be with them because, as luck would
have it, he was on his way to Moscow. The winter weather was too bad
for a journey by aeroplane, so they sailed from the Clyde on the brand-new
battleship *Duke of York*, not yet 'worked up' (in landsmen's language, 'run

in'). The crossing took eight stormy days, and he was at the White House on 22 December.

The Grand Alliance was the title Churchill gave to the third volume of *The Second World War*, which concluded with the entry of both Russia and the United States into the war. What 'alliance' might mean with regard to the Soviet Union was yet to be discovered; it would cost Britain and her allies many lives and ships and much material, but until the end of 1943 it allowed no military collaboration and is a relatively simple story to tell. The American side of the story is altogether richer. Military collaboration was expected from the start – there had indeed already been secret staff discussions – and in due course it would attain gigantic proportions. Fixing the terms of the collaboration and planning joint action was not, however, achieved without argument and friction. What else could be expected? Wartime alliances by definition are fragile creations. The Americans had no previous experience of them (their army had acted in the Great War as an independent force), the British had too much. Fighting in alliances brought brickbats as well as bouquets. The British were used to the charge that they were willing to fight to the last Prussian or Russian or Frenchman; Churchill had to make sure his generals' plans did not make it look as if Americans were being added to the list.

The questions that arose to disturb the harmony of Britain's alliance with the United States would have done more damage than they did had relations between the two national chieftains not been amiable and, on the whole, trusting; an easy working relationship, which Churchill went to endless pains to create and sustain. It is very clear that Churchill was not always the mastermind in their relationship that he wanted to be, that he did not always understand what was going on, and that experience in the relatively straightforward ways of Westminster afforded no clues towards understanding the mental workings of the magician of Washington. The Churchill-Roosevelt relationship was special, no doubt about that, but, not being coextensive with the Special Relationship of Churchill's historical imagination, it could never achieve as much as Churchill imagined.

The actual relationship between the two allies was subject to many strains. Of these there were two clusters of causes, which might be called the attitudinal and the strategic. By attitudinal I mean the ways the respective policy-makers and service chiefs were culturally conditioned to regard each other. British military men and diplomats generally thought of Americans as novices in war and international relations, sure to benefit from the guidance of their more experienced allies. Americans were quick to resent this, even if they were not already Anglophobic. Endemic among Irish-Americans, Anglophobia was patchily present all over; the lectures at the

US Army and Navy War Colleges, it has been discovered, were much more likely to make American staff officers suspicious of Britain than friendly towards it.[9] Fighting for the President's Four Freedoms might have to include fighting to save Britain but it certainly needn't include saving the British Empire. Americans generally, not least some in high office, were amazingly ignorant about what actually went on within the British Empire, but that didn't stop them doing what they could towards dissolving it. Churchill reassuringly declared in a Mansion House speech that he 'had not become the King's First Minister in order to preside over the liquidation of the British Empire',[10] but there was little he could do to stop what was happening by natural process, and nothing he could do to resist the hard bargain the Americans actually struck – Lend-Lease and other support on condition of Britain's opening the Empire and Commonwealth to Free Trade (in other words, American trade) as soon as the war ended, and speeding the process of self-government in India and the Colonies. The two leaders had more than enough statesmanship between them to realise that, since with regard to the British Empire they could only agree to differ, their difference of opinion must not be allowed to disturb their good relationship as co-belligerents; and it didn't.

The danger, however, was very real. It was only natural that mutual suspicions and contempts should have threatened to disturb the working relationship between the two nations' armed forces. Armed services of one country being accustomed to play at rivalry with one another, they inevitably play at rivalry with those of a foreign ally. Churchill and Roosevelt were well aware of the problem and did something towards overcoming it by appointments of just the right men to two crucial style-setting jobs. Churchill's appointment, more by luck than judgement, was of Field Marshal Sir John Dill to be his and the British Chiefs of Staff's representative on the United States Joint Chiefs of Staff Committee, the American counterpart of the British Chiefs of Staff; a sort of Washington version of London's Ismay. Too gentlemanly to stand up to Churchill as he needed to be stood up to, Dill had not been a happy Chief of the Imperial General Staff through 1941, but he blossomed in Washington, where Churchill took him when he went to that city in December. He adapted so surprisingly well to American ways and manners that, where so much might have gone wrong, his presence made it go right. 'His tact and persuasiveness became renowned, and he won the trust and friendship of Roosevelt and his Chiefs of Staff', being accorded in the end the unexampled honour of burial alongside America's national heroes in Arlington cemetery.[11]

The crucial Roosevelt appointment was of General Dwight Eisenhower to be Supreme Commander of the first major Allied combined operation, the landings in Vichy-controlled French North Africa in November 1942; and then, two years later, of the biggest ever such operation, to land in German-defended Normandy in 1944. (Churchill would have preferred Brooke, but he bowed to the political reality that required an American.) 'Ike', as he became popularly known, had no experience of active service, but he was politically astute, good-tempered and fair-minded, and absolutely determined that the Americans and Britons on his Combined Staff should learn to collaborate. 'I don't care who calls who a son-of-a-bitch', he admirably said, 'but I will not have them called an American son-of-a-bitch or a British son-of-a-bitch.' His naval Commander-in-Chief was the Nelsonian Andrew Cunningham. It was asking quite a lot of a dyed-in-the-wool navy man of high seniority to serve under a then unknown foreign general of a few months standing, but they soon became friends and Cunningham subsequently paid Ike generous tribute:

> From the very beginning he set Anglo-American unity and friendship as his aim ... The Staffs were closely integrated, and it was not long before the British and American members ceased to look at each other like warring tom-cats, and came to discover that nationals of both countries had brains, ideas and drive.[12]

It was too much to expect that the Eisenhower spirit would hover dovelike over every battlefield all the time, and it certainly didn't. Military historians can point to plenty of instances of rivalry, jealousy and uncooperativeness and, in consequence, flawed victories or worse. The long Italian campaign was bedevilled by bickering, the drive from Normandy towards Germany was accompanied by ugly arguments and recriminations, Mountbatten as Supreme Commander in South-East Asia was not quite as good as Eisenhower at discouraging quarrels and calming stormy waters. Whether these rows did more harm in the long run than did spats between commanders of the same nationality is, however, an open question. Their total certainly pales into insignificance when weighed against the tremendous record of successful military working together which lasted until the war was finished.

The second hazard in the conduct of military alliances is always the question of what they are to work at. Was there a shared grand strategy as well as a grand alliance? Churchill, needless to say, was full of ideas, but the Americans had ideas too – or, rather, with regard to the war in Europe they had one idea and they were reluctant to budge from it. The giant difficulty that might have spoiled all, American concentration on the Pacific theatre, did not actually exist. The President and his advisers had already concluded that Nazi Germany was more dangerous than Japan to the peace of the world and to American security and prosperity within it, and that

Britain was a more necessary ally against the first than the second. They also supposed that the defeat of Germany would not take long. The Americans therefore were all set to bring airmen and soldiers, such of the latter anyway as were more or less trained, to Europe. Churchill and the British Chiefs of Staff were astounded to discover that the one idea in the minds of General George Marshall, the US Army Chief of Staff, and his men was to go straight for an assault on German-occupied Europe. It proved curiously difficult to persuade them that this would be suicidal and was in any case wholly impractical, not least because there was simply not the shipping to bring enough American soldiers and their voluminous stores across the Atlantic, on top of what was needed to rush Lend-Lease materials to Russia. Space could be found in Britain for the US Army Air Force to prepare to bomb Germany, but where could the US Army begin? Domestic pressures for it to begin fighting somewhere were strong. If it did not do something on the European side of the world, American public opinion would press for its removal to the Asian theatre. Stalin, moreover, was demanding military action as well as military supplies; sympathy for Russia spread wide beyond the British and American Communist Parties and would go on demanding a Second Front until it got one.

The way out of these difficulties was found along the western side of North Africa. British and imperial forces had been engaged along its eastern side since Italy entered the war. The net profit from the ding-dong of successes and failures (the latter mostly since the arrival of Rommel's Afrika Korps early in 1941) was nil; worse than nil, if you bring into the account the disastrous adventures in Greece and Crete. Churchill had already toyed with the idea of a collaboration with the more anti-German of Pétain's generals and admirals. Now he sang the merits of a plan to effect landings along the coasts of French Morocco and Algeria, was happy to accede to the Americans' desire to bear the brunt of it, had no doubt that their chance of blandishing the Vichy French into cooperation was much better than his, and looked forward to catching Rommel in the jaws of a conjunction with Montgomery's army advancing from the other side. This hopeful project he managed to sell to Roosevelt even while the American Joint Chiefs of Staff were still arguing that a cross-channel assault in 1942 was not impossible. Roosevelt accordingly pressed it on them (incidentally taking a stronger line with his Chiefs of Staff than Churchill ever took with his). The idea of a Second Front that year was at last abandoned, and Operation Torch was duly launched on 8 November 1942.

There was more to Churchill's advocacy of Torch than Roosevelt at first realised (although General Marshall rumbled him quite early); it was a further variation on the theme of offensive action in the Mediterranean theatre which had been on his brain since the late summer of 1940. Ever since then he had been urging his generals to get on with it, and now he was persuading the Americans to commit themselves too. Ever since Dunkirk, and excepting only the hastily-formed Commando units' raids on mainland Europe, the British and Commonwealth troops in the Middle East were the only ones in a position to do any fighting. The Italian invasion of Egypt in September 1940 gave them their opportunity. Chivvied by Churchill, and bolstered by a convoy with tanks which a more defence-minded leader would have kept at home in case of invasion, Wavell and his field commander General O'Connor pushed the Italians back the way they had come and counter-invaded Libya. What, by the end of January 1941, had looked like becoming an extraordinary clearance of enemy power from the southern coast of the Mediterranean then came to a halt and never regained momentum until, twenty-one months and several generals later, Montgomery won the battle of El Alamein and began the drive westwards which would meet up in Tunisia with the armies of Operation Torch.

During those twenty-one months the Mediterranean came to assume peculiar importance in Grand Alliance strategy. This could not have been predicted – but then, as Churchill himself never tired of emphasising, what can? He accompanied the most forward-looking of the three strategic memoranda he placed before the President in December 1941 with these instructive reflections:

> War is a constant struggle and must be waged from day to day. It is only with some difficulty and within limits that provision can be made for the future. Experience shows that forecasts are usually falsified and preparations always in arrears. Nevertheless, there must be a design and theme for bringing the war to a victorious end in a reasonable period ... [13]

At that date his 'design and theme' anticipated landings in 1943 all round the periphery of occupied Europe, the Mediterranean side as well as the Atlantic. It was not long before he was made aware of the very different expectations of General George C. Marshall, whose importance in Washington may be measured by saying that he mattered even more to the President than General Sir Alan Brooke mattered to the Prime Minister. To Marshall and the Joint Chiefs of Staff the Mediterranean initially meant nothing, unless it was as a British imperial region wherein the British throughout 1941 suffered more reverses than victories. But to Churchill, notwithstanding those reverses, it was rich in memories, possibilities and temptations.

Churchill's Dardanelles memories were part of the Mediterranean mosaic in his mind. It had been a good idea to try to get round the back of the enemy in 1915. Could anything similar be hoped for now? Some other old pieces of the mosaic were still in place. Turkey was one of them. Could Turkey be persuaded to join hands with the Allies? The Foreign Office, to which Churchill had moved the trusted Anthony Eden in December 1940, never gave up trying, but never got anywhere. As for the Balkans generally, they recovered their old interest when, at the end of October 1940, Mussolini unexpectedly launched an attack on Greece. In principle, this activated the British military guarantee offered to Greece in the spring of 1939; but the Greek government, proud of its people's military prowess and anxious not to attract German hostility needlessly, at first proved reluctant to accept other help than that of a few RAF squadrons. But whether the Italians beat the Greeks or not, British interest in the Balkans was now bound to intensify. As it happened, the Greek army promptly repulsed the Italian and began a counter-invasion of Albania, annexed by Italy in April 1939. This inevitably intensified German interest. Movements of Wehrmacht and Luftwaffe to their north concentrated the Greeks' minds to the extent of accepting the collaboration of a mainly Anzac force hastily extracted from Wavell's Cairo Command.

It was the kind of bold and risky venture dear to Churchill's heart but, in the exceedingly muddled event, he had more hesitations about it than others. Eden believed (mistakenly) that foolproof arrangements had been made with the Greek Commander-in-Chief; Dill acted as if anxious to give the lie to his Churchillian nickname 'Dilly-Dally'; and Wavell never doubted that Middle East security began in the Balkans. The tumultuous events that followed came to a stark and simple conclusion. Within the first five months of 1941, the forces of the Axis had occupied or gained as allies the whole of the Balkans. The Anzac and British divisions which had at last, in early March, been allowed to join the Greek army in seeking to stem the German onrush had been driven successively from Greece and from Crete (those that escaped, that is; over 11,000 were taken prisoner). The British navy in valiantly attempting their rescue had suffered terrible losses, mostly at the hands of the Luftwaffe: three cruisers and six destroyers sunk, and bad damage suffered by two battleships, an aircraft carrier, five cruisers and seven destroyers. On 7 May 1941 Churchill for the first time had to vindicate himself and his government in the House of Commons.

'So ... came to an end at last the Greek adventure and the concomitant fantasy of a Balkan front.'[14] Correlli Barnett's verdict invites slight modification. The Balkan front idea had a continuing half-life in the mind of Winston Churchill as part of his belief that 'the under-belly of the Axis' (as he misleadingly conceptualised it) was where Allied armed force could profitably be applied; and that it was not an altogether foolish fantasy is suggested by the fact that, although the Allies never seriously considered major landings in Greece or up the Adriatic, Hitler never ceased to fear that they might. In contrast, the Americans were never in the slightest bit interested. They suspected the existence of Churchill's Mediterranean obsession even before its diagnosis was confirmed. As early as mid 1941 the American dignitaries who came over to give their prospective ally the once-over questioned the apparent wisdom and disliked the presumed rationale of the military build-up in the Middle East. So long as the British military record there remained unimpressive, Churchill could hope for no more than to persuade them that it would not forever be so. The Americans were not the only people just then to wonder whether Churchill's style of war management was as effective as it should be. The depressing series of disasters and defeats from December 1941 through to the autumn of 1942 – the sinking of the battleships *Prince of Wales* and *Repulse*, the surrender of Singapore and retreat to the borders of India, the definitive loss of Australian trust, the loss of Tobruk and the disaster of convoy PQ17 – made early and mid 1942 his unhappiest time and fomented through several months public unease and parliamentary criticism, even to the point of hysterical talk of proposing that he be replaced by the curiously charismatic Labour dignitary Sir Stafford Cripps. His desperate search for a general who could defeat Rommel had many motives besides the *arrière-pensée* that only thus could he maintain influence with the American President.

Montgomery at El Alamein, fought between 23 October and 4 November 1942, gave Churchill the victory he needed. Through 1942 he had striven, and striven successfully, to persuade Roosevelt and his as yet untried generals to share his belief that the Mediterranean was where the action ought to be. This belief burgeoned *pari passu* with the Allies' successes in the Mediterranean theatre from the autumn of that year onwards. One thing led to another. The Americans were persuaded to site their first Cisatlantic operation in North Africa. That operation after many vicissitudes had a happy ending, duly effecting the planned junction with Montgomery's Eighth Army coming from the east and successfully expelling the last of the Germans and Italians from Tunisia in May 1943. The obvious next step was to cross the Mediterranean and invade Sicily, as had in fact been planned at the Casablanca summit and Combined Chiefs of Staff conference earlier that year. And once through Sicily, Italy beckoned. By the middle of 1943, Italy was on the brink of surrendering; the unseen sort of event which changes the scene and invites changes of plan. Mussolini was sacked by the King and replaced by Marshal Badoglio towards the end of July. What the Allied attitude to this ought to be was unclear. Could the Italian armed forces be turned to join the Allies? It proved unhelpful, as Churchill had foreseen, that the Casablanca conference had ended by demanding the 'unconditional surrender' of Italy equally with that of the other Axis powers; even if the insistence on including Italy had been the War Cabinet's work, not his. By the time a secretly negotiated armistice was announced on 8 September, and the Salerno landings were begun on the 9th, all hope of an easy take-over of Italy had gone. Not the Allies or a newly friendly Italian government had taken over but the Germans; and the long drawn out, painful and costly Italian campaign had begun.

By now the American high command, which had so far strung along hopefully in the Mediterranean but which had never let out of sight its original purpose to storm Hitler's French fortress, was beginning to wonder how far Churchill's Mediterranean enthusiasm (zealously seconded by Brooke) was taking them. They began to shuffle their feet, preliminary to putting them down. Italy for them would never be more than a sideshow. Stalin also put his foot down. He shared the Americans' fears that the preparation of Operation Overlord, as the Normandy landing plan was now known, would suffer from the demands made by Churchill on behalf of the Italian campaign (or some optimistically imagined subsequent Balkan breakthrough) and other operations in the Aegean Sea supposed to nudge Turkey tardily into co-belligerence. Churchill recorded how, at one of the dinners during the Tehran summit conference, at the end of November 1943,

> Stalin looked at me across the table and said, 'I wish to pose a very direct question to the Prime Minister about Overlord. Do the Prime Minister and the British Staff really believe in Overlord?' I replied, 'Provided the conditions previously stated for Overlord are established when the time comes, it will be our stern duty to hurl across the Channel against the Germans every sinew of our strength.' [15]

At last, on 6 June 1944, D-Day came. Churchill praised and (once it was launched) publicised the virtues of Overlord for all he was worth, and was so keen to participate in the event itself that nothing less than the command of his monarch could stop him. Nor was he in any respect lacking in zeal for its success, following the immensely complicated preparations with intelligent interest and contributing good ideas of his own. At the same time, he voiced fidgety hesitations about its viability as late as March 1944. He remained absolutely insistent that those 'conditions previously stated' should be fulfilled. In *The Second World War*, he showed himself defensively sensitive on the subject, insisting with some disingenuousness that he had never not been a supporter of the Overlord plan to which (under earlier provisional names) the Allies committed themselves at the Casablanca

9. Churchill in office. Note the perfect, even dandyish attire: black jacket and striped trousers, gold watch-chain, lowest waistcoat button undone, white handkerchief in breast pocket, and the inevitable spotted bow tie. (*Imperial War Museum*)

10. Giraud and de Gaulle reluctantly shake hands at Casablanca, January 1943. Churchill can hardly contain his amusement. (*Imperial War Museum*)

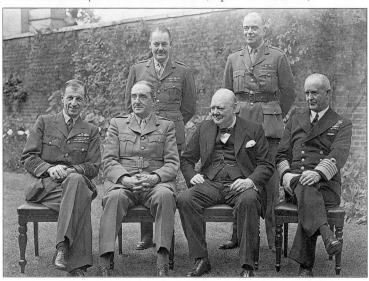

11. The Chiefs of Staff Committee, VE Day, 1945. Left to right (front): Portal, Brooke, Churchill, Cunningham; (back) Hollis and Ismay. (*Imperial War Museum*)

12. In the Western Desert, August 1942. Churchill's eccentric rig-out and easy-going stance make a remarkable contrast with the near-naked soldier's rigidity. (*Imperial War Museum*)

13. Churchill meets President Franklin D. Roosevelt for the first time, on the USS *Augusta* in Placentia Bay, 9 August 1941. Churchill presents a letter from King George VI to Roosevelt, who is supported by his son Elliott. (*Imperial War Museum*)

14. Enjoying a joke with Stalin at Yalta, February 1945. On a man to man level, Churchill and Stalin liked and respected one another. (*Imperial War Museum*)

15. Winston and Clementine on his return from Moscow, 22 October 1944. Clementine is wearing the convenient 'turban-bandana', signifying her solidarity with working women. (*Imperial War Museum*)

16. Churchill and President Dwight D. Eisenhower. There is no mistaking the genuineness of good feeling between the two men. Mamie Eisenhower beams between them. (*Conservative Party Archive and Bodleian Library*)

17. Churchill enjoying himself on the rostrum at the Conservative Party rally in May 1955. (*Conservative Party Archive and Bodleian Library*)

conference of January 1943 and the Washington one of May. Feasibility studies had promptly been begun under General Sir Frederick Morgan's direction and from that time on the President and the Joint Chiefs of Staff had their minds directed to Overlord as the magnetic needle to the pole, adding as time went by a landing in the south of France to support it (Operation Anvil). No more Allied divisions were kept in Italy than were necessary to keep the Germans from disengaging the many divisions they had moved there in mid 1943 and continued to introduce thereafter. Since Overlord in the event did succeed, it remains a matter of speculation, and an inexhaustibly fertile field of argument for military historians and biographers, whether Churchill's and his Chiefs of Staffs' conviction that Anvil (later named Dragoon) was a distraction of resources from where they could have been used to greater advantage – in Italy, and thereafter in Istria and Slovenia – was justified.

This disagreement about the Mediterranean strategy was probably the most serious of the many potential areas of disagreement Churchill and Roosevelt had to negotiate lest the Grand Alliance be gravely disturbed by them. Their differences of opinion about de Gaulle and about how to handle Stalin were more easily got over. But just as troublesome as the war in the Mediterranean might have been was what the British called the War in the Far East and the Americans the War in the Pacific. In this theatre of operations, the national interests and war aims of the two parties to the Grand Alliance had nothing in common. The United States was determined to make the whole Pacific Ocean region safe for American-style democracy and to put down for once and for all, in alliance with China, Japan's challenge to American hemispheric hegemony. Understanding, as every sensible Briton could, that in the long run the Pacific must matter more to Americans than Europe, Churchill was immensely relieved to find in 1941 that the President was prepared to sell his electorate the slogan 'Europe First!', and for over a year thereafter to follow Churchill's lead as to how the war in Europe should be conducted. When it came to Asia and the Pacific, however, Churchill was in no position to do more than struggle to recover for Britain and its European allies the many colonies the Japanese had overrun (Burma, Malaysia, and what were then called French Indo-China and the Dutch East Indies) and to make sure that British India was not added to the Japanese bag. These were not war aims about which Americans could enthuse. Roosevelt and Americans generally, even well-informed ones, deplored Britain's failure to grant India autonomy or, better, independence; they disapproved of the European colonies in that part of the world as they disapproved of them everywhere; and they nourished a special regard for China, feeling that the European imperial powers had never treated it fairly.

Churchill and Britons generally found the American obsession with China and high regard for its national leader Chiang Kai-Shek unreasonable, but were compelled to go along with it; nothing annoyed Churchill more than to find Roosevelt bringing Chiang along to summit meetings and insisting, in the planning of the United Nations Organisation, that China must be counted as one of the Great Powers.

The differences of opinion were so fundamental that the two men could not happily discuss them. Churchill thought Roosevelt infatuated about China; Roosevelt thought Churchill antediluvian regarding India. Most of Churchill's colleagues in the Cabinet thought that too; but, while he could be argued and stonewalled into reason on most other subjects, on this he was immovable. He would sanction no attempt to appease the Indian political leaders until the more pressing need to appease the American political leaders induced him to authorise the prestigious and high-minded Sir Stafford Cripps to go to India, in March 1942, with an offer of Dominion status after the war (or even, certain conditions being fulfilled, independence) in return for India's total support for the war against Japan until it was won. Why Cripps's mission came to grief is not entirely clear – Churchill's failure fully to back him is certainly part of the explanation – but its consequences were momentous. The Congress Party dropped all collaboration with the Raj and its 'Quit India!' movement quickly degenerated into a fragmented mosaic of popular violence, put down by the authorities with an efficient show of force. The immediate military advantage to Britain was that India became, through the remainder of the war, a safe base for launching the campaigns to recover Burma and Singapore, and to support General Stilwell's American mission in South-West China. Politically, however, the consequences were as counter-productive as could be. Cripps's offer could be neither forgotten nor undone. Even Churchill had to recognise, by the end of the war, that 'India was lost', just as Americans with less justification were soon going to have to mourn 'the loss of China'.

It galled Churchill that Britain's means of vindicating its imperial claims in Asia were so limited until the end of the war in Europe, by when it was too late to make much of a show. It is difficult to feel that he had much to complain about. He bore a share of responsibility for the inadequacy of Singapore's defences – not that even much better defences would have saved a place with so much ineptitude in its administration. His absorption in the war in Europe and the Atlantic was so total that he could never give the other side of the world his full attention. But even his full attention could not have averted the penalties of imperial overstretch, now painfully enforced. He was unreasonably cross when Australia insisted on withdrawing its soldiers (though, thankfully, not its airmen) from the European theatre and moreover made it clear that the United States, not the United Kingdom, was henceforth to be regarded as Australia's protective big brother.

Churchill was nevertheless responsible for two important interventions in the conduct of the war in South-East Asia. The first was to persuade the President at the Quebec summit in August 1943 to agree to the formation of South-East Asia Command with Admiral Lord Louis Mountbatten as its Supreme Commander. From this position Mountbatten was able in due course to give valuable backing to General William Slim's campaign to drive the Japanese from Burma and then, in mid September 1945, to receive in style the Japanese surrender at Singapore. Churchill's second notable intervention followed on his enthusiasm for the guerrilla enthusiast, Orde Wingate. This neurotic character, having done remarkable things in Palestine before the war and in the campaign that expelled the Italians from Ethiopia, came out of eclipse in 1943 as the leader of a dashing jungle exploit behind the Japanese lines in Burma. The British public took him up as a hero, and Churchill took him up as the protagonist of a promising new way to undermine the oriental enemy. He successfully interested the Americans in Wingate and made sure that massive backing was given to his second venture in early 1944, which was not without its effect. Just how much effect, continues to be debated. There would, however, be nothing to debate if Churchill had not seen in the man a second T. E. Lawrence, making sure that he had his opportunity.

Rangoon, the Burmese capital, fell without a shot fired to an advance detachment of General William Slim's multinational army just one week before D-Day in Europe. With Burma well on the way to liberation, the Malay peninsula and Singapore island were the next theatre of operations for Mountbatten's amphibious forces. Churchill had it in mind that, after reconquering those places, they would add to the lustre of their arms (as the Royal Navy was already doing off Okinawa) by fighting side by side with the Americans in the invasion of Japan, which, until the last days of July 1945, looked as if it would be the only way to bring the Pacific war to an end. But upon that grim prospect there suddenly dawned, as Churchill put it, 'a miracle of deliverance'.[16] Of course he had long known of the work going ahead in the United States towards making an atomic bomb (as it was always known in those days), but he had no idea until 17 July that the thing was actually known to work. He was at Potsdam when the coded news came through. Neither he nor President Truman, nor any of the highest-level military and political decision-makers, could find any reason not to use it, seeing it as likely to push the rulers of Japan over the bridge between putting out feelers for a negotiated peace, which they were already doing, and making up their minds to surrender, which the

Allies were determined to make them do. Churchill never doubted that the decision to use the bomb was right. But he also understood the awful significance of the event, and had a statement of explanation ready for delivery to the British people when it happened. By that day, 6 August, he was out of office, but his statement was issued by Downing Street all the same. Its conclusion opened a line of thought that was to stir him to noble endeavours ten years later:

> This revelation of the secrets of nature, long mercifully withheld from man, should arouse the most solemn reflections in the mind and conscience of every human being capable of comprehension. We must indeed pray that these awful agencies will be made to conduce to peace among the nations, and that instead of wreaking measureless havoc upon the entire globe they may become a perennial fountain of world prosperity.[17]

18

Special Operations and Bombing Offensive

'It is very disputable whether bombing by itself will be a decisive factor in the present war.'

Churchill to the Chief of Air Staff in later 1941

The obvious and ordinary way to meet the challenges of Britain's situation in June 1940 was to concentrate all resources on the defence of the British Isles. Churchill's way was the eccentric one of finding means to go on the offensive, even though that meant, as did the opening of the Mediterranean strategy, a diversion of heavy equipment away from home defence. Less resource-consuming were the Special Forces which he immediately set about recruiting with the purpose, as he imagined, of making it difficult for the Germans to think they were secure in their military occupation of nearly every continental European land. In common with many others in those early days, he innocently underestimated the strength of the German hold and was as yet incapable of imagining how efficiently and ruthlessly it would be maintained. On 6 June he put it to the Chiefs of Staff, through Ismay, that the Australians who were about to arrive in Britain would make first-rate

Striking Companies ... equipped with grenades, trench-mortars, tommy-guns, armoured vehicles and the like ... We have got to get out of our minds the idea that the Channel ports and all the country between them are enemy territory. What arrangements are being made for good agents in Denmark [and elsewhere in occupied Europe] and along the French coast? Enterprises must be prepared, with specially trained troops of the hunter class, who can develop a reign of terror down these coasts, first of all on the 'butcher and bolt' policy; but later on ... we could surprise Calais or Boulogne, kill and capture the Hun garrison ... and then away. I look to the Chiefs of Staff to propose to me measures for a vigorous, enterprising and ceaseless offensive against the whole German-occupied coastline. Tanks and AFVs [Armoured Fighting Vehicles] must be made in flat-bottomed boats, out of which they can crawl ashore, do a deep raid inland, cutting a vital communication, and then back, leaving a trail of German corpses behind them ... The following measures should be taken:

Proposals for organising the Striking Companies.

Proposals for transporting and landing tanks on the beach.

A proper system of espionage and intelligence along the whole coasts.

Deployment of parachute troops.[1]

This document, first of a flurry thrown from the express train of his thought, incidentally illustrates the truth about Churchill observed by so many, that the Prime Minister's 'strategic vision veered wildly between the patently absurd and the stunningly brilliant'.[2] In the document just quoted, mixed up with romantic recollections of cavalry forays and trench raids, and a convenient mental blockage about the Luftwaffe, can be seen the germs of several of Churchill's most original innovations: the Special Operations Executive, the Combined Operations organisation, and those specialised fighting men soon known respectively as the 'Paras' and the Commandos.

Churchill initially supposed that the peoples of the occupied countries needed only some encouragement and assistance to rise up against their invader. This was the rationale behind the formation of the Special Operations Executive, rather awkwardly inserted into the war machine as a dependency of the Ministry of Economic Warfare. Its tasks of undercover operations, liaison with resistance movements and sabotage being of the dashing and dangerous kind to which Churchill was temperamentally addicted, it might seem strange that he did not retain as close and continuous an interest in it as might have been expected. To begin with anyway, this was partly because he didn't want to see more than he could avoid of the Minister of Economic Warfare, Dr Hugh Dalton, and also because the SOE, itself the victim of bureaucratic jealousy and infighting, was quite unable to deliver the instant results Churchill looked for. There were more serious reasons. He did not let his boyish enthusiasm for dashing adventures blind him to the possibility that independent and covert operations in foreign lands could cut across the main lines of grand strategy and diplomacy, producing the sort of unsavoury messes in which the CIA has sometimes landed the US government. There was also his unreasonable disappointment that the peoples of occupied Europe did not come up to his expectations. It was not SOE's fault that it had little to point to in the way of massive resistance before 1943, when the Yugoslav partisan leader Tito attracted Churchill's favouring eye (and when moreover Randolph Churchill was one of SOE's Balkan agents), and 1944, when the by now well-organised French resistance gave Eisenhower, so he reckoned, six divisions' worth of support. SOE's gallant and varied activities have been much written about, not least because it included a surprising number of historians, but Churchill figures no more in their narratives than they do in his. He set it going, then left it to its own and others' devices.

It was quite otherwise with Combined Operations and the Commandos. Churchill, a good soldier who believed he had also made himself a good navy man, had always been interested in amphibious warfare. Soldiers and sailors generally speaking were not. Their respective professional formations kept the land and the sea separate. This was an aspect of that inflexibility and lack of vision about which he never ceased to complain. The Combined Operations HQ, wrote one of its distinguished alumni, 'broke the log jam of tradition'.[3] This was not the only way it promoted flexibility. It was a challenge to innovating and inventive spirits. We have seen how Churchill backed and protected military inventors like Jefferis and Hobart. Nowhere does his genius for war show itself more than in the way his mind played over the matter of amphibious operations. If he was not himself an inventor, he was certainly fecund in ideas for inventions; and many of these were for facilitating landings on hostile shores. Other minds were simultaneously busy on the landing craft problem, but in the conception of the portable 'Mulberrry' harbours he really does seem to have had an original share.

The Combined Operations organisation had two chiefs, a Marine general and one of Churchill's First World War heroes, Sir Roger Keyes, before it was entrusted in October 1941 to the much-publicised and royally related Captain Lord Louis Mountbatten. (Valued by Churchill for his leaderly qualities and infectious panache, he was soon a vice-admiral with an independent place on the Chiefs of Staff Committee, to the lasting indignation of experienced senior admirals who had got to the top the hard way.) The organisation's greatest contribution towards victory was probably its intensive study of landings on defended coastlines and its mixed experience of them. With regard to the particular exciting business at the forefront of Churchill's mind when he created it, its overall achievement was full of enterprise and bravery but mixed both in effects and in results. Army and marine commanders thought their regiments' fighting powers diminished by the siphoning off of their toughest men. Many Commando operations were so small-scale as to be invisible in all but the specialist literature. The most successful of the visible ones were the actions at St-Nazaire (navy and Commandos) to put out of action its giant dry-dock, at Bruneval near Le Havre (parachutists) to seize vital parts of a German radar station, and in the Norwegian mountains (Norwegian SOE parachutists) to sabotage part of the German atomic-energy project. Among the least successful and most costly was the biggest, the Canadian-led raid on Dieppe on 19 August 1942, for his insistence on launching which Mountbatten has been much criticised.

An unwanted though not wholly unpredictable consequence of Churchill's hearty endorsement of the Commandos was the gift it gave to the Nazi propaganda machine. The Nazi propaganda minister Goebbels never tired of presenting to the subject peoples of Europe and to the few remaining neutrals a characterisation of Churchill as a gangster and the British armed forces as law-breakers. His network made tremendous use of the photograph which Churchill allowed to be taken of himself holding a tommy-gun in a Chicago gangster pose. British spirits may have been lifted by the blood-and-guts hype surrounding the Commandos – blackened faces, unarmed combat, karate and knives and so on (especially the knives, still popular among young males of violent disposition) – but on the other side of the Channel the Wehrmacht, anxious to observe the laws of war vis-à-vis the British, was bound to wonder whether these trumpeted terror-merchants were going to fight fair. Atrocity stories always spread like wildfire in armies, and it is difficult to sort out what actually happened; but some of their methods, binding and gagging prisoners particularly, were pushing legality close to the limits. The Wehrmacht's attitude towards them increasingly hardened until Hitler put an end to dithering in October 1942 with his 'Commando Order': any Commandos taken prisoner in the future should be handed straight over to Himmler's men and be done away with.

The third line of offensive action that could at once be undertaken in the early summer of 1940 was bombing, and the RAF's Bomber Command appeared to be ready to undertake it. Bomber Command was the most ambitious and expensive part of the air force. Until now it had not been able to do much. Chamberlain's government and Hitler's had equally shied off bombing any but exclusively and distinctly military objectives on each other's territory; fearful not so much of being branded as international law-breakers as of initiating a city-bombing tit-for-tat that neither was confident of winning. Fighter Command had monopolised the limelight during the Battle of Britain. Steadily thereafter, however, bomb by bomb and raid by raid, the bomber barons moved into the dominant position they had indoctrinated themselves to expect ever since the RAF had become an independent force just after the Great War. Bombing of the enemy heartland was what it had been formed for, and now at last it had the chance to show what it could do.

Churchill had been enthusiastic about the capability of long-range bombers in the Great War and, as the Secretary of State for War and Air in the first post-war government, he had presided over the RAF's bomber-orientated birth. Nothing had happened since then to diminish his belief in the potential of bombing, or its inevitability. It was predictable that in 1940 he would unconditionally back Bomber Command to take the war to Germany, especially after the Luftwaffe had begun so emphatically to bring it to England. It was not so predictable that he would privately begin to have doubts about Bomber Command twelve months or so later. Through the remainder of the war his confidence in it was marked by hesitations and ambiguities paralleling those which showed more obviously among the British public as the Strategic Air Offensive got into its stride. That campaign, from early 1942 until the spring of 1945, proved to be the most controversial of all the major campaigns fought by British, Commonwealth and Allied forces, and it has remained so. The official history of it excited extraordinary controversy when it came out in 1961, even though it was co-authored by a distinguished international historian and a rising historical star who knew the business from the inside, having survived a full tour of bombing duty.[4] Although reputable and scholarly books about it have since then become available, criticisms are still likely to touch Bomber Command loyalists on the raw. Where so much controversy is in the air, it can hardly be expected that Churchill's relationship with Bomber Command should be immune from it.

As a good soldier and a civilised man, Churchill was very well aware of the fundamental principles of the laws of war: that attacks should be made only on military objectives, and that injury to civilians should be avoided as far as possible. As a well-read military historian and a student of current affairs, he was equally aware that these principles could be more faithfully observed in limited wars guided by prudent self-interest and controlled by diplomats than in revolutionary and people's wars guided by ideologists and zealots and fired by popular passion. By the twentieth century, limited wars were becoming things of the past. The principles of civilised warfare were still there and good men tried to keep faith with them, but the difficulties could be great. Nowhere were the difficulties greater than when the use of a new military technology offered advantages hitherto inaccessible or unobtainable but pressed hard on the principles in doing so. The submarine was one such novelty. The bomber was another.

Churchill had taken it for granted throughout the 1930s that the next war, if it could not be averted by the liberal democracies' collective pre-emptive action, would witness bombing by every belligerent with the capability to do it. But he kept his head. He had never believed that war could be won by bombing alone, as the bolder aficionados of the new weapon liked to claim. Nor had he found attractive the use of bombers simply to terrorise civilian populations, as practised by the Italian and German squadrons sent to support Franco in the Spanish Civil War and boasted of by the dictators. On the other hand, he still believed, as he had in the Great War, that manufacturing and communications centres were legitimate military targets, and he accepted it as a fact of life in modern industrial nations that, although civilian populations could not come within the military objective category *de jure*, their enthusiasm for a war and economic activity in support of it made their *de facto* involvement impossible entirely to ignore. In the Great War and now again in this war he never doubted the legitimacy of economic blockade, which was bound to hurt civilians even if they were not its primary target. The parallel with strategic bombing was exact. When the Blitz began, he was neither surprised nor indignant. His two chapters about it in *The Second World War* contain not a word of complaint. Along with the Chiefs of Staff and everyone else at the top, he expected Coventry to be one of the first targets outside London, and took it for granted that its factories could not be hit without much collateral damage. Such was war. The human aspect, which he repeatedly emphasised in these chapters, was not any illegality or unfairness done to the civilians but their resilience under fire, their fighting spirit. They had been done the honour of sharing with their men in the services the dangers of the front line. Looked at in that light, it seemed no more than justice that German civilians in due course should be given the same opportunity. (In parenthesis, this is the place to nail the story, springing from the inaccuracies of the earliest British writer about Ultra, that Churchill, faced with the alternatives of revealing the existence of Ultra or letting Coventry be bombed, opted for the latter. He did no such thing.) [5]

Churchill's initial approval of Bomber Command's operations was the heartier for there being at that time, and for much time to come, no other means of showing the German people that they were not immune within their own borders, nor of letting the occupied peoples know that they were not being forgotten. That was valuable, whether much damage to the German war effort was done or not. But the Air Ministry kept reporting that its raids (night raids, because daylight ones had proved suicidal) were successfully hitting the military and economic targets aimed at; every militarily educated person understood that there would be collateral damage, but that was deemed no more significant than had been the damage to the civilian areas of Coventry, London and other British cities. If it helped the British cause at all it would only be because, if Bomber Command's amateurish psychological prediction was to be believed, the German people could not take it as the British could.

For its first twelve months of operations, Bomber Command carried on to Churchill's satisfaction and indeed in close collaboration with him, to the virtual exclusion of the Chiefs of Staff. He would talk fiercely about bombing Germany to bits. He sought to maintain morale among the courageous bomber crews, professing to share the airmen's faith that the RAF was the one of the three armed services most likely to win the war; understanding at the same time that great results could not be achieved until the big four-engined bombers prudently conceived before the war came into service, as substantial numbers of them would be doing in 1942. But Churchill's faith in the leadership of Bomber Command had by 1942 been shaken. Cherwell made another of his dramatic entries into the story. Sceptical about Bomber Command's claims, he had instituted in mid 1941 an inquiry into the reliability of its methods of assessing success. The results were devastating. His researcher, Mr Butt, showed to Lindemann and his master's satisfaction what some independent-minded airmen, including John Slessor, had already realised, that its night bombing was so generally inaccurate as to be damaging Germany's war effort hardly at all. The bomber barons indignantly rebutted Butt's statistics, but Churchill preferred the judgement of his scientific guru, and was absolutely right to do so. Either night bombing had to be given up or the plan of night bombing had to be changed. To give up the bombing of Germany was unthinkable. It was still the only way that Germany could be hurt in its heartland, it still promised to damage (even, according to its most devout high-priests, to wreck) the German war economy, and – what became a dominant factor in Churchill's reasoning until 1944 – it was a way of demonstrating to Stalin that, although it was not yet possible to open the Second Front Stalin urgently demanded, Britain was doing something aggressive and painful to help Russia and, despite what Russian generals liked to insinuate, was willing to take heavy losses in the process. Therefore a new plan was adopted, and a new chief appointed in February 1942 to execute it. The plan, which Portal had long been maturing, was for area bombing, and the new chief of Bomber Command was Air Marshal Sir Arthur ('Bert') Harris.

The theory of area bombing was an inversion of the bombing theory which had guided Bomber Command so far. Instead of aiming at particular targets and often missing them, the object now was to drop bombs within particular areas which they could hardly miss. These areas, it was presumed, could in a double sense be described as industrial: they would contain factories, railway yards and other economic targets, and they would con- tain the homes of the people who worked in those places. The workers would be, in Cherwell's euphemistic language, dehoused and demoralised. They would also probably be killed, but that was not, in the practised speech of Air Ministry spokesmen, the primary purpose of the operation or even a principal one. Right up to when Bomber Command at last went out of business, in mid April 1945, the official justification of its hugely destructive and death-dealing operations was that it was targeting military objectives and thus directly and legitimately weakening Germany's power to go on fighting.

This justification was at the same time true and not true – which is one of the reasons why the Strategic Air Offensive has always been controversial. Behind this more or less lawful-sounding screen Sir Arthur Harris (popularly known ever since as Bomber Harris but within his Command as 'Butch' Harris, because huge RAF casualties never deterred him from his purpose) and his subordinates pursued their own agenda of methodical city destruction within which the military-objective justification became increasingly difficult to perceive. The last generation's disputes about how much of a contribution they made towards winning the war have quietened down to a consensus opinion that indeed they did make a great contribution, though not entirely in the manner expected. Churchill himself put his finger on a less expected effect when he told the last of his series of talented private secretaries, 'the fact undoubtedly was that large numbers of German aircraft and vast resources of manpower and material were tied up in their air defence'.[6] An eminent authority on the subject sums up thus:

> The important consequence of the bombing was not that it failed to stem the increase in arms production, but that it prevented the increase from being very considerably greater than it was. [The] amount of war material that Germany might have been able to produce for the crucial battles of 1944 and 1945 without bombing would have meant a longer and far more costly battle for the final defeat of fascism, and might have made necessary the use of atomic weapons in Europe as well.[7]

The word 'decisive' has acquired crucial significance in this debate, because it was what the dedicated bombers claimed they could be. Those who insist on saying that Bomber Command played 'a decisive part' in Hitler's downfall may fairly do so in as much as the ultimate victory is unimaginable without it, but the same could be said of other commands and campaigns. Bomber Command, for all the resources it absorbed and for all the men it lost (about 56,000, a fearful total), did not play *the* 'decisive part' Harris hoped for, and which by his reckoning it only failed to achieve because it never received the first call on resources, and the giant's share of them, that he demanded. So many German cities were wrecked and civilian losses of such enormity were caused that it was not difficult for anyone outside the range of Harris's authority and influence to ask whether the British bombing of Germany had not to some extent become disproportionate and barbaric. Churchill himself, while watching at Chequers an Air Ministry film of German cities burning under Harris's assault, once burst out, 'Are we beasts? Are we taking this too far?'.[8]

What *did* Churchill think about it? There has been some confusion about this. Because he sometimes was heard to regret what was being done to

German cities and because, whatever he loyally said to Harris or Harris's critics, he never uncritically subscribed to the Harris belief in air power's ability to win a war over the heads of the other services, critical historians have wondered how much he approved of the man. A major item of evidence must be his 28 March 1945 minute to the Chiefs of Staff, beginning 'It seems to me that the moment has come when the question of bombing of German cities simply for the sake of increasing the terror, though under other pretexts, should be reviewed. Otherwise we shall come into control of an utterly ruined land ...' After the pregnant observation that 'The destruction of Dresden remains a serious query against the conduct of Allied bombing', it concludes: 'The Foreign Secretary has spoken to me on this subject, and I feel the need for more precise concentration upon military objectives, such as oil and communications behind the immediate battle-zone, rather than on mere acts of terror and wanton destruction, however impressive.'[9]

This much-quoted minute surely has some puzzling aspects. The evident facts about it are, first, that Portal objected to it, on the very reasonable ground that Bomber Command had done no more than Churchill and the War Cabinet had told them to do and approved of their doing for the past three years; and, secondly, that on 1 April a much milder minute was substituted for it, omitting the references to 'terror' and Dresden and focusing solely on the self-interested accommodation argument. At first glance the story of these minutes suggests that Churchill would have liked to discipline Harris but, just as Portal had done when similarly inclined not long before, drew back from the brink. But evidence sometimes brought forward to support that theory does not stand up, while other evidence points in the opposite direction. The refusal to allow Harris to do what was normal for Commanders-in-Chief at the end of successful campaigns, to issue a celebratory despatch about it, came from the Air Ministry and its rationale was a security one. That Harris was denied a peerage would appear to have been due not to Churchill but to Attlee. The decision to single out for distinction only the airmen who had fought in the Battle of Britain ('a gilt rose emblem to be worn on the ribbon of the 1939–45 Star') was not unreasonable, nor can it have been Churchill's sole responsibility. It is true that he may have been thought to do Bomber Command less than justice in his Victory world-broadcast of 13 May; so much being packed into that oration, the omission is equally noticeable and regrettable. It is true also that he retained an awareness that the Dresden raid could justly be criticised; when the draft of Harris's memoirs came to his hand twelve months or so later, he advised careful handling of it, and his mention of it in *The Second World War* seems inadequate and evasive. On the other hand, he professed indignation at the Attlee government's slights to Harris, and he boldly affronted *bien-pensant* opinion as soon as he returned to Number Ten by giving Harris the highest honour he would accept, a baronetcy. (Apart from living in South Africa, Harris thought the House of Lords was 'a morgue'.) [10]

His attitude towards Harris and bombing while the war was going on was of a piece with these gestures of loyalty and admiration after it had ended. For his backing of Bomber Command, Lord Cherwell had some responsibility. He was consistently enthusiastic for bombing and optimistic about its results. He played a conspicuous part in the introduction of the valuable navigational aid H2S, from which much improvement in accuracy was correctly anticipated. He also presented Churchill with damage-estimates that were encouragingly impressive, although they were not as scientific, nor as accurate, as he claimed. (His figures were in fact queried at the time by experts outside the magic circle, and therefore discounted within it – one of the several instances where 'The Prof's' influence worked to ill effect.) But apart from the personal influence of a trusted adviser and friend, there were many reasons why Churchill remained, or could not bear not to remain, a supporter of the area-bombing campaign. Like most other Britons, he got satisfaction from contemplating the initiators of city bombing being repaid in their own coin; 'tasting and gulping each month a sharper dose of the miseries they have showered upon mankind'.[11] There was nothing wrong with retribution. He believed the British public demanded it. He was sure Stalin appreciated it. Ever anxious to keep Stalin sweet, he was thankful that Bomber Command enabled him to claim that Britain was doing something that could broadly be understood to weaken German resistance to the Russian offensives. And in the absence of hard evidence to the contrary, which could not appear till the war was over, he could not contradict Harris's claims that great damage was being done to the German war-machine. He had to hope that the possibly greater damage to non-military places and persons, which the humane and sentimental sides of his mind regretted, was thereby justified. A few concerned Britons of social eminence raised their voices to question what was going on; Lord Salisbury in private, for example, and Bishop George Bell of Chichester very bravely in the House of Lords on 9 February 1944. Churchill and his government stood by Harris, laying the usual 'military objectives' smokescreen over the city-destruction realities; and it was universally believed that Bell's principled gesture ruled him out of consideration for the succession to the see of Canterbury, which became vacant later that year.

'Bert' Harris was one of the military commanders of whom Churchill saw most. He frequently received visits by Harris to Chequers (which was only a few miles from Bomber Command's headquarters at High Wycombe) until, after D-Day, it became more exciting to visit Eisenhower and Montgomery; and he allowed Harris a freedom of approach to him, and a freedom of speech upon great issues, often without prior reference to the Air Staff, denied to any other Commander-in-Chief. The official historians found that they could not write their book without spelling out the facts and consequences of this special relationship.

> Thus was the position of the Commander-in-Chief vis-à-vis the Air Staff enhanced beyond the theoretical limits of the constituted system of command. [This] relationship with the Prime Minister was an important factor in the extraordinary position which Sir Arthur Harris occupied ... Never, indeed, in British history had such an important Commander-in-Chief been so continuously close to the centre of government power as Sir Arthur Harris was to Mr Churchill.[12]

That having been the actual situation, it can no longer surprise that Churchill took no steps to pull Harris back into line – to lay off area-bombing and focus more on oil and transportation targets – during the autumn of 1944 and the winter following. When Portal, the Chief of Air Staff, Harris's only superior within the service, 'directed' him to do this, Harris refused and defied Portal to sack him. After that, only Churchill had the authority to intervene, and Churchill chose not to. He later told Anthony Montague Browne that the bombing 'did go on too long, and I pointed it out to the COS'. But mere 'pointing out' did not amount to much. It is difficult to believe that the already-cited minute of 28 March signified, what would have suited the image Churchill was proud to cultivate, that here was the civilian war leader unafraid to put in his place even so popular, press-favoured a warrior chief. But how did that minute come to smack of that image and to contain elements of the standard critiques of Harris? It may be that some sensible person, aware of issues likely to be raised in the war crimes trials fast approaching, sensed the need for pre-emptive action in advance of the possibility that British area-bombing, known in Germany (and in Sweden and Switzerland) as 'terror' bombing, might embarrassingly be cited in a *tu quoque* defence. Churchill was not unaware of the risks he and Harris ran. In a post-war letter which admitted to some unease about Dresden, he wrote that Harris

> should be very careful in all that he writes not to admit that we ever did anything not justified by the circumstances and the actions of the enemy in the measures we took to bomb Germany. We gave them full notice to clear out of their munition-making cities. In fact, they had very good shelters and protection, and the position of the civilian population was very different from that of London,

Coventry, Liverpool etc. when they were bombed in the second year of the war ...[13]

That was an unusual and not an ineffective line of justification; but of its bearing on Churchill's place in the history of the Bombing Offensive, each reader must judge for himself.

19

France and de Gaulle

'The Almighty in His infinite wisdom did not see fit to create
Frenchmen in the image of Englishmen.'

Secret Session Speech on 10 December 1942

One of the major difficulties dumped on Churchill in the early summer
weeks of 1940, a difficulty destined to run on until the very end of the war,
was how to handle the self-appointed representative of the Free French
people based in London, Général de Brigade Charles de Gaulle. By the
middle of June 1940 the mainland French government was asking for an
armistice, and Hitler's armies were on their way to controlling the French
coast from Dunkirk to Biarritz. What else could be done in London, it
might be asked, but to give up France for lost; to hope its purported
neutrality would not turn into German vassalage; to incorporate such armed
forces as de Gaulle might gather to himself within the Allied war effort;
and (in terms of the political cartoons of the period) to wait until John
Bull and, hopefully, Uncle Sam could liberate Marianne from the dragon's
chains? It was not as simple as that.

Churchill flew five times to France between 16 May and 13 June, striving
by this device or that to keep up the spirits of the Prime Minister, his friend
Paul Reynaud, and, once the government had left Paris for the south, to
urge it not to give up the fight but to carry it on from across the Mediterranean, where its immense African territories sheltered most of its navy
and over 400,000 of its soldiers. His encouragement was unavailing, not
least because the French leaders believed that Britain had let them down
by not bringing all its fighter aircraft across the Channel to help defend
France (in which Churchill thought them unreasonable: British losses in
May and June 1940 amounted to a thousand aircraft and four hundred
pilots and invasion was looming) and by sending an Expeditionary Force
inadequate in size, equipment and training (in which Churchill had to
acknowledge they were right, though this military feebleness was not of his
doing). There was even, at the last moment, his astonishing offer of an
'indissoluble union' between the United Kingdom and the French Republic

'against subjection to a system which reduces mankind to a life of robots and slaves'. But it was all to no avail. Reynaud was brought to the end of his tether on 16 June and made way for the defeatists headed by the aged Great War hero Marshal Pétain. Terms of armistice (a word more acceptable to the honour-obsessed military mind than surrender) were agreed on 22 June. Germany's armed forces were to control all France's western and northern regions, including Paris. Pétain's government established itself at Vichy early the following month, with sovereign authority over no more than an interior block of France and no coast other than the Mediterranean. Within Hitler's Europe France was now of little consequence, but it still cut a figure in world politics, with its overseas empire intact, as well as a large army and, within the terms of the armistice, a navy.

This conclusion to the Anglo-French alliance, grievously unsatisfactory to Churchill, would sooner or later seem unsatisfactory to many French people. It is difficult to know how many of those who remained obedient to Vichy did so in hope that the German domination would not last long or even that the Marshal, a patriot by his lights, would in course of time be able to break out the colours of restored national honour. The readiness of many Vichy Frenchmen to change sides when it became possible or profitable to do so makes it clear that many officers and administrators kept a corner of their minds open to such thoughts. Such people would have perfectly understood Churchill when, in his first broadcast to the French people on 21 October 1940, he recalled Gambetta's advice about what France had lost to Germany in 1871: 'Think of it always: speak of it never.'[1] Other Frenchmen and women of course definitively distanced themselves from Vichy. Jean Monnet, for example, subsequently architect of the European Union, was one of them; being already in England, he stayed there. Soon he was joined by the man who was to become the leader of them all and, many people would say, the greatest Frenchman of the century.

Churchill mentions in *The Second World War* how, in the hectic days before the armistice, he several times came across this 'impassive, imperturbable ... very tall, phlegmatic man', a junior general and junior minister, and how on the last of those occasions he said to himself (prompted no doubt by a recollection of the strongest and best French character in Shakespeare's *Henry V*), 'This is the Constable of France'.[2] He was therefore delighted when de Gaulle dramatically flew to Britain on 17 June ('carrying with him, in this small aeroplane, the honour of France'), and used his authority to enable de Gaulle to broadcast to the French people the very next day.

It was de Gaulle's primary task, and one which the British government was happy to help him get on with, to rally to his banner as many as he could of the French servicemen who had come to Britain from Dunkirk and the other ports of escape from the panzers. At this early stage he was not very successful, but 'ce n'est que le premier pas qui coûte'; the foundations were laid for the armed forces of France Libre recruited from all round the empire which, under the flag of Joan of Arc's cross of Lorraine, became strong enough in due course to combine with his Forces Françaises de l'Intérieure in the liberation of their own country and to go on to be in at the kill of Nazi Germany. Churchill was pleased to see de Gaulle beginning this long and difficult process, but more on his mind through the second half of June was the question of what was going to happen to the French fleet, almost every vessel of which accepted the armistice as ordered by its chief, Admiral Darlan. The French navy was very well trained and equipped and the fourth largest navy in the world: if its vessels became available for German use, as Churchill thought possible, the Royal Navy might lose the mastery of the seaways on which British survival depended. That prospect was a nightmare. Nothing in his whole life seems ever to have worried Churchill more. He had tried to persuade the French government not to sign anything until its fleet had sailed to British ports. Now the terms of the armistice required all French warships away from their home ports to return to them forthwith and then to disarm. The disarming would take time. What if Germany were to seize them before it had been done?

Churchill, with the War Cabinet solid behind him, was determined not to risk that happening. A tense and tragic drama ensued. Vichy was pressed for undertakings that would keep the warships away from all risk of German seizure. All it would give were assurances that the Germans would never be allowed to seize them – or, if the worst came to the worst, would find them unusable. The British naval officers involved were on the whole inclined to trust their French counterparts, whom they believed to dislike the Germans even more than they disliked the British. Churchill, having witnessed at first hand what he considered the moral weakness of Pétain, Weygand and the other defeatist soldiers to whom Admiral Darlan was tied, concluded they could not be trusted, and gave orders to the admirals commanding respectively in the eastern and western Mediterranean to bring pressure on the French fleets in Alexandria and Mers-el-Kebir, the port of Oran. If this could be done by negotiation, so much the better. But time was critical. If negotiation and a choice of options including sailing to comfortable demilitarisation in Martinique or luxurious internment in the United States didn't appeal, force would have to be used. At Alexandria, where he was in a strong position vis-à-vis Admiral Godfroy, Admiral Cunningham ignored Churchill's importunities to tough action to good effect; the operation was achieved without bloodshed. At Mers-el-Kebir, where the French were on French territory, Admiral Somerville was less fortunately placed. With Churchill's latest message in his pocket, commiserating with him on having to carry out 'one of the most disagreeable and difficult tasks that a British Admiral has ever been faced with', Somerville took his fleet from Gibraltar to Oran early on 3 July, arriving off the harbour at about half-past nine. Negotiations with Admiral Gensoul went on throughout the day, but seemed to be getting nowhere. It was an awful time for everybody, with the clocks ticking in the Admiralty as well as on the ships outside the Algerian port. Somerville had been given no choice but to settle the matter by nightfall. Nothing being settled as six o'clock approached, he opened fire not long before the arrival of the last signal of the day: 'French ships must comply with our terms or sink themselves or be sunk by you before dusk.' Most of them were put out of action within only a few minutes, and fifteen hundred French sailors were dead.

Was Churchill right or wrong? The question has been debated again and again, and there is no generally agreed conclusion. Churchill believed he was justified but took no pleasure in a 'hateful decision, the most unnatural and painful in which I have ever been concerned'. (Which was saying something.) The fundamental fault-line that lay, and still lies, beneath the debate concerned those most inflammatory of matters, honour and trust. The French admirals, perceived from London as 'the Vichy French', could not see why they should not be trusted; London could not see why they should be. On the surface, the debate was largely in terms of the reliability of the French naval officers' assurances and the intuitions of British naval officers regarding that reliability. Mentalities formed at public schools and in professional training institutions were not well equipped to understand what was going on in French official minds three weeks after a huge national humiliation; and, in any case, no matter how seriously the French assurances and British intuitions were taken, they could not eliminate all elements of risk. As for the Admiral-in-Chief, Darlan, Churchill had formed a poor opinion of a man who, after talking tough about never surrendering, had overnight become a prominent Pétainist. He felt he could not trust Darlan to keep his navy safe from German hands, any more than he could trust the Germans not to try to get their hands upon it. With the advantage of hindsight, it may be said that, if Somerville had been given another twenty-four hours for his negotiation with Gensoul, he might have come to an agreement that would have been satisfactory. In those desperate days, however, even twenty-four hours was too much for an all but overwrought Churchill to wait. He would not take the risk of shortening the odds against his country's survival. It was, he well knew, a most unwelcome way out of a totally unprecedented and unwanted difficulty. The British sailors who disliked it so much were not in a position to understand the global spread of political, economic and strategic considerations that lay upon the War Cabinet's table. To the world's watchful and wondering neutrals, no less than around the Empire and Commonwealth, it sent the message that Britain was not going to go the same way as France, and it had for Churchill a quite unexpected though very welcome by-product in the House of Commons, to which without a day's delay he explained what had happened: for the first time since his replacement of Chamberlain, the Conservatives cheered him to the echo.

For de Gaulle, who nobly swallowed whatever may have been his feelings about it, its immediate consequences were disastrous. Mers-el-Kebir came as manna from heaven to all who wished to convince themselves, or who were ready to be further convinced, that Britain was still *perfide Albion*, ever an untrustworthy ally, and that Marshal Pétain had been right to sever the tie. Sailors in French warships still at large, and French soldiers from Casablanca to Cochin China, from Martinique to Madagascar and in Britain too, who might have been persuaded to side with de Gaulle suffered a patriotic revulsion. The beginnings of his campaign to put France Libre on the map were enfeebled. And perhaps the honeymoon of his relations with Churchill came to an end sooner than it might have done.

Their relations with one another soon became fraught with tensions and touchiness. The touchiness was more on de Gaulle's side than Churchill's. On top of his own proper self-respect and Gallic pride, de Gaulle found himself in circumstances that would have tried the temper of a saint. The British government encouraged him boldly to denounce the Vichy administration as the betrayer of his nation's interest and honour, but he was not himself recognised as head of a government either in exile or *in posse*. Pétain's administration was still there, recognised by all neutrals as legitimate (the United States and, oddly, Canada maintained embassies at Vichy) and also by some belligerents, including the British, as at any rate a *de facto* administration with whom business might have to be done. By that administration, de Gaulle was denounced as a traitor and his life was declared forfeit. He was utterly dependent on hand-outs from his British hosts. The not very numerous French men and women who first joined him constituted a mercurial and, to the anxious eyes of British security, irresponsible anomaly – not at all like the sober governments-in-exile who were glad to be in London and who knew on which side their bread was buttered. Towards all these embarrassments his hosts were not unsympathetic. What they found difficult to be sympathetic about was de Gaulle's posture of hauteur and dignity, even calculated standoffishness, which he deemed necessary to maintain the great status of France among the nations. Churchill so greatly admired de Gaulle and so much wanted him to succeed in his rallying enterprise that he showed more patience towards him than towards any other bothersome person, and was able to empathise with his feelings.

> He had to be rude to the British to prove to French eyes that he was not a British puppet. He certainly carried out this policy with perseverance. He even one day explained this technique to me, and I fully comprehended the extraordinary difficulties of his problem. I always admired his massive strength.[3]

The two men never absolutely fell out with one another. Each appreciated the other's quality and at bottom they knew they had to stay on good working terms. Their relationship was punctuated by rows, some so bad that each privately said he would like to cut loose from the other if only circumstances permitted it. But circumstances never did. The rows were regularly followed by reconciliations, de Gaulle's cause steadily prospering in inverse proportion to the decline and disgrace of Vichy. Its satisfactory conclusion was General Leclerc's place at the head of the Allied entry into Paris, on 24 August 1944, and de Gaulle's own march along the Champs Elysées two days later. Even that happy ending (as it should have been) to his four years' exile was marred by one of their worst rows. On the eve of Overlord de Gaulle blew up because he had not been told of it earlier, Churchill and everyone else in SHAEF having been convinced by experience that any secret confided to the people around de Gaulle would be leaked. De Gaulle kept up the huff for weeks but it ended, as usual, with the return of kindness; his Committee of National Liberation having been, however tardily, recognised as the provisional government of France, he invited Churchill to visit Paris in style on 11 November 1944. Clementine and Mary accompanied him and had the gratification of seeing the two great men processing around the most famous public places together and hearing them make complimentary speeches about each other. Next day, the pair of them went to Besançon hoping to observe General de Lattre de Tassigny's army in action, but the weather was so terrible that the operation had to be postponed. What Churchill was able to observe, and enjoyed observing, was 'the awe, and even apprehension, with which half a dozen high generals treated de Gaulle in spite of the fact that he had only one star on his uniform and they had lots'.[4] Another formidable row blew up in May and June 1945 when de Gaulle quite mistakenly got the impression that Churchill was trying to manoeuvre the French out of the Levant, but that too blew over, and was indeed the last of the series; de Gaulle learned how Churchill had actually stood up for him at Potsdam, and Churchill was not a man to nurse grievances. Their mutual regard (it can hardly be called a friendship) continued until the older man died. In November 1958 de Gaulle, newly empowered as President, conferred on Churchill the honour, rare for a foreigner, of the Croix de la Libération. At Churchill's funeral seven years later, 'the Constable of France' stood tall among the mourners from abroad. He wrote to Clementine on the anniversary of her husband's death every year until he too passed into history.

The dimension of their relationship which gave Churchill the most grief was the three-cornered relationship between Britain, de Gaulle and the United States. Of course it was not in the General's mind when he raised his flag in London that he would ever become embroiled with Washington, but that inevitably happened once the United States was in the war. The Free French became co-beneficiaries with everyone else of the Lend-Lease programme, and had to be thankful that American armed forces would in due course add to the strength of the anti-German alliance. At the same time the American connection came with an awkward price tag. President Roosevelt had not, indeed had no opportunity to acquire, the personal rapport, the fellowship of comrades in arms, that bound Churchill and de Gaulle together. On the contrary, Roosevelt disliked whatever he heard of de Gaulle. Most of what he heard came from the State Department (which, because it maintained 'normal' diplomatic relations with Vichy, turned a cold shoulder towards Vichy's enemies). The American Joint Chiefs of Staff necessarily followed those leads as they shared in the planning of Operation Torch, the Anglo-American (in fact, mostly American) landings in North Africa early in November 1942 under the supreme command of General Eisenhower. With a view to minimising resistance, covert contacts were made with the more tractable and anti-German Vichy dignitaries, above all General Giraud with whom the Americans ill-advisedly hoped to trump Britain's French ace.

To simplify a tortuous and intricate story, these hopes of Vichy French neutrality or even assistance were largely realised, but less immediately through the wooden Giraud than through the slippery Admiral Darlan, who turned up unexpectedly, took charge, and entered into a ceasefire arrangement with Eisenhower which appeared to make him a sort of ally. This pragmatic deal with the Devil, although militarily convenient, was so repulsive to British opinion, and so tricky to explain to the House of Commons, that the embarrassed Churchill felt he could do so only in one of its rare secret sessions. But if it was unpalatable to Churchill, how much more so was it to de Gaulle. He said to Churchill,

> I don't understand you. You have fought since the first day. One could even say that you personally symbolise this war. Your armies are victorious in Libya. Yet you allow yourself to be towed along by the United States whose soldiers have

never even seen a German. It is up to you to take over the moral direction of the war.[5]

The particular Darlan difficulty disappeared as unexpectedly as it had arisen when he was assassinated by an anti-Pétainist zealot, but to Churchill's burdens was henceforth added that of bringing harmony into two troubled relationships: that between de Gaulle and Roosevelt; and that between de Gaulle and those of his compatriots who were ready to change horses in mid war. Churchill and Roosevelt got some amusement, and so did Churchill's family, out of their 'match-making' in respect of de Gaulle and Giraud. The 'shot-gun marriage' they joked about (with Eden as 'best man', Churchill himself as 'the heavy father', etc.) was consummated with the world's press as witness on the last day of the Casablanca conference, in January 1943: 'de Gaulle and Giraud were made to sit in a row of chairs, alternating with the President and me, and we forced them to shake hands in public before all the reporters and photographers'.[6] The gesture meant as much and as little as most such staged scenes usually mean. Giraud did not stay long in the limelight. He lacked de Gaulle's political sense and personal grandeur, and he had none of the rapport with the Forces Françaises de l'Intérieur that de Gaulle was painfully building up. Churchill realised long before Roosevelt that the Council of National Liberation, another Gaullist creation, was the natural and proper body to assume the provisional governance of France as its liberation progressed. His efforts to persuade Roosevelt and his State Department to see this European sense made extra work for him in the busy summer of 1944. Relations thereafter improved remarkably, and in October Washington, with that lack of sensitivity towards an ally perceptible on other occasions, announced its recognition of de Gaulle's provisional government without having first informed the British Foreign Office.

20

Russia and Stalin

'Trying to maintain good relations with a Communist is like wooing a crocodile. You do not know whether to tickle it under the chin or to beat it over the head.'

Churchill as reported by Alan Brooke, 24 January 1944

The news of Germany's invasion of the Soviet Union on 22 June 1941 came as a surprise to all Britons and a moral perplexity to some. There seemed to be advantage in the German military machine's commitment on another front, but what if Germany were to defeat Russia and return with doubled strength to the assault on Britain? Hitler would not have launched the operation named Barbarossa had he not expected his armies to outclass Stalin's, and the greater part of British military opinion reckoned that indeed they would. Churchill for many months feared that they might. The only sector of British opinion which knew exactly what to think about the prospect was the Communist Party. Since September 1939 it had denounced the war as a capitalists' war. Its instant new line was that Britain should do all it could to help the Soviet Union. Non-Communists might come to the same conclusion, but some of them only with difficulty and embarrassment. Soviet Communism having been judged bad for so long, how could it so quickly become good?

Churchill made his mind up at once. He distinguished between the Russian people and the Soviet regime. He had disliked what he persisted in calling Bolshevism as much as anyone and more than most. He had immensely resented the material aid that the Soviet Union had given to Germany over the past eighteen months, aid that among other things had rendered nugatory the British blockade. What made him ready now to rally to Russia, as he liked to call it, was above all his urgent desire to keep Hitler's armies engaged. Commando pinpricks, Bomber Command's nuisance raids and even the weightier blows that he kept hoping for in the North African deserts were small beer beside the giant clash of arms promised on the broad plains of western Russia. His mind was not unprepared for this somersault. Respecting the principles of the balance of power and national self-interest, he had long maintained that Russia had much to fear from a resurgent Germany. Once Germany had come under the domination of Nazi ideology, Churchill supposed that the makers of Soviet foreign policy, if they were sensible, would be as ready for a military alliance with 'the West'; and 'the West', if it was sensible, ought to be ready for a military alliance with the Soviet Union. There were elements of the fanciful and the risky in this policy prescription but it cannot be dismissed as having been *less* likely to have served the security of Europe than the policies actually followed under the premierships of Baldwin and Chamberlain; there was no way out of the 1930s with guaranteed safety, not even the way of dishonour. To most Conservatives in that decade, the idea of compromising with Communism was odious. Their idea of the Soviet Union was not of a state that might be an ally against Germany but rather of a state which Germany ought to be allowed to beat up whenever it thought the time had come to do so.

The Nazi-Soviet Non-Aggression Pact of 23 August 1939 – the moment when, as a Foreign Office wag memorably put it, the isms became wasms – shunted this anti-Soviet attitude temporarily into limbo, but it became tenable again from 22 June 1941. Whatever Churchill and the War Cabinet decided to do with regard to the Soviet Union was bound to be controversial twice over: both at the time they did it and in the coming time when its consequences would become clear. Some have argued that British interests would have been better served in the long run had Germany and the Soviet Union been left to fight it out; but that only makes sense on the very shaky assumption that Germany would not have won such a victory or come to such terms as would have given Hitler everything he wanted: the oil of the Caucasus, the grain and minerals of the Ukraine, a land-route to India outflanking the Middle East, and much more. Such an outcome would have been enormously to Britain's disadvantage. But alliance with the Soviet Union undoubtedly had distasteful aspects. Conservatives who were prepared to believe Churchill's decision the right one never got over their discomfort at finding themselves fighting on the same side as 'Asiatic hordes' who were 'barbaric' as well as 'Red'. Churchill not only understood those prejudices, he actually shared them; but, so long as the war was still to be won, he sternly suppressed their expression by himself and in the press and in any other public places where they threatened to appear. He would offer support to Stalin as a fellow-fighter in the same good cause – and one who, it was generally feared, would need it. Even if Hitler's armies should in the end prove the better, Churchill felt sure that Barbarossa was Hitler's biggest mistake yet, just as the invasion of Russia had been Napoleon's. The important thing was to keep the Russians fighting for as long as possible.

What happened on 22 June came as no surprise to Churchill. British Intelligence had been predicting Barbarossa for many weeks. Churchill had warned Stalin to get ready for it, as had some of Stalin's own informers, but he paid no heed, for reasons which are still not absolutely clear. Poised to offer the hand of military friendship, Churchill had prudently ascertained that the American President would be sympathetic. The BBC was instructed to clear the way for a Prime Ministerial broadcast at 8.45 p.m. that same evening. It was not one of his most persuasive orations, because he had to get round the fact, which he saw no point in denying, that he had never liked Communism and still didn't. Implicit was the judgement that Nazism was even wickeder than Communism. The explicit grounds for entering into alliance with the world's one Communist state lay in his distinction between its official creed and its people's common humanity. It needed a very hard Conservative heart to reject the latter plea. Churchill concluded with an expression of conviction that 'the Russian danger is our danger, and the danger of the United States, just as the cause of any Russian fighting for his hearth and home is the cause of free men and free peoples in every quarter of the globe'.[1]

His hope or expectation that this broadcast would elicit a grateful response was disappointed. In early July therefore he did with Stalin what he always did when new stars appeared in his constellation; he sought to 'put himself in close personal relations' and 'friendly touch' with the man whom he would soon be describing as the 'profound Russian statesman and warrior'. He succeeded, but the relationship thus begun gave him more exasperation and grief than any other, even that with General de Gaulle. With de Gaulle, after all, he could release his feelings in a good row, but with the ogre of the Kremlin and his implacable Foreign Minister Molotov he felt it necessary to keep his temper, and he usually succeeded in doing so. (He admitted that Molotov did once tell him to calm down.) He found them 'surly, snarling, grasping, and [what especially irked him] so lately indifferent to our survival'. The Russia which by his reckoning owed gratitude to Britain and her Allies proved unreasonable in its demands and ungrateful for the sacrifices made on its behalf.[2]

Stalin's demands were comprised under two main heads, of which the first was military supplies. He wanted everything that Britain and America could send: tanks, aeroplanes, trucks, guns, rubber, aluminium, boots, and all sorts of other stuff in vast quantities. Britain itself was short of most of these things and the United States was still gearing up to begin its Lend-Lease deliveries. Churchill nevertheless held that it was supremely important to try to meet these demands; initially because he really feared that Russia would have to capitulate, and as time went on because Russia was seriously fighting back. Aid for Russia involved a double measure of sacrifice. There were no routes from Britain to Russia other than around the north of Norway or across some part of Asia, Persia for preference. Its Shah proving reluctant to cut his German connections, British and Russian military action in August backed a coup which opened the way for supplies to go by rail from the Persian Gulf to the Caspian Sea. Getting it going took months. It was possible, however, to open the sea-route round the North Cape at once. The first convoy sailed even before Persia was brought onside. Thus began one of the most courageous and painful campaigns of the war. In winter, when ice prevented the ships from getting further than Murmansk, the weather conditions were frightful. In the summer months, when Archangel became accessible, almost unbroken daylight gave the Germans (U-boats, surface warships and Luftwaffe) ideal opportunities to find and sink them. The Royal Navy protected the convoys as best it could, but its own resources were already overstretched. The Russian navy hardly helped at all. The worst of many bad experiences was the tragic (and arguably mismanaged) convoy PQ17, which lost twenty-six out of its thirty-seven ships in midsummer 1942. Summer hazards and winter weather sometimes enforced cancellations. Stalin's monotonous complaints that the British weren't trying hard enough or giving enough struck Churchill as extraordinarily unreasonable, but what hurt him most was a human, or rather inhuman touch: Stalin's refusal to relax his regime's obsessively suspicious attitude towards foreigners for the benefit of the brave sailors (volunteers, moreover) who had survived long enough to attain the Russian ports. Churchill thought they were entitled to a good time on shore; the Russian authorities didn't.

Stalin's second demand was for the opening of a military diversion in western Europe; a Second Front, as it very soon became popularly known. Until it really happened, Stalin and his generals could not be persuaded that the British (and from 1942 the Americans with them) did not privately share the resolve to fight to the last Russian. Churchill was willing to see merchant sailors and bomber crews hazard their lives in his three-year effort to persuade Stalin otherwise. But he was unable to produce, until June 1944, the Second Front that alone would have definitively convinced him. When this demand was first formulated, before June 1941 was out, Churchill was characteristically excited by it and for several weeks put it at the top of the list of offensive operations he drove the Chiefs of Staff to consider. It was not long before they had persuaded him that any operation of the desired weight was utterly out of the question in what remained of 1941 and improbable for the foreseeable future. The Russians persisted in seeming not to understand what the obstacles were – how far they really couldn't and how far they were being disingenuous and contemptuous, it is impossible to estimate – and their expectations were boosted when the Americans came into the war proclaiming their purpose to make a landing on the Continent before the year 1942 was out.

We have already seen how this idea was, with much difficulty and only after a presidential veto, squashed, and how the Torch landings in North Africa were substituted for it. For Churchill that was very satisfactory; for Stalin most unsatisfactory. His hopes had been raised only to be dashed again, and the German armies were still smashing their way into the Russian heartlands. Churchill resolved to break the news to him personally, and with a suitable military entourage undertook the 10,000 miles round-trip. He admitted that on the last leg of the flight, from Tehran to Moscow, on 12 August 1942, he felt as if he was 'carrying a large lump of ice to the North Pole'.[3] His conversations with Stalin passed off better than they might have done (unlike those between their respective military chiefs), and the visit ended with one of the interminable dining- and drinking-sessions which favoured visitors to Russia had to go through; Churchill proving better able to handle it than most. He returned to Britain 'with new resolve to aid Russia to the very limits of our power'. But if he thought that his brief encounter with 'Uncle Joe' would conjure more geniality into the correspondence regarding the Arctic convoys, he was to be disappointed. It actually became so much more unreasonable, so distressing to Churchill that it fills most of a chapter of *The Second World War*. The chapter however ended on a happier note: the defeat of the German Sixth Army at Stalingrad which, taken in tandem with a success at last for British and Commonwealth arms at El Alamein, marked (as he stylishly put it), if not the beginning of the end of the war, at least the end of the beginning.

The only worthwhile cards in Churchill's hand at the Kremlin talks were the British Bombing Offensive (just then beginning to be joined by the Americans) and the Allied commitment to Operation Torch with its promise to take the pressure off Russia by 'attacking the soft belly of the [Axis] crocodile'. He put it to Stalin that, if the North African operations went as hoped and were vigorously exploited, Hitler would find his forces under as much pressure from across the Mediterranean as they ever could from across the Channel. With this alternative, and an accompanying vague hope that a Second Front might be undertaken in 1943, Stalin for the time being had to be content. The decision to postpone it yet again at the Casablanca conference in early 1943 was accompanied by a positive commitment to launch a Second Front in May 1944, no matter what Mediterranean or other operations might by then be going on.

Stalin was helped to find this acceptable by the fact that the Great Fatherland War was going his way at last. Ever-increasing quantities of supplies were arriving from the USA and his armies were beginning to win victories. Churchill would have found it more acceptable had there not continued to lap around the foundations of his authority a popular agitation under the banner 'Second Front Now'. Fomented by the Communist Party, whose object was purely political, it attracted the support of a broad band of the left-inclined and the warm-hearted who had not a clue regarding the strategic and military issues involved. Failure to open a Second Front before 1944 became a common item in popular and, needless to say, left-wing post-mortems on the war. In the third volume of his own account, published in 1950, Churchill complained that 'Niagaras of folly and misstatement still pour out on this question of the Second Front'. The agitation had galled him on several grounds. He had known, though he was not able to publicise the fact, that aid went to Russia at the expense of the British and imperial forces in Burma and North Africa, and probably contributed to his country's humiliations and failures in those theatres, not to mention the groundswell of criticism of his leadership in early and mid 1942. He had done his best to suppress the publication of matters injurious to Stalin's reputation, without receiving anything in return. With five years' sobering experience of the post-war world, and 'Without in the slightest degree challenging the conclusion which history will affirm, that the Russian resistance broke the power of the German armies', his memory of the 'Second Front Now' agitation was understandably bitter.[4]

The Arctic convoys, the Bombing Offensive and the Mediterranean surrogates for a Second Front were Churchill's three means of satisfying Stalin that, contrary to what he and the Russian people generally believed or were led to believe, the Red Army was not being left to fight the Wehrmacht on its own. Churchill had a good case, and found plenty to say about it. What he did not like discussing with Stalin was the other big matter on Stalin's mind: what the Soviet Union could look forward to when the war was brought to a victorious conclusion. This meant, to put it with forcible bluntness, what Churchill and Roosevelt had in mind regarding Poland.

In every philosophy of war and peace, states engaged in war are presumed to have war aims; success or failure in war being measured in proportion as those aims are achieved or not, perhaps also as to whether they are rational or not. Churchill has been criticised for pursuing no aim beyond survival until it was too late to plan for anything else; implying that the other principal belligerents did better, having war aims that went beyond mere survival and pursuing them successfully. This line of criticism is somewhat unreasonable. War aims, if they are to be realistic, have to be shaped in relation to situations and events. The Polish element in Britain's initial war aims put them in a peculiar situation from the start, while the diversity of Britain's interests, European as well as imperial, placed its aims peculiarly at the mercy of unpredictable turns of events.

America's and Russia's war aims were comparatively simple and stayed so. Before the former was attacked by Japan, which gave it a straightforward war aim on its Pacific side, the aim of the United States in joining Britain's war against Germany was to make sure that the post-war world would be one in which Americans and their business could be safe and prosperous: a world certainly freed of Nazism but also, so far as could be secured, of imperialism. The Soviet Union's war aim was the simple one of repelling the Germans and securing its borders against renewed attack by them on its European side and by Japan, a bad neighbour, on its Asian. With the latter, which Roosevelt and Stalin easily settled between them, Churchill had little cause to interfere; his long-term worries were less about Japan than America's protégé China, potentially inimical to Hong Kong. But the post-war settlement in Europe was very much his business. Britain had gone to war against Germany in September 1939 not so much to protect its Empire but to prevent the continental hegemony of Germany and to protect the independence of the lesser states of Europe, eastern as well as western. Embracing the Soviet Union as a co-belligerent in June 1941, an event totally unforeseeable in September 1939, brought with it the problem that the Soviet Union had its own ideas about what should happen to those states after the war, especially Poland. Poland therefore became, in the context of war aims, Churchill's biggest headache.

Pre-war Poland in itself had been of no interest to Britain other than as an unusual piece in the balance of power chess game. Poland's inter-war government liked to present its country as a militarily formidable one, a valuation which its larger neighbours were to begin with, and for propaganda purposes, prepared to accept. But what had been plausible in the 1920s was totally implausible by the later 1930s. Hitler planned to take over Poland as soon as he judged it diplomatically safe to do so. After Czechoslovakia had been devoured in mid March 1939, Poland was obviously next in line. Therefore the Chamberlain government, moved to make a stand at last, guaranteed Poland's territorial integrity at the end of that month; a verbal guarantee given paper backing on 25 August, two days after the signing of the Nazi-Soviet Pact and to all appearances a stout response to it. True, there was not the slightest chance of Britain or the co-guarantor France protecting Poland's territory if and when Hitler attacked it, but the guarantee was more than an empty one in as much as, first, it gave Britain a lawful pretext for declaring war on Germany and, secondly, it made Britain the obvious destination for the Polish government-in-exile, which naturally looked to Britain to see it safe home when the war was over.

Churchill had enormous admiration for Polish military gallantry, and he often expressed gratitude that Polish combatants made such a fine showing among the continental contingents in the anti-German coalition, but he knew too much about history, strategy and statecraft to be surprised by the German-Russian partition of Poland completed by the end of September 1939; nor was he outraged by Stalin's subsequent seizures of Lithuania, Latvia and Estonia. He understood them to be justified as projections of Russia's line of defence against its likeliest attacker; and if anyone had pointed out to him the parallel with the strong-arm policies he regularly urged with regard to obstructive or unresponsive little neutrals, he would have found it impossible to disagree.

Poland, at the same time, was a special case. Churchill was caught between a rock and a hard place, with his head on the first and his heart on the latter. Stalin intimated at the first opportunity that he expected Russia's post-war western boundary to lie where it had done at the end of September 1939; which was in fact rather like the line that had been proposed by the British Foreign Secretary, Lord Curzon, in 1919. So long as the outcome of the war was in doubt, Churchill avoided or evaded this Polish problem, leaving it (as he sought to leave all dealings with the governments-in-exile) to his confidential agent Desmond Morton and the Foreign Secretary, Anthony Eden. The topic was scarcely raised – how could it have been while the Russian armies were still retreating? – during his visit to Moscow in August 1942. By the time 'the Big Three' met at Tehran in November 1943, however, the tide of war had turned and the Russian armies were grinding their way westwards. Poland's post-war borders therefore needed to be discussed. Churchill found himself unable to reject Stalin's case for a return more or less to the 'Curzon Line'. They agreed that Poland could be compensated at Germany's expense with a western frontier further west than it had been before the wars, on the line of the rivers Oder and Neisse. This was old-style Great Power diplomacy and statecraft, as was the 'percentages' deal in October 1944 by which Churchill and Stalin agreed upon spheres of influence in the Balkans. It had the singular merit of recognising facts of power and possession, but it did not look good to those who knew their Atlantic Charter and who hoped for great and good things from the improved version of the League of Nations, which (so increasing numbers of democrats everywhere believed) was going to set the tone for the post-war world and make its rules. Churchill's attempts to persuade the London Poles that their country's sidestep westwards was a reasonable and realistic solution to the problem they inadvertently presented were unsuccessful;

partly because they persisted in regarding not themselves but the Soviet Union as the problem, but also because they had friends in press and Parliament among unreconstructed Red-haters and former Chamberlainites, as well as support in the Dominions.

National territory was one thing; form and composition of government something else. Churchill had strong principles regarding the latter, but no more than any other national leader was Churchill able to magic perfect matches between order and freedom. Stalin would have been difficult about the form and composition of Poland's post-war government anyway, but the difficulties were magnified by the intransigeance in this respect of the Poles in London. Churchill was willing to take great pains to edge them towards acceptance of the changed boundaries which history inexorably pressed on them, insisting that the leaders of the London Poles should join him in Moscow in October 1944 and try to come to an accommodation with the Moscow-backed Poles in Lublin. But he was not willing to believe that history also condemned their country to become Communist. He understood that the leader of a Great Power with a disastrous modern history of invasions from the west was entitled to take steps to prevent their continuation, and that this must mean the making of defensive arrangements with the neighbours on that side. But he did not want to accept Stalin's axiom that the political system of a liberated country should as a matter of course be determined by its liberator. This point was embarrassing to argue about, however, in as much as Britain and the United States accepted the axiom as the guide for their own liberating conduct. The only way to argue about it was on the ideological ground that Britain and America were entitled to impose their idea of a democratic regime but Stalin was not entitled to impose his, because theirs was good and his was bad. Which is indeed what Churchill believed and, now that the war was nearly won, could admit to believing. From that view of the situation, there was no way out but a trial of strength, of which he was now and then driven darkly and desperately to mutter during the war's last months.

To this final phase of the war, when he came to it in the closing volume of his memoir-history, he gave the title *Triumph and Tragedy*. Squeezed between so many uncongenial *faits accomplis*, Churchill did not enjoy the last nine months of the war as much as he had expected to do. The Red Army was doing most of the hard fighting on the ground. At some moment in the summer of 1944, Britain and its imperial partners became, in numbers of military personnel, what they had long been in terms of war materials: junior partners to the United States in the western European war. (Of course they had always been junior partners in the Pacific one.) Churchill continued gamely to fight Britain's corner in the Grand Alliance, but he

had ever fewer good cards in his hand and, showing signs of fatigue here
as in domestic affairs, he was playing them less skilfully. The young William
Hayter noted at the final summit:

> Churchill was tired and below his form. He also suffered from the belief that he
> knew everything, and need not read briefs ... Stalin and Molotov, always very
> well briefed, would put pointed questions. 'What's the answer to that?', the Prime
> Minister would say, turning round with difficulty to his advisers sitting behind
> him. We could not say 'if you had read our brief you would know ...'[5]

His fears about the Soviet regime had been confirmed in the unending
course of his involvement with the Polish question. In the spring of 1943
the Germans unearthed at Katyn the graves of many thousands of Polish
officers and dignitaries massacred three years or so earlier, they alleged, by
Stalin's NKVD; believing this to be probably the case, Churchill was pained
to feel obliged nevertheless to advise the London Poles not to publicise the
matter. They persisted however in doing so – with the predictable consequence that Moscow broke off relations with them, and began to organise
a provisional government of its own, the Lublin Committee. In the later
summer of 1944 there was the tragic affair of the Warsaw Rising. The Polish
'Home Army', loyal to the London Poles, by extraordinary covert endeavours
had gathered strength to liberate the national capital before the Red Army
got there. To Churchill and to everyone else in the West, where the news
about it was freely available, it seemed that the Poles' gallant action only
needed some Russian assistance to make it complete and permanent; and
the Red Army was indeed very close. But Stalin proved unsympathetically
immovable, declining either to order his soldiers to advance or to allow
Allied planes landing facilities in Russian territory so that they could drop
supplies on Warsaw without running out of fuel in the process. Churchill's
outrage vented itself in an exceptional output of telegrams, some of minor-
speech length. Stalin's responses being consistently negative, most of these
telegrams went to the American President, whose responses were discouraging too; he was *not* going to be driven into a row with Stalin and he was
not going to allow any distraction from the great military operation progressing under General Eisenhower's supreme command in France.

The Polish question was prominent on the agenda of the Yalta summit
meeting in February 1945. Yalta in the Crimean Riviera was the furthest
from home that the Russian dictator would agree to travel, so Churchill and
Roosevelt were again the ones who had to make long flights. Churchill
had now turned seventy. Sarah and Lord Moran, accompanying him, were
concerned when he developed a temperature of over 100 degrees Fahrenheit
en route, but he rapidly got over it (with the aid of Moran's mysterious

medications), as he almost always did. By the middle of the conference he was 'drinking buckets of Caucasian champagne which would undermine the health of any ordinary man', noted one of the Foreign Office mandarins in his entourage.[6] The boundaries of the major Allies' prospective zones of military occupation of Germany were finalised and, by Churchill's insistence, France was given a zone too, carved out of the British and American allocations. Churchill had a brush with Stalin about reparations, arguing as he had done in 1919 that Germany must be allowed to recover its natural economic place in Europe and that, once Nazism was done away with and the power of 'Prussia' (his imaginary bugbear) diminished, magnanimity was the best treatment for the German people. Roosevelt, by now visibly failing, gave less support than his friend had hoped for. What was likely to happen in Europe was less interesting to the USA than what it wanted to happen in Asia, which meant fixing the terms for Russia's entry into the war against Japan. It was also important to Roosevelt to get confirmation of the terms of the Soviet Union's participation in the United Nations Organisation, the inaugural meeting of which was scheduled for San Francisco only two months later. Churchill and the Foreign Office were not as keen on this great venture as Roosevelt and the State Department; the British did not share the American confidence that issues difficult to decide about now would become less difficult when the UN was up and running. All that they could do with regard to Poland, the subject of no fewer than seven out of the eight plenary meetings of the Yalta Conference and the interchange of nearly eighteen thousand words between Stalin, Roosevelt and Churchill, was the Declaration on Liberated Europe, recapitulating the Atlantic Charter's promise of 'free elections' to all the liberated or (in the case of Axis allies) 'purified' countries.[7] But Stalin's idea of free elections was not Churchill's, and the Russian dictator made it clear that he would not tolerate any government in Warsaw that might be 'unfriendly'.

Between the Yalta summit and the final one at Potsdam, at the end of August 1945, relations with the Soviet Union became worse, not better. Churchill could not escape the impression that it was all give on the western side, all take on Stalin's. He had not expected this when he embraced the Russians as comrades-in-arms four years earlier. It looked as if the whole of Eastern, Central and Balkan Europe was on the way to becoming Communist. Poland was only the most acute and longest-running of his political concerns. The constant grinding of anxiety and distress about the future of the lands in the grasp of the Soviet armies was aggravated from time to time by flare-ups arising from the Russians' singular fears and suspicions. They suspected that Britain and the USA would be tempted to come to an armistice arrangement on their western fronts which would work to the

Russians' disadvantage. Their fears took three forms. Either the German divisions which surrendered in the west would reinforce their comrades on the eastern front (which was what the German military opposition, such as it was, always held out as a carrot in its sporadic communications with London); or they would be encouraged to surrender en masse to the Allies rather than the Russians (which all German soldiers who knew what was good for them wanted to do); or their surrender would simply enable the British and Americans to romp eastwards without opposition, as Churchill would have liked to do given favouring circumstances and (by this stage of the war) indispensable American backing.

Churchill's sense of honour and obligation prevented him from contemplating any deal with Germans, but he did become obsessed with the idea of establishing a victory line as far eastwards as possible, and preferably beyond Berlin; not because he anticipated holding that line ad infinitum – it would be far beyond the West's zones of occupation as provisionally agreed long ago – but because he thought it would provide bargaining chips for the next summit, which he hoped to turn into a showdown. Nothing, after all, could be more predictable.

> As a war waged by a coalition draws to its end political aspects have a mounting importance. In Washington especially longer and wider views should have prevailed. It is true that American thought is at least disinterested in matters which seem to relate to territorial acquisitions, but when wolves are about the shepherd must guard his flock, even if he does not himself care for mutton.[8]

But his pleadings and arguments, telegram upon telegram, aroused no sympathetic response in Washington. (It is impossible to avoid the impression that the more he wrote, the less the recipients paid attention.) The last communication he ever received from Roosevelt, despatched indeed on the very day of the latter's death, 12 April 1945, expressed the same unruffled magisterial optimism Roosevelt had shown with regard to Stalin since their first encounter at Tehran, nearly eighteen months before:

> I would minimise the general Soviet problem as much as possible, because these problems, in one form or another, seem to arise every day, and most of them straighten out ... We must be firm, however, and our course thus far is correct.[9]

Churchill, understanding how unfamiliar with high affairs of state an American Vice-President was likely to be, especially when he had been in office for less than three months, sought to arouse in the new President Harry S. Truman a greater sense of urgency, but with little success. He longed to do his usual thing of 'establishing friendly contact', but the times were not propitious. He was fully occupied with the German surrenders on 8 and 9 May; Victory celebrations and speeches; the end of the British coalition government on the 23rd; and, soon afterwards, the onset of campaigning for the general election which would happen on 5 July. Truman for his part was more than fully occupied, learning the ropes of presidential authority in Washington and assuring his Chiefs of Staff that, now the war was won in Europe, there should be no distraction from hastening to win it in the Pacific and to get the boys home. Churchill longed for the end of the Pacific war as ardently as Truman or anyone else, but he could not take the same easy view of the situation in Europe, and he sought to convey to the American President his pessimistic appreciation of it. On 12 May 1945 he sent the telegram containing the most famous phrase he contributed to world history. The Allies' armed forces, he remarked, were fast disappearing from Europe. Under present arrangements, all of them would soon have departed except for 'the moderate forces' required to occupy Germany. 'Meanwhile, what is to happen about Russia?' He summarised the still-spreading extent of Soviet influence over eastern Europe and the Balkans (excepting Greece, where Stalin had given him a free hand and where he had dashingly intervened at Christmas 1944), and reminded Truman that the Russian armies were not in any haste to disband. Then came the punch-line:

> An iron curtain is drawn down upon their front. We do not know what is going on behind ... Surely it is vital now to come to an understanding with Russia, or see where we are with her, before we weaken our armies mortally or retire to the zones of occupation.[10]

'Understanding' and 'seeing where we are' were euphemisms for what he was perhaps afraid to spell out too precisely – his thoughts during these first weeks of peace that a show of strength would make Stalin more tractable. To some extent, no doubt, these thoughts were prompted by the criticisms, of the unreconstructed Chamberlainites, that he was appeasing Stalin. And there was truth in the charge, although in its simpler form it took no account of the difference between appeasing a dictator who was sure to become your enemy and appeasing a dictator who had for a while been your valued friend. He kept these dangerous ideas about confronting Stalin to himself and his closest friends, and conveyed them only in elliptical terms to the American President. Since the latter paid little attention to them, they never came out in public at that time, and Churchill was spared the shock he would have surely have had if the British armed forces had been instructed to halt demobilisation and to devote themselves to martial pursuits all over again, this time against the people they had for four years been admiring as their gallant allies. In this respect, as in some others, he was thoroughly out of touch with public opinion. There could be no repetition of the magic that had worked in the summer of 1940.

His hope that he could repeat with Truman what he had achieved with Roosevelt was dashed before they met at the last wartime summit at Potsdam, near Berlin, between 17 July and 2 August 1945. Truman believed, as already did most non-Communists, that Stalin had defaulted on his Yalta undertakings regarding the eastern European countries. But there was a limit to how far he and his Secretary of State, James Byrnes, would go in continuing the dispute. Preoccupied with the war against Japan, Truman was unwilling to give Stalin an excuse to welsh on his promise to declare war on Japan three months after the war in Europe ended: on 8 August. Churchill felt discontented and out of it. The background presence of the leader of His Majesty's Opposition, whom he had chivalrously taken with him just in case the election went Labour's way, was a reminder of political mortality. He hated becoming the minor partner and thought that the other two were mean not to bring into their current account what they owed to the Britain of 1940. One of the Foreign Office contingent described the meeting as not so much the Big Three as the Big Two-and-a-Half. Churchill didn't like the compromise bargains proposed by the American and Russian Foreign Secretaries about Poland's western border and German reparations, and in the closing chapter of *The Second World War* he recalls how he was gearing up 'to come to grips with the Soviet Government' and 'to have a show-down at the end of the Conference'.[11] That was how he looked back on it after five years of the Cold War. Was he really so determined at the time? An expert comments: 'It is hard to see what he could have done, beyond perhaps insisting that British dissatisfaction was recorded in the Protocol in some form of words that did not wreck the whole conference.'[12]

The world however was never to know what he would actually have done, and to what effect. He and Mary went back to London on the 25th, to be there for next day's announcement of the general election results. Not Winston Churchill and Anthony Eden would go back to Potsdam, but Clement Attlee and Ernest Bevin.

21

Victory Overcast

'The decision of the British people has been recorded ... I have therefore
laid down the charge which was placed upon me in darker times.'

Churchill's message to the nation on 26 July 1945

Events in Britain from May to July 1945 brought Churchill back with a
bump from his global soaring. He had to give his mind to domestic
matters which he had been glad to leave to others since the formation of
his coalition five years before. The terms on which the coalition had been
formed required it to come to an end with the achievement of victory in
Europe; a commitment that Churchill confirmed when in October 1944 he
proposed yet again the prolongation of the Parliament. With great issues
of world order queuing up to be settled, victory over Japan still to be won,
and in any case preferring to withhold from party what was meant for
mankind, Churchill was far from eager to return to the ding-dong of
ordinary parliamentary politics, but there was no avoiding it now. The
Conservatives who had acclaimed him as leader in 1940 had no objection
to being in a government labelled 'National' or 'Coalition' so long as they
dominated it, but Labour unsurprisingly thought differently. The Labour
Party's annual conference was scheduled for mid May 1945, and although
Clement Attlee and Ernest Bevin might personally have been willing to
carry on in coalition for a bit longer, their party gave them no choice. It
had long been looking forward to the return of peacetime politics and
wanted to get on with them. The latter days of May therefore witnessed
the resignation of the Labour ministers. Hugh Dalton recalled how, at a
farewell party at Number Ten, Churchill inimitably told them, with tears
streaming down his cheeks, that the light of history would shine on all
their helmets.[1] Then came the formation of a caretaker government, without
Labour content, and the announcement of 5 July as the date for the general
election.

For this election, now fast approaching, Churchill's former Labour colleagues were the better prepared. This was not because they had been less
than properly supportive of the national war effort. On the contrary, they

had been prominent and efficient in the front lines of government, incidentally getting experience as 'an effective governing party for the first
time'.[2] Churchill had been glad to embrace them as co-governors for the
same reasons and with the same single-mindedness as, twelve months later,
he embraced the Russians as co-belligerents. The all-important things in
Churchill's anxious mind in those dark days had been to survive and, that
once assured, sooner or later to conquer. His mind did not readily run
beyond that mark, and he did not like to see other people giving it too
much attention if they were people who ought to be concentrating on
winning the war. It is not true to say that he never thought about the
aftermath of victory. Sometimes his colleagues made him think about it.
Sometimes he volunteered thoughts of his own, and they could be extremely
impressive; for instance his broadcast of 21 March 1943, printed under the
title 'A Four Years' Plan', a masterly survey of what was likely to be the
condition of the nation at the end of hostilities, and what mixture of
necessities and opportunities would press upon it.[3] But, for all that, it is
true to say that the details of planning for post-war Britain had no firm
lodging in his mind until the early summer of 1945. He had more important
things to think about.

Others meanwhile were (to borrow the title of a Pelican Special famous
in those days) thinking to some purpose.[4] Whether they did so as politicians,
as administrators or as academics, they had one thing in common: their
thoughts about the problems and possibilities of post-war Britain were
bred within and borne along by the tide of collectivist organisation and
communitarian experience created by the war itself. The logic of total
war – comprehensive economic and social mobilisation of a people in desperate self-defence – led inexorably in this direction. The loosely laisser-faire
Britain of the 1930s had, in not much more than the twinkling of an historical
eye, turned (in effect) into a showpiece of war socialism; which was nothing
strange to Churchill who, we may remember, had recommended something
of the same sort during the nation's last great emergency, though he never
used the word socialism itself to describe it. Those who were already socialist
liked what was happening; academics and intellectuals recruited to thicken
the senior civil service – powerful figures like Keynes and Beveridge – were
happy to promote it. Conservatives, even if they didn't like it in principle,
could hardly oppose what was evidently necessary for survival.

Churchill's libertarian tendencies caused him to dislike the idea of needless
or excessive controls. He repeatedly fired minutes at ministers on the
'civilian' side, especially the long-suffering Ministers of Food, demanding
that they be relaxed. He certainly hoped that the Britain he was leading to
victory would become a Britain liberated with all prudent speed from the

bondage of a militarised command economy. But he was also mindful, as of course were millions more, of the post-war disappointments last time and its reckless 'bonfire of controls'. There must not be such a mess this time. The public gage of his seriousness about this was the formation in November 1943 of a Ministry of Reconstruction, but in fact planning for the peace went on throughout the non-military establishments. Such was the predictable awfulness of the economic situation awaiting the nation at the end of hostilities that the solidarity bred by coalition did something to minimise the differences between party points of view. The consequence was that 'Between 1942 and 1945 the coalition government committed its successors, in a series of White Papers, to major initiatives in the fields of education, health, housing, employment, social security, industry and environmental planning.'[5] Addressing the Conservative Party conference before the coalition had broken up, but after election expectations had begun to electrify the air, Churchill represented those wartime White Papers as blueprints for filling out the Four Years' Plan he had adumbrated two years before, and which he now had to hold out as an election winner.

As push came to shove in the election contest, Churchill sounded a less centrist, more aggressive note. His party expected no less, and he was not the man to disappoint its expectations. He was determined to show that he was the man in charge. Distrust and dislike of him had never been eradicated among erstwhile Chamberlainites and retired brass hats. As the *Manchester Guardian*'s respected parliamentary correspondent, Harry Boardman, commented on the eve of the party conference, it would cheer him but 'He is not bone of their bone, flesh of their flesh. The Tories smell an infidel. Or rather, they suspect, and rightly, that he is not of the hundred per cent true Faith.'[6] Churchill was aware that in such company it was prudent to watch his back. But, looking outwards, he could rely on the party's support in finding fault with Labour's programme and with the Labour Party itself. He could argue that Labour's ambitious programme of socio-economic reforms was not seriously costed, a risky shortcoming given the unpredictabilities of the economic future of a country impoverished by war and dependent on the unreliable charity of Uncle Sam. These questions were not new to him or to his wartime colleagues; they had several times been before the coalition Cabinet, not least apropos of William Beveridge's Plan for Social Security (whose merits Lord Cherwell, ultra-Conservative in most matters, surprisingly pressed upon his friend). No one who knew anything about the young Churchill's social-reforming partnership with David Lloyd George could fairly accuse him of indifference to the Condition of England question.

What was reasonable in his four big broadcast speeches in June 1945 was however outweighed in public estimation by what was unreasonable; and that was much. Ancestral demons returned to possess him. The Labour politicians with whom he had worked harmoniously belonged, after all, to a party proudly called socialist. They sang 'God Save the King' whenever they had to, which in those days was on many public occasions, but among themselves at party conferences they sang 'The Red Flag'. Behind the Labourites whom Churchill more or less trusted were others he very much distrusted. The most personally disagreeable of these was the eloquent and energetic, though diplomatically uninstructed, MP for Ebbw Vale, Aneurin Bevan, whose conception of a democratic war effort included the less successful sides of the government's management of it being freely and publicly subjected to challenge and criticism. Less personally offensive but more dangerous appeared to be Harold Laski. Besides being a professor at the London School of Economics, which it was the fashion of those who had been to Oxford and Cambridge to deride, Laski was also Chairman of the Labour Party's National Executive. In the latter role he offered hostages to fortune by appearing to instruct the leader of the Parliamentary Labour Party (and Leader of His Majesty's Loyal Opposition) Clement Attlee, when Churchill invited him to join the party going to Potsdam, not to make up his mind about anything until he had cleared it with the National Executive. This enabled Churchill to conjure up the spectre of a parliamentary party responsible less to the electorate than to non-elected ideologues. Since there undoubtedly were leftist ideologues around who would have welcomed such an opportunity, and Laski being one of the Right's favourite bogeymen, Churchill's taunts were not ineffective. But his accompanying charge that a Labour government's programme would entail such unaccustomed restrictions of civil and political liberty as to make Britain into a really unfree society were altogether too far-fetched, proving counter-productive. That impetuous liability to go over the top at the wrong moment produced, in the very first of his broadcasts on 2 June, this fatal passage:

> I declare to you, from the bottom of my heart, that no Socialist system can be established without a political police ... No Socialist Government conducting the entire life and industry of the country could afford to allow free, sharp, or violently-worded expressions of public discontent. They would have to fall back on some form of Gestapo ...[7]

Clementine, as usual the more commonsensical of the two, when she read the draft of the speech urged him to cut this bit out; but, as so often, he ignored her advice, preferring that of party advisers who had excitedly been reading Hayek's The Road to Serfdom and that of Lord Beaverbrook with whom he was again very thick. One might have said that this broadcast alone lost the Conservatives the election, did one not know from the last twenty-five years of historical research that the election had been lost to them long before. Whatever the people's affection and respect for the hero who had won the war, too many of them did not trust the party he had come to head. They were not going to have what remained of the present decade mismanaged by the men whom they, fairly or unfairly, believed to have mismanaged the previous one.

It was a strange general election, unlike any other in the history of the British Parliament. Parliament was dissolved on 15 June and the poll was held on 5 July. Then – except of course for the hundreds of thousands of servicemen grimly gearing up for the final assault on Japan, all unaware of the surprise deliverance to be given them by the atomic bomb – came three weeks of curious suspense while the armed forces' votes were collected from all over the world and brought into the count. Winston and Clementine seized the opportunity for a week's holiday in southern France, the first holiday he had chosen to take since 1939. Then, with Mary as the daughter-in-waiting, he went direct from Bordeaux to Potsdam for the last of the wartime summits. He came back home on Wednesday the 25th to prepare for Thursday's count. Throughout the rest of the watching world, it was taken for granted that a grateful nation would confirm its great captain's continuation on the bridge. Opinion in Britain tended towards the same conclusion, but there were those who thought otherwise. Two such were very close to him: his daughter, Sarah, and his companion-in-arms 'Bert' Harris. Both of them (and others) had tried to prepare him for a shock. That Wednesday night, his slumber was curiously disturbed.

> Just before dawn I woke suddenly with a sharp stab of almost physical pain. A hitherto subconscious conviction that we were beaten broke forth and dominated my mind. All the pressure of great events, on and against which I had mentally so long maintained my 'flying speed', would cease and I should fall. The power to shape the future would be denied me. The knowledge and experience I had gathered, the authority and good will I had gained in so many countries, would vanish.[8]

He managed to get back to sleep and stayed so until nine, when he went to the Map Room in the Whitehall bunker which had been cunningly rearranged to show the results as they came in.

> They were, as I now expected, unfavourable. By noon it was clear that the Socialists would have a majority. At luncheon, my wife said to me, 'It may well be a blessing in disguise'. I replied, 'At the moment it seems quite effectively disguised.'[9]

He could have waited for the meeting of Parliament 'and taken my dismissal from the House of Commons', but the head of the government was urgently needed to represent Britain back at Potsdam, and the voters' verdict seemed peremptory. 'At seven o'clock therefore, having asked for an audience, I drove to the Palace, tendered my resignation to the King, and advised His Majesty to send for Mr Attlee.' [10]

He had come to the fifth great turning-point of his life. Falling for Clementine in 1908 was surely the first; Gallipoli, and his consequent panicky scramble back to the political heights, the second. The third was his decision to contest the National Government's Indian policy in the early 1930s; world history might have gone differently, had he not thus got himself excluded from consideration for office through the remainder of the decade. The King's commission to form a government on 10 May 1940 was obviously the fourth. And now came the moment when it seemed reasonable and proper that he should retire. He was nearly seventy-one, and everyone close to him could see that he was very tired. His wife and children wanted him to retire. Clementine thought it possible he would die, worn out and with no purpose in view after six such high-pressure years. But there might be calm after the storm. For so long as he survived, Chartwell, the home of his heart, awaited him. He would receive honorific invitations to go to interesting places, all expenses paid. The south of France was becoming accessible again; friends and connections would enable him to stay there cushioned by the comforts and conveniences he liked, and free from the sterling exchange controls that restricted the travels of the common man. He would be able to write his war memoirs, and to paint to his heart's content.

He did not retire. He would not, he could not leave the stage upon which for so long he had played a leading part. When the new Parliament met six days later he would be in place as leader of the chastened Opposition. National and world affairs would continue to claim him. But for the moment he did feel devastated. The pain and shock of transition from the old life to the new were very great. Mary Soames affectingly describes the family's last week-end at Chequers.

> After dinner there were films; Clementine quite firmly went to bed before the cinema; she was exhausted ... The hardest moments were when, after the film, Winston came downstairs; normally, then he would get all the latest news; there might even be a 'box', brought down by despatch rider with some urgent and secret communication. Now there was nothing. We saw with near desperation a cloud of black gloom descend. [Next day, Sunday 29 July] before we went to bed we all signed the Chequers Visitors Book. My Father signed last of all, and beneath his signature he wrote: '*Finis*' ... That is how he and my mother and all of us felt then. [11]

Clementine found him very difficult through the next few weeks, during which she had to do all the work of moving them into the Westminster flat lent to them by Diana and her husband while she prepared for their occupation the house they had bought at 28 Hyde Park Gate on the south side of Hyde Park, and, the heavier task, began to restore Chartwell to inhabitability. Her letters to Mary tell how his spirits were temporarily revived by the cheers that greeted him when he was spotted around Westminster. 'The crowds shout "Churchill for ever" and "We want Churchill". But all the King's horses and all the King's men can't put Humpty Dumpty together again.' She begged Mary (still months away from demobilisation) to apply for a London posting so that she could be at home sometimes, 'Because I am very unhappy and need your help with Papa'. During the war, of course, their way of living had been protected and exceptional – servants, transport, the extra rations and fuel required for official entertainment and so on, not to mention the gifts of visitors from North America – but now with no preparation they were on their own and having to live as others did. She was mightily relieved when it was arranged that he and Sarah should go for a short holiday to Lake Como where his favourite general, Harold Alexander (a field marshal now), had requisitioned a villa. He got his brushes and canvasses out again, drove a speedboat about the lake, told Clementine that he missed her, and began to unwind. 'This is the first time for very many years that I have been completely out of the world.' From Como, the two young officers whom Alex had placed at his disposal drove him to Monte Carlo (where he virtuously resisted the call of the casino) and then on to Ike's villa at Cap d'Antibes. By now, he was ready to drop the pretence of detachment from the world. His last letter before coming home showed how wrong Clementine had been about Humpty Dumpty:

I have all this batch of newspapers now up to the 21st ... I was sure there would be a complete deadlock at the Foreign Ministers' conference ... The Bolshevization of the Balkans proceeds apace and all the cabinets of Central, Eastern and Southern Europe are in Soviet control, excepting only Athens. This brand I snatched from the burning on Christmas day [1944]. I regard the future as full of darkness and menace. Horrible things must be happening to millions of Germans hunted out of Poland and Czechoslovakia ... There will be no lack of topics to discuss when we all come together again.[12]

On return from the Mediterranean he began to pick up again the threads of life as statesman, politician, writer, painter, landowner and family man. He continued his activities with surprisingly little variation for nearly ten years to come, the first six during the Labour Party's tenure of office, the next four as Prime Minister again. The achievements of these years were very considerable. His continuing activity as a statesman with international expertise, respect and celebrity made him a unique global personality: one of whom it was thought unsurprising that his closely followed speeches on world affairs should more often than not be delivered in countries other than his own. Less obviously, he continued to share in shaping his own nation's character and to guide its course through the difficult post-war years. And besides all that, there was his life at home and the new activities and recreations he took up on top of renewed exploitation of his skills as writer and painter. The post-war Churchill in fact appeared to be even more multi-faceted an individual than the pre-war Churchill had been and, until the early 1950s, not much less active.

The world with which his mind compulsively involved itself was in a bad way. To an experienced statesman like Churchill 'the world' meant the society of states into which the peoples of the world were politically organised, the health or otherwise of that society being measured by the ease or otherwise of states' relations with one another. The events of the past five years suggested that its ill health could become so bad as to approach the terminal. The task now was to establish a regimen of recovery and to hit upon a better and less danger-prone way of living for the future.

The immediate outlook was both puzzling and discouraging. Through the past three hundred years European statesmen had been accustomed to play the Great Powers game on an exclusively European board, with four, five or six players, aiming to keep any one of them from dominating for long the others. Now, at the end of the war, there were only three, the greatest of them was not European at all, and the next most powerful was half-Asian. Moreover, these three victorious states, on whose influence and powers of leverage international order depended, were at odds with one another; or, to be more precise, two of them were at odds with the third. We have seen how they failed to agree about some essential items of peacemaking policy before the war was won. Now that it was won, the disagreements only got worse, and they were more serious than they had been since the wars against Revolutionary France, in as much as one of the three had become possessed of an ideology that made it a doubly uncomfortable partner; its official creed held that between it and the others relations must be hostile until such time as the others too became true believers, and its missionaries and adherents in those other countries were committed to working for that conversion, by violent means if no others would do.

Churchill found none of this surprising. He had prophesied that the Bolshevik state would be bound to act in this way, and the 1920s and 1930s had witnessed the Soviet Union, within the limits of its capacity, starting to do so. That capacity had been enormously magnified by victory in the war just concluded. Churchill realised, earlier than most, that Stalin and Molotov's words regarding free elections in the eastern and central European States within the Soviet sphere of influence did not mean what they meant to himself and to the American Presidents. With the exceptions only of Austria, under continuing shared military occupation until its neutralisation in 1955, of unhappy Greece whose monarchical government was soon imperilled by Communist insurgency, and of Turkey upon which Russia was leaning menacingly, every state in eastern and central Europe would by 1948 be a Communist-run one. To the Communist parties of western Europe and to their fellow travellers (numerous enough for the term to become popularised in description of them) these political developments to the eastwards encouraged the hope that their own countries might be moved in the same direction. Not a lot was possible through constitutional processes, using which non-Communist parties might muster to block revolution, but more could be hoped for in consequence of the conditions of ruin and deprivation in which, as the war ended, the populations were plunged. Western European democrats wondered, even before the dreadful winter of 1946–47, how they could ever get their countries back on their feet again, and whether liberal democracy itself could stand such strain.

It was in Germany that Europe's post-war crisis was at its worst and politically most dangerous. The Allies had made only provisional arrangements. These were that, first, the victorious armies should distribute themselves within designated zones of military occupation (before the French were given a small one for themselves, it was pleasantly observed that Russia would have the agriculture, Britain the industry and the United States the scenery); secondly, that overall supervision of some sort should be exercised by an Allied Control Commission; thirdly, that what was left of Berlin should be divided into four sectors, one for each occupier; and, fourthly, that the Soviet Union, whose homeland the Germans had most comprehensively depopulated and wrecked, was entitled to immediate reparations in kind, drawn from the western zones as well as from its own. Progress towards a peace treaty was left for the Foreign Ministers to get on with at the regular meetings expected of them. In the event, they were able to agree on next to nothing. Reparations became a major source of grievance. Relations between the eastern and western occupiers deteriorated, the western zones found more and more common interests among themselves, and already by 1947 the outlines of the two Germanies which the world knew until the early 1990s were clear to be seen. The only way to solve Europe's longstanding problem of containing giant Germany seemed to be, for the time being anyway, to cut it more or less in half.

22

The Iron Curtain

'A friend of mine ... was in Zagreb when the results of the late General Election came in. An old lady said to him, "Poor Mr Churchill. I suppose now he will be shot". He said the sentence might be mitigated to one of the various forms of hard labour which are always open to Her Majesty's subjects.'

Churchill's first speech in the new Parliament, 16 August 1945

When several years later Churchill got to writing the final volume of his war memoirs, the volume running from D-Day, 6 June 1944, to the Potsdam summit in July 1945, he set out its theme thus: 'How the Great Democracies Triumphed, and so were able to Resume the Follies which had so nearly Cost them their Life.' By the early 1950s it was all too clear to everyone that the Second World War had no more brought about a safer world than had the First. Cold War had succeeded to hot, Europe was once again divided between two hostile groups of states, and hot war itself was soon to be back in several other parts of the globe. From 1944 the great matter with which Churchill's mind most constructively concerned itself was how to create an international order that would prove disaster proof; one that would prove itself more effective, one might add, than the United Nations Organization, whose principles and standards he admired while realistically reckoning that Great Power disharmony would restrict its usefulness. The greatest barrier to begin with was his listeners' reluctance to believe that disaster might happen. Communists and fellow travellers were not the only elements of western European public opinion that found it difficult to think ill of Stalin and the Soviet Union. It was unnatural and distasteful to most people, it was a sort of affront to human nature, to be asked to view yesterday's acclaimed friends as tomorrow's probable foes. Churchill took no pleasure in hoisting storm signals: he was not looking for a fight, although most of the Left from the Pyrenees to Manchuria, not to mention places southwards, understandably accused him of doing so. (It was quite something to be called a warmonger by Hitler in one decade and by Stalin in the next.) It is truer to say that he was peacemongering in the only way he knew – finding for the nations he most valued a solidarity among themselves and a consequent impregnability in defence that would make attack on them unthinkable.

This message, already spelled out to the House of Commons before 1945 was out, and dramatically laid before the American and world publics in March 1946, drew upon him criticism not only from those who thought what he said abhorrent but also, at first, from those who thought it alarmist. To leftist writers and to revisionist historians, Churchill has appeared to have been giving a kick-start to the Cold War. The charge is not unjust, though whether he is thereby made a worse or a better man remains subject to ideological interpretation. Within two years the fears which he had been nearly alone in voicing had become widely shared by others well capable of judging for themselves, and the foreign policies of the western democracies had been adjusted accordingly. It was he who gave the first big public push to the process of rethinking that made the West (as it was soon called) willing to combine in resistance to the Soviet Union's imperialism and Communism's seemingly limitless capacity for expansion. From Poland and the Baltic states in the north to Bulgaria in the south Communism had taken over. Greece, Turkey, Iran were the next to be threatened; France, Italy and, perhaps, as soon as political life resumed there, Germany were politically at risk. So far as economic or military support could help to restore and sustain these countries, Britain had none to spare of the first and not much of the second. The USA had plenty of both, but between them and the places where they were needed lay a great obstacle. The American people were accustomed to think little of the problems of Europe. In 1917 their country had been drawn away from its hemisphere to fight what the American people were persuaded to regard as a crusade in Europe to set Europe to rights. In 1941, with more conscious self-interest but also with the idealism and altruism inseparable in those days from intervention overseas, Americans had gone to Europe again to perform, apparently, the same service. That war in Europe, which in any case never came as close to American hearts as the war in the Pacific, was now over and done with. The sooner American soldiers finished with their occupation duties in Germany, the better. The problems of the rest of the world were for the rest of the world to deal with, and the new world organisation (as Churchill and others at that time described the infant United Nations) would help them do it. Such was the general drift of American public opinion through the months immediately following the end of the war, and of course it was reflected in Congress. If American attention was to be recalled to the political problems of the world at large, and to Russian Communist expansion in particular, it would require some doing.

The inclination to do it was in fact stirring in a few select circles through the winter of 1945–46, but none could tell how long it would take to get anywhere or whether it might not come too late for the countries most at risk. It was as natural that American statesmen and diplomats should be reluctant to think ill of the Soviet Union as that they should nourish suspicions that the British were still playing the game Americans were prone to suspect them of playing – manoeuvring the USA into helping preserve British overseas interests under the noble cover of saving the world. Churchill was determined to persuade the people of the United States that their suspicions were unjustified, that the world was indeed in need of salvation, and that Britain and the United States side by side could save it.

He did this in the latter days of a visit to the United States early in 1946. This was by no means his only lengthy trip abroad in the post-war years, as was observed with mixed feelings by the Conservative Party, most of them stuck with Britain and Parliament. No party leader has ever absented himself more often from the Commons than Churchill during his last ten years in it. He was usually there for the big occasions, and he still showed fine form both in set-piece speeches and, what he had not always been so good at, debating chamber repartee. He enjoyed roasting the socialists and exposing the fallacies, as he argued, of their programmes of social welfare and nationalisation. But he felt more at home with old political allies like Brendan Bracken and Lord Beaverbrook than with party managers and enthusiasts, and he would not hang about outside the Chamber to chat with the foot-soldiers. Clementine as usual did her best to compensate for his failings, by giving party lunches at Hyde Park Gate (by mid March 1949 there had been twenty-six of them), but grumbles about his social aloofness rumbled on into the next decade, mingling by then with the question unanswered for too long: when would Winston retire? [1]

What the historian is better able to understand than Tadpole and Taper understood at the time is that he never ceased to feel most at home in the society of states, and that the main interest of the last phase of his political life is that he continued to care about its health. Whether as Prime Minister lost or Prime Minister regained, his stature in world affairs was unrivalled. F. D. Roosevelt could have rivalled him, had he survived and stayed in good health; but after that great man's death, in the spring of 1945, Churchill stood alone. He was a global political educator as no one had been before unless it was Woodrow Wilson (and what a mess he had made of it). Freed from personal responsibility for the management of national affairs, Churchill made the most of his opportunities to write, to travel and to talk. His wartime speeches had been heard all over the world and much admired. There now arose a demand, far greater than he could satisfy, for him to address foreign bodies of distinction: universities, cities, legislatures, elite clubs and associations. Most of these were in Europe but the one which history has made the most famous was on 5 March 1946, at Fulton, Missouri.

He was away from Britain on this occasion for nearly two months. The Churchill party, Clementine in it as she was not always, sailed on the *Queen Elizabeth* on 9 January and went from New York straight to an old friend's mansion at Miami Beach. In February he and Clementine and Sarah spent some days in Cuba, an island especially close to his heart. Back in Miami, he received an honorary degree from its university and began to think about the trip to Fulton, with whose modest Westminster College President Truman had connections close enough to move him to escort Churchill there and share his introduction. On 3 March the Churchills went to Washington, met Harry Truman and trundled in the presidential train to Missouri. At some point of the ride Churchill asked Truman to take a look at his draft (whether Truman saw the whole of the final version is unclear) and not surprisingly Truman said it was fine, though he added that it was sure to make a stir.[2]

The stir was chiefly because of this passage, about half way through:

> From Stettin in the Baltic to Trieste in the Adriatic, an iron curtain has descended across the Continent. Behind that line lie all the capitals of the ancient states of Central and Eastern Europe. Warsaw, Berlin, Prague, Vienna, Budapest, Belgrade, Bucharest and Sofia, all these famous cities and the populations around them lie in what I must call the Soviet sphere, and all are subject in one form or another, not only to Soviet influence but to a very high and in many cases increasing measure of control from Moscow.[3]

The 'Iron Curtain' expression was in fact not new, though Churchill in the manner of many receptive and restless minds may have thought it was; he himself had used it in the 1945 letter to Clementine already quoted. It was a striking expression and it was no wonder that it went straight into universal usage. But it was the substance of the speech that gave it instant notoriety and power to offend and to disturb. To the rulers of the Soviet Union and the Communist parties of the world, their members and their well-wishers, and beyond them the political innocents who added to the numbers of their marches and demonstrations, Churchill's measured analysis of Communism's incompatibility with the freedoms of the Atlantic Charter and the Charter of the United Nations was simply offensive. Many members from one or other of those categories had seats on the governing party benches of the House of Commons, and the Prime Minister and Foreign Secretary (the latter, nevertheless, privately sharing Churchill's views) had to point out, what indeed Churchill himself had plainly stated, that he spoke only for himself.

Not many people in America were positively offended by what he said, but many were disturbed by his message that the menace of Soviet and Communist expansion and the risk of western Europe's inability to prevent it were together such that the United States, for its own sake as well as everyone else's, should stop disarming, drop thoughts of pursuing happiness again in traditional isolation, and realign with the only reliable ally available, the British Empire and Commonwealth.

Here were two uncomfortable ideas for the Americans to digest. The idea that the United States had to start gearing up for a return to Europe and defensive alliance there provoked much criticism. Truman himself found it politic to deny that he had any foreknowledge of what Churchill was going to say: surely an excusable fib, given that he could not without extreme impoliteness have either refused to see the draft when offered a sight of it, or have asked so distinguished a visitor to alter it. From the positions advanced at Fulton, Churchill withdrew not an inch in the addresses that remained to be delivered before embarking to go home on the *Queen Mary* on 20 March. Indeed he took the opportunity to extend his argument and to humanise it. For example, from his speech at the Waldorf Astoria reception given by the Mayor of New York:

> If any words that I have spoken have commanded attention, that is only because they find an echo in the breasts of those of every land and race who love freedom and are the foes of tyranny. I certainly will not allow anything said by others to weaken ... my earnest desire that Russia should be safe and prosperous and should take an honoured place in the van of the World Organisation ... We all remember ... how Russia survived and emerged triumphant from injuries greater than have ever been inflicted on any other community. There is deep and wide-spread sympathy throughout the English-speaking world for the people of Russia ... If the Soviet government does not take advantage of this sentiment ... the responsibility will be entirely theirs.

Later in the speech, after expressing his conviction that misunderstandings between peoples would diminish in proportion as they became able to 'mingle freely with one another', the fact that an unusual number of Russian ships were in New York harbour prompted him to hope that their crews would receive 'a hearty welcome to the land of the free and the home of the brave'. No doubt he was recalling the frosty non-welcome that American and British sailors had been wont to receive, only a few years before, when they arrived (if they lived to arrive) in the land of people's democracy.[4]

Through the months that followed, Churchill had the satisfaction of seeing his Fulton analysis turn from an alarming novelty into a commonplace. 'If I repeated the Fulton speech in America today,' he told his constituency in September 1947, 'it would be regarded as a stream of tepid platitudes.'[5] The Iron Curtain remained part of the furniture of the western mind for the next forty years.

The subsequent history of the other idea that disturbed his American hearers was not so happy. They could not feel as excited as Churchill did about being tied into alliance with Britain, its Empire and (so far as the concepts were separable) its Commonwealth. This idea was of course the political wing of his belief in the mutual affinities of the English-Speaking Peoples, a concept he continued to deploy like a magic charm. It is impossible to avoid the conclusion that he suffered from a romantic, sentimental delusion in this respect. Its roots were various. As a young man he had subscribed to the then dominant belief in the superior virtues and inborn qualities as rulers of the Anglo-Saxon Races; the belief in the solidarity of the English-Speaking Peoples which succeeded it may be seen as a humanised version of it, more appropriate to the eras of the League of Nations and the UN. Its intellectual strength, so far as it had any, lay in the version of English history (in fact, from the seventeenth century, British History) he had part learned, part constructed; he could not believe that any society steeped as the American one was in Magna Carta and Shakespeare would not equally relish the Statute of Westminster and Rudyard Kipling. In more political vein, it was beyond his comprehension why Britain's white cousins in the United States (such terminology came naturally to him) should show such an interest in helping the Indian people remove themselves from the blessings of British rule and should want the Arabs to become independent of it. From time to time persons close to him heard him say things that showed he knew very well how ready the United States had been and still was to override British interests when its own interests, especially economic ones, were at stake. Perhaps he discounted those thoughts in gratitude for the United States' role as saviour in the war; his old-fashioned principle of loyalty responded instinctively to the call of the bugle. Whatever the reason, this confusion of cultural affinities with *Realpolitik* considerations remained with him to the end of his days and, as is well known, it has survived through more recent times under the title of the 'Special Relationship'.

There was no follow-up to the Fulton speech. In fact he only went back to the USA four more times; although he operated in the grand manner on three of those occasions (by the fourth in 1959 he was too feeble), none of them produced or was hoped to produce anything like the same effect.

The 'Iron Curtain' oration did its work; that is, it gave confidence and direction to a body of opinion about Soviet policy which was forming anyway on the basis of observation and experience. Churchill like others observed the mounting spikiness, suspicion and hostility of Soviet foreign policy with regret, but the Americans' sturdy response with satisfaction: the Truman doctrine, the Marshall Plan, the resumption of military interest in the defence of Europe dramatically signalised in the Berlin airlift of 1948, and to crown it all the North Atlantic Treaty Organization of 1949. From 1950 the NATO countries were ready to defend themselves and their friends from Russian menaces. Historians continue to debate whether NATO, and the USA in particular, themselves now became menacing. They certainly became prone to exaggerate the extent of Soviet menace and, in the poorer parts of the world, to confuse insurgent nationalism with it – but that was none of the ageing Churchill's business. What he did make his business to do was to seek to do from strength what had not been possible while weak – to find out, when the clear and present danger to western Europe had been averted and a solid and formidable front including the threat of nuclear attack presented to the Soviet Union, whether it had not become time to move towards an accommodation with western Europe's uncomfortable eastern neighbour.

The development of Churchill's ideas about the Soviet Union was quite straightforward and offered little room for misunderstanding. The development of his ideas about the parts of Europe that had not come under Stalin's shadow was not so straightforward, and from the beginning there has been argument about what exactly he meant at each successive stage of his engagement with the European Movement (to use its conveniently vague early name). He was for a while the leader of that movement, by far the greatest public personality giving it countenance and encouragement. He made as great a contribution to post-war history by his speeches at Zürich, Brussels, The Hague and London as he did at Fulton and New York. Non-Russian-dominated Europe in the later 1940s – incredible as it may seem, fifty years on – looked to Britain for a lead. Churchill stepped forward to give it, and for a few years seemed to know where he was going and who was going with him. Then doubts began to arise. The more eager spirits of western Europe and its constructive statesmen found that Churchill was after all not ready or, after he became Prime Minister again in 1951, able to keep company with them. The Churchill of the early 1950s showed little of the zeal for Europe that had marked him in the later 1940s. Two explanations seem obvious and may together be sufficient: his ageing, and the dedication of what remained of his energy to the search for improved relations with the Soviet Union. But enough questions remain about his

Opposition years to keep the questions coming. Was there consistency in his earlier pronouncements on Europe, and what exactly did he mean by them? Did this energetic founder of the European Movement and the star speaker of its early years become Europe's lost leader?

Misunderstanding awaits the person who takes Churchill's post-war European speeches on their own, neglecting the fact that the same Churchill had delivered himself of thoughts about Europe for many years already. And very strange some of them had been. The Foreign Office, catching those fired off during the war apropos of post-war arrangements, found them to be exactly the same mixture of the wise and the foolish as the Chiefs of Staff had found his daily barrage of ideas about strategy and operations to be. His notion of strengthening the political structure of the Continent by grouping its states into regional 'councils' (the most egregious of them, a Danubian one to be managed by Turkey) was fantastic. Ideas about splitting up or otherwise downgrading Germany which sometimes beset him were incompatible with his more usual principle, that it was important to bring a denazified Germany back to its historic key position at the heart of Europe. More fortunate than the Chiefs of Staff in being at a greater distance from him, the Foreign Office ignored his ideas as much as it could, merely noting that he gave no thought to the all-important question of the mechanics of the coupling between his regional councils and the still-gestating world organisation which he was unenthusiastically having to accept because he had to go along with the United States.

Late 1945 brought big changes in Churchill's position vis-à-vis Europe. Once he had bounced back from the distress and disorientation of being ousted from office, he began to enjoy the freedom of Opposition at home and the opportunities which came from his unrivalled celebrity abroad. A statesman in Opposition is free to play around with plans and proposals beyond the reach of one in responsible office, and he was still as capable of mischievous behaviour as he always had been. It amused him to bait the Foreign Office and to steal Labour Foreign Secretaries' thunder. He was also curiously self-indulgent about making difficulties for the long-suffering Anthony Eden, the Shadow Foreign Secretary and Conservative leader apparent, and he enjoyed provoking the Labour government. Hence the 'somewhat bizarre affair' that Harold Macmillan described as following close on the heels of Churchill's stirring address to the United Europe Movement at The Hague in May 1948, an address always and rightly placed somewhere in the foundations of what much later became the European Union. Macmillan, one of Churchill's closest coadjutors in this endeavour, recalls how a dozen or more of them met in his room in the House of Commons, then marched in solemn procession ... up Whitehall till we reached Downing Street. Churchill led, with the usual cigar and the equally inevitable V-signs. The police-men on duty seemed a little surprised as we dutifully followed our leader, two by two, like a school crocodile. But the traffic stopped for our benefit, and we reached No. 10 ... in reasonably good order. The Prime Minister and the Foreign Secretary (with a number of other Ministers) received us with appropriate courtesy and gravity. Churchill deployed the case [for a European assembly] with eloquence ...[6]

It is advisable always to watch out for the boyish element in his make-up when analysing the more extraordinary things he said and did. The way he said them requires to be thought about too. The grander the theme, the higher rose his eloquence to meet it. When he was rousing people to a grand design, he would not let the foreground be cluttered by the nuts and bolts of achieving it. R. A. Butler, who was in and out of government with him from 1941 to the end, addressing the Winston Churchill Foundation of Switzerland, cleverly spotlighted 'the vague magnificent way' in which Churchill presented his European proposals.[7] The Foreign Office's Gladwyn Jebb thought it a pity that Churchill allowed his stirring generalities to mislead the continental leaders of the movement, for whom supranation-alism was an article of belief, into believing he would go all the way with them, when he actually had principles and commitments that would keep him from doing so.[8] What was it about Europe that led him onto these heights, and why did some of his early companions end up disappointed in him?

Heights and disappointments are both prefigured in the first of his series of noble orations about Europe, at Zürich on 19 September 1946. This was the real beginning of the series, rather than the speech at Metz on 14 July preceding, because that speech was to a great extent focused on France, concerned to encourage that nation along the road back to its proper self-respect and fortitude in the van of European recovery. In little multi-national neutral Switzerland he could say what he couldn't, so far, helpfully say in any other European land.

We all know that the two world wars through which we have passed arose out of the vain passion of a newly-united Germany to play the dominating part in the world ... crimes and massacres have been committed for which there is no parallel since the invasions of the Mongols in the fourteenth century ... The guilty must be punished ... But when all this is done, as it will be done, as it is being done, there must be an end to retribution. There must be what Mr Gladstone many years ago called 'a blessed act of oblivion' ... Can the free peoples of Europe rise to the height of these resolves of the soul and instincts of the spirit of man? If they can, the wrongs and miseries which have been inflicted will be washed

away on all sides by the miseries which have been endured. Is there any need
for further floods of agony? ... I am now going to say something that will astonish
you. The first step in the re-creation of the European family must be a partnership
between France and Germany ...

While his audience was still recovering from this pronouncement, revolutionary indeed at that date, he rendered its state of shock complete by
saying that 'under and within [the] world concept' of the United Nations
Organization, 'we must re-create the European family in a regional structure
called, it may be, the United States of Europe. The first step is to form a
Council of Europe.'⁹

United States of Europe, a Council of Europe, a partnership between
France and Germany – it was not only or even principally his Swiss auditors
who were astonished by Churchill's espousal and linkage of these concepts,
it was the whole of the Continent. Macmillan remarked that a later speech
in the series displayed 'the wonderful combination' of prophetic foresight
and moral courage which so often inspired him'.¹⁰ It was certainly at work
in Zürich. The epigraph of his memoir-history, what he called its 'Moral',
concluded: 'In Victory, Magnanimity. In Peace, Goodwill.' The reference
to the need for France and Germany to get onto good terms with one
another (it has to be understood that he was speaking of a Germany that
was yet to be reconstructed), and the plea that wartime animosities should
be overcome, was something no one else could have got away with at that
time. He kept on at it until, not long after, it became political reality. At
the Council of Europe's Consultative Assembly in Strasbourg in September
1949, he memorably broke out of his prepared speech to glare around the
chamber with the challenge, 'Where are the Germans?' By then in fact 'the
Germans' (that is, the West Germans) were well on the way; their representatives were sitting alongside the French and everyone else by the time
the council next met.

With regard to the Germans and their nation, Churchill's European
campaign was brilliantly successful, entirely helpful to the progress of the
European movement. Helpful to not much lesser a degree was his contribution to the metamorphosis the movement had to go through if it was
to become, as its continental founding fathers were determined that it
should become, a permanent and indissoluble company of states committing themselves to one another in unprecedented ways and embarking on
experiments with pooled sovereignty. When Churchill talked of a United
States of Europe and a Council of Europe, it was natural that the
supranationally-minded planners should think he meant what they
meant when they used the same terms. But he didn't. The misunderstanding
was natural and confusing. Churchill gave the European Movement a

tremendous lift-off, but he didn't go into orbit with it, and we must now see why.

The workings of Churchill's mind regarding Europe may be made out by contrasting what he said and did about Europe while he was in Opposition with what he said and did when he was in office again, which he was not until the end of October 1951. Although Churchill was the biggest name in the European Movement in the later 1940s, no more than the other weighty participants could he tell where it was going or how far it would get. As a politician in Opposition he was in no position to commit his country to anything. It was commonplace politics to espouse causes pooh-poohed by the government of the day, as the European Movement unfortunately was. And in any case his own party was divided on the issue. It is probable that the need to get the accessible European countries restored and reconstructed pressed so heavily on him that to begin with he felt justified in adopting more of a federalist stance (the word 'federalist' had not then the sinister connotation put upon it by British Conservatives now) than fairly represented his views. But by the summer of 1950, anxious to clear up lingering misunderstandings, he plainly told the House of Commons when it was debating the Schuman Plan for a coal and steel community: 'In our European Movement we have worked with federalists and we have always made it clear that, although they are moving along the same road, we are not committed to their conclusions.'[11]

Some of the great pathfinders of European Union, Jean Monnet, Paul-Henri Spaak and others, had hoped that the Council of Europe which Churchill had done so much to promote would evolve into the groundworks of the supranational organisation they dreamed of. Finding that it wouldn't, and that Churchill was not going to push it in that direction, they didn't linger shivering on the brink but boldly launched away via the Schuman Plan of 1950 to Europe's first supranational institution, its Coal and Steel Community of 1952. Gladwyn Jebb, prominent among those who regretted his country's missing the European bus at its first stop, opined 'that Churchill decided to have it both ways; that he was not really, as it proved when he came into power a second time, in favour of joining anything like a supranational Europe'.[12] In that debate about how Britain should respond to the French invitation to join in the preliminaries to the Schuman Plan, Churchill and Eden both went out of their way to poke fun at the word 'supranational'. Had they paused to think about it, they might have recalled that in the desperate days of mid June 1940 Churchill had gone beyond mere supranationality so far as to propose an organic constitutional union of Britain with France; also, that the substance of the word they made fun of was present in the Supreme Command over Allied forces later confided to

General Eisenhower. But no such precedents entered Churchill's head. It was enough that he simply could not think of Britain as a part of Europe by itself and on its own. When he thought of Britain he thought simultaneously of its supporting Empire and of the USA, with which his country had a 'Special Relationship', and to whose Presidents he was proud to have direct access.

It is not difficult therefore to understand why Churchill, for all his rhetoric and sincerity about 'the European family' and a 'United Europe', never thought of Britain as integrated within it. No matter what he said about Britain being part of Europe, Europe as a whole was not as potent an idea for him as either the British Empire and Commonwealth or the 'Special Relationship', nor had his affinities with the other European nations the same depth and richness as those with 'the English-Speaking Peoples' (by which incantation he actually meant above all those on both sides of the Atlantic). His language about Europe was so warm in these years that it is easy to misunderstand what other affections cohabited with it in that capacious mind. At Zürich, he began with a rendering of the well-educated European's hymn to the excellence of his inheritance.

> I wish to speak to you today about the tragedy of Europe. This noble continent, comprising the fairest and the most cultivated regions of the earth, enjoying a temperate and equable climate, is the home of all the great parent races of the western world. It is the fountain of Christian faith and Christian ethics. It is the origin of most of the culture, arts, philosophy and science both of ancient and modern times. If Europe were once united in the sharing of its common inheritance, there would be no limit to [its] happiness ... Yet it is from Europe that have sprung that series of frightful nationalistic quarrels, originated by the Teutonic peoples, which ... wreck the peace and mar the prospects of all mankind.[13]

But nowhere in the speech or at any time later did he take the opportunity to insist that Britain was a European country in the full sense that the continental ones were. In spite of all temptations to belong with other nations, he remained an Englishman; and within a few minutes indeed at Zürich he was talking about an already existing 'natural grouping in the Western Hemisphere' which can only have meant the Special Relationship and, explicitly, the British Commonwealth of Nations as another such. The secret of this alchemy was Churchill's magical invocation of 'the three intersecting circles'. A distinguished retired diplomat, Oliver Franks, recalled how Churchill once said to him,

> 'Young man, never let Great Britain escape from any of them.' Now [went on the diplomat], if you come to the question of priorities, that is more difficult. If you are thinking in strategic and military terms there is no question that our

relationship with the United States was the priority. On the other hand, in terms of tradition, emotion and affection, the Commonwealth came first; and in terms of our neighbours without whom we were literally not safe or secure, then Europe came very much into the picture.

That seemed clear enough. But on another occasion he described these 'mighty and august' circles thus: 'the circle of the British Empire and Commonwealth, the circle of the English-speaking world, and the circle of united Europe'.[14]

The truth of the matter was that Churchill's affections were coming increasingly to rule his intellect. The three intersecting circles were not so much a magic charm to make Britain forever safe and cosy as a mesh of tripwires in which Britain could find itself isolated. The three circles trick could only work so long as Britain was no less needed by the inhabitants of the other two than they were needed by Britain. Once hard decisions and delicate choices had to be made, one or possibly even both of the other circles could be neglected. The dilemma soon showed in Britain's relations with the United States. Churchill was anxious to keep America interested in Europe and to bring its armed forces back to Europe. America for its part wanted Europe to become strong and united so that it would not have to stay too long or to spend too much on Europe's behalf. Americans would have been happy for Britain to throw itself into the movement for a European Union; a United States of Europe with Britain as an integral part of it was the best thing Washington could imagine. But that was exactly what neither Attlee's Britain nor Churchill's wanted or would accept.

For all the muddles of the 'three circles' fantasy and the limitations in his commitment to Europe, Churchill performed two enormous services for Europe in the years that followed the war. The first service was to get the European Movement going. What he did for it in the later 1940s was of incalculable value. The Council of Europe remained for many years a useful forum of pan-European debate, and its European Convention on Human Rights and accompanying commission and court became important organs of the supranational European identity. By the early 1950s, however, the serious Europeans were forging ahead on the track that would take them, via the European Coal and Steel Community, to the Treaty of Rome's European Economic Community of 1957, leaving Britain far behind. Churchill was not interested in all that. The other big thing he had been interested in, his other signal service to the recovery of Europe, was his early advocacy of reconciliation between French and Germans; his insistence that democratic West Germany, once it had been conjured into existence, should be received into the western European family of nations; and (within the limits allowed by his Foreign Secretary) his steady backing of the movement to get a West German army into NATO. All this was consistent with his famous belief in the magnanimity of victors, and it was of incalculable service to the reconstitution of western European self-confidence (and, within the limits set by national peculiarities, solidarity) that so widely respected a political celebrity as Churchill publicly and ardently supported it all. The only inconsistent blip came before the war was ended. This was the foolish and discreditable moment in September 1944 when his urge to please President Roosevelt and 'The Prof's' whispers in his ear combined to lead him to support for a short while the idiotic 'Morgenthau Plan' for de-industrialising Germany (it was a lapse he regretted ever after). Once the war was over, magnanimity reigned again; if it was less heard of after 1951, that was partly because there was by then less need for it.

There were other reasons why he seemed to be less involved with the continental drift. Political circumstances close to home were working to the same effect. The Foreign Secretary in the administration he formed after winning the election of October 1951 was again Anthony Eden. Eden, who had never shared Churchill's enthusiasm for Europe in the later 1940s and who, moreover, had suffered a good deal from Churchill's interference while he was at the Foreign Office during the war, was not about to let the old man dominate him again. The Conservative Party was not as pronouncedly anti-European as Labour (whose proclaimed policy was not to think supra-nationalism at all unless it was socialist supranationalism), but only one of its weighty pro-Europeans, Harold Macmillan, was in high office, and he had his hands full with the government's ambitious housebuilding programme. The party indeed had several worrisome overseas concerns – the Korean War, upsurges of anti-British nationalism in Iran and Egypt, Communist insurgency in the Malay States, Moscow's 'peace offensive' to push a wedge between the United States and its European partners – but the economics and politics of continental Europe were only of concern (as for Churchill also) in so far as they bore on the question of western European defence, and the core business of bringing West Germany into it. Churchill himself went to France often but not to Paris or with diplomatic intent; the Midi was where he liked to go, to write, paint and enjoy himself.

23

Summitry and the Bomb

'There is time and hope if we combine patience and courage. All deterrents will improve and gain authority during the next ten years. By that time, the deterrent may well reach its acme and reap the final reward.'

Churchill in the House of Commons, 1 March 1955

The general election of October 1951 brought the Conservatives back into power with a small but sufficient majority and with Churchill still at their head, determined, although now in his later seventies, to lead from the front. There were domestic crises to be dealt with immediately but, as soon as he could get clear of them, he turned with new energy to what had become the most intractable and momentous international problem of the age: the Soviet Union and the nuclear arms race. His trumpet-blast at Fulton, once the message had sunk in, had the effect of rearming the West, and he was proud to have figured so prominently in it. For a few years, western Europe had been able to begin to put itself into order again. Stalin showed no interest in extending his sphere of military influence beyond where it had reached in early 1948 (Czechoslovakia), but the language in which the Soviet Union conducted its external relations continued to be hostile; and the Berlin Blockade from June 1948 to May 1949 was an unmistakably hostile act of a carefully controlled kind. Churchill lost no sleep over the fact that the Americans had atomic bombs and were prepared in certain circumstances to use them. He even thought it might be helpful if they were used pre-emptively. Pending the West's recovery of means of 'conventional' defence, the Bomb was presumed to warn Stalin off hostile gestures that could get out of control.

By the time Churchill returned to Number Ten, however, he might well have begun to lose sleep about Soviet-American relations if he had been of the sleep-losing kind. The shift in his thinking, a shift which was to go very far, began with the Soviet Union's explosion of its first test atom bomb in late August 1949. The brief age of American nuclear hegemony, a hegemony Churchill never doubted to be beneficent, was nearly over. Looking back on it from the early 1960s, Tom Lehrer sang

> First we got The Bomb, and that was good,
> 'Cause we love peace and motherhood.
> Then Russia got The Bomb, but that's okay,
> 'Cause the balance of power's maintained that way.
> – Who's next? [1]

But could the balance be stabilised? The point of Tom Lehrer's catalogue of nuclear acquisitions and aspirations was the 'Who's next?' repeated at the end of each verse. As it happened, Britain was next after Russia; its first test being carried out in 1952, fifty miles or so off the coast of Western Australia. Churchill rejoiced that the Labour government, despite its none too adequate resources, had set in train what was necessary for Britain to acquire the weapon, not least because it cemented the country's claim to continuing Great Power status. But it was proper to continue to worry about the new pattern and tendencies of international relations. 'Who's next?' was not the only question to be asked. For those who preferred a more peaceable world, there was also 'What's next?' Churchill was the last person in the world to subscribe to the aims of the emerging Campaign for Nuclear Disarmament, but what would lead it towards the historically prescribed goal of disarmament led him towards what would soon be called Arms Control. From regarding the Bomb as just the latest in the long line of ever more powerful weapons of war, which was quite a common view of it in those early years, he began to realise that it was a weapon *sui generis*, with potential consequences far beyond those of any previous weapon. Its use in war was therefore not to be contemplated with the old sangfroid, and the premium on peace was raised accordingly. Better to begin to think afresh about the question that had activated the hopeful endeavours of international conferences before both world wars: how to prevent it happening all over again. When it came to the general election of 1951, and his party's demand for a more robust response to an anti-British movement in Iran caused him to be again pilloried as a 'warmonger', he indignantly denied the charge, calling it

> a cruel and ungrateful accusation. It is the opposite of the truth. If I remain in public life at this juncture is is because, rightly or wrongly, but sincerely, I believe that I may be able to make an important contribution to the prevention of a third World War and to bring nearer that lasting peace settlement which the masses of the people of every race and in every land fervently desire. I pray indeed that I may have this opportunity. It is the last prize I seek to win.[2]

Since Churchill remained as hostile towards Communism as he always had been, and was unbudging in his resolve to prevent it spreading beyond its present borders, his last campaign requires a bit of explanation. Churchill did not go into this delicate, complex and (one of his favourite words) grave matter without principle and theory to guide him. He distinguished between ideology and national interest. The Soviet Union was possessed of a bad ideology but Russia was a Great Power, greater indeed than it had ever been before, and Churchill's principles of statecraft instructed him that the national interests of states were a study in themselves which the managers of their external relations were wont to handle in technical, not ideological, terms. Revolutionary ideologies and the powers of the media had made statecraft a more difficult business than it used to be but its principles hadn't changed since he had picked them up from Salisbury and Grey at the start of the century. A strong sense of national interest might yet do what calls to virtue or the UN couldn't. He believed the truth of this principle had been demonstrated by Stalin's readiness to enter into a military alliance with Britain in 1941, and he regretted that what he thought had been a good 'man of the world' sort of understanding with Stalin had not survived the end of the war. Now it was time to try again.

It would not have been in Churchill's nature to express himself with the same concision as Charles de Gaulle – 'States are cold monsters' – but, way down beneath the strata of sentiment and romance which coloured his thinking, and which sometimes misled himself as well as others, that seems to have been what at bottom he actually believed, except with regard to the USA to which he attributed an extraordinary faculty of altruism. States were organisations of power and their way of life in the peculiar society they inhabited was to use power: to keep what they already had, to get more if they could. (For those which hadn't much power there was no choice but to propitiate those which had, or let the latter look after their interests.) Negotiation from weakness was doomed to fail. Successful negotiations between states began from positions of strength or bargaining opportunity. Whether the UN would provide new channels for power to flow through, and a better chance that it would be applied in the interests of justice as well as peace, remained to be seen. Until it was seen, Great Powers had to get on with their business in the old way.

A variety of demanding domestic political circumstances and the deliberations of his own mind, impossible to plot precisely, delayed the public development of his new line of thought until the winter of 1952–53. What certainly facilitated his venture was that public opinion in Britain did not become so frenzied about Communism as it did in America, nor was it in the tradition of British diplomacy to demonise states with which, however bad relations might now be, better relations might be possible in the future.[3] Churchill's personal peace initiative, whenever it came, would be more welcome in Britain than it could be in the America of Joseph McCarthy and John Foster Dulles. But there was an obstacle to his launching it nearer home: his own Foreign Secretary, heir-designate and friend, Anthony Eden. Eden, a Foreign Office man through and through, was not keen on what he regarded as Churchill's amateurish interventions in the domain of diplomatic professionals. He did not share the ageing Premier's complacency about his wartime summits and, along with most of the Cabinet and a yearly growing proportion of the parliamentary party, he was longing for the moment to come when he would be able to take over. Out of office, Churchill had been able to say and to plan more or less whatever he liked, regardless of Eden's feelings; now that he was head of the government again, he had to mind what Eden and the Cabinet said; and, on matters of diplomacy, Eden's voice normally carried more weight than his.

Then came two unexpected and, for Churchill, most welcome surprises. The first of these was the election in November 1952 of General Eisenhower as President of the United States. The two of them had been happy warriors together through three eventful years, and they had seen something of each other while Ike was back in Europe as NATO's first Supreme Allied Commander in 1950–51. Churchill felt sure that he could establish as cordial a relationship with this President as the one he had had with Roosevelt, and that he might hope to exercise a similar influence. The thought of having direct access again to the White House had its familiar intoxicating effect on him, and he did exactly what he had done when the same opportunity offered, eleven years before; post-haste, he invited himself to meet the President (not actually in office until mid January) and on 31 December embarked on the Queen Mary with a typical entourage: Clementine, Mary and her helpful husband Christopher Soames, private secretary, secretary-typist, valet, bodyguard and so on. In New York (where he took the opportunity to visit for the first time the house where his mother had been born), he stayed with the venerable financier-statesman Bernard Baruch, a friend and financial adviser since the 1920s, and there had the talk with Eisenhower from which he expected so much benefit to flow. Twice more would he make the pilgrimage while he was still in office: in December 1953, to meet Eisenhower in Bermuda, and at the end of June 1954 when he was privileged to stay three days and nights in the White House.

Here obviously was a Special Relationship of some kind, but it was not what Churchill thought it was. His judgement, so shrewd and sound in most respects, was *not* reliable regarding the USA. His and his friend's respective perceptions of their relationship could not have been more different. President Eisenhower, a perfect officer and gentleman and naturally a kindly man, was unfailingly courteous and considerate on private occasions. He genuinely liked and admired 'my old friend', and was sad to see the signs of ageing: how Churchill for instance wouldn't wear his hearing-aid and therefore had to be shouted at, and how he was liable to nod off when not himself energetically holding forth. Eisenhower also perceived how fixed Churchill's ideas were. The unusually long entry in his diary for 6 January 1953, just after Churchill's introductory visit, is of exceptional interest.

> Mr Churchill is as charming and interesting as ever, but he is quite definitely showing the effects of the passing years. He has fixed in his mind a certain international relationship he is trying to establish – possibly it would be better to say an atmosphere he is trying to create. This is that Britain and the British Commonwealth are not to be treated just as other nations would be treated by the United States in our complicated foreign problems.
>
> I assured him that I am quite ready to communicate with him personally, on our old basis of intimate friendship, where discussion between us would help advance our common interests. But I made clear to him that when official agreement or understanding must be reached, it must be done through those channels that will establish proper records for the future ...
>
> He is unquestionably influenced by old prejudices or instinctive reactions. [The President and his Secretary of State designate John Foster Dulles had tried to get him to understand their concerns about European union, but had got nowhere.] It is almost frustrating to attempt to make Winston see how important it is [that Britain should exert] leadership in bringing about this development.
>
> He talks very animatedly about certain other international problems, especially Egypt and its future. But so far as I can see, he has developed an almost childlike faith that all of the answers are to be found merely in British-American partnership ...
>
> Winston is trying to relive the days of World War II.[4]

It is clear from the Churchill-Eisenhower correspondence that followed that Churchill hadn't taken in a word of what the President was quite plainly seeking to get across to him: that notwithstanding what might have been the case during the war, there was to be 'No More Mr Nice Guy'. Churchill subjected Ike to the friendly-letter treatment ('My Dear Friend') that had informed and entertained Roosevelt in more desperate times. Ike wished that his letters did not arrive so often but patiently replied ('My Dear Winston'), sometimes at great length, politely explaining why he disagreed with Churchill's diagnoses of international situations, and why American foreign policy was not going to be influenced by them. These letters of course had a lot of official input, but that doesn't mean that they didn't say exactly what Ike wanted said. The very fact of their correspondence, a correspondence between leaders of Great Powers with no parallel other than that between Churchill and Roosevelt, obviously symbolised and embodied Anglo-American amity; and, so far as it went, that was good for both parties. Something unusual was certainly happening when a President showed the draft of a speech to the UN ('Atoms for Peace') to a Prime Minister and accepted several of his proposals for improvement. But so far as 'substantial matters of policy [were concerned], the evidence of the correspondence suggests that the two nations were growing further apart'.[5] They could not agree on how to handle the problems presented by China, Korea, French Indo-China, Iran, Europe or, closest to Churchill's imperial heart, Egypt. Above all, they were not of the same mind about Churchill's idea that the Big Three should have a summit meeting to talk together about the Bomb.

Churchill was already thinking of this in an unspecific sort of way long before the event in March 1953 that brought his thoughts abruptly to a point. Stalin died. The new man, or men as it surprisingly turned out to be, could only mark an improvement in the government of the Soviet Union, and there was a possibility that its foreign relations would become warmer. Then came another unexpected event, with advantageous consequences for Churchill although neither he nor anyone else would have wanted it to happen as it did. The Foreign Secretary Anthony Eden, who had long been unwell, was pronounced by his doctors to need an operation on his gall bladder. Performed in mid April, the operation was so badly bungled that another and more complicated operation – to be done preferably by the world's expert in it, an American – was imperative. The suffering Eden was flown over to Boston and operated on in June. He would not be back before the autumn. The work of his office was done in the meantime not by Eden's deputy at the Foreign Office but by – the Prime Minster himself.

The way once cleared by Eden's misfortune, Churchill opened his campaign. On 11 May, without consulting the Cabinet, the Foreign Office or the American President, and having treated the House of Commons to one of those *tours d'horizon* that he loved and did well, he concluded by arguing that it would be a pity not to seize the opportunity of Stalin's death to explore the possibility of improving East-West relations, and finding out just where that improvement might begin. In the language of the next generation, he was pioneering détente, which he did not believe the normal processes of diplomacy would easily discover. Cognoscenti of that recondite science and of Foreign Office orthodoxy would have recognised who was being got at when he said:

> It would, I think, be a mistake to assume that nothing can be settled with Soviet Russia unless or until everything is settled ... It certainly would do no harm if, for a while, each side looked about for things to do which would be agreeable instead of being disagreeable to each other.

He recalled how, eight years before, in one of his many attempts to check the falling of the diplomatic temperature, he had pleaded with Stalin not to let their disagreements harden into a global West-East conflict; 'It is quite obvious', he had said, 'that their quarrel would tear the world to pieces, and that all of us leading men on either side who had anything to do with that would be shamed before history.' What he had felt then, he felt again now.

> I believe that a conference on the highest level should take place between the leading Powers without long delay. This conference should not be overhung by a ponderous or rigid agenda, or led into mazes and jungles of technical details, zealously contested by boards of experts and officials drawn up in vast cumbrous array ... It might well be that no hard-faced agreements would be reached, but there might be a general feeling among those gathered together that they might do something better than tear the human race, including themselves, into bits ... If there is not at the summit of the nations the will to win the greatest prize and the greatest honour ever offered to mankind, doom-laden responsibility will fall upon those who now possess the power to decide. At the worst the participants ... would have established more intimate contacts. At the best we might have a generation of peace.[6]

The House was moved to hearty enthusiasm, the press followed suit; and, until the next sensation came along, Churchill enjoyed being a popular hero again. Here was initiative, here was hope! Might not the simple gesture, man to man within four walls, succeed in breaking the diplomatic ice? The professionals doubted it. The unfortunate Eden on his sick-bed felt worse when he heard of it, while his understudy at the Foreign Office, Lord Salisbury, thought of resigning. They were upset not least because this pulled out the rug from under the feet of the continental neighbours whom they had been patiently shepherding towards a European Defence Community. The Americans especially were not amused. If 'Special Relationship' meant anything, it surely meant that the partners did some consultation before launching an extravagant initiative, especially when it was the junior partner who wanted to launch it. The deed was done, however, and Eisenhower and Dulles had to make the best of it. They agreed to a preliminary meeting in the middle of June, accepting Churchill's suggestion that it should be in Bermuda but disappointing his hopes for a Special Relations private party by insisting that the French should be invited too.

Nothing happened for some weeks. First, there had to be a postponement because of changes in France. Then fate and illness struck again. On 23 June 1953 Churchill had a stroke, more serious than any of the little ones he had almost got used to over recent years. The Bermuda summit had to be postponed again, and only took place in early December. When at last it did happen, it gave Churchill little satisfaction. American policy towards the Soviet Union and (what they now bracketed with it) 'Red China' appeared to be as rigidly suspicious and hostile as ever. Unwilling to believe that he could not bring Ike round to his point of view, he turned his rage onto the Secretary of State. His doctor, who saw him every morning, recorded these remarks on 7 December, the day before the party came home.

> 'This fellow preaches like a Methodist Minister, and his bloody text is always the same: That nothing but evil can come out of meeting with Malenkov.'
>   There was a long pause.
>   'Dulles is a terrible handicap.' His voice rose. 'Ten years ago I could have dealt with him. Even as it is I have not been defeated by this bastard. I have been humiliated by my own decay ...'
>   When I turned round he was in tears. That was the last I heard of Moscow while we were at Bermuda.[7]

There the matter of a summit remained until the early summer of 1954. But the nuclear concerns prompting it moved on fast. The first American hydrogen bomb was exploded in November 1952; Russia's first followed, rather more quickly than had been expected, in August 1953. Britain would clearly be next. (The political decision to make one was in fact taken in mid 1954.) As the nuclear arms race speeded up, so did the production of estimates of what would happen to the cities and civilians involved in nuclear war, whether they chose to be or not. The terrifying facts about the effects of the American hydrogen bomb tests in the South Pacific became known. Churchill could reckon as well as anyone else what war with nuclear weapons would mean for Britain; the Special Relationship began to look not so good from the place of the relation nearer to the Soviet Union. In April 1954, Clement Attlee opened a debate on a motion requesting the convening of

> high-level talks between the Prime Minister, Mr Eisenhower and Mr Malenkov to discuss not just the question of the hydrogen bomb and of disarmament, but to discuss the problem that faces the world in the existence of the hydrogen bomb.[8]

Churchill agreed with Attlee as to the horrendous powers of the new superweapon but, unwilling to upset the Anglo-American apple-cart and in any case believing that its production had to be perfected before it could be halted, declined to ask the President to halt the experiments, which his scientific advisers had assured him would not get out of control. After reviewing the several routes towards disarmament currently being surveyed, he concluded with a brief affirmation of hope that something along the lines of Attlee's motion might be achieved and a reminder of the circumstances in which alone it might succeed.

> As we go forward on our difficult road, we shall always be guided by two main aims of policy. One is to lose no opportunity of convincing the Soviet leaders and, if we can reach them, the Russian people, that the democracies of the West have no aggressive designs on them. The other is to ensure that until that purpose has been achieved we have the strength necessary to deter any aggression by them and to ward it off if it should come. We shall continue at the same time to seek by every means open to us an easement [détente] in international tension and a sure foundation on which the people of the world can live their lives in security and peace.[9]

His last shot at it came two months later, in the summer of 1954. There was a certain desperation about it. His colleagues in government and everyone else who came close to him knew that his powers were intermittently failing. They also felt that it was very hard on Anthony Eden to be kept on a string month after month wondering if he would ever succeed to the premiership that had been marked out for him for so long. The possibility of a summit with détente to follow was by now the old man's main argument for carrying on. Still nursing the hope that he might persuade the President to support him, he began by inviting himself to Washington before April was out, and finally got there, with Eden as an apprehensive minder, at the end of June. Ike refused to be persuaded, but of course could not stop Churchill going ahead with an attempt to get himself invited to Moscow if he insisted on doing so. Even such minimal acquiescence sufficed a very old man in a very great hurry. There were elements of tragic farce about what happened next. Sailing home on the *Queen Elizabeth*, Churchill and Eden had a huge row. Churchill wanted to send his telegram to Malenkov straightaway, Eden didn't want him to send such a telegram at all. The compromise they reached was that Churchill would send the telegram and tell the Cabinet what he had done, and that Eden would say he had approved. The telegram was duly despatched, but Churchill deviously kept it from the Cabinet. When business resumed as usual in London, the Cabinet found out what had happened and there was another row. The possibility of a Churchill-Malenkov twosome continued to come and go like the Cheshire Cat until the Russians shot it down, several weeks later.

Churchill reported to the House of Commons as soon as he could after his return to England. Much of his speech on 12 July 1954 was designed to cement his Anglo-American Special Relationship on its pedestal above the inevitable and, he thought, insignificant ground-level bickering over minor details. At last he came to what Members had been waiting for: West-East relations under the shadow of the Bomb. His speech so far had necessarily reviewed many fields of conflict, some of them very violent, but he was able to end on the note of 'peaceful co-existence', an expression just then coming hopefully into use on both sides of the ideological divide. Herein, he prophetically said, lay the best hope for the future and (though he didn't explicitly mention it, probably lest he seem to upstage the President) his hope of advancing it.

> What a vast ideological gulf there is between the idea of peaceful co-existence vigilantly safeguarded, and the mood [sic] of forcibly extirpating the Communist fallacy and heresy. It is indeed a gulf. This statement is a recognition of the appalling character which war has now assumed and that its fearful consequences go even beyond the difficulties and dangers of dwelling side by side with Communist States.
>
> Indeed, I believe that the widespread acceptance of this policy may in the passage of years lead to the problems which divide the world being solved or solving themselves, as so many problems do, in a manner which will avert the mass destruction of the human race and give time, human nature and the mercy of God their chance to win salvation for us.[10]

He never got the summit on which he had set his heart. But he had yet to make his last and most lasting contribution to the debate about international security. His thinking about nuclear weaponry had moved on a long way from when he mentally classified it as the latest advance in the long history of explosives. The American hydrogen bomb tests had set his thoughts going along quite novel lines. His first disclosure of these in November 1953 had attracted little attention, perhaps being passed off as an instance of the old man's peculiar sort of humour. Tucked into a speech covering a variety of topics, he had admitted to the Commons that he 'sometimes had the odd thought that the annihilating character of these agencies may bring an utterly unforeseeable security to mankind ... and that when the advance of destructive weapons enables everyone to kill everybody else nobody will want to kill anyone at all'.

This light touch had gone when he returned to this theme in his final performance in the House of Commons on 1 March 1955. By now even he had acknowledged that, as an octogenarian unmistakably going downhill, he ought at last to retire, and he had promised to do so on 5 April. The 1 March speech, on whose composition he took enormous pains, was to be his swan song and, grand old trouper that he was, he made sure it would be a good one. The House of Commons was packed by 3.45 p.m. for the Prime Minister to move the approval of his government's statement on defence, a statement that would include the decision to make the hydrogen bomb. What the House got was as searching a review of defence and security in the nuclear age as had yet come before the world, and one that was to leave its mark on all subsequent discussion. He began with a bang.

> We live in a period, happily unique in human history, when the whole world is divided intellectually and to a large extent geographically between the creeds of Communist discipline and individual freedom, and when, at the same time, this mental and psychological division is accompanied by the possession by both sides of the obliterating weapons of the nuclear age ... We have force and science, hitherto the servants of man, now threatening to become his master.

The fearful powers of the hydrogen bomb had been made clear in the American tests and nothing could stop the Soviet Union from arming itself comparably. War with these weapons could not be 'won' in the conventional sense. Talks on disarmament, though earnestly pursued, were not getting anywhere.

> A curious paradox has emerged. Let me put it simply. After a certain point has been passed it may be said, 'The worse things get, the better'. The broad effect of the latest developments is to spread almost indefinitely ... the area of mortal danger. [Thus widely-spread-out countries become as vulnerable as crowded, tight-packed ones.] Here again we see the value of deterrents, immune against surprise and well understood by all persons on both sides – I repeat 'on both sides' – who have the power to control events. That is why I have hoped for a long time for a top level conference where these matters could be put plainly and bluntly from one friendly visitor to the conference to another.
>
> Then it may well be that we shall by a process of sublime irony have reached a stage in this story where safety will be the sturdy child of terror, and survival the twin brother of annihilation.

This became the central and lasting message. It baptised the strategy of nuclear deterrence which professionals of defence and strategic studies were beginning to articulate in a realm of technical discourse of which he can hardly have been aware, except in so far as echoes of it may have filtered through to him from the Chiefs of Staff. The theory was not comfortable; as he himself remarked, 'Imagination stands appalled'. But it was not unhopeful either, and in any case it was the only way ahead, until the process attained its natural conclusion in stalemate and (to adapt expressions coined thirty years or so later) mutual and balanced force reduction. To something of this sort, he looked forward in his peroration:

> To conclude, mercifully, there is time and hope if we combine patience and courage. All deterrents will improve and gain authority during the next ten years. By that time, the deterrent may well reach its acme and reap its final reward. The day may dawn when fair play, love for one's fellow men, respect for justice

and freedom, will enable tormented generations to march forth serene and triumphant from the hideous epoch in which we have to dwell. Meanwhile, never flinch, never weary, never despair.[11]

Churchill's search for a summit was controversial and has remained so. Eden disliked Dulles even more than Churchill did, and had to see a lot more of him but they both shared a dislike of Churchill's attempted summitry: Eden, chiefly because he shared the Foreign Office's preference for well-prepared and limited agendas on which the actors would be thoroughly briefed; Dulles partly because he could not trust the Soviets not to pull a fast one. Each of them had a good point. The history of the post-war series of summits (the first of which took place in 1955, not long after Churchill's retirement) has many disappointments in it. On the other hand, it also has remarkable and wholesome successes. Summits could work in the beneficial way Churchill maintained. One might reckon that the successful ones did more good than the unsuccessful ones did harm. But whether the Churchill of the 1950s was really up to managing a summit has to be doubted. By that time he had become notoriously reluctant to study briefs. His powers of concentration could still be formidable when he had nothing to distract him and when he felt well and motivated, but how could those conditions be guaranteed at critical moments? More than ever, he was liable to be tearfully swayed by emotions, perhaps emotions that would be inappropriate in summit circumstances. One has to conclude that his pursuit of a summit for quiet private talk about the arms race was a magnificent endeavour – but that Eden was right to be glad that Churchill did not manage it.

24

Return to Downing Street

'that characteristic British Parliamentary principle cherished in both Lord and Commons, "Don't bring politics into private life".'

Churchill in Westminster Hall, 30 November 1954:
his eightieth birthday

The later 1940s were good years for Churchill. Having, so to speak, won the war, he was free to help win the peace. The three campaigns that most obviously marked his doing that on the world stage – the European Movement, the rally to resist Soviet and Communist expansion, and the beginnings of nuclear arms control – have already been described. Now we must attend to his activities nearer home. The Conservative defeat in the 1945 Election turned out to be just what Clementine hoped it would be, a blessing in disguise. He was freed from the fears, demands and disappointments that had been his companions for the past five years: disasters reported, opportunities missed, demands that could not be met, inefficiencies and bungles more numerous than his minutes could correct, the sense of his beloved country's resources in manpower and everything else being squeezed till the pips squeaked. That squeaking (far from stopping in August 1945, it went on remorselessly) now ceased to be his responsibility. He would observe the work of those whose responsibility it had become from the seat he had never occupied before, that of Leader of His Majesty's Loyal Opposition. Beyond that, he was free to do what he wished.

As Leader of the Opposition, Churchill was no more than intermittently active: too intermittently to satisfy the more fiery spirits within his party. Notwithstanding that his prepared speeches struck some newcomers as pompous, what he did in the Commons he did well; but he didn't do a great deal until the approach of the next general election. He had other work to do that seemed just as important to him: the Cold War and European Movement work on the one hand, the writing of his war memoirs on the other; the latter had the dual value that, besides establishing his side of the story before the others got their versions out, his contracts for the books and the American journalism associated with them would produce income for the present and capital to invest for the family's future. His rich way of living and liking for luxury again depended, as they had done throughout his earlier life, on the generosity of friends and on what he earned with his pen.

Those fiery Conservative spirits who were passionate to fight socialism tooth and nail, and to throw down an ideological gauntlet, began dreaming of a more full-time and forward-looking leader quite early on, and covertly talked of persuading or pressing him to retire. To that there were two obstacles. First, he had no intention of retiring until he chose; and, secondly, the respect he commanded both in and out of Parliament was such that he could truly say that the rank and file of the party wanted him to carry on. It was widely supposed that Churchill had not been the great vote-winner in 1945 in large part because of socialistic bias in the educational branches of the armed forces; now the war was over, why should he not be a vote-winner, next time round? Moreover, it could be expected that the socialists would make themselves unpopular. Churchill the hammer of socialism was scarcely less potent a totem than Churchill the hammer of the Nazis. Churchill himself confidently expected Attlee's government to dig its own grave. In peace as in war he didn't like planning for too far ahead; you never knew what unforeseen opportunities and problems might turn up in the meantime. He therefore resisted the enthusiasts' call for, as he viewed it, a premature declaration of Conservative policy and settled for keeping the party's commitments to principles and generalities while Labour's popularity burned itself out.

It was indeed difficult to see what else could profitably have been done. Labour had come into Parliament with 184 more seats than the Conservatives. It set about its ambitious legislative programme without a week's delay. The first of its series of nationalisations, that of the Bank of England, was one with which in fact Churchill had a good deal of sympathy; a nationalised bank would not, he thought, have leaned on him to make the wrong decision in 1925. And that was only one of Labour's measures he had no stomach to oppose. He had favoured nationalising the railways since the Great War. He would not have been sorry if the coal industry had been nationalised in the troublesome 1920s. He could not find any good arguments against the case for keeping or bringing into public ownership public utilities that were also natural monopolies. He did not bother to participate in any of the debates about them, and when the intellectuals of the party with his encouragement produced an Industrial Charter in early 1947, it accepted that category of nationalisations as *faits accomplis*. Then there was the government's legislation establishing the National Health Service and comprehensive social insurance. This latter did bring him into action, but only to claim for himself when young, for pre-war Conservative governments and for his wartime coalition most of the credit for what he picked out as the schemes' more sensible, affordable and discriminating elements.

The truth was that Churchill could bring himself to dislike only part of the Labour government's legislation and only some Labour politicians. That did not keep him from harrying, and encouraging his sharp-shooters to harry, the party in power by every available parliamentary device and convention, including some which might have been labelled sharp practice, even blows below the belt in any other game than the parliamentary one. Attlee, victim of one such, was surprised to find himself able to forgive its perpetrator; Cripps, a more sensitive soul who suffered from another, found it much more difficult.[1] When Churchill did take the offensive, it was no holds barred. The socialists had ousted him from the front bench, he would not rest until he had ousted them. But, because of his mixed feelings about them personally and what they were doing, he got more satisfaction from the fight with some of them than others. Ernest Bevin's conduct of foreign policy in most respects he admired and approved, and when he was in Washington he sought to back it; he would have had more reservations about Bevin's policy regarding Palestine, had his pro-Zionism not received a bad knock when Jewish terrorists assassinated the British minister in Cairo, his and Clementine's friend Lord Moyne.

India was another matter. This was something about which Churchill's ideas had essentially remained unchanged over the years – a strange phenomenon in a man who could move with the times in so many respects. Attlee, who had long believed in the granting of independence and took a leading part in promoting the legislation that brought the Raj to an end on 15 August 1947, concluded that, in this part of his mind, Churchill was still the subaltern of Victoria's Diamond Jubilee year. No exchanges between the leaders of the two sides were more sharp than those about India. Churchill made a carefully prepared speech early in March 1947, pointing out how precipitate the pending withdrawal appeared to be (although it was going to be even more precipitate after Mountbatten got going as Viceroy), and forecasting with more accuracy than the ignorant and doctrinaire liked to hear the tumults and massacres that were sure to ensue. But, having consistently over so many years refused to listen to those of his own party who had constructive ideas about how to hand India back to the Indians more or less painlessly (supposing such a thing ever to have been possible, which may be doubted), he was in no position to criticise a government that did at last grasp the nettle and do the necessary thing. In private he spoke of the loss of the jewel in Britannia's crown as if it was a personal deprivation, and predicted that the Indians would not be up to governing their own country. He was man enough to recognise, over the next few years, that in that respect at least he had been wrong; the bitter pill being sweetened by India's decision to remain within the Commonwealth.

Their differences over India notwithstanding, Churchill respected Clement Attlee. Because certain fabricated Churchillisms at Attlee's expense had currency in those days, and because some continue to appear in the more popular kinds of Churchill literature, it is worth recalling that, when John Colville ventured to tell Churchill about them, he was indignant and instructed Colville expressly to deny them.[2] Churchill certainly did not dislike the captain of the other team. But he did dislike some of the people in that team. (Attlee privately disliked some of them too, but that is another matter.) A type of socialist that curiously irritated him was the well-educated intellectual, subject of repeated jibes. But the socialist individual he most disliked (even more than his 1945 bugbear Harold Laski) was the Welsh miners' MP Aneurin Bevan, famous for his journalism and oratory, and for giving Churchill a hard time in the wartime Commons, before achieving high office as Labour's Minister of Health. In Bevan was distilled and transparent the class antagonism that the consensus-minded, coalition-preferring, one-nation Tory detested and feared. Always politically on the boil, Bevan was the idol of the more romantic, the more revolutionary and the more unaccommodating part of the Labour Party. The language that Aneurin Bevan, Michael Foot and their kind used about Conservatism was sometimes as extreme as the language Churchill had used about Bolshevism in 1919–20. The Bevanites and some of the more primitive Labour types who were swept into Parliament by the 1945 landslide made no attempt to conceal their hostility to Churchill; an observer of the Commons might find it a sad spectacle to see him baited by them, an ageing monarch of the glen at bay among the hounds, though it may be that the ageing monarch himself didn't feel so bad about it.

Dislike of socialist personnel and style was, however, not sufficient ground on which to maintain a Parliamentary Opposition. Until the time came for the formal presentation of Conservative policy in preparation for the next election, Churchill left the ideological and City-based opposition to those with greater expertise in it. He himself focused on the issues of bureaucracy, controls and the people's hardships under the continuing reign of austerity, the great theme of the time. He had regretted these concomitants of a centralised command economy in the years when total war made them necessary; now that the fighting war was over, he felt free to come out strong as representative of the plain man and woman's feelings about rationing, shortages of what wasn't rationed, and an excess of civil servants.

Rationing was in some respects tighter than it had been during the war; such basics as housing and coal were in short supply, the latter most painfully during the grim winter of 1946–47 with consequent power cuts. The supply of civil servants on the other hand seemed to be excessive and some of their powers, if not as menacing as predicted in the 'Gestapo' speech, were at any rate unprecedentedly intrusive. These were the years when the dark-suited bowler-hatted 'men from the Ministry' became figures of radio fun and Ealing Studios' topical comedies.

It was easier to excite indignation about these unpopular things than actually to do something about them, especially when they hung on the strings of the nation's overall economic situation and its fluctuations. When the Conservatives returned to power in October 1951, one of the promises they held out was for easier and better times. But one of the first things an economic crisis forced them to do was to reduce the meat ration. Churchill's imaginative empathy with the lives of the poor and ordinary was at its most sensitive in respect of food-rationing, but his privileged existence and self-indulgent habits kept him from understanding much about the matter. Harold Macmillan recalled how, when Churchill returned to Number Ten, he demanded to be shown what a single adult's food ration amounted to. A week's rations were accordingly set out on a tray for his inspection. What's wrong with that, he asked; you could get a good meal out of that.[3]

The government he formed and the policies it pursued were of the most un-Thatcherite character, purposefully non-divisive and conciliatory; by no means can the Iron Lady seriously claim his policies as a precedent for hers. The Tory rhetoric superficially suggested something of the sort – 'Set the People Free' and so on, and such Churchillian aphorisms as 'the ladder not the queue' and 'competition upwards not downwards' – but once he entered Number Ten he became the consensus-seeking politician his heart had always wanted him to be. The Cabinet was both the most harmonious and the most lordly there had been for a very long time. So far as possible he filled it with wartime colleagues, friends and relations. One son-in-law, Duncan Sandys, the second husband of Diana, became Minister of Supply; another son-in-law Christopher Soames, Mary's kindly, clever and capable husband, who seems in these years to have stood in for the supportive son Randolph unfortunately couldn't be, became his Parliamentary Private Secretary. The ever-faithful Lord Cherwell was Paymaster-General, from which point of ease and vantage he again set up a Statistical Section and acted informally as minister for atomic weapons development. 'Pug' Ismay was roped in, to his great astonishment, and so was 'Alex' (Field-Marshal Lord Alexander). Lord Woolton became Lord President of the Council;

Lord Salisbury, Lord Privy Seal. Lord Bracken, as Brendan Bracken now became, was offered the Colonies but said he was not fit enough; that office went instead to Oliver Lyttelton. Anthony Eden of course was Foreign Secretary, Sir Walter Monckton (the Duke of Windsor's former legal adviser) Minister of Labour. R. A. Butler was Chancellor of the Exchequer, well trusted since 1942 but with a Chamberlainite prehistory still to live down. As Minister of Housing and Local Government, Harold Macmillan had the onerous task of trying to build the 300,000 houses each year promised at the 1950 Party Conference. This was an elderly, respectable and soothing administration. Conservatives who had hoped for one with plenty of anti-socialist pepper in it were disappointed.

Churchill did not mind disappointing them. He was happy to leave the pepper of argument and abuse to the Labour Party which, although it had remarkably achieved a larger number of votes than the Conservatives (that familiar effect of the first-past-the-post system), was entering one of its recurrent phases of civil war, with the dissident Bevanites denouncing the leadership in the Parliamentary Party from their stronghold of dominance within the National Executive Committee. Conservatives did not like that sort of thing – their present leader's having done it himself in the 1930s was something the true-blue faithful never quite forgot – which made it easier for them to claim to be the more comprehensively 'national' party. This was a note that Churchill enjoyed sounding. It had come out clear and strong in his speeches during the campaign; not least when speaking at Plymouth on the eve of the poll on behalf of his son Randolph, contesting Devonport against the ultra-peppery Michael Foot. After commiserating with his opponents on being worn out and dried up, and expressing generous sentiments about 'their principal figures' Bevin and Cripps, now gone from the scene, he concluded:

> let me tell you how much I look forward to the time when this loud clatter and turmoil of party strife dies down for a spell and gives us a good, long, steady period in which the opposing parties may be able to see some of each other's virtues instead of harping on each other's faults ... Let us rise to our full height above class and party interests, and guard with growing comradeship and brotherhood the land of hope and glory we all love so well.[4]

In a political language more familiar now than it was then, Churchill was a 'wet'. The term already had some currency, and the general 'wetness' of his administration was explicitly lamented by Conservatives of 'dry' disposition. But Churchill wanted it that way. It fortified his aspiration to national unity and ran closer to the socio-parliamentary pattern he had always imagined to be the best; no doubt it also flattered his idea of himself as a national leader. At the opening of the 1953–54 session, after commenting on the near equivalence of the two main political parties in the country, he remarkably said:

> It is not really possible to assume that one of these fourteen million masses of voters possess [sic] all the virtues and the wisdom and the other lot are dupes or fools, or even knaves or crooks. Ordinary people in the country mix about with each other in friendly, neighbourly relations, and they know it is nonsense for party politicians to draw such harsh contrasts between them.[5]

His government's policy therefore was to take over as many of the preceding government's institutional innovations as it could, and to disturb as little as possible the social and industrial relations it inherited. The National Health Service, for all that it was the odious Bevan's baby, and the rest of the Welfare State institutions were taken over en bloc and maintained with only minor, financially prudent modifications. The major nationalisations were left untouched; only those late and most controversial ones of the steel industry and of road transport being painfully and, in the case of steel, unsatisfactorily undone. The abolition of rationing took longer than expected, not least because Churchill came into office just as a balance of payments crisis was coming to its climax; his worst wartime moments may have been recalled by the appearance on his domestic doorstep, only a few hours after he had become Prime Minister, of the Permanent Secretary to the Treasury and the Secretary to the Cabinet with the information that Britain was about to go bust unless Churchill and his team did something very quickly. The most sensational of the measures consequently taken was a 25 per cent rise in the bank rate, taking it to 2.5 per cent, followed by an even more enormous jump to 4 per cent in the budget of March 1952. Among the economies enforced were cuts in ministers' salaries and even in defence expenditure. This was a disappointing beginning. But the same rises and falls of economic pressure that enforced these early embarrassments soon turned round to work on the government's behalf. The progressive abolition of food rationing was complete by the middle of 1954, by which time the shades of austerity were yielding to the dawn of relative affluence. Work was plentiful, real wages were going up, people were acquiring homes and cars as never before. Sailing before the same fair wind, the second in line of Churchill's successors would after no long interval be able to congratulate the British people on 'never having had it so good'.

It was a matter of some annoyance to true-blue believers and would-be reformers with 'dry' credentials that Churchill and many of his Cabinet colleagues showed themselves more interested in Transport House than in the City. This again was because of the policy of avoiding social unrest and maintaining, so far as possible, full employment. Already before the poll two sweeteners had been thrown in Labour's direction: an excess profits levy on defence contracts, and an undertaking not to tinker with the law on trade disputes. Once in office, it was a major concern of Churchill to avoid industrial disputes which might lead to strikes in the nationalised industries. His emollient Minister of Labour, Monckton, was picked precisely with that end in view. The result was 'a series of inflationary wage settlements ... as public sector unions campaigned for comparability with the private sector'.[6] Miners and railwaymen did particularly well in this genial industrial climate. Churchill had indeed in his old age become an 'industrial appeaser'. The wisdom of his policy was questioned by fearless colleagues within the governing circle and by frustrated 'drys' outside it. Strong arguments have been mounted by critical historians, social scientists and (with their own agenda to pursue) radical politicians, to the effect that it did British society no good in the long run to continue cushioned in a culture of dependency, also that so complacent a regime could not assist what the British economy very much needed: modernisation of its material base, sharpening of its employment habits, and reappraisal of its products and markets. To which may be added, in the wider dimension already glanced at, a neglect of all the opportunities that might have come with early entry into the uniting institutions of Europe. These have been and remain serious questions.

Defence was predictably an area in which Churchill took a special interest, but it was not an area offering much room for manoeuvre or gratification. The potential demands of the three services were limitless, given that Britain was striving to do so much: to keep the Union Jack flying all round the world and especially in the Middle East, to convince the western European allies that Britain would be with them in the event of an invasion from the east, and to acquire an independent nuclear capability. On permanent guard against the service ministries stood the Treasury brandishing the balance sheets of national finance. Britain was not economically secure and rich enough to play the Great Power without cutting corners and cheeseparing. Clement Attlee's government in the winter of 1950–51 had valiantly embarked on a rearmament programme to encourage American confidence in Britain as a worthwhile ally, but even that modest pace was too fast for the economy to maintain; Churchill's government had to cut the programme as part of the early economies already mentioned. Within eighteen months the same bitter draught had to be swallowed again. The Chiefs of Staff having produced estimates unacceptably high for a war they thought Britain might survive on the winning side, they were instructed by an ad hoc Cabinet committee, Churchill in the chair and his son-in-law Sandys putting on the pressure, to make cheaper plans for the only sort of war the country could afford: to put no fine point upon it, a war in which the Soviet Union would quickly be bombed into submission by the USA.[7]

The heart of the matter was nuclear weaponry. It was as unthinkable for Churchill and his military men not to go in for these armaments as it had been for Attlee and his Chiefs of Staff a few years earlier. The latter had early decided that Britain had to begin the quest for nuclear capability if British foreign and defence policy was to retain the option of independence and if Britain was to be valued as an ally of worth. This decision, at first known only to a small and totally trustworthy group of ministers officials and, of course, scientists, had been revealed to Parliament in May 1948. Churchill's initial inclination, when he found out how far the work had progressed, was to put the Bomb's further development on hold, in the belief that once he had applied his unique bellows to the embers of the Special Relationship, the US would generously save Britain the trouble and expense of going it alone. Discovering in the course of his visit to Washington in January 1952 that things were not so simple, but given an exciting view of the possibilities of strategic air power in his talks with the American air chiefs, he thought that it was best after all to carry on where Attlee had left off. Work on Britain's atomic capability continued.

How far to go along the line of nuclear preparedness, and how to integrate nuclear weaponry into Anglo-American and NATO strategy, were the most important defence questions Churchill and his government had to deal with through the remainder of his term of office. It is right to say Churchill and his government because he could not be as dominant now as he had been during the war. In the Cabinet he was more like what the original theory of his office supposed, *primus inter pares*. The Treasury's opinion swayed the majority. There was no national emergency to induce his countrymen to lend him their ears. His attempt to create a sense of emergency by conjuring up the spectre of Britain overwhelmed by Russian paratroops unless the Home Guard re-formed to confront them was a flop, and there were other signs of the nation becoming less war-minded, more war-worried. His friend Alexander, unsuitable as Minister of Defence (or indeed as a politician of any sort), had no aptitude for presenting the Chiefs of Staffs' papers to the Cabinet. The Chiefs, for their part, lacking the direction of such a master as Churchill had once been, were doing their usual thing of fighting their own service's corners and angling for strategies that would bring the most benefit to their respective constituencies.

The more the Chiefs of Staff and the Defence Committee (the one Cabinet Committee Churchill always chaired) mulled over the nuclear questions, the more unenviable the British situation seemed and the more desirable therefore that nuclear war should at all costs be avoided. They had to take note, as Churchill and every other sensible person by then had done, that the progression from atom bomb to hydrogen bomb took nuclear weaponry and planning for nuclear warfare through a quantum leap. Since there was as yet no prospect of halting, let alone reversing, the arms race, the only hope of avoiding war lay in deterrence. The Chiefs' thinking was already beginning to run along this line before Churchill re-entered Number Ten; their 1952 Global Strategy Paper for the first time brought it clearly to the fore, where it stayed. Under relentless pressure from the Treasury, and well before Churchill had given deterrence his valedictory blessing in March 1955, defence policy was en route to becoming at once more nuclear and more economical; money spent on adding a British hydrogen bomb (ordered in 1954) to the British atom bomb (successfully let off in October 1952) finding the additional justification that it facilitated a massive reduction of conventional armed forces.

Churchill had turned eighty by the time he quit Number Ten on 5 April 1955, bringing to a close at last the long drawn out saga of his retirement. From several standpoints, his retirement was by then years overdue. His wife and family had wanted him to retire in 1945. They thought, and the world in general agreed with them, that he had earned a rest. It would not have been a rest in the ordinary sense of the word, because it was not in his nature to be inactive or purposeless; but there was his memoir-history to write, his painting to resume, his estate at Chartwell to improve, and the company of his family and friends to enjoy. And indeed those were things he wanted to get back to and did get back to with great success. But he would not give up Parliament and all its opportunities for usefulness (and, of course, enjoyment; he loved the House of Commons) while he could still carry on.

This was going to make problems for those whose standpoint was not the preferences of private but the amenities of public life. The problems became most apparent in their convergence on the unfortunate person of Anthony Eden. Eden was acknowledged and respected as Churchill's political heir and successor, which Churchill himself was happy for him to be. In 1945 he was still under fifty. So long as the old man continued in robust health and did not overmuch neglect his Opposition duties, Eden did not let the question of succession bother him. Six years later, the relative situations of the two men were in rapid process of change. With a majority over Labour of no more than twenty-six, the party had to hope that the next election would move it into a stronger position, and it was natural that the man who would lead it at that election (it could only be Eden) should soon begin to talk about needing time to 'play himself in'. Eden was still in his early fifties, but he was not the healthy and happy man his debonair appearance suggested, and, until after his second marriage in 1952, he had a wretched home life. It was not surprising that he shared the opinion of those in party and government who judged that Churchill was getting past it and that Eden should be given his chance.

This awkward question lay dormant through the first two years of the government's life. Churchill was managing the job adequately; in fact, rather well for a man of his age. Admittedly he was becoming deafer, he took longer over business and he had less energy for interfering with other people's business than formerly, but with the support of one of the century's best Cabinet Secretaries, Norman Brook, the Cabinet's work went on as good constitutionalists expected it to do, and most of the departmental ministers were efficient. Then came some transfiguring events in 1953. The year began pleasantly enough. Eden's serious illness through the summer gave Churchill the opportunity to manage the Foreign Office while his friend and deputy was on sick leave. In early summer came an occasion he very much enjoyed. Elizabeth II had been Queen since her father's death in February 1952 but now, the vast array of necessary imperial arrangements having been made, she was to be formally crowned. The splendid Coronation ceremony on 2 June of course became the great event of the year, perhaps of the decade, making all the more of an impression on the nation because it was televised. Monarchs from all over and dignitaries of every kind and colour were there in full fig, Churchill himself contributing to the show by putting on his fanciest costume, that of Lord Warden of the Cinque Ports, and gilding the lily with his martial ancestor the great Duke of Marlborough's king-size badge of the Order of the Garter. All the Commonwealth Prime Ministers came to London for the great occasion, and Churchill had to take the lead in their official entertainment. All this, on top of carrying on the Queen's government and doubling for the Foreign Secretary, was a terrible strain for a stoutish *bon viveur* of seventy-nine. His doctor, his family and his colleagues all worried lest it should prove too much.

On Tuesday 23 June 1953, it did. Mary Soames was there.

It happened towards the end of a large dinner at No. 10 ... given in honour of Signor de Gasperi, the Prime Minister of Italy, and his wife ... In proposing his guest's health, Winston made a singularly delightful and witty speech, but as the company was leaving the dining-room Christopher suddenly noticed that his father-in-law was having difficulty in standing up.

Clementine also had spotted that something was wrong. She and Mary's husband helped him to a chair in the next room and tactfully explained to the guests that their host had been overdoing things and had to retire early. But the truth was that Churchill had had a stroke more serious than any of the minor strokes and spasms that went back to the early 1940s and from which he had always quickly recovered. Churchill himself, completely *compos mentis* all the time, was as anxious as everyone else at the apex of the pyramid of power to keep the matter secret. Dinner guests who had noticed something wrong with his articulation were allowed to go on attributing it to over-indulgence. The family got him to bed and anxiously awaited Lord Moran's visit next morning.[8]

Early next morning, Moran and the suitably named brain specialist Lord Brain duly appeared, and the stroke was formally diagnosed. Churchill having said he didn't want to miss Questions in the House that afternoon, he was advised not to go, lest he find himself at a loss for words. He seems not to have mentioned to the doctors that a Cabinet was scheduled for that very morning. The doctors departed. Then the illustrious patient put on one of the most extraordinary shows of his life. He had himself properly dressed, went downstairs to the Cabinet and got through it without anyone noticing more than that there was something odd about his mouth, that he was unusually quiet and, instead of his usual pink complexion, was very pale. It was magnificent but it may not have been wise. There were no signs of the usual rapid recovery. In fact he became rather worse. It was decided to move him down to Chartwell where he could more easily be quiet and unseen. He was desperately anxious that the world should not know what had happened, and, by the prodigies of secrecy and discretion still possible in those days, the world believed what the medical bulletin told it, namely, that he was simply worn out by the Coronation activities and was under doctor's orders to rest.

Over the next few weeks, he steadily recovered both speech and movement, until by August the doctors said he could ease himself back towards work if that was what he insisted on. It was. On 18 August he presided again at Cabinet, and claimed to be as good as new. But of course he wasn't. From this time on, his health was a major political concern, his competence to do the top job indubitably questionable, and his reluctance to retire a source of unhappiness and disquiet to his Cabinet colleagues. But still the inevitable was delayed, for several reasons. First, the only person in the world who could have made him give up wouldn't do so; Clementine had wanted him to retire years ago and knew that his colleagues all wanted him to give up now, but this was the one thing she would not tell him to do, on the loving ground that to give up politics would be, for him, to give up life itself; she couldn't even bring herself to tell him, eight years later, that he ought to give up being an MP. Secondly, he was not yet incapable enough for the case for retirement to be obvious even to his obstinate self. On occasion, and with Lord Moran's mysterious pills inside him, he could still produce a grand effect; the 'balance of terror' speech as late as 1 March 1955 proved it. Apart from special occasions, however, his powers of concentration and his will to work were evidently weakening by the month. And, thirdly, given that Clemmie wouldn't and the Queen constitutionally couldn't press him, and that he was far too much of the grand old man and iconic hero for his party to presume to push him, the decision lay with no one but himself. The British public, seeing the flattering pictures of him which were all that editors at that time printed and in particular the scene of him thanking the House of Commons for the eightieth birthday gift of the Graham Sutherland portrait, flanked by beaming Cabinet colleagues, had no idea that those colleagues were privately fuming with annoyance at his egoistic determination to believe that he was still indispensable.

Even to the very last days Churchill was finding reasons for hanging on. Eden thought that he was home and dry at last when Churchill summoned him on 14 February 1955 and said that he really would go on 5 April. But as late as 29 March he was finding reasons why the date should be put off again. This time, however, it was for real. On the eve of his retirement there was a big farewell dinner at Number Ten, unprecedentedly distinguished by the presence of the Queen and the Duke of Edinburgh. Next day, after chairing his last Cabinet, he was driven to Buckingham Palace to present his resignation. He finally quit Downing Street for Chartwell on the 6th, receiving popular plaudits at both ends of the journey. It was somehow sad and predictable that Clementine had to stay behind, to supervise the clearing up.

25

Sunset and Nightfall

'I feel like an aeroplane at the end of its flight, in the dusk, with the petrol running out, looking for a safe landing.'

Churchill to R. A. Butler, March 1954

Churchill's family and friends experienced his second retirement from the Premiership as a rerun in slower motion of the first retirement ten years before. By now a great deal slower and frailer, he took longer to emerge from the initial period of depression and a kind of bewilderment; as in 1915 and again in 1945, everyone close to him could see, what he himself was all too aware of, that his mind and body worked together best when he was under pressure and in a state of permanent excitement and high tension. On the two previous occasions when he seemed to suffer from the release of pressure (he vividly likened it to what happened to a deep-sea creature brought suddenly to the surface), a high road to recovery had been the justification of the historical role he had just been playing and its publication at the earliest opportunity. In 1955, no such work of justification was called for. The only literary task remaining to be done was to finalise the draft of his *A History of the English-Speaking Peoples*. For that, and for a tired old man's epilogue (drafted for him by one of his regular assistants and his private secretary) to *The Second World War*, done for a huge sum of money early in 1957, he had just enough vitality left.[1]

The vitality was now flowing much less strongly than in 1945, and his family would have suffered sorely had this not been the case. The immediate prospect then was of a return to his earlier situation of having to live by his pen. Every prop that his high office and privileged status had put beneath him through nearly six years suddenly disappeared. What he had humorously described as living from mouth to hand through the 1930s really had been a touch and go time of surviving financially from month to month, and the end of that decade found him grievously in debt. It was to remove that incubus that early in 1938 he had contracted to produce the ambitiously long *History of the English-Speaking Peoples* in record quick time, by December 1939. With the help of assistants he had 500,000 words duly drafted before fate or destiny (his preferred reading of the workings of accident and chance) called him to duties to which even the most demanding publisher had to defer. Within a few months of the end of the war, he was looking into the abyss of debt again. It is a measure of its darkness and his consequent need for publishers' advances that he allowed his *Secret Session Speeches* to come out in *Life* magazine before they came out as a book in Britain. From the same source – *Time-Life's* owner Henry Luce had long been an admirer – came $25,000 dollars for reproduction of a batch of his pre-war paintings. The team of research and writing assistants reassembled early in 1946. Churchill was having to return to the old grind as an out of office politician obliged to write to make ends meet, and he was again having to consider putting Chartwell on the market.

Then friends and admirers took a hand. Lord Camrose, a press magnate and one of Churchill's long-time friends, was astounded and shocked when he learned the facts. This was no way to treat a national hero, the saviour of civilisation. Three arrangements were made that transformed Churchill's situation and which freed the hero from financial worry for the rest of his life. First, a deal was made whereby Chartwell would be purchased for the National Trust, with the condition that it should remain the Churchills' country home for as long as Winston and Clementine were alive. (In the event, Clementine left it as soon as she was on her own, and it was opened to the public in 1966.) Camrose and his benevolent syndicate, the only untitled members of which were J. Arthur Rank and James de Rothschild, easily raised £85,000; £50,000 for Churchill (that was a lot more than he had expected to get in a forced sale) and the rest for the National Trust as a maintenance endowment. Now the Churchills had only their London home at 28 Hyde Park Gate to maintain. The second arrangement was to secure good contracts, with fat advances, for the war memoirs. Camrose fixed this in concert with the cosmopolitan literary agent who had marketed Churchill's journalism before the war, Emery Reves. Before 1946 was out, their star performer was assured of over a million dollars from Henry Luce for serialising his memoirs in *Life*, and £250,000 from Houghton Mifflin for them in book form. Contracts with Cassell for their UK publication followed soon after. The third arrangement was necessitated mainly by the British rates of taxation, then rising to 95 per cent (and driving many high earners to work abroad). With the generous payment for Chartwell in his pocket and sundry incomings from his literary labours in view, income for himself was the lesser part of Churchill's financial concern. He wanted to ensure his family's security, especially that of Clementine, who would, he correctly believed, outlive him. There was therefore established, with Cherwell, Brendan Bracken and Oliver Lyttelton in charge, the Chartwell Literary

Trust, to receive the war memoirs' profits and to use them for Clementine's and his descendants' benefit.[2] By the end of 1946, the financial troubles that had recurrently dogged him were over for good.

The riches just listed were not, as things turned out, the only source of the affluence that soon marked his way of living. It was not easy for the honest rich to live up to their income in Britain for many years after the war, so steep was the taxation and so fine-meshed the tax net. Nor was it easy for British subjects who had money to take out of the country for holidays actually to take it, currency exports being severely restricted and the British traveller's exchange allowance meagre. Means soon evolved to enable Churchill to indulge his love of living on the Continent, especially the French Riviera. Money earned in America could be spent in France, for example at Monte Carlo's Hôtel de Paris or the Hôtel Roi René in Aix; the irrepressible and generous Beaverbrook had a lovely villa, La Capponcina, at Cap d'Ail, where the Churchills could stay whether Beaverbrook himself was there or not. From 1956, Churchill was also often at Emery Reves's lush villa, La Pausa, near Roquebrune, where he met the man who would be the richest and most surprising of all the hosts of his sunset years, Aristotle Onassis. There were also well-heeled admirers whose interest or pleasure, or both, it was to have him and his company to stay at their expense. They needed to be rich, because Churchillian visits didn't come cheap. 'When he went abroad, [he] was literally treated royally.'[3] The Swiss banker who placed his lakeside villa at the Churchills' disposal for three weeks in the summer of 1946 also had to accommodate, as a minimum, Mary, Diana and her husband, two secretaries and Churchill's valet.[4] Churchill liked to travel in style, rather like an eighteenth-century nobleman on the Grand Tour or a high-up colonial administrator in Africa. The amount of luggage was colossal. It was burned into Mary's memory that, when she and Christopher and her parents made an unpremeditated move from Annecy to Venice, there were over one hundred items of luggage.[5] The climactic venture was to Marrakesh in January 1951, courtesy of Henry Luce. It was meant to be on a generous scale but, even so, Luce's European agent became concerned about the costs of accommodating, dining and wining Churchill and 'his large entourage' of family, friends, servants and writing assistants.[6]

These latter were integral to Churchill's method of book production. He relied upon assistants to locate and to bring to the building site materials relevant and necessary for the story he wished to tell. What that story was he had a pretty good idea before he started. Its outline and its 'moral' (to use a concept better understood in his time than ours) at any rate were clear in his head. Besides the building stones, he also sought from his assistants supplies of local colour and accurate detail to enable him, the master builder, properly to deck out the grand impressive whole. He did not want materials or ideas that would spoil his story, or suggestions that it should be altered. Since his assistants were generally men (always men, never women) of culture, experience and academic accomplishment, there was theoretically a possibility that differences of opinion would disturb the relationship, but from the testimonies left by several of them it is clear that the terms of service were so well understood on both sides that harmony prevailed. His assistants helped him to write well what he wanted to write, and, so far as the facts of his version were concerned, they made sure that he would get them right. They did not feel compromised by the personal tone of his final versions, which in the case of The Second World War was nobly self-justificatory and in the case of A History of the English-Speaking Peoples was gloriously old-fashioned.

It is well to emphasise all this in an age when the 'ghosting' of books has become promiscuous and the criteria of scholarly respectability fastidious. Churchill had read widely in classics of British, European and American history and had mastered them so well that the young Oxford historian F. W. Deakin, a regular assistant from Marlborough onwards, paid Churchill the tribute of saying that he learned 'in evenings and early morning hours in [the] study at Chartwell ... vastly more of the sense of history than my formal university education as a student, and later as a teacher, ever taught me'.[7] All the same, it must be remembered that Churchill's education lacked instruction in critical method, he had little or no acquaintance with contemporary historical scholarship, and whatever may have been the 'sense of history' that excited the young Deakin, it did not include those senses most useful to the true historian of sensing when he was on shaky ground and knowing how much he didn't know. In the case of The Second World War he already knew nearly as much as he needed for what he wanted to write, and what he didn't already know the assistants under his direction would find out for him. They might present their findings in the form of a draft narrative, but that would be thoroughly 'Churchillised' on its way to the finalised text. If this was ghosting, it was no more than might be done for any historian prosperous or otherwise fortunate enough to have research assistance. The case of The History of the English-Speaking Peoples is different. Ghosts do haunt its pages, though not at all obviously; perhaps because his style was so imitable. In both phases of its composition, 1938–39 and 1955–56, Churchill felt intense pressure to get it finished and he commissioned or, as happened with his last private secretary, commanded the writing of sections on episodes he knew nothing about. What he then did or did not do to fit them into his grand design was his affair. The pen of Churchill ruled over the whole, just as the brush of Rubens ruled over mighty canvases painted partly by his numerous assistants. We recognise them as 'by Rubens', all the same; but some may be not such good Rubenses as others.

A feature of *The Second World War*, much commented on and somewhat complained about as the books rolled out, was the great quantity of official documentation presented raw. Since much of it was the product of Churchill's own dictation through the war years, it was quite easy to weave his retrospective narrative around it, and the style stayed consistent throughout. Attlee's Cabinet gave permission for him to use all this material, so far and for long after denied to others, with only minor provisos about not making difficulties for Ernest Bevin's conduct of foreign affairs and not upsetting the Americans. ('When you see the documents', he told a prospective assistant, 'you will be amazed to see how often I was right.')[8] The most legitimate element in the complaints about all those documents, and the way they were presented, was that it was difficult to discern how often he had been wrong. Whether that was a reasonable criticism at that time may be questioned. After all, he was not engaged in a dispassionate analysis, he was reliving a world-historical drama in which he had taken the lead; and, in true historian's style, he was providing a mass of documentation to support the contentions in his argument. Participants who believed he had sometimes been wrong, and who lacked the affectionate loyalty felt for example by Ismay, thought it unfair that he should have had privileged access to official papers and have used them to his advantage. Their time would come; and when it did, they would find their task the easier for the guidelines and documents Churchill's *The Second World War* provided. (And if they had any interest in fairness, they might like to compare his ability to admit error with that displayed by certain other war celebrities who set down, as soon as they could, what *they* had done to win the war.)

A History of the English-Speaking Peoples was something else. In the war memoir he had taken pains to check the facts or to have them checked, he put in nothing that was not objectively verifiable unless it was a frank admission of his own opinion, and he took notice of relevant and up to date literature, such as there was of it at the time of his writing. In his broad-gauge history book he was willing to retain national stories and legends of doubtful historicity, he included virtually none of the economic and demographic history that alone made serious historical sense of the whole, his sources were old-fashioned and by scholarly criteria out of date, and he sought verification only of what would improve the story he enjoyed telling. Concept and substance were both familiar in the standard 'Whig' history of England: 'the struggle of its gentlemen against the Crown for their liberties, and then, when these had been won [their] harmony with it on their forward march to wealth and Empire', to civil and political liberties and 'the decencies of human life'.[9] It had the peculiar attraction of his own style and commitment; and, being moreover a self-congratulatory story that Britons and Americans liked to hear, it sold in hundreds of thousands (like the similar stories told by the high-class Whig historian G. M. Trevelyan and the patriotic populariser Arthur Bryant) and mightily increased. Clementine correctly assured him that 'ordinary people' would love it.[10] It went down particularly well in the United States because, unlike the Trevelyan and Bryant versions, it included so much about America, most of it flattering. His account of the American Civil War's campaigns and battles was especially admired. But military campaigns and battles as usual were lavishly and excellently covered throughout, whether they had much to do with his main theme or not. In short, it was not history as it is known in the groves of academe. It was *Our Island Story* plus some exciting Americana grandly done up for readers in the fields outside, and it ended around 1900, when the British side of the story ceased to be confident and encouraging. Churchill perhaps understood little of the deeper currents and manifold complexities that shape historical development. But the book was more than just a four-volume money- spinner. It was a serious expression of the history-steeped patriotic faith that its author had lived by and fought for; it told a tale of noble achievement even if it offered only superficial explanations; and it therefore made a reasonable call on the attention of men and women who adhered to the same admirable faith, or who would have done so had they been around at any of the times it had to be vindicated by arms.

Organising and writing (or, in the case of the last one, 'writing') these big books would have taken even longer had Churchill not worked at them in the intense, concentrated way that he could always manage until some time in his seventies. Until the years of his first retirement, he generally followed the rule he prescribed for others during the war, that a change was as good as a rest. Only one of his habitual occupations combined concentration with relaxation, and now he had time for more of it: painting. Only once during the war had he found time to put brush to canvas: when convalescing at Marrakesh in January 1944. His first post-war painting was done at Alexander's villa by Lake Como in August 1945. From then until the inevitable slowing-down towards the end of the next decade he was at his easel as often as he could get there, whether it was in his studio at Chartwell or out of doors, preferably on the French Riviera and under one or other of his two painting hats ('a grey felt hat ... and a cream, wide-brimmed, gangsterish fedora') or, when the sun was really fierce, under a great umbrella.[11] Now his painterly talent became revealed to the wider world, through the agencies of the Hall-Mark Cards company in the United States, which reproduced a few every Christmas and had earlier shown the originals in travelling shows, and of the Royal Academy in Britain. In 1947 he submitted two paintings under a pseudonym, and they were exhibited. The secret soon got out and from 1948 he exhibited annually under his own name. The Academy made him an Honorary Academician Extraordinary in 1948 and his status as an interesting amateur was sealed by a 'one-man show' in 1959. The Tate Gallery had already acquired one of his paintings for its permanent collection: *The Loup River, Alpes Maritimes*. He liked strong, bright colours. Water, whether still and silent in green-shaded pools, stagnant and sinister in Venetian canals, or brisk and bubbling in lively rivers, was one of the subjects he most enjoyed. Another was sunny landscapes with hills in the distance. He was not bad at still life. He had happily and shrewdly written about his enjoyment of painting in the *Strand Magazine* for 1921–22, subsequently made into a small book, *Painting as a Pastime*. His analysis of the painting process, from perception to performance, was thoughtful enough to attract the commendation of Ernst Gombrich.[12]

No one ever claimed that he was a great artist but it was difficult not to recognise that he had some talent and impossible not to be astonished that he had this on top of everything else. He liked to meet other painters and he could talk sensibly enough to retain the attention of tolerant professionals like William Nicholson, Walter Sickert and Paul Maze (since 1914–18 an Anglophile friend), although the company of the crass Sir Alfred Munnings, President of the Royal Academy in the later 1940s, brought out the worst in him. His tastes in modern painting were fairly conventional, though he admired the landscape-painting Impressionists, Cézanne especially. Cézanne was one of the contemporaries plentifully represented on the villa walls of Emery and Wendy Reves and their rich Riviera friends. Picasso, who was another, was the subject of some well-publicised Munnings vulgarities, and it is fortunate that he and Churchill never met. When Picasso learned that they had just missed doing so, he expressed regret. 'After all his *conneries* about my painting', said Picasso, 'he should hear what I think of his.'[13]

These post-war years were a good time for Churchill, and who could say that he did not deserve it? Once rescued from that early brief brush with relative deprivation, he had all the money he needed and some to spare; he bought a couple of farms adjacent to the Chartwell estate and, encouraged by his son-in-law Christopher Soames, whose help was indispensable in managing these rural enterprises, he acquired racehorses and had some winners; the name of one of them, High Hat, suggests that one of the many films seen on Saturday and Sunday nights had been the Marx Brothers' *A Day at the Races*. Honours and pleasures showered upon him. His own country gave him the highest honours it had to offer – Knight of the Garter, Order of Merit, Companion of Honour – and a dukedom was his for the asking. Great cities vied to offer him their freedom, their traditional gesture. Universities competed to give him honorary degrees; his very suitable response in kind was to launch, in 1958, the fund to found in Cambridge the college bearing his name, revolutionary in its dedication to science and technology and in being the first men's college to open its gates to women. (Mary Soames attributes this admirable progressiveness to Clementine's influence.) In Paris, he received the Médaille Militaire in 1947 and, an extraordinary honour, the Croix de la Libération from the hand of President de Gaulle in 1958. In West Germany, his promotion of the European Movement and especially the reconciliation of Germany and France earned him the Charlemagne Prize, received in Aachen in 1956. The Nobel Prize for Literature came to him in 1953; unable himself to go to Stockholm, because of the twice-postponed 'Western Summit' in Bermuda, Clementine and Mary received it on his behalf. A great American honour arrived a good deal later than it might have done, in 1963, when Congress voted to make him an honorary citizen of the United States. Churchill being by then incapable of travelling so far or of making a speech, Randolph Churchill went instead, managed to commit no *faux-pas* on his own account, and no doubt enjoyed delivering an acceptance speech that included a defiant affirmation of the sovereign equality with the United States of Great Britain.

Randolph, by now a successful journalist, clever, combative and controversial, and an unsuccessful politician, was far from ideal as his father's deputy. He was wilful, explosive, capable of being very rude, and much given to drink. Relations between father and son can be summed up as a series of rows, which neither could prevent happening and which both immediately regretted. Never however doubting Randolph's loyalty and literary ability, Churchill was happy that the 'official' biography should be undertaken by him. In the event it was only begun by him, Randolph's intemperate lifestyle bringing about his death in 1968 before he had taken the story further than 1914. The rest of the family managed to show their love and admiration in less disturbing ways. Everyone in the family, whatever his or her personal troubles, made it a priority through Winston's declining years to pamper and protect him: pamper, because although he had always received pampering he now really needed it, and protect, because he hated the unstoppable decline of his powers and with understandable vanity or pride or a mixture of both wanted the world to continue to think of him as he had been in his long-protracted prime.

Clementine was still fiercely watchful but was herself often unwell; she had given her strength without stint throughout the war and her nervous constitution had been more worn down by it than his. Her judgement was as excellent as ever but the two of them were apart from one another so often that it more often reached him through the mail than from her own lips. Anyone who reads Mary's daughter's biography of her mother and, alongside it, her edition of the careful and loving letters her parents kept exchanging, is likely to suspect that their mutual affection flourished the better through these years for their not being always under the same roof. When Winston was being entertained and looked after somewhere else, the nervous strain of attending to his needs and making sure he was kept happy rested on other shoulders, and her own could take a much needed, well-earned rest. She could also give the more attention to the younger members of the family, two of whom trod precarious paths. Diana's second marriage, that to the talented Conservative politician Duncan Sandys, had broken up around 1957. She had been subject to 'bouts of nervous ill-health' and remained so. These did not keep her from doing good work for, among other charities, the newly-established Samaritans or from finding some happiness with her two grown-up daughters; but something went very wrong one week-end in October 1963 and she took her own life. No less tragic was the later life of the gifted, humorous, sensitive and romantic Sarah. The war over and her first husband gone for ever, she returned to the commanding passion of her life and chosen means of livelihood: stage and screen. An affectionate soul, she naturally also hoped to marry again. In 1949 and, to her parents' annoyance, in Hollywood, she did. Such careers as hers notoriously make difficulties for matrimony, and her second marriage was over by 1955. Living alone at Malibu Beach, she took to drinking more than was good for her in public places and suffered what was to be the first of several embarrassing arrests. A third marriage in 1962 to a nice man whom everybody liked ended when he died of a heart attack only fifteen months later. Sarah gamely struggled on for another twenty years.[14] Of Mary it might be said that in these years, as in earlier ones, she alone seemed to be happily normal and relatively untroubled, although it is clearly unreasonable to imagine that there were no troubles in the life of a young woman married to a rising Conservative politician, raising five children, sharing her parents' worries and helping them and her sisters whenever she could.

The family, then, had its problems, but it remained solid in loyalty to Papa and in keeping intact around him such a protective screen that the extent and nature of his steady decline after 1955 was not generally under-stood. It could not be kept from those who came close to him, and who could not fail to realise how slow in speech he was becoming and how increasingly silent, how little he heard unless unwillingly wearing his hearing aid, how dependent he was from 1958 on the attendance of full-time nurses, how little he now knew of what went on in the world, and how little that worried him.[15] Those who were closest to him were few and loyal, and astonishingly he could still, until quite near the end, put on a good show on public occasions or family festivals, when beaming and waving his hat were more required than speaking.

One of those faithful few towards the end was of such questionable character that Churchill's connection with him requires explanation. This was Aristotle Onassis, to whom Randolph introduced him when he was staying with the Reveses. Onassis was an unscrupulous Greek commercial buccaneer of immense wealth who took pleasure in hosting celebrities and whose own ultimate celebrity, after a long affair with Maria Callas, would come with his marriage in 1968 to Jacqueline Kennedy. He was also owner of the *Christina*, the largest, most luxurious and showy pleasure-yacht that sailed the seas – seas to whose whale population, it might be added, his ruthlessly illegal operations in the earlier 1950s had done great damage. Between 1958 and 1963 Churchill sailed on the *Christina* no less than eight times, not only in the Mediterranean but also around the Caribbean and once even up to New York, where however he wasn't well enough to disembark. Churchill found life on the *Christina* and in Onassis's Monte Carlo hotel entirely to his liking. He could have with him his whole entourage and as many of his family as were free to come. He could play bezique, his favourite, and other card games for hours on end. He was fussed over, rested, and as securely protected from intrusive eyes and unsympathetic strangers as he could desire. (In his whole life, he had never liked strangers.) Onassis, for his part, must have valued the kudos that came with entertaining such a celebrity, but credible witnesses testify that he was also an attentive, sympathetic and discreet host. The family found no cause to fear that Papa was being exploited, and the Onassis connection kept him in the luxury and climates he most enjoyed. Mary reckoned that from 1956 to 1962 her father spent on average seventeen weeks each year in the sun.[16]

His last sight of the Mediterranean and last holiday on the *Christina* were in the summer of 1963. By this time he had undergone and survived a number of 'strokes' (my word for the variety of incidents recorded by his medical attendants) and several accidents, from all of which he made some sort of recovery; but the recoveries each time took longer, and the level to which he returned was ever lower. The world at large had little opportunity to realise what was happening. 'All his outings and public appearances were carefully prepared and stage-managed so that, impeccably attired, he gave a debonair impression.'[17] He persisted in occasionally attending the House of Commons until June 1964, but could only do so with his son-in-law on one side of him and a safe pair of hands on the other. A general election being scheduled for not later than the autumn of that same year, his Woodford constituency committee, from whom his unfitness was not concealed or indeed concealable, had been wanting since the last election in 1959 to be free to go ahead with selecting someone to succeed him. By 1963 a triangular impasse had been reached: the veteran parliamentarian, solipsistically obstinate as old persons notoriously can be, would not undertake to resign; the constituency party was hoisted with its own imprudent petard of having proclaimed it would never ask him to do so; and Clementine, although she knew very well that he ought to resign, and who had actually been doing what she could to fill in for him in the constituency, felt unable to intervene. After much trouble and anxiety that upset Clementine considerably, and much persuasion by his son-in-law Christopher Soames, Churchill at last told Woodford that he would stand down. The day after his last visit to the House of Commons on 28 July 1964, the Prime Minister and a select group of senior worthies came to Hyde Park Gate to present the House's unanimous resolution of admiration and gratitude.

That event may be regarded as the beginning of the end. He spent the summer at Chartwell, returned to London in October and remained there. Clementine had to represent him at the opening of Churchill College in Cambridge and at the British Embassy in Paris when a portrait bust of him by Oscar Nemon was presented; she also had lunch with President de Gaulle and found him 'very mellow'. The family assembled in the usual way for his ninetieth birthday and for Christmas, wondering how much longer the tottering patriarch could go on. A few days later, they knew. On 10 January 1965 he had another stroke, became completely helpless, and could only have been kept alive by artificial means, which the family rejected.[18] The last coherent words he spoke to anyone of his family were, thought Mary Soames, to her husband when the latter hopefully suggested a glass of champagne: 'Winston looked at him vaguely. "I'm so bored with it all", he said.'[19] He lingered for surprisingly many days after ceasing to take nourishment and passed away peacefully, his hand held by Clementine and his family gathered around the bed, shortly after eight o'clock on the morning of Sunday 24 January 1965.

The funeral was announced to take place on Saturday, 30 January. Remarkable mourning rituals preceded that final event. All in all they marked an epoch in British history: the end of a great Englishman's life, and the end of much more besides. Her Majesty the Queen had decreed well in advance of the event that her most illustrious subject should have a state funeral, a distinction normally reserved for royalty. (The only precedents were in respect of Viscount Nelson in 1806, the Duke of Wellington in 1852 and Mr Gladstone in 1898.) Making the arrangements for it was the responsibility of the Earl Marshal, the Duke of Norfolk. It is a perfectly credible Churchill story that he planned the whole great show himself, but his secretary says that he didn't, that he knew he was destined to receive this singular honour, and was pleased to hear it, but the only thing he said about the arrangements was that he wanted 'plenty of bands'. He certainly got them – nine, in fact – and a great deal more besides.

The first act of the state funeral was a lying-in-state in Westminster Hall. Churchill's lead-lined, quarter-ton coffin was taken there with due military ceremony on the evening of Tuesday the 26th, and remained there until Saturday, covered with a Union Jack (the Order of the Garter gleaming on top of it) and guarded at its four corners by officers of the armed services. The great gloomy hall, illuminated only by the tall candlesticks around the catafalque, stayed open almost round the clock; over 300,000 people queued in the bitter cold to pay their tributes, the queue at times stretching back along Millbank and over Lambeth Bridge.

The funeral proceedings on Saturday began with a procession from Westminster to St Paul's. Herculean Guardsmen carried the coffin to its traditional vehicle, a gun-carriage, drawn by 120 naval ratings slow-marching, like all the other detachments of all branches of the armed services in the procession, in that marvellous sustained symmetry for which British military parades were world famous. The men of the family followed the gun-carriage on foot, Clementine and the women in carriages provided by the Palace. The procession took an hour to get to St Paul's. Deliberately it passed along Whitehall, the Strand and Fleet Street, then up Ludgate Hill to St Paul's, the sound of silence (perfected by the hushing of Big Ben for the day) broken only by the solemn music and drums of the bands and by the guns in Hyde Park firing once a minute, ninety shots for the ninety years of his life. All of this was immediately heard and seen by television viewers throughout almost the whole of the Continent, an estimated three hundred and fifty million viewers. On radio, it was heard worldwide.

Everyone who was going to have a seat in the cathedral was already there, including Queen Elizabeth II and her family, an unprecedented gesture. The representatives from other countries, many of whom came out with the Queen and Prince Philip onto the west end steps after the service to salute the coffin's departure towards its burial place, helped to make such a show as had rarely been seen before and has never been seen since. Every European monarch was there, and many non-European leaders including the founding father of Israel, David Ben-Gurion. The most conspicuous non-royal head of state was President de Gaulle, taller than most and not in a grey greatcoat like the British generals but in a buff one. Layfolk supposed that General Eisenhower, in civilian clothes, was the official American representative, but he was there in a private capacity; there are various theories of explanation why President Johnson was represented only by the Chief Justice of the Supreme Court and the American Ambassador. The Soviet Union sent a member of the Politburo and Marshal Koniev, West Germany Chancellor Erhard. From Ireland came only the Minister for External Affairs.

Over the remaining acts of the funeral, the limelight slowly dimmed. The coffin was taken through quieter streets to Tower Steps at the eastern corner of the City, transferred to a Port of London Authority launch for its short voyage along the grey, choppy River Thames to Waterloo Station, from which a locomotive named 'Battle of Britain' pulled the sombre train to the little station of Long Hanborough, the station nearest to Bladon, close by the walls of Blenheim Palace, the country churchyard where he had wished to be buried. For a former private secretary privileged to be in the small party that went with the family to the interment, there was no forgetting the 'two single figures' he saw from the train: 'first on the flat roof of a small house a man standing at attention in his old RAF uniform; and then in a field, some hundreds of yards from the track, a simple farmer stopping work and standing, head bowed, and cap in hand'.[20] For the millions whose link with the funeral had to be television, the most unforgettable moment was probably (as it certainly was for me) the great cranes along the south side of the stretch of river between Tower Bridge and London Bridge, dipping their masts in tribute as the launch went by, 'like giants bowed in anxious thought'.

> Now is the stately column broke,
> The beacon-light is quench'd in smoke,
> The trumpet's silver sound is still,
> The warder silent on the hill.[21]

26

Epilogue

'I am prepared to meet my Maker. Whether my Maker is prepared for the great ordeal of meeting me is another matter.'

On the occasion of his seventy-fifth birthday

I undertook this book from a desire to satisfy my curiosity about Winston Churchill. Now that I've finished, it seems reasonable to summarise what I've found and to acknowledge that it has been worth the effort. I found the great man I had always supposed to be there; less great in some respects that were new to me, and with many more idiosyncrasies than I could have thought possible, but with a title to a place in any pantheon not wholly reserved for stars of screen, song and stadium; and, besides all that, an extraordinary many-sided human being whom it has been exhilarating to study.

What sort of a great man was he? Greatness, as commonly attributed, comes in such a variety of colours and contexts that it is as well to state at the start that his title to greatness rests on achievements in the fields of war and politics. It is of the kind that often accompanies dramatic episodes in the histories of nations and peoples, episodes almost always of armed struggle, sacrifice and heroism. Every nation has (or should one say, in our unprecedentedly demilitarised society, has had?) its warrior heroes and champions, accorded greatness for their embodiment of qualities collectively most admired. Biographers and historians who wish to recognise the existence of Great Men in history have to meet the challenge of critics who insist that who these alleged great men were, and what they did, must be explained by the hard historical work of ascertaining whom they represented, what they stood for, and what irresistible movements were sweeping humanity along at the time when they were part of it. Much indeed can be done along those lines, and should be. But there often comes a point at which these lines of explanation part from reality, the point where inner-directed elements of individual thought and action defy explanation in terms of social context.

An eminent authority has acutely observed that 'Consciously or unconsciously it was Churchill's aim in life to evade classification'.[1] Much of his rich and complex personality nevertheless is explicable in terms of his social context but the most important elements in it are not. He can be classified as a late Victorian Liberal Imperialist, as an Edwardian humanitarian and national efficiency enthusiast, and in the 1920s as the holder of several ministerial posts which he filled in an unexceptional way. His ideas about race, other than his sympathy for Zionism, were those of commonplace white-superiority Anglo-Saxonism; his ideas about class were basically those of the Tory Radical tradition, and his ideas about gender scarcely differed from the patriarchal norm, despite his marriage to an intelligent and liberal-minded woman. In these areas, he is explicable in conventional terms. In other areas of personality he certainly is not. No one else in the political class believed in his own patriotic destiny and persistently followed its star as he did; no one else's mind was furnished with so much dramatic history or with such a compulsion to place himself in its evolving future. No one else's thoughts found their natural expression in a form of rhetoric that he had the talent to craft into oratory which made him the most remarkable political speaker of his generation. No one else who could function so effectively as a man of peace had in him such exceptional capacity to function also as a man of war. No one else capable of grand solemnity of utterance was also given to humour and witticism. And no one else in the political firmament provoked such mixed and conflicting attitudes among his own class and kind: admiration and disapproval, affection and distaste, amusement and boredom, loyalty and repudiation.

All this made Churchill a man of individuality so pronounced and peculiar that what he did for the good of his country and, it is not extravagant to say, for western civilisation was what no other person on the political stage at those times could have done. He did what the more dogmatic critics of 'great man theory' doubt that even the greatest of men can do: he changed the apparent course of history.

That was in 1940, when he led his countrymen and women, as the famous phrase had it, to 'stand alone'. They did and they survived, their country and its values and civilisation's with them. How much of a gamble it was, and how narrow the margin of that survival, has been a revelation to me. Whether the subsequent outcome is better regarded as victory or avoidance of defeat may be debated. When that victory was certain though not quite yet sealed, he reminded his party that though Britain had 'avoided annihilation ... years of torment and destruction have wasted the earth, and victory with all its brilliant trappings appears to our strained and experienced eyes as a deliverance rather than a triumph'. All the same, avoidance of defeat can be as glorious as victory, and Churchill was not only at the centre of this one, he *was* the centre. 'If it had not been for Winston, anything might have happened. He steadied the ship.'² As good a summary as any of his achievement comes from the pen of one of his most intractable opponents and critics, and is the more impressive on that account. Aneurin Bevan concluded a memorial essay:

> He cast himself in the role of the great advocate who put the case of Britain to the world and the destiny of Britain to the British. His name will stand ... as a symbol of what inspired words can do when there is a strong, brave and devoted nation free and willing to back them up with deeds.³

That was when he fitted for a while the literary historians' definition of an epic hero: 'fully human, fallible therefore, but "superior in degree to other men [with] authority, passion and powers of expression greater than our own"'.⁴

It is arguable that once Churchill had guided Britain through that desperate, heroic first phase of the real war, his greatness as a national leader continued on a less exalted plane. Bevan certainly thought so. Although the way he kept saying so from 1941 onwards annoyed, even shocked many members of his own party as well as every member of Churchill's, some of his criticisms were no more than what others on both sides of the House also thought but felt it more patriotic not to say out loud for fear of giving comfort to the enemy and discouragement to their own side. Was it, for example, better or worse for the morale of a democracy's armed forces that the general inferiority of British tanks – an inferiority that British and Allied soldiers painfully experienced at first hand – should be aired in the House of Commons? The working-class Welsh democrat didn't like the English patrician's long speeches on the war situation in which, he complained, failure and follies were incorporated as obstacles successfully overcome rather than as what he thought they should be, matters for regret and stimulants to self-criticism. It was certainly possible to hear in Churchill's majestic speeches the voice that, once the war was over, would be dictating his self-justificatory published version. On the other hand, those speeches were meant to serve, and did serve, the purpose of maintaining popular morale, that confidence in ultimate victory necessary to an increasingly exhausted people in a war that disappointingly took longer to win than most people expected, even with such mighty allies as were picked up along the way. Churchillian oil was better than Bevanite vinegar for helping a democratic people together through a difficult war. When it ended, and notwithstanding the domestic turnabout at the 1945 general election, Churchill received universal gratitude and admiration as the pilot who had weathered the storm. The greatness established in 1940 was not eroded by the mixed fortunes of the years that followed.

Keeping Britain going in 1940–41 and directing the war effort to victory thereafter constituted Churchill's main claim to respect as a maker of history. Another claim, less weighty but still substantial, comes from his interventions in international affairs after the war. His contributions towards the new international order have been less noticed than they deserve to be, perhaps because he had quit the scene before his seeds came to flower. All of them shared the same purpose: to secure the peace so hardly won and the liberal values that the English-Speaking Peoples had fought for. Very few Britons and Americans just after the war wanted to believe that their Russian wartime ally was going to become a peacetime menace, but Churchill early perceived that this was very likely to happen and accordingly called the West's attention to the disagreeable prospect. He took advantage of his unique status to sound the trumpet (Fulton) and to stimulate the democratic countries of western Europe to find strength in community (Zürich, Brussels, Strasbourg). His mind sprang back to the great global themes of peace and war that had always possessed him, and he did not allow it to be distracted by the optimistic clamour surrounding the United Nations, whose Security Council, he anticipated, would be little more than a puppet show mimicking the Great Power relationships of the real world at large. Just as he had emerged from the First World War with a sombre conviction that the peace settlement would sooner or later be disturbed by Germany, he emerged from the Second with a similar conviction regarding the Soviet Union. Inevitably he was accused of being 'provocative' by leftists and pacifists, and the western posture of self-defence and policies of containment and deterrence he did much to promote would later be placed by 'revisionist' historians of the Cold War among its causes; alleging in one form of words or another that 'The West started it'. The question is complex, and continues to be vigorously debated. For my part, I cannot see that Churchill is particularly to blame. Although provocations and extravagant alarmism may be seen on the American side in the early 1950s, they were not conspicuous in the later 1940s. Western statesmen's fears of Soviet and Communist expansionism in those years were not unreasonable.

By the early 1950s, the groundwork of western European defensive preparedness and of 'containment' elsewhere in the world was well laid. Peace then appearing to be endangered also by the western bellicosity and intransigence epitomised from January 1953 by John Foster Dulles, Churchill's thoughts turned to the need to calm things down and to explore the possibility of co-existence between West and East. He thought a summit meeting might make a breakthrough, and remarkably strove to set one up. No summit happened while he could attend it, but it was largely by summitry that East and West came in the end to coexist, until Communist power collapsed under the weight of its own untruths and misjudgements. Churchill's sterling performance in the earliest stages of this post-war saga is too often neglected by biographers and historians mesmerised by his wartime achievements, perhaps finding it difficult to believe that anything thereafter merited serious respect.

All these great achievements in the field of international relations, a field wherein war and peace are of equal importance, were the work of a human being whom it is impossible to describe as other than extraordinary in his mixture of qualities. Not all of them were attractive. Egotism is not usually counted among the moral pluses. His egotism – and it was something to which he frankly admitted – was 'of Himalayan vastness'; but the historian who wrote that nevertheless went on to assert Churchill's 'uncontestable superiority over every other twentieth-century occupant of his office'.[5] He was better at saying he could admit error than at actually admitting it. He was spoiled and self-indulgent. He could be rude and hurtful. He was often inconsiderate and demanding, not least towards his wife; his loving letters to her are full of protestations of dependence and indebtedness, but it is hard to believe he ever really took in the extent to which she sacrificed herself for his sake. Yet that vast egotism was inseparable from the originality, the energy, the willpower and the courage both physical and moral that made him unique. Harold Macmillan observed that in Churchill's last months in office 'he was obsessed by his hopes of going down to history not only as the greatest War Minister but as [also] the greatest peacemaker in the world', and what better use could there be for egotism than that?[6] His wife never fell out of love with him, his daughters loved him and helped look after him, and all of his children including Randolph cherished him as a father. The several varieties of secretary and aide who slaved for him, and most of the senior civil servants and military men who worked with him during the war, were devoted to him. The closer you were to him, the greater the chances that he would appear in a good light, and the likelier it was that you would be fascinated and won over by him.

Everybody who came close to him during the war and after it sooner or later recorded his or her opinion. Dwight Eisenhower, Supreme Commander and President and no soft touch, said Churchill 'came nearer to fulfilling the requirements of greatness in any individual that I have met in my lifetime. I have known finer and greater characters, wiser philosophers, more understanding personalities, but no greater man.'[7] The philosopher and historian Isaiah Berlin wrote in 1949:

> Mr Churchill sees history – and life – as a great Renaissance pageant ... something between Victorian illustrations in a child's book of history and the great procession

painted by Benozzo Gozzoli in the Riccardi Palace ... The units out of which
his world is constructed are simpler and larger than life ... painted in primary
colours.[8]

Clement Attlee agreed about the pageant and procession and added the
point that Churchill saw himself as one of the figures in them.

He was always, in effect, asking himself, 'How will I look if I do this or that?'
and 'What must Britain do now so that the verdict of history will be favourable?' ...
He was always looking around for 'finest hours', and if one was not immediately
available, his impulse was to manufacture one.[9]

Of all the obituary essays, Attlee's is the most impressive. He wrote it for
a 1965 memorial collection, *Churchill: By His Contemporaries*, published by
the *Observer*. Having no doubt thought about it for many years in advance
of the event, Lord Attlee (as he became in 1955) took the opportunity to
distil into about 7000 words the observations and reflections of nearly half
a century. He was famous for his matter-of-factness, being neither a wordy
man nor an emotional gusher, but he put into this essay his whole heart
and mind and produced a persuasively honest, close-up, critical, perceptive
sketch of a man at various times his opponent, his colleague and his chief.
He saw the lights and shadows with an equal eye, and concluded thus:

By any reckoning, Winston Churchill was one of the greatest men that history
records. If there were to be a gallery of great Englishmen that could accommodate
only a dozen, I would like to see him in. He was brave, gifted, inexhaustible and
indomitable ...
 Energy, rather than wisdom, practical judgement or vision, was his supreme
qualification ... However, it is not the full story of what he did to win the war.
It was the poetry of Churchill, as well, that did the trick. Energy and poetry, in
my view, really sums him up.
 He was, of course, above all, a supremely fortunate mortal ... And perhaps the
most warming thing about him was that he never ceased to say so.

Attlee himself was nearing his end when Churchill died. One of the most
moving sights at the funeral was of the deceased Prime Minister's wartime
deputy and Downing Street successor at the foot of the cathedral's western
steps, crunched up in the chair that had been specially brought out so that
he could share with the other dignitaries their last farewell. Hatless in the
bitter cold, his huddled meditative posture brought to mind what was in
any case apparent to anyone who reflected on the meaning of the event,
that it wasn't just a great man and a national hero who was being mourned,
it was an Empire and an Age.

'We met all the tests, but it was useless.'[10] The sometime subaltern of
the 4th Hussars had been less well prepared for the second half of the

twentieth century than the sometime mayor of Stepney. The Empire had gone, that 'empire that spread its wings wider than Rome', being replaced by the more workaday Commonwealth. In his splendid 'Epilogue to an Empire', written in the 1960s, John Stallworthy hears 'the Admiral' say, from his eyrie high above Trafalgar Square,

> My one eye reports that their roads
> remain, their laws, their language
> sowing all winds.[11]

The Commonwealth survives and flourishes as an intergovernmental organisation of independent states with a representative Secretary-General and an active Secretariat, upholding good standards of governance for its members and committed to ensure that those standards are taken seriously. But what of Britain itself, a Britain already fast changing through Churchill's sunset years and by now, at the turn of the new millennium, revolutionised in ways 'the greatest Englishman of his age' could not have dreamed of or understood? So violently have the continuities of British culture and politics been ruptured since the 1960s, so totally have the conditions of international relations been transformed since 1945, that it is impossible to imagine either another Churchill as national leader or circumstances that could make such a leader necessary. Through most of his lifetime the people of Great Britain still had a good idea of what collectively they amounted to and what was their place in the world, and the only way in which their survival could be seriously threatened took exactly the same shape as it had taken for many centuries past – foreign invasion, legitimising national military preparedness and calling on the King's subjects to assist in national defence. Threats to national survival are still conceivable (for example, from climate change, asteroids, epidemics, nuclear disaster) but they are not of a kind to offer people what Churchill called the moral satisfaction of fighting for your country and the glory of dying in battle on its behalf.

'Glory' to Churchill's way of thinking was not only something within the reach of individual fighters and cohesive small groups like regiments and crews of warships, it was what entire peoples could attain through shared achievement and self-assertion in the world, which historically meant by force of arms. That war-accepting state of mind has become frowned on in the era of the United Nations and no longer commends itself to peoples who, having acquired as large a share of the good things of the world as they can reasonably expect, prefer to think of peace not war. A Briton may nevertheless wonder how much of larger value has gone with the cult of arms. One might not lament the end of 'glory', but what about 'chivalry' and 'honour'? There must be improvement of some kind in the fact that the concept of 'dying for your country' no longer provides the model of an ideal death; but there may not be much of an improvement in not knowing whether there is anything in your country worth fighting for, whether you belong to this country or to that, or even whether you belong to any distinctive country at all.

By the time Churchill died, Britain was fast turning into a land in which such a man as he was would never again find room to flourish, with a popular culture increasingly inimical to his values and likely therefore not to notice or properly appreciate his achievements. I hope my book may help to make his values intelligible and his achievements respected. In the years 1940 and 1941 he was indeed the saviour of the nation. His achievements, taken all in all, justify his title to be known as the greatest Englishman of his age. I am persuaded that, in this later time, we are diminished if, admitting Churchill's failings and failures, we can no longer appreciate his virtues and victories.

Notes

Churchill's own works are cited without his name first.

Notes to Chapter 1: Unwillingly to School

1. Oscar Wilde, *The Importance of Being Earnest* (1895), Act III.
2. *My Early Life*, ch. 7.
3. John Mather, 'Lord Randolph Churchill: Maladies et Mort', in *Finest Hour: The Journal of the Churchill Center and International Churchill Society*, 93 (Winter, 1996–97), pp. 23–28.
4. Gilbert, *Churchill: A Life* (1991), p. 16.
5. Clare Sheridan, *Nuda Veritas* (1927), p. 14.
6. Martin Gilbert, *Winston S. Churchill*, Companion Volume, i, pt 1, p. 221.
7. *My Early Life*, ch. 5.
8. Henry Pelling, *Winston Churchill* (1974), p. 33.
9. *My Early Life*, ch. 3.

Notes to Chapter 2: Willingly to War

1. *My Early Life*, ch. 4. The usually accurate Henry Pelling, *Winston Churchill* (1974), p. 41, states that he was twentieth out of 130. I cannot explain the difference and see no need to; both results were commendable.
2. Ibid., ch. 9. Martin Gilbert, *Churchill: A Life* (1991), pp. 55, 67, 68, 70.
3. Paul Addison, *Churchill on the Home Front* (1993 edn), p. 10.
4. *My Early Life*, ch. 6.
5. Rudyard Kipling, 'The Young British Soldier', in *Barrack Room Ballads* (1898).
6. *My Early Life*, ch. 12.
7. Ibid., ch. 14.
8. Gilbert, *Churchill: A Life*, p. 92.
9. Randolph S. Churchill, *Winston S. Churchill*, i, pp. 485–502. Gilbert, *Winston S. Churchill*, Companion Volume, i, pt 2, pp. 1087–1136, for the whole escape episode and the controversies that came in its wake.
10. *My Early Life*, ch. 22. Gilbert, *Winston S. Churchill*, Companion Volume, i, pt 2, p. 1091.
11. *My Early Life*, ch, 16.
12. Gilbert, *Churchill: A Life*, p. 80.
13. *My Early Life*, ch. 16.

14. Ibid.

15. One of the pieces collected in *Thoughts and Adventures* (1932). Gilbert, *Winston S. Churchill*, v, p. 50, corrects Churchill's date of original publication.

16. Gilbert, *Churchill: A Life*, p. 122. Also Gilbert, *Winston S. Churchill*, Companion Volume, ii, pt 2, p. 912.

17. Cited by Peter Gretton, *Former Naval Person* (1968), p. 31.

Notes to Chapter 3: Clementine and the Commons

1. *Monthly Review*, 13, pp. 28–30.

2. Mary Soames, *Clementine Churchill* (1974), ch. 4.

3. Cited by Ronald Hyam, *Elgin and Churchill at the Colonial Office* (1968), pp. 17–18.

4. Martin Gilbert, *Winston S. Churchill*, Companion Volume, ii, pt 1, pp. 496–500.

5. *Parliamentary Debates*, 22 February 1906, fourth series, 152, cols 554–72.

6. Gilbert, *Winston S. Churchill*, Companion Volume, ii, pt 2, p. 701.

7. Sir Francis Hopwood, in Gilbert, Companion Volume, ii, pt 2, pp. 729–30. Hopwood remained an enemy until he left Whitehall.

8. Henry Hesketh Bell, *Glimpses of a Governor's Life* (1946), pp. 167–70.

9. Gilbert, *Winston S. Churchill*, Companion Volume, i, pt 1, p. 593.

10. Beatrice Webb, *Our Partnership* (1948), p. 416. Diary entry for 16 October 1908.

11. Entry by E. T. Williams, who after distinguished war service ended his Oxford career as Warden of Rhodes House.

Notes to Chapter 4: Board of Trade and Home Office

1. Cited by Addison, *Churchill on the Home Front* (1993 edn), p. 59, in his chapter headed 'The Cause of the Left-Out Millions'.

2. *My Early Life*, last words of ch. 6.

3. Paul Addison, *Churchill on the Home Front* (1993), p. 79.

4. Martin Gilbert, *Winston S. Churchill*, Companion Volume, ii, pt 2, p. 863.

5. Ibid., p. 898.

6. David Cannadine (ed.), *The Speeches of Winston Churchill* (Penguin edn, 1990), p. 45.

7. Ibid., pp. 49, 51, 54.

8. Mary Soames, *Clementine Churchill* (1974), ch. 5.

9. Ibid., ch. 6.

10. *Parliamentary Debates*, 20 July 1910, fourth series, 19, col. 1347.

11. For correction of the myths attaching to these events, I rest on Addison, *Churchill on the Home Front*, pp. 142–43.

Notes to Chapter 5: First Lord of the Admiralty

1. *The World Crisis*, i, near end of ch. 5.

2. Ibid., early in ch. 4.

3. The exchange with Limpus is in Randolph S. Churchill, *Winston S. Churchill*, ii, pp. 643–46. For Limpus's genial letter, see Martin Gilbert, *Winston S. Churchill*, iii, p. 482.

4. Mary Soames (ed.), *Speaking for Themselves: The Personal Letters of Winston and Clementine Churchill* (1998), pp. 99–100.

5. *Parliamentary Debates*, 16 February 1922, fifth series, 150, cols 1270–71, moving the second reading of the Irish Free State Bill.

6. *Gallipoli Memories*, beginning of ch. 1.

7. *The World Crisis*, i, ch. 9, second paragraph.

8. Ibid., end of ch. 10.

9. Ibid., near end of ch. 9.

10. 'Churchill and the First World War', in Blake and Louis (eds), *Churchill* (Oxford, 1994), p. 133.

11. Gilbert, *Winston S. Churchill*, iii, pp. 111–12.

12. A view shared by C. R. M. F. Cruttwell, *A History of the Great War, 1914–1918* (1934), pp. 95–96.

13. Mary Soames, *Clementine Churchill* (1974), near end of ch. 8.

14. M. Davidson, *The World, the Flesh and Myself* (1997), p. 315. Gilbert, *In Search of Churchill* (1995), p. 232, evidently thinks it apocryphal, but I don't see why.

15. Gilbert, *Winston S. Churchill*, iii, p. 111n.

16. See in particular the many pages devoted to it in Gilbert, *Winston S. Churchill*, iii, pp. 96–134.

Notes to Chapter 6: The Dardanelles

1. *The World Crisis*, i, ch. 14.

2. Ibid., ii, ch. 3.

3. Ibid., ii, ch. 1.

4. Ibid., part 2, ch. 2.

5. Martin Gilbert, *Winston S. Churchill*, iii, p. 242.

6. Peter Gretton, *Former Naval Person* (1968), p. 209.

7. Gilbert, *Winston S. Churchill*, iii, p. 233.

8. Ibid., p. 234.

9. *The World Crisis*, ii, ch. 12.

10. C. R. M. F. Cruttwell, *A History of the Great War, 1914–1918* (1934), p. 216.

11. Mary Soames, *Clementine Churchill* (1974), ch. 9.

12. *Thoughts and Adventures* (1943), p. 13.

13. Soames, *Clementine Churchill*, ch. 9.

14. 'Painting as a Pastime', initially in the *Strand Magazine*, December 1921 and January 1922, was next published in *Thoughts and Adventures* (1932).

15. Gilbert, *Winston S. Churchill*, iii, pp. 562–64.

Notes to Chapter 7: Recovery

1. Extracts from Lucas, *Quoth the Raven* (1919), pp. 15, 16, 17, 20.
2. Martin Gilbert, *Winston S. Churchill*, iii, p. 633.
3. Ibid., p. 648.
4. Mary Soames (ed.), *Speaking for Themselves: The Personal Letters of Winston and Clementine Churchill* (1998), p. 119.
5. Ibid., p. 111.
6. Ibid., p. 195.
7. Soames, *Clementine Churchill*, ch. 12.
8. Soames (ed.), *Speaking for Themselves*, p. 196.
9. Ibid., p. 194.
10. *Churchill as I Knew Him* (1965), p. 448.
11. *The World Crisis*, iii, ch. 12.
12. *Parliamentary Debates*, 25 April 1918, fifth series, 105, cols 1156–57.
13. *My Early Life*, ch. 18.
14. *The World Crisis*, iii, ch. 7.
15. Trevor Wilson, *The Myriad Faces of War: Britain and the Great War, 1914–1918* (1986), p. 350. Supported by Ian Beckett in Brian Bond (ed.), *The First World War and British Military History* (1991) p. 108.
16. *The World Crisis*, iii, ch. 14.
17. A. J. P. Taylor, *English History, 1914–1945* (1965), p. 65.
18. Gilbert, *Winston S. Churchill*, iii, p. 801.
19. Both short quotations from *The World Crisis*, iii, ch. 12.
20. *The World Crisis*, iii, appendix N. The 'hiatus' bit is in paragraph 15.
21. Hew Strachan in Bond (ed.), *The First World War and British Military History* (1991), pp. 53–61, demonstrates that Cruttwell was not perfect but concedes that he deserves a place among the top few.
22. C. R. M. F. Cruttwell, *A History of the Great War, 1914–1918* (1934), pp. 626–67.
23. Soames (ed), *Speaking for Themselves*, p. 214.

Notes to Chapter 8: Bolsheviks and Irishmen

1. Frederick Sykes, *From Many Angles* (1942), p. 267.
2. *Parliamentary Debates*, 3 March 1919, fifth series, 113, col. 72.
3. Martin Gilbert, *Winston S. Churchill*, iv, p. 196.
4. *The World Crisis: The Aftermath* (1929), p. 263.
5. Paul Addison, 'The Political Beliefs of Winston Churchill', *Transactions of the Royal Historical Society* (1980), pp. 23–47.
6. Mary Soames (ed.), *Speaking for Themselves: The Personal Letters of Winston and Clementine Churchill* (1998), p. 232.
7. In his 1924 article, 'The Irish Treaty', in *Thoughts and Adventures* (1943), p. 189.
8. *The Aftermath*, pp. 305–6.

9. Gilbert, *Winston S. Churchill*, iv, pp. 678–81, cites large chunks of it. For the original, see *Parliamentary Debates*, 16 December 1921, fifth series, 149, cols 169–83.

Notes to Chapter 9: Eastern Questions

1. *Thoughts and Adventures* (1943), p. 39.
2. Martin Gilbert, *Winston S. Churchill*, iv, p. 402.
3. For Churchill's speech, see *Parliamentary Debates*, 8 July 1920, fifth series, 131, cols 1719–33. Gilbert, *Winston S. Churchill*, iv, pp. 404–10, gives some of the best passages.
4. Gilbert, *Winston S. Churchill*, iv, illustration no. 50.
5. Ibid., p. 599. Original in *Parliamentary Debates*, 14 June 1921, fifth series, 143, cols 265–99. Winterton spoke directly after.
6. A. V. Lawrence (ed.), *T. E. Lawrence by his Friends* (1937), pp. 204–5, the essay by M. H. Coote, Churchill's orderly officer at the Cairo Conference.
7. Stephen Roskill, *Hankey: Man of Secrets*, ii (1972), p. 295.

Notes to Chapter 10: Tory Chancellor

1. Martin Gilbert, *Winston S. Churchill*, iv, p. 873.
2. *Thoughts and Adventures* (1943) p. 180. He calls them mill 'girls' but, if they were going to vote, they must have been at least thirty.
3. Gilbert, *Winston S. Churchill*, iv, p. 887.
4. *Thoughts and Adventures* (1943), p. 181.
5. Mary Soames, *Clementine Churchill* (1974), ch. 14.
6. *Thoughts and Adventures* (1943) pp. 182–3.
7. Mary Soames (ed.), *Speaking for Themselves: The Personal Letters of Winston and Clementine Churchill* (1998), p. 290.
8. Gilbert, *Winston S. Churchill*, v, pp. 97–98.
9. Sidney Pollard, *The Development of the British Economy, 1914–1967* (1973 edn), p. 194.
10. Paul Addison, *Churchill on the Home Front* (1993 edn), p. 243.
11. Gilbert, *Winston S. Churchill*, v, p. 116.
12. Ibid., p. 218.
13. *The Second World War*, iv, bk 1, ch. 4.

Notes to Chapter 11: Empire and India

1. Martin Gilbert, *Winston S. Churchill*, v, p. 350.
2. Mary Soames, *Clementine Churchill* (1974), ch. 15.
3. Cited in Gilbert, *Winston S. Churchill*, v, p. 339.
4. *The World Crisis*, i, ch. 2.
5. Churchill gives an amusing account of this encounter in *The Aftermath*, p. 152.

6. Judith M. Brown, *Modern India: The Origins of an Asian Democracy* (1990 edn), p. 277.
7. Ibid., p. 198.
8. Gilbert, *Winston S. Churchill*, v, p. 358.
9. Ibid., pp. 390, 401.
10. *The Times*, 13 December 1930.
11. Gilbert, *Winston S. Churchill*, v, p. 467.
12. Ibid., pp. 356, 376.
13. Ibid., pp. 370, 600.
14. Clement Attlee in *Churchill by his Contemporaries* (1965), pp. 28–29. It looks as if he mellowed in this respect in his later years. John Colville, *Fringes of Power*, 3 December 1953, notes Churchill insisting, when he was in Bermuda, that two coloured dignitaries be invited to a Governor's Banquet. Andrew Roberts has an excellent chapter on Churchill and 'the magpie society' in his *Eminent Churchillians* (1994).
15. Gilbert, *Winston S. Churchill*, v, p. 601.
16. Gilbert, *Winston S. Churchill*, v, p. 617.
17. Speech by Stanley Baldwin at the Queen's Hall, 17 March 1931. Keith Middlemas and John Barnes, *Baldwin: A Biography* (1969), pp. 599–600.

Notes to Chapter 12: Chartwell and Hitler

1. Mary Soames, *Clementine Churchill* (1974), ch. 15.
2. *The Second World War*, i, bk 1, ch. 5.
3. Martin Gilbert, *Winston S. Churchill*, v, p. 866.
4. *The Aftermath*, pp. 41, 51.
5. *The Second World War*, i, bk 1, ch. 1. In the same paragraph, the remarkable description of Hitler that follows.
6. 'Hitler and his Choice', reprinted in *Great Contemporaries* (1937).
7. Gilbert, *Winston S. Churchill*, v, pp. 566–67.
8. *The Second World War*, i, bk 1, ch. 18.

Notes to Chapter 13: 'Winston is Back!'

1. *The Second World War*, i, bk 2, ch. 22.
2. Ibid., ch. 25.
3. Correlli Barnett, *Engage the Enemy More Closely* (1991), p. 105.
4. Hastings Ismay, *Memoirs* (1960), ch. 8.
5. *The Second World War*, i, bk 2, ch. 35.
6. Paul Addison, *The Road to 1945* (1975), pp. 89–90.
7. John Wheeler-Bennett, *King George VI: His Life and Reign* (1958), p. 444.
8. *The Second World War*, i, bk. 2, ch. 38.
9. A. J. P. Taylor, *English History, 1914–1945* (1965), pp. 488–89. I have inverted his sentences in order to make the point clearer.

10. Cited in Andrew Roberts' biography of Lord Halifax, *The Holy Fox* (1997), p. 179.

11. *Into Battle* (1941), p. 133.

12. Mass Observation, *War Begins at Home* (1940) p. 5 (tenses changed).

13. *Into Battle*, p. 169.

14. Ibid., p. 134.

15. Ibid., pp. 145–46, for this and the preceding reference to the United States.

Notes to Chapter 14: His Finest Hour

1. Mary Soames, *Clementine Churchill* (1974), ch. 19.

2. Andrew Roberts, *The Holy Fox* (1997), pp. 213–28, gives an admirable terse summary of these tense days; John Lukacs, *Five Days in May 1940* (1999), devotes a whole book to them.

3. John Charmley, *Churchill: The End of Glory* (1993), p. 649.

4. Clement Attlee, *As It Happened* (1954), p. 118.

5. Ismay, *Memoirs* (1960), p. 170.

6. See John Keegan, *Churchill's Generals* (1992 pbk), p. 7; and Ronald Lewin, *Churchill as Warlord* (1973), p. 34.

7. W. Averell Harriman and Elie Abel, *Special Envoy to Churchill and Stalin, 1941–46* (1975), p. 59. That decisions were thought to be taken 'promptly' might have surprised some participants, but it was true, first, that they were taken a lot more quickly than in Washington; and, secondly, that they were decisive.

8. Ismay, *Memoirs*, p. 159.

9. John Colville, in *Action This Day* (1968), pp. 50–51.

10. *The Second World War*, ii, bk 1, ch. 4.

11. Mary Soames (ed.), *Speaking for Themselves: The Personal Letters of Winston and Clementine Churchill* (1998), p. 454.

12. James Marshall-Cornwall, *Rumours of Wars* (1984), pp. 166–71. It may also be found in Max Hastings (ed.), *The Oxford Book of Military Anecdotes* (1987 pbk), pp. 406–9.

13. Robert Rhodes James, *Anthony Eden* (1987 pbk), p. 283.

14. Colville, in *Action This Day*, p. 117.

Notes to Chapter 15: Democratic Warlord

1. *The Second World War*, iv, bk 1 ch. 5.

2. *Secret Session Speeches* (1946), p. 21.

3. Ibid., p. 44.

4. David Reynolds in Blake and Louis (eds), *Churchill* (1994), p. 255. It is appropriate here to notice the story, put into circulation principally by David Irving and Clive Ponting, that a few of Churchill's wartime broadcasts were actually imitations of him by the actor Norman Shelley. That is a myth; but Shelley may well have later *recorded* his admired impersonations for the BBC and

Decca. See Sian Nicholas in *History Today*, 51 (February 2001). The matter is given a searching examination by D. J. Wenden in his contribution to Blake and Louis (eds), *Churchill*, pp. 236–39.

5. Asa Briggs, *The History of Broadcasting in the UK*, iii (1970), pp. 205, 325.

6. *Into Battle*, p. 224.

7. Paul Addison, *Churchill on the Home Front* (1993), p. 334.

8. Isaiah Berlin's essay first appeared in the *Atlantic Monthly* (1949) and the *Cornhill Magazine* (1949) as 'Mr Churchill and FDR'. The London publishing house of John Murray then brought it out as the little book, *Mr Churchill in 1940*, undated; my quotation comes from its p. 29.

9. Speech of 30 November 1954, acknowledging the House of Commons' eightieth birthday gift, the portrait by Graham Sutherland which drew from him the ambiguous comment that it 'is a remarkable example of modern art. It certainly combines force and candour'. He hated it on sight, and the picture was never again seen in public. After it had languished for some years in a basement, his wife – by then his widow – destroyed it. See Mary Soames, *Clementine Churchill* (1974), ch. 30.

10. Berlin, *Mr Churchill in 1940*, pp. 26–27.

11. *Into Battle*, pp. 221 (Dunkirk), 280, 299.

12. Ibid., pp. 223 (Dunkirk), 234 ('Finest Hour') and 262.

13. Hastings Ismay, *Memoirs* (1960), pp. 183–84.

14. *The Second World War*, iv, bk 2, ch. 26.

15. Mary Soames (ed.), *Speaking for Themselves: The Personal Letters of Winston and Clementine Churchill* (1998), p. 469.

16. Soames, *Clementine Churchill*, ch. 23.

17. These exchanges and the letter from Malta are in *Speaking for Themselves*, pp. 508–13.

18. Soames, *Clementine Churchill*, ch. 23.

Notes to Chapter 16: 'Action this Day'

1. John Colville, *Fringes of Power*, 5 August 1941.

2. Hastings Ismay, *Memoirs* (1960), p. 174. P. James Grigg, *Prejudice and Judgement* (1949), p. 390.

3. Alanbrooke in John Keegan, *Churchill's Generals* (1992), p. 7; Ismay in Roberts, *The Holy Fox* (1997), p. 240.

4. The minutes being printed chronologically, it is necessary only to indicate the volumes from which my examples are taken. 29 August and 22 November 1940 are in ii; 17 July and 27 November 1941 in iii; 12 December 1942 and 2 March 1943 in iv; 16 July and 27 September 1943 in v; 1 September, 20 November 1944 and 18 March 1945 in vi.

5. *The Second World War*, ii, bk 2, appendix A.

6. John Colville, *Frontiers in Time* (1985 pbk), p. 100.

7. *The Second World War*, ii, bk 1, ch. 8.

8. Ibid., iv, minute dated 10 March 1943.

9. This quotation and the next come respectively from minutes in *The Second World War*, ii, 17 October 1940; and iv, 4 September 1942.

10. Alanbrooke, *Triumph in the West*, diary entry for 25 January 1944.

11. Cited by Malcolm Smith, *Station X* (2000), p. 80.

12. F. H. Hinsley, in Blake and Louis (eds), *Churchill* (1994), p. 409.

13. Ronald Lewin, probably his *Ultra Goes to War* (1978). I regret having lost track of the source of this quotation.

14. Paul Addison, *Churchill on the Home Front* (1993), p. 355.

15. A phrase of Arthur Bryant in his fine introductory chapter to *Triumph in the West*.

16. A. B. Cunningham, *A Sailor's Odyssey* (1951), pp. 683, 647–48.

17. The need for a more complete version has been clearly stated by Gerhard L. Weinberg, *A World at Arms* (1994), p. 928, where he notes that the text has been 'seriously tampered with'.

Notes to Chapter 17: America and Roosevelt

1. *Step by Step*, p. 254.

2. *Into Battle*, pp. 54, 57.

3. *The Second World War*, i, bk 2, ch. 23.

4. Warren F. Kimball in Blake and Louis (eds), *Churchill* (1994), p. 300.

5. *The Second World War*, ii, bk 2, ch. 28.

6. *The Unrelenting Struggle*, p. 63.

7. Andrew Roberts, *The Holy Fox* (1997), ch. 22. A fellow Dickensian may be allowed to suggest that, if Churchill was Micawber, Halifax was Perker.

8. *The Second World War*, iii, bk 2, chs 32 and 33.

9. John Gooch, in Laurence Freedman (ed.), *War, Strategy and International Politics* (1992), pp. 155–75.

10. Speech of 10 November 1942, in *The End of the Beginning*, p. 215.

11. *Oxford Companion to the Second World War* (1995), p. 300. Dill is the subject of Alex Danchev's biography, *Very Special Relationship* (1986).

12. Cited in Oliver Warner, *Cunningham of Hyndhope* (1967), pp. 184–85.

13. *The Second World War*, iii, bk 2, ch. 34.

14. Correlli Barnett, *Engage the Enemy More Closely* (1991), p. 364.

15. *The Second World War*, v, bk 2, ch. 20.

16. Ibid., vi, bk 2, ch. 38.

17. *Victory*, p. 224.

Notes to Chapter 18: Special Operations and Bombing Offensive

1. *The Second World War*, ii, bk 1, ch. 12.

2. Well put by Michael Simpson in his edition of *The Somerville Papers* (1996), p. 355.

3. Bernard Fergusson, *The Watery Maze* (1961), p. 415.

4. The couple in question were Charles Webster and Noble Frankland. The latter

has published a very interesting account of its stormy gestation in *History at War* (1998).

5. John Colville, *The Churchillians* (1981), pp. 62–63. For a full explanation of the sequence of events preceding the Coventry raid, see Ronald Lewin, *Ultra Goes to War*, ch. 3 (1980 pbk), pp. 99–103.

6. Anthony Montague Browne, *Long Sunset* (1995) p. 201.

7. Richard Overy, *The Air War, 1939–1945* (1981 pbk), pp. 122–25.

8. Gilbert, *In Search of Churchill* (1995), p. 185.

9. This strange minute and its replacement, which together were given their first airing in Webster and Frankland, *The Strategic Air Offensive against Germany*, iii, p. 112, are printed in full in Gilbert, *Winston S. Churchill*, vii, p. 1257. The file in the Public Record Office containing them (PREM 3/12) offers no clues relative to my speculations.

10. A full and almost certainly definitive account of the tangled facts about Harris's (as it would seem) refusal of a peerage, and his indignation at the failure to recognize the services of his air- and ground-crews, may be found in Henry Probert, *Bomber Harris: His Life and Times* (2001).

11. Speech of 22 June 1941, in *The Unrelenting Struggle*, p. 129.

12. Webster and Frankland, *The Strategic Air Offensive*, iii, pp. 79–80.

13. Martin Gilbert, *Winston S. Churchill*, viii, p. 259.

Notes to Chapter 19: France and de Gaulle

1. The whole speech is given in *The Second World War*, ii, bk 2, ch. 26, as well as in *Into Battle*, pp. 295–97.

2. Ibid., ii, bk 1, ch. 10.

3. Ibid.,ii, bk 2, ch. 26.

4. Ibid., vi, bk 1, ch. 16. Churchill was mistaken about the one star; pictures show de Gaulle with *two* stars on his cap.

5. Thus translated in François Kersaudy, *Churchill and de Gaulle* (1990), p. 223.

6. *The Second World War*, ii, bk 2, ch. 38.

Notes to Chapter 20: Russia and Stalin

1. Broadcast of 22 June 1941, in *The Unrelenting Struggle*, pp. 176–80.

2. *The Second World War*, iii, bk 2, ch. 22; iv, bk 2, ch. 27; and ii, bk 2, ch. 25.

3. Ibid., iii, bk 2, ch. 27, for 'the lump of ice', and (in the next paragraph), 'the soft belly'.

4. Ibid., iii, bk 2, ch. 21.

5. William Hayter, *The Kremlin and the Embassy* (1966), p. 29.

6. *The Diaries of Sir Alexander Cadogan, 1939–1945*, ed. David Dilks (1971), p. 707.

7. *The Second World War*, vi, bk 2, ch. 27.

8. Ibid., vi, bk 2, ch. 27.

9. Ibid., ch. 26.

10. Ibid., vi, bk 2, ch. 24.
11. Ibid., vi, bk 2, ch. 40.
12. Robin Edmonds, *The Big Three: Churchill, Roosevelt and Stalin in Peace and War* (1991), p. 434.

Notes to Chapter 21: Victory Overcast

1. High Dalton, *The Fateful Years* (1957), p. 462.
2. Paul Addison, in Anthony Seldon and Peter Hennessy, *Ruling Performance* (1987), p. 5.
3. *Onward to Victory*, pp. 32–45.
4. L. Susan Stebbing, *Thinking to Some Purpose* (Pelican Books, 1939: reprinted 1945 and susbsequently).
5. Addison, in *Ruling Performance*, p. 6.
6. Harry Boardman, *The Glory of Parliament*, ed. Francis Boyd (1960), pp. 92–93.
7. *Victory*, p. 189.
8. *The Second World War*, vi, bk 2, ch. 40.
9. Mary Soames, *Clementine Churchill* (1974), ch. 24.
10. *The Second World War*, vi, bk 2, ch. 40.
11. Soames, *Clementine Churchill*, ch. 24; also the quotation in the next paragraph.
12. Mary Soames (ed.), *Speaking for Themselves. The Personal Letters of Winston and Clementine Churchill* (1998), pp. 535, 540–41.

Notes to Chapter 22: Iron Curtain

1. For those lunch parties, see Martin Gilbert, *Winston S. Churchill*, viii, p. 461.
2. John Charmley, *Churchill's Grand Alliance* (1996 pbk), p. 222.
3. The Fulton speech is no. 28 in David Cannadine (ed.), *The Speeches of Winston Churchill* (Penguin edn, 1990). It is also of course in *Sinews of Peace* (1948).
4. *Sinews of Peace*, pp. 116–17, 119.
5. *Europe Unite* (1950), p. 143.
6. Harold Macmillan, *Tides of Fortune* (1969), p. 163.
7. R. A. Butler, *Churchill's Personality and Europe*. The first Winston Churchill Memorial Lecture, Zürich, 1967, p. 2. I would never have known about this clever piece but for the excellent library of the Churchill Archives Centre.
8. Jebb, cited in Michael Charlton (ed.) *The Price of Victory* (1983), pp. 56–57.
9. *Sinews of Peace*, pp. 201–2.
10. Macmillan, *Tides of Fortune*, p. 175.
11. *Parliamentary Debates*, 27 June 1950, fifth series, 476, col. 2156.
12. Charlton (ed.), *The Price of Victory*, p. 56.
13. *Sinews of Peace*, p. 198.
14. The Franks version of the three circles is in Charlton (ed.), *The Price of Victory*, p. 58. The other version is in a speech of 20 April 1949 at the Economic Conference of the European Movement. *Complete Speeches*, vii, p. 7811.

Notes to Chapter 23: Summitry and the Bomb

1. 'Who's Next?', in *Too Many Songs by Tom Lehrer* (1981), pp. 120–23. The copyright is dated 1965.
2. Speech at Plymouth, 23 October 1951, *Complete Speeches*, viii, p. 8282.
3. For this important point I am indebted to John Charmley, *Churchill's Grand Alliance*, p. 265.
4. R. H. Ferrell (ed.), *The Eisenhower Diaries* (1981), pp. 222–23.
5. Peter G. Boyle (ed.), *The Churchill-Eisenhower Correspondence, 1953–1955* (1990), p. 209, verb endings modified. Churchill's suggestions for improvement appear on p. 110.
6. *Parliamentary Debates*, 11 May 1953, fifth series, 515, cols 895–98.
7. Lord Moran, *Churchill: The Struggle for Survival* (1966), 7 December 1953.
8. *Parliamentary Debates*, 5 April 1954, fifth series, 526, col. 36.
9. Ibid., col. 60.
10. Ibid., 12 July 1954, fifth series, 530, col. 47.
11. Ibid., 1 March 1955, fifth series, 537, cols 1893–1905. Also in David Cannadine (ed.), *The Speeches of Winston Churchill* (Penguin edn, 1990), no. 33. This speech is with reason referred to as Churchill's last, his swan song, but in fact he contributed to debates on two more occasions, on 14 and 28 March, before the end.

Notes to Chapter 24: Return to Downing Street

1. Clement Attlee, in *Churchill by his Contemporaries* (1965), p. 29. Regarding Stafford Cripps, my source is private.
2. David Hunt, *Churchill at Work: An Address to the Churchill Society for the Advancement of Parliamentary Democracy* (Toronto, 1990), pp. 9–10.
3. Harold Macmillan, *Tides of Fortune* (1969), p. 491.
4. Speech at Plymouth, 23 October 1951, *Complete Speeches*, viii, p. 8282.
5. *Parliamentary Debates*, 3 November 1953, fifth series, 520, cols 21–23.
6. Paul Addison, *Churchill on the Home Front* (1993), p. 493.
7. This relies largely on John Baylis, *Ambiguity and Deterrence* (1995), pp. 184–85.
8. Mary Soames, *Clementine Churchill* (1974), ch. 26.

Notes to Chapter 25: Sunset and Nightfall

1. This Epilogue, drafted by Denis Kelly and the last of his private secretaries, Anthony Montague Browne, according to the latter's *Long Sunset* (1995), p. 222, brought in £20,000.
2. Financial details digested from many references spread about in Martin Gilbert, *Winston S. Churchill*, viii. The staggering outcome of the trust arrangements, brought to completion in the spring of 1949, is revealed in ibid., p. 461: 'For

the first time an author had been allowed to set his annual literary income into a trust fund without it being counted as income as each payment was made by the publishers. From the capital sum, an annual payment was then made to Churchill for his living and literary expenses.' That payment amounted to an annual £20,000.

3. Henry Pelling, *Winston Churchill* (1974), p. 580.

4. Gilbert, *Winston S. Churchill*, viii, p. 260, and Mary Soames, *Clementine Churchill* (1974), ch. 25.

5. Mary Soames, *Winston Churchill: His Life as a Painter* (1990), p. 180.

6. K. Alldritt, *Churchill the Writer* (1992), p. 156.

7. F. W. Deakin, *Churchill the Historian* (Winston Churchill Memorial Lecture, Zürich, 1969), p. 12.

8. Gilbert, *Winston S. Churchill*, viii, p. 270.

9. J. H. Plumb, in *Four Faces and the Man* (1969), pp. 139, 149.

10. Mary Soames (ed.), *Speaking for Themselves: The Personal Letters of Winston and Clementine Churchill*, p. 596.

11. Adrian Searle in the *Guardian*, 17 January 1998.

12. Gilbert, *In Search of Churchill*, pp. 71–72.

13. John Richardson, *The Sorcerer's Apprentice* (1999), p. 231.

14. Diana and Sarah, as mentioned in Soames, *Clementine Churchill*, passim.

15. Ibid., ch. 27. Lord Moran, 25 May 1958, writes of 'two nursing orderlies'.

16. Soames, *Winston Churchill: His Life as Painter*, p. 202.

17. Soames, *Clementine Churchill*, ch. 28.

18. W. Russell Brain, 'Encounters with Winston Churchill', in *Medical History*, 44 (2000), p. 18.

19. Soames, *Clementine Churchill*, ch. 29, places these words after the stroke; Montague Browne, *Long Sunset*, p. 325, places them before it and writes: 'Several versions exist of Winston Churchill's last words. No one knows what they actually were.'

20. Leslie Rowan, *Action This Day*, p. 265.

21. Sir Walter Scott, *Marmion*. (I had this verse in mind before I discovered that it had already been used, with much appropriateness, by John Charmley.)

Notes to Chapter 26: Epilogue

1. Paul Addison, *Churchill on the Home Front* (1993), pp. 432–33.

2. Norman Brook in Lord Moran, 24 June 1956.

3. Aneurin Bevan, in *Churchill by his Contemporaries: An Observer Appreciation* (1965), pp. 56–63.

4. Andrew Rutherford citing Northrop Frye, in *The Literature of War* (1989 edn), p. 3.

5. Ben Pimlott, in 'Domestic Mr Churchill', his review of Paul Addison's *Churchill on the Home Front*, in *Frustrate Their Knavish Tricks* (1994), p. 9.

6. Harold Macmillan, *Tides of Fortune* (1969), p. 533.

7. Dwight Eisenhower as cited by Kimball in Blake and Louis (eds), *Churchill* (1994), p. 406.

8. Isaiah Berlin, *Mr Churchill in 1940*, p. 13.

9. Clement Attlee, 'The Churchill I Knew', in *Churchill by his Contemporaries* (1965), pp. 14–35.

10. Lord Moran, 7 December 1947.

11. John Stallworthy, 'Epilogue to an Empire, 1600–1900: An Ode for Trafalgar Day', in *Rounding the Horn: Collected Poems* (1998), pp. 72–73.

Bibliography

This is a bibliography of Churchill, with some suggestions for further reading. The publishing history of Churchill's books is a study in itself: see Frederick Woods, *Bibliography of the Works of Sir Winston Churchill* (1975), and Richard M. Langworth, *A Connoisseur's Guide to the Books of Sir Winston Churchill* (1998). Interested readers should note that differences in the text sometimes occur between one edition and another, that later editions of his earlier writings are often abridged, and that the titles of American editions offer differ from the English ones, cited here.

CHURCHILL'S WORKS

Writings before the First World War

The Story of the Malakand Field Force (1898).
The River War (2 vols, 1899).
Savrola (1900).
London to Ladysmith (1900).
Ian Hamilton's March (1900).
Lord Randolph Churchill (2 vols, 1906).
My African Journey (1908).

Collections of Speeches before the First World War

Liberalism and the Social Problem (1909).
The People's Rights (1910).

Writings between 1914 and 1939

The World Crisis, 5 vols respectively titled '1911–1914', '1915', '1916–1918', 'The Aftermath' and 'The Eastern Front' (1923–1931).
My Early Life: A Roving Commission (1930).

Thoughts and Adventures (1932).
Marlborough: His Life and Times, 4 vols (1933–38).
Great Contemporaries (1937).
Step by Step (1939).

Collections of Speeches between the Wars

Arms and the Covenant, compiled by Randolph S. Churchill (1938).

Writings after 1939

The Second World War, 6 vols respectively titled 'The Gathering Storm', 'Their Finest Hour', 'The Grand Alliance', 'The Hinge of Fate', 'Closing the Ring', 'Triumph and Tragedy' (1948–54).

A History of the English-Speaking Peoples, 4 vols respectively titled 'The Birth of Britain', 'The New World', 'The Age of Revolution' and 'The Great Democracies' (1956–58).

The War Speeches of Winston Churchill. Their first appearances in book form were in successive wartime volumes (the ones I have used), each compiled by Charles Eade, under the titles *Into Battle* (1941), *The Unrelenting Struggle* (1942), *The End of the Beginning* (1943), *Onwards to Victory* (1944), *The Dawn of Liberation* (1945) and *Victory* (1946). Churchill's *Secret Session Speeches* (only five of them) were added in 1946. A three-volume compilation, also by Eade, was published in 1953.

Post-war Speeches, all in volumes edited by his son.

The Sinews of Peace (1948).
Europe Unite (1950).
In the Balance (1951).
Stemming the Tide (1953)
The Unwritten Alliance (1961).

All of the above, and a great many more, may be found in an eight-volume edition by Robert Rhodes James, *Winston S. Churchill: His Complete Speeches, 1897–1963* (1974). A useful introductory selection has been edited, with good commentary, by David Cannadine: *The Speeches of Winston Churchill* (Penguin edition, 1990).

WORKS ON CHURCHILL

Biographies of Churchill

Churchill has predictably been the subject of the most magnificent biographical project ever devoted to a British statesman, *Winston S. Churchill*, in eight volumes. His son Randolph began it with volumes I and II, published respectively in 1966 and 1967, covering the years 1874–1900 and 1900–1914. Martin Gilbert then carried it on to completion in six more volumes: vol. III covers 1914–1916, vol. IV 1917–1922, vol. V 1911–1939, vol. VI 1939–1941, vol. VII 1941–1945 and vol. VIII 1945–1965. This series of large volumes carries so much documentation that it is a generous source of material for other historians, like myself, as well as being a mega-biography in its own right; yet there is also an accompanying series of equally large *Companion Volumes* of documents, not yet completed: vol. I is in two parts, vol. II in three, vol. III in two, vol. IV in three, and vol. V in three, the last of which deals with the years 1936–1939.

Of what comes next, only two volumes have so far appeared of *Churchill's War Papers*; the first on his months at the Admiralty, the second on the months May to December 1940. The chapter headings and elaborate indices of these monumental volumes are the obvious place for beginning any particular inquiry.

Other biographies are available in all sizes. The largest and most elaborate, as yet incomplete, is that by William Manchester: its first volume, *The Last Lion: Winston Spencer Churchill. Visions of Glory, 1874–1932*, came out in 1983; his second, *The Caged Lion: Winston Spencer Churchill, 1932–1940*, in 1988. Going down the scale we have, at 1088 pages, Martin Gilbert's *Churchill: A Life* (1992); Roy Jenkins, *Churchill: A Biography* (2001), 1000 pages; Clive Ponting, *Churchill* (1994) at 900 pages; John Charmley, *Churchill: The End of Glory*, 742 pages (1993); Henry Pelling, *Winston Churchill* (1974), 724 pages; François Bédarida, *Churchill* (in French) (1999), 572 pages; Norman Rose, *Churchill: An Unruly Life* (1994), 435 pages; Piers Brendon, *Winston Churchill: A Brief Life* (1984), 234 pages; Keith Robbins, *Churchill* (1992), 186 pages; Martin Gilbert again, *Churchill* (1966), 112 pages; and Robert Blake, *Churchill* (1998), 110 pages. Gilbert is also the producer of *Churchill: A Photographic Record* (1999); another is Randolph Churchill and Helmut Gernsheim, *Churchill: His Life in Photographs* (1955).

Exceptional in every respect, and proper to include here, are two books which, although incomplete as biographies, are so wise and perceptive that one must regret they are not fuller: Robert Rhodes James, *Churchill: A Study in Failure, 1900–1939* (1970), and Paul Addison, *Churchill on the Home Front, 1900–1955* (1992; enlarged edition, 1993).

The Churchill Family

A. L. Rowse takes *The Early Churchills* (1956) to the death of Sarah the first Duchess of Marlborough in 1744; his *The Later Churchills* (1958) goes up to 1940. For Winston's father, see Robert Rhodes James, *Lord Randolph Churchill* (1959), and Roy Foster, *Lord Randolph Churchill: A Political Life* (1981); for his mother, Anita Leslie, *Jennie: The Life of Lady Randolph Churchill* (1969), and Peregrine Churchill and Julian Mitchell, *Jennie: Lady Randolph Churchill. A Portrait with Letters* (1974).

Winston's wife is admirably portrayed in two books by her youngest daughter, Mary Soames: *Clementine Churchill* (1979); and *Speaking for Themselves: The Personal Letters of Winston and Clementine Churchill* (1998). Their son Randolph may be read about in *his* son Winston S. Churchill's book *His Father's Son: The Life of Randolph Churchill* (1996), and in Kay Halle (ed.), *Randolph Churchill: The Young Unpretender* (1971). Their daughter Sarah made a charming little contribution to the literature with *A Thread in the Tapestry* (1967).

Books of Essays about Churchill

King of them all is Robert Blake and William Roger Louis (eds), *Churchill* (1993), a collection of twenty-nine essays by (mostly) first-rate authorities, covering most major aspects of his life. R. A. C. Parker, *Winston Churchill: Studies in Statesmanship* (1995), makes up for the last-mentioned's gaps on the international relations side. *Churchill: Four Faces and the Man* (1968), by A. J. P. Taylor and four others, remains instructive. Martin Gilbert, *In Search of Churchill* (1995) is charming. Peter Stansky (ed.), *Churchill: A Profile* (1973) is a good collection of essays and extracts.

Andrew Roberts, *Eminent Churchillians* (1994), Ben Pimlott, *Frustrate their Knavish Tricks* (1994), Peter Clarke, *A Question of Leadership* (1992), and David Cannadine, *History in Our Time* (1998), all contain good essays on Churchill.

Books by Officials and Others Close to Churchill

John Wheeler-Bennett (ed.), *Action This Day* (1968). One of its contributors, John Colville, kept diaries which became *The Fringes of Power: Downing Street Diaries, 1939–1955* (1985), covering the years 1940–41, 1944–45 and

1951–55. He also wrote *The Churchillians* (1981) and the autobiographical *Footprints in Time: Memories*, with Churchill weaving in and out of it. Indispensable for the last years is Anthony Montague Browne, *Long Sunset* (1995). Another official observer was David Hunt, *Churchill at Work* (1990). Observing from different angles are Phyllis Moir, *I Was Churchill's Private Secretary* (1941), Elizabeth Nel, *Mr Churchill's Secretary* (1958), W. H. Thompson, *Guard from the Yard* (1958), Robin Fedden, *Churchill at Chartwell* (1969), and Gerald Pawle, *The War and Colonel Warden* (1963).

Uniquely interesting, and still the subject of controversy as to whether he should have written it at all, or at least have given it a less misleading title, is the book his personal medical attendant Dr Charles Wilson, Lord Moran from 1941, published very soon after Churchill's death: *Winston Churchill: The Struggle for Survival* (1966). To it may be added, on the medical side, Anthony Storr, *Churchill's Black Dog and Other Phenomena of the Human Mind* (1989), the Churchill chapter being an improved version of what Storr contributed to *Four Faces and the Man*. Also, for those who can get hold of it, W. Russell Brain, 'Encounters with Winston Churchill', *Medical History*, 44 (2000), pp. 3–20.

Churchill as Painter and Writer

D. Coombs, *Churchill: His Paintings* (1967); Mary Soames, *Winston Churchill: His Life as a Painter* (1990); Keith Alldritt, *Churchill the Writer: His Life as a Man of Letters* (1992); Maurice Ashley, *Churchill as Historian* (1968); J. H. Plumb in *Four Faces and the Man*; John Ramsden's 1996 Inaugural Lecture 'That Will Depend on Who Writes the History …'; and David Reynolds, 'Churchill's Writing of History …' in the 2001 *Transactions of the Royal Historical Society*.

Churchill before 1914

Beyond his own excellent book *My Early Life*, there are: E. D. W. Chaplin (ed.), *Winston Churchill and Harrow* (1941); Violet Bonham Carter, *Winston Churchill as I Knew Him* (1965); Ted Morgan, *Churchill: Young Man in a Hurry, 1874–1915* (1982); Malcolm Hill, *Churchill: His Radical Decade* (1999); Ronald Hyam, *Elgin and Churchill at the Colonial Office* (1968); the early parts of Tony Paterson, *A Seat for Life* (his Dundee constituency) (1980); John Campbell, *F. E. Smith* (Churchill's friend) (1983); Paul Addison, *Churchill on the Home Front* (1992; enlarged edition, 1993); Robert Rhodes James, *Churchill: A Study in Failure* (1970); and Stephen Roskill, *Churchill and the Admirals* (1977).

Churchill and the First World War

Churchill's own story of it, *The World Crisis*, is copious, exciting and informative but necessarily partial, in both senses of the word. (Robin Prior, *Churchill's 'World Crisis' as History* (1983), demonstrates that Churchill would not have got a Ph.D. with it!) The retired admiral Peter Gretton, *Former Naval Person* (1968), takes a more relaxed view of Churchill at the Admiralty than Roskill. Valuable books on the Dardanelles episode are Trumbull Higgins, *Winston Churchill and the Dardanelles: A Dialogue in Ends and Means* (1963); Robert Rhodes James, *Gallipoli* (1965); Geoffrey Miller, *Straits: British Policies towards the Ottoman Empire and the Origins of the Dardanelles Campaign* (1997); and Michael Hickey, *Gallipoli* (1995).

Churchill between the Wars

Paul Addison, *Churchill on the Home Front* (1992; enlarged edition, 1993), and Robert Rhodes James, *Churchill: A Study in Failure* (1970) as before, joined by Martin Gilbert, *Winston Churchill: The Wilderness Years* (1981). The first half of vol. I of Churchill's *The Second World War* is about the inter-war years. For the Chartwell courtiers, see R. W. Thompson, *Churchill and Morton* (1976), and R. F. Harrod, *The Prof: A Personal Memoir of Lord Cherwell* (1959); also, for one who was close to Churchill in these years, Anne Chisholm and Michael Davie, *Beaverbrook: A Life* (1992). The issue of 'appeasement' continues to be argued and written about; the most recent contributions are Andrew Boxer, *Appeasement* (1998), a brief survey in the series 'Questions in History', Graham Stewart, *Burying Caesar: Churchill, Chamberlain and the Battle for the Tory Party* (1999), and R A. C. Parker, *Churchill and Appeasement* (2000), the sage conclusions of a lifetime's study.

Churchill and the Second World War

For the opening months, Patrick Cosgrave, *Churchill at War: Alone, 1939–1940* (1974), Arthur Marder, *Winston is Back: Churchill at the Admiralty, 1939–1940* (1972), a supplement to *the English Historical Review*, and David Irving, *Churchill's War: The Struggle for Power*, i, *1939–1941* (1987), which contains much interesting matter but is wilfully disparaging. For relations with France, Eleanor M. Gates, *The End of the Affair: The Collapse of the Anglo-French Alliance, 1939–1940* (1981), P. M. H. Bell, *A Certain Eventuality: Britain and the Fall of France* (1974), and François Kersaudy, *Churchill and de Gaulle* (trans. 1990). Kersaudy has also a fine book on *Norway 1940* (trans. 1990). John Lukacs has gone over the mid-1940 drama at two levels of intensity: *The Duel: Hitler v. Churchill, 10 May–31 July 1940* (1992) and *Five Days in London, May 1940* (1999).

Churchill's Wartime Coalition

Obvious starters on the domestic side are J. M. Lee, *The Churchill Coalition, 1940–1945* (1980), Stephen Brooke, *Labour's War* (1992), Kevin Jeffreys, *The Churchill Coalition and Wartime Politics* (1995), Brian Gardner, *Churchill in Wartime: A Study in Reputation, 1939–1945* (1968), Paul Addison, *The Road to 1945. British Politics and the Second World War* (1975), and of course his *Churchill on the Home Front* (1992; enlarged edition, 1993). Correlli Barnett, *The Audit of War: The Illusions and Reality of Britain as a Great Nation* (1986), commands respect but tips over on the gloomy side.

On the strategic and military sides, three books stand out: Ronald Lewin, *Churchill as Warlord* (1973); John Keegan (ed.), *Churchill's Generals* (1991; and Stephen Roskill, *Churchill and the Admirals* (1977). (As already observed, there is not a book on Churchill and the Air Marshals. Perhaps indeed it would not be worthwhile to attempt one.) Invaluable inside views of how decisions were made are in Hastings Ismay, *Memoirs of General the Lord Ismay* (1960), Arthur Bryant's edition of Lord Alanbrooke's war diaries in two volumes, *The Turn of the Tide* (1957) and *Triumph in the West* (1959), and the recollections of General Leslie Hollis, co-authored with James Leasor as *War at the Top* (1959). Alex Danchev, 'Waltzing with Winston: Civil-Military Relations in Britain in the Second World War', is delightfully readable in Paul Smith (ed.), *Government and the Armed Forces* (1996).

For the conduct of foreign and strategic affairs generally, Elizabeth Barker, *Churchill and Eden at War* (1974). On the Middle East and Mediterranean, Elizabeth Barker, *British Policy in South-East Europe in the Second World War* (1976), and Lord Chandos (Oliver Lyttelton), *The Middle East in World War Two* (1962). No small book has ever said more than Michael Howard, *The Mediterranean Strategy in the Second World War* (1968). For North Africa, John Strawson, *The Battle for North Africa* (1969), and Barrie Pitt, *The Crucible of War: Western Desert, 1941* (1980). For Greece and Crete, Sheila Lawlor, *Churchill and the Politics of Power, 1940–1941* (1994) (analysing what lay behind the ill-fated expedition), Charles Cruickshank, *Greece, 1940–1941* (1996), and Callum MacDonald, *The Lost Battle: Crete 1941* (1993). For Italy, Dominic Graham and Shelford Bidwell, *Tug of War: The Battle for Italy* (1986), and Richard Lamb, *War in Italy: A Brutal Story* (1995). Richard Woodman, *Malta Convoys, 1940–1943* (2000) is on an episode that, like Crete, cost the Royal Navy dear.

America and Roosevelt

On Churchill's relationship with Roosevelt, Joseph P. Lash, *Roosevelt and Churchill, 1939–1941: The Partnership that Saved the World* (1974), David Stafford, *Roosevelt and Churchill: Men of Secrets* (1999), and Warren Kimball, *Forged in War: Roosevelt, Churchill and the Second World War* (1997). Warren Kimball is editor of their *Complete Correspondence*, 3 vols (1984). See also Robin Edmonds, *The Big Three: Churchill, Roosevelt and Stalin in Peace and War* (1991), David Reynolds, Warren Kimball and A. O. Chubarian (eds), *Allies at War: The Soviet, American and British Experience* (1994), and John Charmley, *Churchill's Grand Alliance: The Anglo-American Special Relationship, 1940–1957* (1995).

Special Operations and Intelligence

On Special Operations see Hilary St G. Saunders, *The Green Berets: The Story of the Commandos, 1940–1945* (1949), J. G. Beevor, *SOE: Recollections and Reflections* (1981), Ronald Atkin, *Dieppe 1942: The Jubilee Disaster* (1980), David Stafford, *Britain and European Resistance, 1940–1945* (1980), and *Churchill and Secret Service* (1991). On Code-breaking see Malcolm Smith, *Station X: The Codebreakers of Bletchley Park* (1998), and Ronald Lewin, *Ultra Goes to War* (1978). Brian Johnson, *The Secret War* (1978), covers several of Churchill's special interests, as do Thomas Wilson (an economist in the Statistical Branch), *Churchill and the Prof* (1995), R. S. Macrae, *Winston Churchill's Toyshop* (1971), and Kenneth Macksey, *Armoured Crusader* (1967), on Hobart.

The Battle of the Atlantic

Stephen Roskill digested his three-volume Official History into one volume, *The Navy at War, 1939–1945* (1960). Ministry of Defence, *The U-Boat War in the Atlantic, 1939–1945* (1989). For this, the Royal Navy's biggest battle, and for everything else it did, Correlli Barnett, *Engage the Enemy More Closely: The Royal Navy in the Second World War* (1991), is very good.

The Bombing Offensive

Noble Frankland, *Bomber Offensive: The Devastation of Europe* (1969), digesting into a small space the Official History he co-authored with Charles Webster. Anthony Verrier, *The Bomber Offensive* (1968). Particularly readable and judicious is Max Hastings, *Bomber Command* (1979). For overviews of the war in the air, see Richard Overy, *The Air War* (1980), and John Terraine, *The Right of the Line: The RAF in the European War, 1939–1945* (1985).

Singapore and the Far East

Christopher Thorne, *Allies of a Kind: The United States, Britain and the War against Japan, 1941–5* (1978); David Day, *The Great Betrayal: Britain, Australia and the Onset of the Pacific War, 1939–1942* (1988); Alan Warren, *Singapore 1942* (2002); Joan Beaumont, *Australia's War, 1939–1945* (1996); Robert Rhodes James, *Chindit* (1980); and John Bierman and Colin Smith, *Fire in the Night: Wingate of Burma, Ethiopia and Zion* (2000).

The Holocaust

David Cesarani, *Britain and the Holocaust* (1998), and Bernard Wasserstein, *Britain and the Jews of Europe* (1999).

Questioning the Necessity or Wisdom of the War, and its Management

John Charmley, *Churchill: The End of Glory* (1993); John Grigg, *1943: The Victory that Never Was* (1985); Richard Lamb, *Churchill as War Leader: Right or Wrong?* (1991); Tuvia Ben-Moshe, *Churchill: Strategy and History* (1992).

The Years after 1945

Paul Addison, 'Churchill in British Politics, 1940–55', in J. M. W. Bean (ed.), *The Political Culture of Modern Britain* (1987), and Paul Addison *Churchill on the Home Front* (1992; enlarged edition, 1993). Correlli Barnett, *The Verdict of Peace* (2001). For 1951–55, Henry Pelling, *Churchill's Peacetime Ministry, 1951–1955* (1997), Anthony Seldon, *Churchill's Indian Summer* (1981), and his summary of it in Anthony Seldon and Peter Hennessy, *Ruling Performance* (1989). Michael Charlton, *The Price of Victory* (1983) is exceptionally informative about Britain and the budding European Community.

For foreign affairs and nuclear matters, John Baylis, *Ambiguity and Deterrence: British Nuclear History, 1945–1964* (1995); Ann Deighton (ed.), *Britain and the First Cold War* (1990); John W. Young, *The Foreign Policy of Churchill's Peacetime Administration* (1988), *Britain and European Unity* (1993) and *Winston Churchill's Last Campaign* (1996).

Index

Most men in this index having had more than one title in the course of their lives, I have omitted titles except where they are as or more familiar than original names.